OPEC
Instrument of
Change

OPEC
Instrument of
Change

Ian Seymour

St. Martin's Press   **New York**

Library of Congress Card Catalog Number 80–53646

ISBN 0–312–58605–1

CONTENTS

FOREWORD

The year 1980 heralds the 20th Anniversary of the existence of the Organization of the Petroleum Exporting Countries, better known to the man in the street as OPEC, and what more fitting an occasion to introduce a comprehensive book about this world-renowned Organization.

The period covered in this volume has seen OPEC grow from a membership of five Founder Countries, which laid the foundation stone of the Organization in September 1960 in Baghdad, to that of thirteen Member Countries representing the main oil-producing regions of the world and distributed in four continents, namely Africa, Asia, Latin America and the Middle East. The book recalls the Organization's record of achievements in the oil industry, achievements which initiated a new process, that of transforming a valuable depletable natural resource – oil – into a more permanent asset for the future.

Not very much serious thought was given way back in 1960 to that relatively unknown Organization comprising a group of developing nations, and there were many predictions of an early disintegration. However, the years were to show that OPEC would not only remain a unified group of oil-producing and exporting countries, but would also become a focus for the demonstration of the full exercise of those nations' sovereignty over the exploitation and management of their natural resources. Its unparalleled achievements have also been seen as an appropriate nucleus in current international relations to promote an exchange of views on such vital and delicate issues as energy and development, which could ultimately benefit both the developing and developed countries. For the former this could pave the way for a degree of development towards prosperity, and for the latter it could contribute to the maintenance of such prosperity.

Now that the Organization is celebrating its 20th Anniversary, this book is being published to record OPEC's history since its foundation in September 1960. The author, Mr. Ian Seymour, has been thoroughly acquainted with the Organization throughout this period, both in his capacity as an editor, and as a reporter of petroleum and energy affairs. Furthermore, Mr. Seymour has been able to draw on a wealth of documentation, to which he has added his objective judgement in recounting the events as they occurred. Indeed, the Organization's history is reflected in this book not as a chronological analysis of events, but rather as a factual approach to issues directly related to the OPEC Conference and its decisions, which, incidently, have greatly influenced, and will continue to influence, the course of the petroleum industry, not only in OPEC Member Countries but throughout the world as a whole. The facts recounted in this book have so far not appeared in other literature on OPEC; it also contains a collection of statistics and relates the views of many people who have played an active role in the evolution of the Organization. Furthermore, the book reveals the complexity of the issues OPEC was called upon to handle and highlights the interplay of politics, economics and technology which has determined the changing structure of the petroleum industry and, to a large extent, the future of its Member Countries in world affairs.

As Secretary General of the Organization of the Petroleum Exporting Countries, and as a believer in its aims and objectives, I am convinced of the need for this book to help straighten out the record and to relate the true history of OPEC's development.

Therefore, in celebrating the 20th year of OPEC's existence, I would like to express the sincere hope that the contribution provided by this volume will reach a large number of readers eager to assimilate historical facts and to keep themselves abreast of international events, among them the innovative and expanding role being played by the Members of the Organization of the Petroleum Exporting Countries.

Rene G. Ortiz
Secretary General
of the Organization of the
Petroleum Exporting Countries
(OPEC)

September, 1980

INTRODUCTION

The story of the rise of OPEC from relative obscurity to world eminence over the past 20 years is well worth the telling. There are the moments of high drama when political and economic crosscurrents converged to set the scene for significant changes in the balances of power. At the same time, much of OPEC's work has been on a more mundane technical level, concerned with the complex mechanics of oil pricing.

The objective in writing this book has been to make it detailed and accurate enough on the technical level to pass muster with the most exacting of specialists, while at the same time highlighting the broad sweep of the politico-economic changes which enabled the OPEC oil producers to regain control of their destinies after so many years of subservience to the concessionary system of the major oil companies.

First of all I would like to express my deepest gratitude to all these officials of OPEC and its Member Governments who have helped me with my coverage of OPEC affairs during the past 20 years — in interviews, background briefings or plain friendly conversations. The list is too long to spell out individual names, but their experiences and views inevitably form a significant part of the input of this book.

The writing of this book was made possible through the generous sponsorship of OPEC, and I am especially grateful to the OPEC group which assisted me with information, ideas, comments and suggestions in this regard. However, it should be stressed that such assistance from OPEC was made available freely and without strings or obligations as far as the contents of the book are concerned. The responsibility for all that appears in the book, as regards contents, interpretation or opinion, rests solely with the author, and should not be attributed in any way to OPEC or its Member Governments.

I would also like to express my appreciation for the forbearance of my colleagues on Middle East Economic Survey — particularly Fuad Itayim and Charles Snow — who generously filled in for me during my book-writing absences from the office.

Finally, a particular debt of gratitude is due to Antonio R. Parra who was responsible for preparing Chapter XI on OPEC aid to the Third World.

Ian Seymour
September 1980

PART I

CONTROL OVER PRICES AND TAX REVENUES

CHAPTER I

PRICES AND PROFITS BEFORE OPEC

When the OPEC Member Governments took over full responsibility for the pricing of their crude oil exports in 1973-74, it marked the end of an era as far as the major international oil companies and the industrialized consuming countries were concerned. Some of the implications of this momentous decision took a few more years to work themselves out. But basically it was clear that the time-span of control by the major multi-nationals over the oil resources of the main exporting areas was drawing to a close after nearly three-quarters of a century.

The OPEC battle for control over the main levers of oil power took 13 years from the time of the Organization's foundation in 1960. But for decades before that the governments of the oil exporting countries had been virtually without a voice in decisions affecting the development, production and pricing of their single significant resource. Some background on the world oil scene in these earlier years is therefore essential for a proper understanding of what was to come in the sixties and seventies.

The System of the Majors

It is sometimes difficult in these days to recall just how complete was the dominance exercized by eight major international oil companies* over the world oil industry in pre-OPEC times. By the mid-fifties the majors were in control of over 90% of production, refining and marketing facilities in the non-communist world outside the United States. They owned a smaller portion of the tanker fleet, but overall control through owner-ship and time charters also amounted to over 85%.[1]

In addition to their economic power and technical expertise, the

---

* Namely the traditional "Seven Sisters" plus the Compagnie Francaise des Pétroles of France, which though less important in international terms at that time nevertheless owned a significant share in Middle East production. The Seven Sisters comprise five US firms – Stand-dard Oil of New Jersey (now Exxon), Texaco, Standard Oil of Cali-fornia (Socal), Mobil Oil and Gulf Oil – plus the Royal Dutch/Shell Group (60% Dutch, 40% British) and Britain's British Petroleum (BP).

majors at crucial historical junctures derived invaluable political strength from the backing of their home governments, notably the United States and Great Britain. In fact, the entire concessionary system in the Middle East, from its beginnings in Iran in the early years of the century through its spread over neighbouring countries – Iraq, Saudi Arabia, Kuwait, the Gulf States – in the twenties and thirties, evolved under the political umbrella of a Western imperalism which, though approaching its twilight years, still ruled the roost in the areas of international relations.

Ownership of the concessions was concentrated in the hands of the eight majors in varying combinations. This, together with the existence of substantial long-term supply agreements between individual companies in various areas, provided the majors with a high degree of horizontal integration (that is to say owership of and access to widely diversified sources of crude oil supply) in addition to their vertical integration through ownership of both upstream (crude oil production) and downstream (transport, refining and marketing) facilities.

For example, in Iran British Petroleum (formerly Anglo-Iranian Oil Company) was the sole concessionaire until replaced in the 1953 post-nationalization settlement by a Consortium which included all eight international majors. In Iraq and the Gulf states (Qatar, what is now the United Arab Emirates, and Oman) a British-Dutch-French-US combination of five majors – BP, CFP, Royal Dutch/Shell, Exxon and Mobil – known as the Iraq Petroleum Group of Companies, gradually acquired exclusive oil rights. In Kuwait the concessionaire was an Anglo-American group composed of BP and Gulf Oil, while in Saudi Arabia the all-American Aramco consortium, founded by Texaco and Standard Oil of California in 1933 and subsequently joined by Exxon and Mobil after the second world war, took charge of oil operations. Moreover, the majors – notably Exxon, Shell and Gulf – were also responsible for the bulk of crude oil production in Venezuela.

The early history of these oil concessions has been described in detail elsewhere and need not detain us here. But, taken together, all these concession agreements, mostly concluded in the inter-war period, formed something like a closed system whose salient features were:

Area
The areas of the concessions were generally extremely large, covering in many cases the entire territories of the countries concerned.

Duration
The agreements were of an extremely long duration, stretching up to

and beyond the end of the century.

Prices
The determination of f.o.b. prices for crude oil — both the prices posted for tax purposes and the prices at which the oil was actually sold to affiliates or third parties — was wholly the responsibility of the concessionaire companies.

Production Levels
Subject to certain minimum output levels stipulated in some agreements (often in the form of non-binding "best endeavour" commitments) the companies were also free to determine oil production and export levels, as well as investment programmes for exploration and development.

Payments to Governments
Payments to governments in the form of royalties or taxes were set at given rates for the entire duration of the agreements. In other words, these could not be altered during the span of the agreements without the consent of the concessionaires.

Arbitration
The agreements provided for the settlement of disputies by means of international arbitration, rather than through the national courts of the host country.

In time, of course, some of these company prerogatives became eroded through the force of host government pressure. But the fact remained that, in the concession documents, these host governments had signed away their sovereign powers of action in a number of vital areas, notably decision-making on prices, production and export levels, and tax and royalty rates.* This system of the majors, though perhaps already showing signs of wear and tear, was still largely intact when OPEC came upon the scene in 1960.

It can be argued that the oil reserves of the Middle East and Venezuela could never have been developed at the pace and volume required to fuel the world economic resurgence after World War II had it not been for the expertise, financial resources and downstream refining/

* *Unlike the Middle Eastern producers, Venezuela retained its freedom of action vis-à-vis royalty and tax rates, which it used to good effect in 1948, 1958, 1966 and 1970 when the state unilaterally raised its share of profits to 50%, 65%, 72% and over 80% respectively.*

marketing outlets of the major international companies. On the other hand, that self-same relentless efficiency of the closed integrated system established by the majors served to imprison the newly emerging producing countries in an economic and political straight-jacket which in the long term was bound to prove intolerable to national sovereignty and interests.

Before the emergence of OPEC, there had been two serious rebellions against the system of the majors — the first in Mexico in 1938, and the second in Iran in 1951. There were, of course, wide differences in the historical background of the two nationalizations — in Mexico the impetus came from the oil workers' dissatisfaction with their labour conditions, while in Iran a nationalistically-minded parliament was reacting against the financial inequity of the concession agreement with Anglo-Iranian (BP) — but in both cases the basic motivation showed a broad similarity: on the one hand a deep feeling of suffocation and frustration of national aspirations under the concession system administered by the majors, and on the other a simple desire for a fairer financial deal, that is to say a more appropriate slice of a very large cake.

In both cases, also, the reactions of the major oil companies and their political backers were broadly similar: severance of diplomatic relations by Britain though not by the US in either case, an all-embracing boycott of exports of nationalized "hot" oil to international markets, and the switching of crude oil output to other, more compliant producing areas where the same major companies were in operational control. In the case of Mexico its pre-nationalization exports of 60,000 b/d were rapidly made up through expanded production in Venezuela, while the three-year 1951-54 halt in Iranian production witnessed a compensatory growth in output from neighbouring Saudi Arabia, Kuwait and Iraq. This horizontal integration of the oil companies which enabled them to switch sources of crude supply at will in the event of any conflict with an individual host government remained the most potent weapon in the major's armory until it was finally neutralized by OPEC in the 1970s.

In both countries settlements were eventually imposed on rather humiliating conditions. The Mexican Government was forced to agree to compensation of $180 million — a huge sum in present value terms — the last instalment of which was not paid until 1963. In Iran, although the act of nationalization was never repealed, the 1954 settlement with the Consortium provided for nothing more than the standard 50-50 concession terms which had been generalized in other neighbouring producing countries without the trauma of a three-year shutdown of production.

4

The ill-fated nationalizations in Mexico and Iran cast a long shadow over relations between the major oil companies and their host governments. The memory of these premature efforts to challenge the concession system was certainly one of the motives for the caution exercised by the OPEC Countries in their dealings with the companies during the early years of the Organization's existence. However, by the time nationalization-type confrontations arose between governments and companies in Iraq, Algeria and Libya in the early 1970s, the companies were no longer able to mobilize the same degree of muscle, either in terms of solidarity between themselves, access to alternative sources of supply, or political backing from their home governments. And in today's conditions the type of reactions occasioned in the West by the Mexican and Iranian crisis would be absolutely unthinkable — which is perhaps a fair measure of the extent of the practical and psychological change that has taken place during OPEC's first 20 years.

Prices Administered by the Majors

Perhaps the first thing to make clear in any discussion of the crude oil pricing system maintained, albeit with decreasing efficiency in later years, by the major oil companies during the 30-odd years prior to the formation of OPEC is that these were basically "administered" prices insulated as far as possible from the cut and thrust of pure market-place competition. To put a complex matter in simple and necessarily rather crude terms, this was made possible through a sophisticated, though never entirely successful, effort at cartelization of the international oil industry (outside the United States with its ever-intrusive anti-trust legislation) based on the so-called Pool Association of September 17, 1928, more generally known as the Achnacarry Agreement or "As Is" Agreement. The story of this agreement — how the world's three most powerful oilmen of the time, the heads of Royal Dutch/Shell (Sir Henri Deterding), the Standard Oil Company of New Jersey (Mr. Walter Teagle) and Anglo-Persian (Sir John Cadman) met during a grouse shoot at the Scottish castle of Achnacarry to organize the world oil business — has been told often enough elsewhere.[2] Nor is it germane here to go into the various controversies as to whether or not the Achnacarry and related agreements and understandings constituted cartel activity in the strict sense of the term. Suffice it to say that, after a bout of unusually fierce price competition in the international market,* the big three — themselves accounting for over 50% of total oil sales outside the US (28% for Jersey, 16% for Shell and 11.5% for Anglo-Persian/BP) and later to be joined by most of the other significant world oil traders — agreed in 1928 on the following principles for restoring order in the market:

(1) Acceptance and maintenance of the 1928 status quo in proportional market shares as between the various participants.

(2) Making surplus existing facilities available to participants on a preferential cost bases.

(3) Avoidance of unnecessary duplication in the addition of new facilities.

(4) Maintaining for each producing area the financial advantages of its geographical location, "it being recognized that the value of the basic products of uniform specifications are the same at all points of origin and shipment and that this gives to each producing area an advantage in supplying consumption in the territory geographically tributary thereto, which should be retained by the production in that area."

(5) Drawing supplies for a given market from the nearest production area with a view to achieving maximum efficiency and economy in transportation.

(6) Preventing surplus crude from any given geographical area from upsetting the price structure in any other area.

(7) Discouragement of measures that would materially increase costs.

Insofar as the status-quo division of local markets for petroleum products in various consuming countries was concerned, the Achnacarry principles provided the basis for a number of detailed agreements both of a general and a local character, but few of them seem to have been entirely successful for very long. And by the early 1940s the operation of the US anti-trust laws had put an end to any formal participation by US companies in such arrangements.

However, the Achnacarry principles did have a significant and lasting effect on the pricing of crude oil and refined products moving in international trade, through the consolidation of the so-called "US Gulf-Plus" pricing system under which the delivered price of crude oil or products from whatever source would be equated to the price for comparable oil at the US Gulf of Mexico plus freight from there to the destination

---

* In the words of the preamble to the As Is Agreement: "Excessive competition has resulted in the tremendous overproduction of today, when over the world the shut-in production amounts to approximately 60% of the production actually going into consumption."

concerned. It was this mechanism that facilitated the application of the fourth of the Achnacarry principles to the effect that each producing area should enjoy the financial advantages of its geographical location. In other words, with US Gulf being taken as the sole basing point for world prices, in sales from any other producing area to a nearby location, closer to it than the US Gulf, the buyer would have to absorb, and the seller stand to benefit from what is known as "phantom freight" – i.e. freight charged for in the delivered price but not actually incurred in practice. For example, a cargo of oil delivered to India from the Middle East would be priced on a c.i.f. basis as if it had come from the US Gulf; that is, US Gulf price plus freight to India, with the producer benefiting from the element of phantom freight for the voyage that never was between the US Gulf and the Middle East. Thus, under this system, the f.o.b. realization of the Middle East producer was higher than the US Gulf base price in nearby markets (benefit from phantom freight), equal at a point equidistant between the Middle East Gulf and the US Gulf (i.e. the mid-Mediterranean around Italy), and less in more distant markets west of Italy where the Middle East producer was liable to freight absorption in order to equalize his delivered prices with those of shipments from the US Gulf.

This single basing point Gulf-plus system lasted until 1944-45 when – in response to pressure from the British and American military procurement authorities who objected to paying phantom freight for supplies of Middle East to East of Suez destinations – the companies concerned simply removed the "plus" from "US Gulf-plus" and established the Middle East Gulf as a second f.o.b. price basing point with prices equal to those at the US Gulf. The two identical f.o.b. prices – US Gulf and Middle East Gulf – therefore equalized on a c.i.f. basis for West of Suez deliveries approximately at Italy.

By way of example, if we take the price of 36° API crude at the end of World War II – which was \$1.05/barrel at both the Gulf of Mexico and the Middle East Gulf – we find that the delivered prices of US and Middle East crudes were closely aligned at Naples (\$/barrel):

	FOB	Freight	CIF Naples
Gulf of Mexico	1.05	1.10	2.15
Middle East Gulf	1.05	1.18	2.23

However, following the end of the war, crude oil prices shot up under the impact of sharply increased demand in the US and Europe and the lifting of price controls in the US. By December 1947 the delivered price of Texas sour crude at the Gulf of Mexico reached $2.75/barrel as compared with $1.05 at the end of the war. Prices of Middle East crudes followed the upward trend of US prices, but only part of the way. In the years that followed the ever-widening gap between f.o.b. prices at the Gulf of Mexico and the Middle East Gulf was officially explained in terms of the necessity of widening the competitive scope of ever-increasing supplies of Middle East oil in markets further and further westwards. In fact, in view of the tight control over the market then exercised by the major integrated oil companies, the "competitive model" thesis is difficult to sustain. A more likely explanation lies in the very considerable pressure exerted by a large US government-sponsored buyer of Middle East crude. This was the European Cooperation Administration (ECA) which from 1948 to 1952 financed oil supplies to Europe under the Marshall Plan. As we shall see, the ECA was anxious to see that Middle East oil was delivered to Europe as cheaply as possible and during its years of operation succeeded in bringing about a reduction of over 20% in the Middle East Gulf price level.

While the price at the Gulf of Mexico had risen to $2.75/barrel, the Middle East Gulf price climbed to $2.22/barrel in early 1948 (this being just before the ECA began operations in April 1948). The smaller increase in the Middle East Gulf price was rationalized at the time as being necessary to permit Middle East crude to be delivered to Northwest Europe, rather than only as far as Italy, competitively with oil from the United States. In retrospect this argument looks rather thin, considering that in 1948 the United States became a net importer of oil and in that year supplied only 9,000 b/d of crude oil to Europe as compared with Middle East deliveries to Europe of 220,000 b/d. However, Western Hemisphere crude from Venezuela did become a significant source of supply for Europe with deliveries of 85,000 b/d in 1948. Under this formula, the equalization of delivered prices of 36^O API crude from the two areas at Southampton in the UK worked out as follows[3] ($/barrel with freight at USMC flat):

	FOB	Freight	CIF
Gulf of Mexico	2.75	1.02	3.77
Middle East Gulf	2.22	1.55	3.77

The first anomaly that the ECA fixed upon was the fact that the US Gulf of Mexico was still being used as a price basing point despite the fact that export shipments of US oil had virtually dried up. On the other hand, Venezuelan crude – which was being shipped in significant volumes to Europe – was priced at 10 cents a barrel below US Gulf crude (to offset the amount of the prevailing US import tax on crude) as well as enjoying a 15-cent freight advantage over US Gulf crude in relation to Northwest European destinations. Thus by mid-1948 the ECA had prodded the companies into reducing Middle East Gulf prices by a net 15 cents to $2.03/barrel.

From now on the Western Hemisphere price basing point was to be located in the Caribbean, though the link with US prices was maintained in that Venezuelan crude prices were themselves derived from the US Gulf price. Under this formula the Venezuelan price was to be equivalent to the US Gulf price plus freight to New York minus US import tax minus freight from Venezuela to New York – in other words the delivered prices of US Gulf and Venezuelan crudes were equalized at the US East Coast (New York). The result as regards the equalization of delivered prices of Middle Eastern and Venezuelan crudes at Southampton was as follows* ($/barrel with freight at USMC flat):[4]

	FOB	Yield Diff.	Freight	CIF
Venezuelan Oficina	2.65	–	0.87	3.52
Arabian ex-Ras Tanura	2.03	0.04	1.45	3.52

The ECA's relentless pressure on Middle East crude prices did not stop there. The administration began to argue that since supplies of Middle East oil had started to flow further westwards to US East Coast markets in appreciable volumes (100,000 b/d in 1949), the equalization point for delivered prices of supposedly competitive Middle Eastern and Caribbean crudes should be shifted across the Atlantic from the UK to the US East Coast – thereby most conveniently for Europe and the ECA, slashing both the f.o.b. Middle East Gulf price and the delivered price of Middle East crude supplies to Europe. This was despite the fact that Europe was still overwhelmingly the main market for Middle Eastern oil, accounting for over 80% of the area's exports, and that deliveries of Middle East crude to the US were in no sense the result of competitive

---

* *A change-over from Iranian Light f.o.b. Abadan to Arabian Light f.o.b. Ras Tanura as the marker crude resulted in a saving of 10 cents on freight with a loss of 4 cents in yield differential vis-à-vis Venezuelan Oficina crude.*

open-market penetration, but rather represented a restricted inter-affiliate movement of oil within the integrated system of the majors. Not surprisingly, the ECA proposal met with initial stiff resistance from the oil companies since, at flat USMC freight rates, it would have entailed a 36% reduction in the Ras Tanura price to $1.30/barrel.

However, the early part of 1949 witnessed a dramatic fall in freight rates which permitted the companies to propose a formula, based on a lower freight charge of USMC minus 35%, which would accomodate a shift in the price equalization point across the Atlantic without requiring such a drastic cut in Middle East f.o.b. prices. Thus, by September 1949 the majors had reduced their Middle East Gulf marker price to $1.75/barrel, with the following formula for equalization with Caribbean prices at New York ($/barrel with freight at USMC minus 35.5%)[5]:

	FOB	US Tax	Yield Diff.	Freight	CIF
W. Texas ex-US Gulf	2.75	—	—	0.25	3.00
Venezuelan Oficina	2.65	0.10	—	0.25	3.00
Arabian ex-Ras Tanura	1.75	0.10	0.04	1.11	3.00

Such a neat formula could hardly have been expected to hold up for very long, and in fact it operated satisfactorily only for a year or so after its adoption. It suffered from a number of inherent and inescapable theoretical defects which rendered it incapable of responding to changing market conditions. Had the formula represented a truly competitive model, f.o.b. prices at the basing point areas would have fluctuated with changes in freight rates. In practice they did not. The $1.75/barrel Middle East Gulf price was maintained unchanged right through until the middle of 1953, despite the fact that freight rates more than doubled in 1950-51 under the impact of the Korean war — which would, under the strict application of the netback formula from New York, have reduced the Middle East f.o.b. price by a quite intolerable 85 cents a barrel, or over 50%.[6]

Also in respect of freight rates, the formula contained a theoretical anomaly fatal to its practical functioning. If it had responded to changes in freight rates, it would have had the perverse result of depressing Middle East f.o.b. prices at times of high freight rates (presumably betokening strong demand for oil) and to put them up when freight rates fell (presumably under the impact of slackening demand).

Thus, it can be seen that these were in no sense prices set in the market place by the competitive play of the forces of supply and demand.

Rather, the major companies were endeavouring to maintain a system of administered prices designed to meet their own particular requirements, i.e. an appropriate price for transactions within a highly integrated set-up which at the same time could be justified to the authorities concerned with reference to a "competitive" price.

It is also clear that the evolution of Middle East crude prices in the post-war period was directly influenced by political pressure from the US Government, which was committed to financing and securing plentiful supplies of cheap Middle East oil to fuel the reconstruction of Europe's war-torn economy.[7] For their part, the oil companies responded to the demands of the ECA because:

(a) In the final analysis they could but not be subject to the dictates of their home governments, and acquiescence to ECA demands was a precondition for access to the rapidly expanding markets of Europe.

(b) The huge reserves, output potential and low production costs of Middle East oil (some 10-20 cents a barrel as against 50 cents in Venezuela and around $1.00 in the US) compensated for the relative loss of price income and ensured that profit margins remained substantial.

(c) There was at the time no significant counter-pressure from the governments of the producing countries (which were at the time paid for oil exports on the basis of a fixed royalty per ton regardless of price).

From 1953 onwards the link between Western Hemisphere and Middle Eastern prices gradually weakened until by the end of the decade, and particularly with the imposition of mandatory oil import controls in the US in 1959, it was severed altogether. When Western Hemisphere prices rose during the Korean War and the 1957 Suez crisis, Middle Eastern prices followed to a lesser extent; and when prices fell back again during the post-Suez period, the reductions in the Middle East were greater. The evolution of posted prices for 36° API crude during this period was as follows ($ 1 barrel):

	US Gulf	Venezuela	Saudi Arabia
Start-1953	2.75	2.55	1.75
End-1953	3.00	2.80	1.97
Start-1957	3.25	3.05	1.97
End-1957	3.25	3.05	2.12
April-1959	3.10	2.80	1.94
Aug-1960	3.10	2.80	1.84

Thus, it may be seen that whereas Middle East crude began the post-war period at price parity with the US Gulf, by 1960 the former had dropped to only 59% of the latter. During the fifties the gap between US Gulf and Middle East postings widened from $1.00/barrel to $1.26/barrel by August 1960.

Though masked for a time by the political crises of the Korean and Suez wars, the underlying weakness of the price structure became more and more evident towards the end of the decade when the following factors began to weigh heavily on the market:

— A formidable overhang of surplus capacity, estimated at some 20-25%, had been developed in the Middle East.
— With the imposition of "voluntary" import controls in 1957, followed by a mandatory programme in 1959, the US market was virtually sealed off and insulated from world market trends. Independent companies which had developed crude oil production overseas in the expectation of importing it into the US had to look elsewhere for markets, thereby increasing the competitive pressure on the international scene.*
— In the world market, price competition was growing from new suppliers outside the charmed circle of the eight international majors: US independents which had gained access to production in Iran, Arabia and Venezuela and were now largely cut off from the US market, and the Soviet Union, which re-emerged in the late-1950s as an aggressively competitive oil exporter. Also the majors themselves, with the incentive of handsome profits from incremental output from their prolific Middle East fields, were compounding the market rivalry with sales to third parties at increasingly discounted prices.

All in all, by the end of the fifties the supply and price situation was showing all the signs of getting way out of hand, thereby setting the stage for the active entry on to the scene of the hitherto unconsulted parties — the governments of the oil exporting countries.

* *During the 1960s US prices, bolstered by prorationing of production and import controls, held steady in the $3.00 - 3.50/barrel range, while realized market prices for Middle East crudes were eroded to a low of about $1.30/barrel. However, during this period the elevated and stable level of US prices did provide a target aspiration for the Middle East producing countries.*

Inter-Affiliate Prices

It should be noted that the prices referred to above — what are known as "posted" prices — tell only a part of the story. Posted prices were originally designed to represent the open market prices at which crude oil was available for sale to buyers generally, and until the late-1950s posted prices did in fact fairly closely parallel market levels. However, by the late 1950s discounting of posted prices had become widespread. When, after the creation of OPEC, posted prices became effectively frozen as a result of host government pressure, they became operational only for purposes of calculating the government's tax and royalty income, so the gap between postings and actual realized market prices gradually widened.

However, even in the fifties posted prices did not necessarily represent the prices at which the great bulk of the world oil trade moved within the integrated system of the majors. The Aramco price to off-takers, for example, was 18% below the posted prices — $1.43/barrel in 1951-1953, rising to $1.58/barrel in 1953 — and interaffiliate prices in general were within limits set by individual integrated companies in such a way as to best suit their tax and profit situation. Also there were a number of interlocking long-term crude supply deals between the majors themselves, with prices generally set at below market levels in line with various formulae designed for the purpose.

Profit Sharing

In most of the original Middle Eastern concession agreements, payments to the host governments were set at a fixed royalty per ton of oil produced and exported — generally four gold shillings per ton, which at the time was equivalent to around $1.65 per ton or 22 cents a barrel. This level of payment was perhaps barely defensible in pre-war days when price and production prospects were uncertain, but by the late forties, when prices had risen and the economy of Europe had become totally dependent on Middle East oil supplies, such a meagre recompense to the host governments had become little short of scandalous and it was hardly surprising that a powerful groundswell of agitation for a more equitable share of oil profits should have arisen among the governments concerned. In Iran, of course, the road to a better deal had to pass through a bitter three-year confrontation with the oil companies, but elsewhere the transition progressed more smoothly.

Meanwhile, an example for the Middle East had already been set in Venezuela where, in 1948, the government raised its tax rate to provide for 50-50 division of profits between it and the companies. This formula was extended to most Middle Eastern producing countries in 1951-1952 and had a dramatic impact on the level of unit oil revenue, which rose eventually in the mid-fifties to something in the region of 80 cents a barrel from the flat royalty rate of 22 cents a barrel in 1950.* The full effect of the introduction of the 50% tax on oil income in the Middle East was however delayed, owing to the companies' insistence on granting themselves substantial discounts (around 17-18% in Saudi Arabia and Iraq) off posted prices for tax purposes. Under heavy government pressure these were largely discontinued in the mid-fifties and from then on the calculation of tax liability on the basis of the full posted prices became the norm.

This boost in the revenue of the producing countries was not, however, reflected in any corresponding fall in the production profits of the oil companies. Motivated by considerations of overriding high policy, the US authorities issued a ruling allowing oil tax (but not royalty) payments to foreign governments to be offset against US tax liability, and similar arrangements were later introduced in the UK. As can be imagined, these rulings were absolutely crucial in that they provided the American and British multinationals with an unprecedented financial latitude to facilitate their dealings with the oil producing countries.

For tax reasons it suited the companies very well to keep within the production stage the bulk of their overall profit from integrated operations. After the introduction of 50-50 profit sharing the majors were left with a very comfortable profit margin of 80-90 cents/barrel (something like $4.0-4.5 in 1980 dollars) at the production stage in the Middle East. This provided a very substantial pool of funds, insulated from the demands of any national taxing authority, which more than compensated for the relatively modest level of downstream returns from refining and marketing. Thus, in the post-war period, through the fifties and early sixties, the oil companies were able to make use of these production profits (earned, needless to say, directly from the natural resources of the producing nations) to finance virtually all their investment, downstream as well as upstream, without needing to have recourse to the money markets — a record which no other industry could match.

* Under the new arrangement the royalty — now set at 12.5% of the posted price — was submerged in the 50% tax by being fully creditable against tax liability.

In terms of return on invested capital, also, the companies' investment in Middle East oil production operations was quite spectacularly profitable. According to a study undertaken for OPEC by the international consulting house of Arthur D. Little in the early 1960s, the rates of return on investment in Middle East oil production ventures for the five years 1956-1960 inclusive averaged over 60%. For Aramco in Saudi Arabia, rates of return ranged from a low of 57% in 1958 to a high of 71% in 1980, with a five-year average of 61%. IPC in Iraq registered returns on investment varying between 36% in 1957 and 75% in 1960 for a five-year average of 62%. In Iran, the consortium's figures ranged between 63% in 1956 and 78% in 1957, with an average of 71% for the five-year period. In Qatar, QPC notched up rates of return ranging from 83% (1960) to 150% (1958) for an average of 114%.

In Venezuela, on the other hand, the situation was a good deal less favourable for the companies. In 1953-57 the companies' per barrel net earnings in Venezuela were roughly comparable with the Middle East, ranging between 64 cents and 87 cents (64 cents in 1953, 65 cents in 1954, 70 cents in 1955, 76 cents in 1956 and 87 cents in 1957); but after the 1958 tax increase they fell sharply to between 38 cents and 45 cents in 1958-62 (45 cents in 1958, 42 cents in 1959, 38 cents in 1960, 44 cents in 1961 and 43 cents in 1962). The companies' return on net assets in Venezuela, which had ranged between 20% and 32% in 1953-57, fell to 12-17% in 1958-62.[8]

The Majors' System Analysed

Summing up, it is evident that the system of the majors — magnificent edifice though it was in many ways — was designed first and foremost for the convenience of the companies themselves, then the western industrialized consuming countries (of which the multinationals are an essential offshoot), with the producing countries coming a poor third.

The companies, as a group, were able to ensure for themselves secure and diversified sources of raw material supplies for their international ventures, with a firm financial base from which to finance the totality of their integrated operations.

Although, as the ECA case demonstrated, there were times when Western consumer interests were at loggerheads with the multinationals over oil prices, the consuming countries certainly benefited from the "system" through their guaranteed access to secure and plentiful supplies of relatively cheap oil. In particular, the economic recovery of Europe would not have been possible without availability of Middle East oil in the quantities required and at a price and foreign exchange cost which the Europeans, with American aid, could absorb. On the other hand, it could well be argued that the very cheapness of the oil supplies unduly stimulated demand to the point of dangerous overconsumption of, and overdependence on oil energy, which was to create problems for both consumers and producers later on.

For the producing countries the balance sheet was far less positive. Their status was akin to that of politically subdued raw material depots supplying cheap energy for the insatiable industries of the West, with little or no say in the disposal of their depletable natural resource. Also, the post-war transfer of refining facilities from the centres of production to the centres of consumption — for strategic, technical and balance of payments reasons — left the producers with little chance of profiting from the added financial value or economic development opportunities opened up by the further processing of crude oil. True, unit oil revenues improved substantially after the introduction of 50-50 profit sharing, but the improvement started from a very low base and still left a handsome portion of the economic rent in the hands of the companies. All this would seem to indicate that the oil producing countries were in fact subsidizing the growth of the industrial powers by means of a substantial transfer of wealth.

Just how much of the theoretical economic rent from oil was appropriated by the oil companies and consumers rather than the producers was demonstrated by a study first conducted by OPEC in 1963. The study, the results of which were never contested, found that of the average price of a barrel of refined petroleum products to the final consumer at that time — around $11 — only 6.7% (around 74 cents) was accounted for by government revenues of the producing countries, compared with 52.3% (about $5.75) by direct and indirect taxes on oil imposed by the governments of the producing countries. The full details of this instructive breakdown of this final price of the oil barrel was as follows:

- 45.5% indirect oil taxes in consuming countries.
- 6.8% turnover and direct taxes in consuming countries.
- 6.9% oil company net profits.
- 21.8% storage, handling, distribution and dealer's margin.
- 5.5% tanker freight.
- 4.5% cost of refining.
- 6.7% government revenues of producing countries.
- 2.3% cost of production.

16

In all this, it should be borne in mind that the OPEC Countries were never against the administration of oil prices as such. They, like the oil companies and most consumer governments, agreed that oil was too sensitive and vital an industry to be exposed to the uncontrolled forces of supply and demand. A high degree of organization and administration was clearly essential. What the producers questioned was the advisability of allowing the oil companies to do it all on their own.

CHAPTER II

THE FOUNDATION OF OPEC

As we have seen, signs of price weakness in the crude oil market had been evident way back in the early 1950s, but had been camouflaged by the political upheavals of the Korean and Suez crises. By 1958 the granting of substantial discounts off posted prices in arms-length sales to third parties had become widespread practice. Of course at that time the third-party market accounted for only a small proportion, probably no more than 10% of the whole, and sales between affiliates of the major integrated international companies, which represented the vast bulk of the market, continued in general to be invoiced at posted prices. But rumblings of complaint against the use of such prices in inter-affiliate transactions were already making themselves heard in some consuming countries, particularly those afflicted by balance of payments problems.

All in all, the profit picture of the majors remained healthy enough. In addition to the fat margin of 80 cents/barrel at the production stage there was a slimmer, but at that time still quite positive, return on downstream operations.* Nevertheless, pressure on prices at the margin was undoubtedly mounting.

The big question therefore presented itself as to exactly who should bear the brunt of the impending reduction in income from crude oil sales. In a formal sense, of course, the answer was in the hands of the companies who, under the 50-50 profit-sharing amendments to the concession agreements introduced in the early 1950s, claimed the contractual right to determine the posted/tax reference prices upon which the tax and royalty income of the oil exporting governments was calculated, and this had not yet been subjected to any effective challenge on the part of the producer governments.

Initially, the companies exhibited no qualms about obliging the producer governments to bear part of the revenue effects of the market

* *In a 1958 memorandum to the Saudi Government the Aramco parent companies — Exxon, Texaco, Standard Oil of California and Mobil Oil — said they were making between 6.5 and 12.3 cents per barrel from downstream operations at that time. See interview with Abdullah Al-Tariki in Middle East Economic Survey (MEES), January 8, 1960.*

decline. They therefore unilaterally and without consultation with the producer governments, reduced posted/tax reference prices in 1959 and again in 1960, thereby inflicting a revenue loss of some 15% on the governments concerned. In the long term this was a costly mistake on the companies' part for it served to awaken the actual owners of the oil resources from their inaction. In particular, the 1960 price reduction provided the spark for the emergence of a governmental counter force — the Organization of the Petroleum Exporting Countries (OPEC) — which was eventually responsible for the destruction of the concession system and for bringing about a radical change in an important sector of international economic relations.

The 1959-60 Price Reductions

At the beginning of 1959 posted export prices for crude oil were still at a level reflecting price increases which were introduced as a result of the 1956-57 Suez crisis and the subsequent temporary shortage of supply in Western Europe. The prices of US and Venezuelan crudes, which had been rushed to Europe to make up for the shortage, had risen by as much as 25 cents a barrel. When the Suez Canal was eventually reopened to shipping in May 1957, Middle East crude also registered a price rise, but this was of the order of only 13 cents a barrel. Thus, the traditional link between US/Caribbean and Middle East prices, which had been under strain even before Suez — since 1953 in fact — was further weakened. And with the low freight rates prevailing in late-1957 and 1958 Middle East oil could be delivered to the US East Coast and other Western Hemisphere markets significantly more cheaply than US domestic or Venezuelan crudes.

In 1957-58 indications of crude price weakness in the open market were provided by bids for supply tenders in various Latin American countries (Argentina and Brazil in particular) where the competing suppliers included both major internationals like British Petroleum, and newcomers such as the Soviet Union and various American independents with production in Venezuela (who had been blocked off from their expected markets in the United States owing to the introduction of import restrictions there). As the bids were generally quoted on a c.i.f. basis, it is difficult to determine the level of f.o.b. discount with any precision. But, on the basis of BP sales of 31° API Kuwait crude to Argentina in 1958, the indicated level of f.o.b. discount off the posted price for Kuwait crude ($1.85/barrel) was somewhere between 9 cents and 24 cents, or in the range of 5% to 13%.[1]

Meanwhile, in the United States — despite the introduction of import controls and tight prorationing by the main producing states — a general weakness in refined product prices was translated into pressure on crude oil postings which gradually eroded through 1958. In January 1959 Shell reduced the price of West Texas crude — still at that time regarded as a reference guide for world crude prices — by 15 cents a barrel, and in February followed this up with a similar reduction in the posted prices of comparable Venezuelan crudes. This in itself might have been accepted as a post-Suez shakedown in the Western Hemisphere. However, a few days later British Petroleum initiated an 18-cent cut in Middle East crude postings which was rapidly generalized by other producing companies in that area. In 1957 price increases in the Middle East had been substantially less than in the Western Hemisphere (13-15 cents a barrel in the former, as against 25 cents in the latter), whereas in February 1959 on the downward side the reductions in the Middle East (18 cents) were in excess of those in the US and Venezuela (15 cents). Prices between the Western Hemisphere and the Middle East had by now got thoroughly out of balance, which was by no means fully redressed when the producing companies in Venezuela (apart from BP itself, largely those major international companies which were operating in the Middle East) made a further reactive cut of 10 cents a barrel in April in what was described as a move to "help restore the competitive position of Venezuelan crude in the world market."[2] This time the cut was not reciprocated in the Middle East. Quite apart from the lack of necessity — Middle East crudes were quite competitive enough as it was — the majors were no doubt apprehensive about the mounting reaction in the producing countries against their escalating price cuts, which had begun to take on the ominous appearance of price warfare between the Middle East and Venezuela.

Quite apart from its long-term significance as marking the final demise of the linkage between world crude prices and those of the US Gulf, the 1959 BP-led reduction in Middle East prices could not even be justified in commercial terms. Helmut Frank, an independent observer of the oil price scene in the 1950s and early 1960s, makes this pertinent comment:

"Certainly Middle East prices did not have to be reduced to maintain their competitive market position against US and Venezuelan crudes, even after the prices of the latter had been lowered, because of the low freight rate in the post-Suez period. At USMC minus 50%, representative of new long-term charters in 1957, the delivered price of Middle East

20

crude at the United States East Coast was only two cents above the well-head price of West Texas crudes (ignoring quality differences). And at the still lower spot rates prevailing somewhat later in 1957 and all of 1958, Middle East crude could be delivered at US East Coast ports some 60-80 cents below the Gulf Coast price of domestic crude.

"The relation of Middle East to Venezuelan crude, with its close price link to Texas, was similar. Consequently, Middle East oil was able rapidly to regain and then exceed its former share of the import market, following the reopening of the Suez Canal. In 1958, its share of total US crude imports rose to 31.8% from 27.5% two years earlier. An even sharper shift in favour of the Middle East occurred in the Canadian market, and at the East Coast of South America the delivered price relationships heavily favoured the Middle East at any freight rates below flat USMC. Had they wished to maintain price parity in this market, Venezuelan producers would have had to make deeper cuts in their posted prices than the 15-cent reduction of early 1959. There was, therefore, no strictly commercial reason for Middle East crude prices to follow the downward adjustments in the Western Hemisphere. In fact, the reverse was true: Venezuelan producers pointed to the smaller advances made in the Middle East in 1953, and especially in 1957, as one reason for lowering their prices. *The clue to the post-Suez price reduction must thus be sought in the area of long-range policy decisions rather than in current market pressures.*" [3]

At least part of the explanation may be found in the particular set-up of BP which spearheaded the 1959 Middle East price cuts. The British firm had under its control huge oil reserves in the Middle East — with a developed export capacity far in excess of the requirements of its own refining and marketing outlets — and no production or refining interests whatever in the Western Hemisphere. To a larger extent than any of the other majors therefore, BP was subject to the temptation of indulging in price cutting with a view to enlarging its third-party sales of Middle East crude, even in distant markets like South America, which normally draw their supplies from nearby Venezuela. In this situation where price discounting was prevalent, it was actually to the advantage of the company concerned to make the largest cuts in posted prices it could get away with, firstly in order to minimize its per-barrel payments to Middle East Governments (whose tax and royalty income was calculated on posted prices), and secondly to enhance its competitive position vis-à-vis marginal sales which, even discounted in price, still earned a handsome profit. Thus it is difficult to escape the conclusion that BP deliberately broke what remained of the link with US Gulf prices for the purpose of maximizing its own sales of and profits from Middle East crude.

At the time, one explanation given in the London financial press of the larger price cut in the Middle East than in Venezuela was that since Middle East Governments were likely to demand an increase in exports to offset the price cuts, the greater reduction in Middle East crude prices would help to give Middle East oil a competitive advantage in world markets.[4] However, had the Middle East Governments concerned been consulted about the price cuts — which they were not — they might well have shown more concern about maintaining their unit revenue rather than maximizing sales volume by cutting prices.

The situation for the producing countries was indeed alarming, with the looming spectre of a price war over which they would have no control. For Venezuela the position was even more problematical, for in March 1959, hard on the heels of the February price cuts, the United States Government introduced a system of mandatory oil import quotas to replace the previous, insufficiently effective voluntary restrictions. Venezuela was thus faced with the constriction of its principal market, on top of price competition with the more prolific and lower cost oil reserves of the Middle East.

Venezuela, therefore, embarked upon a series of protective measures, some of which at least bore even greater fruit than was anticipated at the time. These measures included:

— The initiation of a series of contacts and consultations with the producing countries of the Middle East with a view to stabilizing the price and production situation.
— The dispatch of an angry note of protest, via the British Ambassador in Caracas, to the British Government (the majority shareholder in BP) in respect of the British company's unwarranted cuts in Middle East crude postings.[5]
— The forwarding of a memorandum to the United States Government, via the US Ambassador in Caracas, regarding the introduction of mandatory oil import restrictions in that country. The memorandum complained that the mandatory system of US oil import quotas should have incorporated preferential treatment for oil imports from Western Hemisphere sources "with the object of maintaining the normal market structure of the United States for oil received from Venezuela." It pointed out that the lack of such preferential treatment could lead to a loss of markets for Venezuelan oil, "whose place would be taken by lower priced oil from other countries."

This could be interpreted as a reprisal action against Venezuelan efforts to gain a more equitable share of "the excessive earnings of North American capital invested in Venezuela's oil industry" (a reference to the 1958 increase of the Venezuelan Government's share of oil industry profits from 52% to 65%-70%).[6]

- The creation, in April 1959, of a "Coordinating Commission for the Conservation and Commerce of Hydrocarbons" within the Ministry of Mines and Hydrocarbons. The purpose of this new body was to act as a sort of watchdog over the production and sales programmes of the concessionaire companies, these being of particular concern in Venezuela where income tax liability was calculated on realized market prices rather than on posted prices as in the Middle East. As time went on, the Commission gradually tightened its policy as to the level of discounts it was prepared to sanction for tax purposes.

In a press interview in October 1959[7], Venezuela's Oil Minister, Dr. Juan Pablo Perez Alfonzo, made it clear that his government had no wish to enlarge its share of the world oil market or even to maintain its proportionate share of normal market growth; it would be content to see Venezuelan output grow by no more than 4-6% a year (all that was needed for state budgetary requirements) as against a projected 7-8% growth in world demand. He was, however, worried that Venezuela's markets in the United States might also be "progressively captured by cheaper oils" to the point of an actual volumetric drop in Venezuelan production. For this reason, the Venezuelan Oil Minister said, his government was working on a two-point programme:

(i) To persuade Washington to give Venezuela a "guaranteed, fixed market" by allotting it a specific country share of the total import quota. This quota would then be prorated among the companies producing oil in Venezuela, with the proviso that the price should not be lower than that of equivalent US crudes.

(ii) To persuade the Middle East producing countries to join Venezuela in an international compact to prorate production and stabilize prices.

In the event, of course, nothing whatever came of Venezuela's aspiration to obtain a guaranteed hemispheric quota in the US oil import system.* But, by contrast, the second plank in Perez Alfonzo's policy — the approach to the Middle East — was to pay off handsomely.

* It might be interesting to speculate as to how the future course of oil history might have been altered if Washington had been more forthcoming on this particular issue.

Meanwhile, however, the scramble for the uncommitted sector of the world market as between the newcomers — essentially US independent companies on the one hand and the Soviet Union on the other — and the established international majors was continuing unabated, with a consequent further deterioration of realized crude prices. In the trade press discounts off posted prices of 75-80 cents/barrel for Venezuelan crudes and 20-35 cents/barrel for Middle East crudes (presumably sold by the majors) were described as "routine", while Italy's ENI was reportedly able to purchase Soviet oil at a delivered price some 60 cents/barrel below equivalent Middle East crude.[8] As a result of the price weakness in the third-party market, interaffiliate invoice prices (generally still effected at the full posted price) began to come under pressure, particularly from consumer governments afflicted by balance of payments problems. The Indian Government, for example, having been offered Soviet crude at prices substantially below those at which the affiliates of the majors imported oil from their parent companies, made it clear to those companies that, in order to save foreign exchange, they must either themselves process the cheaper Soviet crude or import their Middle East supplies at a more competitive price. The companies declined to use the Soviet oil but did agree to a substantial reduction in the delivered cost of their Middle East crude imports.[9]

Although there had been various indications in the trade press that the major companies were contemplating a further round of posted price cuts in the Middle East, the actual announcement, when it came, appeared to take the Arab governments by surprise, possibly because they were expecting at least to be consulted before hand, in line with a resolution to this effect passed by the Arab Petroleum Congress in Cairo in April 1959 and constantly stressed thereafter by the individual governments concerned. In the event, the price cuts by the companies were as abrupt and unilateral in 1960 as they had been in 1959. This time, however, there were evident differences of approach as between individual major companies. Exxon — the world's largest — led the field with reductions of up to 14 cents/barrel in its Middle East postings on August 9, 1960. On the other hand BP — no doubt chastened by the odium it had incurred in the producing countries by initiating the 1959 Middle East price cuts — issued a public statement saying that it had hoped that action of this kind could have been further deferred by which time conditions might have improved; and when BP finally decided to announce a reduction, it cut its postings only by up to 10 cents/barrel. Of the other majors, Shell, Texaco and Standard Oil of California followed Exxon, while Mobil Oil, Gulf Oil and France's CFP fell into line with BP. Eventually (after the formation of OPEC) the upper-tier group headed by Exxon gave way and realigned its postings on the BP level. The posted/tax reference price of 34° API Arabian Light then settled at $1.80/barrel — where it remained unchanged for the next decade, although realized market prices were to fall as low as $1.30/ barrel at times during the 1960s.

Significantly, the August 1960 cuts in Middle East postings did not spread to Venezuela. There is good evidence that the companies — particularly Exxon and Shell — did originally intend to reduce Venezuelan prices as well, but were deterred from doing so by the certainty of an explosive counter-reaction by the Venezuelan Government. This gives a clean indication of the extent to which the companies were at that time more apprehensive of host government power in Venezuela than in the Middle East.

The overall result of the 1959-60 price cuts was that the per barrel government revenue from a crude oil such as Arabian Light fell by some 14 cents, or over 15%, from around 84 cents in late 1957 to 70 cents after August 9, 1960. In aggregate terms, this worked out at a loss of something like $270 million for the five major Middle East producers — Kuwait, Saudi Arabia, Iran, Iraq and Qatar — on the basis of their 1960 output of 5.2 million b/d. Actual oil revenues of the five countries concerned in 1960 amounted to about $1.4 billion.

In terms of price, the Middle East producing countries thus began the 1960s with their posted/tax reference prices 13 cents per barrel or around 7% lower than they had been in mid1953 (34° API Arabian crude was down from $1.93/barrel in mid-1953 to $1.80/barrel in August 1960 and 31° API Kuwait crude from $1.72/barrel in mid-1953 to $1.59/barrel in August 1960), while the UN world export price index for manufactured goods had risen by 9% during this period. This rate of inflation — a little over 1% a year from 1953 to 1960 — may seem extraordinarily modest when viewed from the standpoint of the galloping 1970s, but when combined with the oil price decline it certainly marked a significant decrease in the purchasing power of the producers' oil barrel in August 1960.

The Broken Link with US Prices

In retrospect, it is difficult to exaggerate the importance of the final breaking of the link between US crude oil prices and international prices, signified by the BP-led reduction in Middle East prices in February

1959. The impact on the producing countries was comparable to the abrupt removal of an essential safety net. And it was perhaps this single development more than anything else which made it inevitable that the oil producing countries would be obliged to get together to defend their interests.

In its strong diplomatic protest to the British Government about BP's action, the Venezuelan Government pointed out that "such an attempt to break the unity of markets and prices is obviously contrary to the common interests of the producing countries, as well as to the long-run interests of the consuming countries."

It also very presciently stressed that the move towards cheaper oil would lull the consumers into a fool's paradise which would have to be paid for later on: "The attempt to separate the prices of oil produced in other regions (ouside the US) tends to ignore a whole historic situation and to base prices arbitrarily on extraction costs alone with serious damage to the countries which own this irreplaceable natural wealth. This procedure seems to have as its only economic purpose a selfish desire on the part of businessmen for fast profits, which apparently also tends to favour the consumers. *But the additional lowering of prices by encouraging consumption could very soon bring oil to the historic cycle of scarcity. This would force consumers to pay much higher prices to finance the exploration and discovery of new areas.*"[10] How prophetic these words now appear!

Another vital and hitherto little-noted fact is that the producing countries regarded the breaking of the link with the US prices as an abandonment of one of the most essential premises on which the 50-50 profit sharing agreements were based. An OPEC position paper put the matter forcefully as follows:

"There was, then, no question either at the time of the signing of the 50-50 agreements or for some years later but that the oil companies set their posted prices both in Venezuela and the Middle East in accordance with US crude postings. In late 1956, US crude prices were advanced by an average of about 25 cents per barrel. For the Middle East the first real break with the tie to US crude occurred in the summer of 1957, when Middle East crudes were advanced in price by an amount equal to only half of the increase in US crude prices. Rapidly deteriorating crude markets thereafter brought pressure to bear on posted prices – a situation that was aggravated by the imposition in early 1959 of mandatory import quotas in the United States. In 1959 and 1960, Middle East crude prices were decreased independently of any movement in US crude prices.

26

"It appears therefore that there was a clear premise at the time of the signing of the 50-50 agreements that the prices to be posted by the major oil companies should remain linked with the prices of crude oil in the United States. As shown above, this was the practice at the time and continued to be the practice for some years thereafter. It could, in fact, scarcely have been otherwise: under conditions where the gross taxable profits of the companies were to be determined solely on the basis of the prices published by the companies themselves, the only protection the signatory governments had against the possibility of a transfer of profits from the crude producing stage to another stage of the integrated operation was the established link with US crude postings. Once that link was effectively broken, there no longer remained any protection for governments in the Middle East against unilateral actions on the part of the companies with respect to their posted prices. Hence the right to which, in all equity, member governments in the Middle East believe they are entitled to, of being consulted before any changes in postings are made."[11]

In other words, with the elimination of the US price link and with the oil companies in sole charge of the level of posted prices on which the revenues of the producing countries were calculated, the latter had no protection of any kind against a collapse of their income levels through price manipulation or otherwise. Under this system crude prices had no floor beyond the bare cost of extraction; and in these circumstances it was obviously incumbent upon the producer governments to construct such a floor through their own efforts based on collective bargaining power and the rights of sovereignty.

Venezuela—Middle East Revenue Disparity

Quite apart from the gap between Venezuelan and Middle Eastern posted prices which had manifested itself by 1960, a very considerable disparity had also developed as between the per barrel revenue receipts in the two regions. This was largely due to the 1958 increase in oil tax rate in Venezuela which boosted the govern-ment's share of gross profits to between 65 and 70% as against 52-53% previously. As has already been mentioned, the Venezuelan Government had no legal difficulty in imposing this increase since, unlike the Middle East producing countries, it was never barred from taking such unilateral action by the terms of its concession agreements.

27

The Venezuelan Income Tax Law of December 19, 1958, increased maximum income tax rates from 26 to 45% of net earnings, in addition to the flat "cedular" income tax of 2.5% which remained in effect. The other component of the government's aggregate oil income was the royalty payments, generally $16\frac{2}{3}$% of crude production valued according to a formula based on US Gulf prices (these being substantially higher than Venezuelan prices), continued unchanged. And this royalty, it should be noted, was treated as an expense item in calculating tax liability, rather than credited entirely against the tax liability as in the Middle East. In other words, in Venezuela the royalty made a positive contribution to the aggregate government revenue over and above the income tax receipts (in fact to the extent of roughly one-half of the royalty payment), instead of being totally submerged in the income tax payment as was the practice in the Middle East.

The higher level of posted prices in Venezuela (roughly one dollar a barrel more than for equivalent Middle East crudes — mainly, though not entirely, attributable to freight advantage vis-à-vis the US East Coast) could, in a comparative revenue calculation between the two areas, be offset by higher Venezuelan production costs (around 50 cents/barrel as against some 20-25 cents/barrel in the Middle East) and the fact that taxes in Venezuela were calculated on realized market prices* as compared with posted prices in the Middle East.**

All this notwithstanding, per barrel payments to the Venezuelan Government were, from 1958 onwards, considerably higher than in the Middle East — by more than 15 cents a barrel an average — despite the fact that the average gravity of Venezuelan output was significantly lower than that of Middle East exports (25° API as against around 33° API). If appropriate adjustment were to be made by the gravity factor, the disparity in per barrel payments would have been much larger.

* *Tempered, of course, over time by the watchdog role of the Coordination Commission, which by 1962 was refusing to accept discounts of over 10% for tax purposes.*
** *Heavy discounts off posted prices for tax purposes (17 - 18% in Saudi Arabia and Iraq) had been phased out by the mid-fifties. But there remained a cost of sale discount, generally 1% of the posted price. And in Saudi Arabia, from 1958 until 1966, third-party sales were invoiced on the basis of realized prices for tax purposes.*

There follows a comparison between per barrel oil revenues in Venezuela and Saudi Arabia (Aramco) between 1953 and 1962.[12] And, as we shall see, one of OPEC's first objectives was to endeavour to correct that evident disparity.

Year	Govt. Revenue ($/Barrel)		Govt. Revenue % of Gross Profits	
	Venezuela	S. Arabia	Venezuela	S. Arabia
1953	0.75	0.69	54	50
1954	0.74	0.81	53	50
1955	0.76	0.78	52	50
1956	0.82	0.78	52	50
1957	0.94	0.81	52	50
1958	1.02	0.79	65	50
1959	0.90	0.73	68	50
1960	0.83	0.70	68	50
1961	0.86	0.69	66	50
1962	0.88	0.69	67	50

Venezuela—Middle East Consultations

Given the circumstances at the time, oil co-operation between the Middle East and Venezuela would most probably have come about regardless of the persons involved. But there can be no doubt that the path towards the formation of OPEC was greatly facilitated by the presence on the scene of two powerful personalities: Dr. Juan Pablo Perez Alfonzo of Venezuela and Abdullah Al-Tariki of Saudi Arabia.

Perez Alfonzo combined the role of a practical man of action with that of a far-ranging thinker on oil matters — a sort of "philosopher of oil." On the practical side, in his first stint as Production Minister in the 1945-48 Accion Democratica Government, Perez Alfonzo spearheaded the introduction of the 50-50 formula in 1948. After the 10-year interregnum of the Perez Jimenez dictatorship, Perez Alfonzo returned in 1958 as Minister of Mines and Hydrocarbons in the new Accion Democratica Government under President Romulo Betancourt, when he was responsible for implementing measures to increase the state's share of oil profits to 65-70%.

As a thinker, Perez Alfonzo saw very clearly from the point of view of an underdeveloped oil exporting country of the Third World, two cardinal facts about oil which Western oilmen from the private multinational companies, preoccupied with the impulsion towards short-term profit maximization, were apt to overlook — particularly in those far-off days when oil was looking for markets rather than the other way round. The first was a deep-seated awareness of oil as a depletable natural resource, a wasting asset with a relatively short life-span. For the oil exporting countries therefore — whose dependence on oil earnings had in most cases become quasi-total — it was essential that the oil money should be used to develop, diversify and transform the domestic economy so as to lay the foundations for long-term survival of the population as oil exports are gradually phased out in the face of declining reserves and growing local energy requirements.

From here it followed, with inexorable logic, that oil exporting countries should gear their production policies towards the maximization of the unit revenue from each exported barrel of this non-renewable resource, rather than laying emphasis upon expanding their exports in terms of volume. In other words, given the satisfaction of essential financial needs, it was absurd for oil exporters to compete for markets in order to sell today at a cheaper unit price what could be sold at a higher value later on.

In the second place, in a sort of corollary to the first argument, Perez Alfonzo had — at a time when such a view was distinctly unfashionable — a lively appreciation of the underlying long-term scarcity of oil as a source of energy and raw material. In 1959 for example, when all the short-term emphasis was on surplus capacity and falling prices, Perez told the Venezuelan National Congress: "Our oil situation is very favourable. World demand is showing progressive increase, yet is not matched by discoveries of new fields which would increase the reserves and guarantee future consumption... Our present situation is not one of begging for markets for our oil. We have information indicating that foreign countries will come begging for it, as they have done in former years... The consuming countries know this very well".[13]

Given the underlying scarcity of oil, its non-renewable nature and the fact that the physical location of the overwhelming bulk of the world's exportable oil reserves was concentrated in a few underdeveloped Third World countries which had a great deal in common politically, economically and socially (to say nothing of the strong religious, cultural and ethnic ties prevalent in the Middle East area), it was clear that the oil exporting countries were potentially in an extremely strong position, if only they could succeed on the one hand in co-ordinating and collectivizing their bargaining power, and on the other hand overcome the political and technological weakness which had led to the imposition of the system of the majors.

These ideas have, of course, long since become part and parcel of basic OPEC thinking. But their initial spread and acceptance was in no small measure due to the influence of Perez Alfonzo.

With this theoretical background, and considering that Venezuela (still at that time the world's largest individual oil exporting country) was producing its slender reserves at a much faster rate than was the case in the more plentifully endowed oil areas of the Middle East, it was not surprising that Venezuela should have offered the Middle East producing countries an international compact to prorate production and stabilize prices, in which Venezuela would be content with a relatively modest share in the growth of world oil demand.

Venezuela's ideas and proposals in this connection met with a sympathetic echo in the Middle East. With their vastly superior oil reserves and lower production costs, the Middle East producers had no logical reason to be afraid of Venezuelan competition in the long term — particularly as the Venezuelans themselves had made it abundantly clear that they had no interest whatever in engaging in any struggle for markets. On the other hand, the Middle East had much to gain from an association with Venezuela and much to learn from that country's experience in the oil industry.

In particular, the Venezuelan Government had clearly demonstrated its effectiveness in imposing its authority on the international companies operating in its territory and in obtaining more equitable financial terms.

In the Middle East, the leading proponent of the Venezuelan connection was Abdullah Al-Tariki, the Director General (later Minister) of Petroleum and Mineral Affairs in Saudi Arabia. A petroleum geologist by training (in Cairo and Texas), Tariki had been Saudi Arabia's top oil official for most of the 1950s. During this period his energies had been directed towards endeavouring to promote Saudi national involvement in the oil industry, as exemplified by the giant Aramco combine owned by four of the largest US multinationals — Exxon, Texaco, Standard Oil of California and Mobil Oil. Among the ideas he advocated were government equity participation in Aramco, and "divorcement" of Aramco from the tight operational control of its four major parent companies, so that a Saudi-based Aramco could enter downstream operations on its own account.

These ideas and efforts came to nothing, and by the end of the 1950s Tariki was heavily disillusioned by his experience with the majors. "They (the companies) do not like us to do anything", he complained bitterly in a 1960 interview. "They prefer that the governments have nothing to do with the business they derive their living from. They do not want the government to have anything to do with the oil business in its own country".[14] On another celebrated occasion during a debate on oil pricing at the 1960 Arab Petroleum Congress in Beirut, Tariki exploded: "They (the companies) can tell two governments two different things. Therefore we cannot accept anything they say now without real investigation. They do not tell us what is going on outside the production phase; they say that this is complicated and is the business of the parent companies. They treat us like children."[15]

For Tariki too, after the 1959 price cuts and the severing of the link with US prices, the prospect of a downward spiral of crude oil prices towards the bare cost of production was an ever-present nightmare. "Our only fear", he said in a 1959 interview, "is that the producing companies will co-operate with the consumer countries and find that it is in their interest to continue to cut crude oil prices. The Middle East share of the percentage increase in world demand for crude, which is estimated at 7-8% a year, will not then be sufficient to make up the losses resulting from the price cuts. If this reduction in oil prices were to continue, it would result in the lifting of oil reserves in the largest possible quantities for sale to consumers at rock-bottom prices without regard to the intrinsic and inherent value of this resource."[16] As a remedy, Tariki enthusiastically espoused the idea of a prorationing agreement between the major oil exporting countries — essentially the Middle East and Venezuela — to divide the projected growth in market demand between them so as to eliminate competitive pressures from surplus capacity. He made it clear at the time, however, that this was his own personal idea, not necessarily representing the view of his government.[17]

There was thus a general meeting of minds between Venezuela and the Middle East which provided a firm foundation for expanding co-operation after the 1959 price cuts. The first concrete step was the arrival in Cairo in mid-April 1959 of a high-powered Venezuelan oil delegation headed by Minister Perez Alfonzo. The ostensible object of this visit was to attend the first Arab Petroleum Congress, which was to be held from April 16 to 22 in the Egyptian capital. But the real reason was to work out a common approach to oil policy questions with the various senior Arab and Iranian oil officials who were attending this function. Informal consultations took place at Cairo's exclusive yachting club between the delegates of Venezuela, Iran, Saudi Arabia,

Kuwait, the United Arab Republic (Egypt and Syria) and the Arab League Petroleum Department.* These informal discussions resulted in the drawing up of a document of understanding which (though it was kept highly secret at the time and was not actually published until 1961) throws much historical light upon subsequent developments in Venezuelan-Middle Eastern relations, the establishment of OPEC and the unfolding of its policies.[18]

According to the document, the delegates concerned agreed to convey to their respective governments a proposal for the establishment of a Petroleum Consultation Commission which would meet at least once a year to discuss common problems and seek solutions to them. Another significant passage speaks of a general agreement to the effect that the oil producing governments should raise their share of oil profits to at least 60%, as had been done in Venezuela and in new concession agreements elsewhere, and that the royalty payment should be considered as a separate element from income tax in calculating the government's aggregate take (rather than being credited entirely against the tax liability). Other recommendations dealt with the need for the oil companies to consult with and obtain the approval of their host governments before making any price change, the participation of producer governments in integrated oil operations downstream, increasing refining capacity in the producing areas, establishing national oil companies, and creating in each country an organization to co-ordinate from the national point of view the conservation, production and exploitation of petroleum.

The proposed Consultation Commission could well be regarded as the harbinger of OPEC, while several of the other recommendations — raising of the government profit share in the Middle East to at least 60%, the expensing of royalties, and the creation of co-ordinating bodies in each country — were clearly designed to bring the Middle East into line

* *The chief delegates concerned were Messrs. Perez Alfonzo of Venezuela (Minister of Mines and Hydrocarbons), M. Farman Farmayan of Iran, Abdullah Al-Tariki of Saudi Arabia (Director General of Petroleum and Mineral Affairs), Ahmed Sayed Omar of Kuwait (Assistant Under Secretary for Oil Affairs in Kuwait's Ministry of Finance), Salah Nessim of the UAR and Muhammed Salman of the Arab League Petroleum Department. Iraq was not represented at the First Arab Petroleum Congress in Cairo owing to its strained relations with the UAR at the time. However, the Director of the Arab League Petroleum Department, Muhammed Salman, was an Iraqi national and subsequently became Minister of Oil in Iraq.*

with the existing situation in Venezuela. In particular, the expensing of royalties in the Middle East was to become a major plank in OPEC's future programme.

In the months that followed working contacts between Middle Eastern and Venezuelan oil officials multiplied until, in May 1960, Tariki and Perez Alfonzo held a press conference in Caracas at which they issued a joint declaration embodying the basis for a proposal for an international petroleum agreement which, they said, would be adhered to by Venezuela, Saudi Arabia, Iran, Iraq and Kuwait. The proposed agreement envisaged that production would be geared to the growth of market demand and prorated among the signatory countries primarily on the basis of proved reserves, but with special provision being made for the participants' current market position and for new oil discoveries in participating countries or new areas. The plan was identical with the proration blueprint which Tariki had outlined a few days previously at the annual meeting in Texas of the Texas Independent Producers and Royalty Owners' Association (TIPRO). On that occasion, too, Tariki was supported by Perez Alfonzo who emphasized that conservation was the keynote of Venezuela's oil policy "as a means of stretching out our reserves over the longest period of time." He explained that "our dependence on oil forces us to hope for an annual production increase, but we do not want our production to rise proportionately to what might now be considered our share of world demand. The annual increase in world demand is expected to be approximately 7%. If Venezuela's production increases at about 4%, we would be leaving an important share of the international market to other producers."[19]

Meanwhile, both Tariki and Perez Alfonzo in their various ways were assiduously maintaining contact with the other leading Middle East producing countries — Iran, Iraq and Kuwait — in order to bring them fully into the picture of the emerging Middle East-Venezuela oil axis. These countries were by and large (particularly Iran) less than enthusiastic about the prorationing scheme, but they all appreciated the benefits of close producer government co-ordination on prices and other oil issues. So when the companies made another unilateral cut in Middle East posted prices, the big five exporters were able after only one month of consultative preparations to set the date for a full-scale conference at oil ministerial level in the Iraqi capital of Baghdad on September 10, 1960.

For their part, the oil companies had been aghast at the developing oil co-operation between the Middle East and Venezuela, with all that implied in terms of greater bargaining strength. In their representations to the Middle East, both to the host governments and to public opinion through the media, the companies lost no opportunity to portray the proposed inter-area compact as a Venezuelan trick designed to deprive prolific low-cost Middle East oil of its rightful expanded share of the market.

Similarly, in Venezuela the Federation of Chambers of Commerce and Industry, a body heavily influenced by the oil companies, persistently lambasted Perez Alfonzo's policy of limiting oil exports. But these attacks were contemptuously brushed aside by Perez Alfonzo whose political backing within the government was rock-solid. "The confusion," he declared imperiously, "results from thinking that in the present market greater exports would bring in more foreign exchange earnings. I consider that we have obtained the most possible under present conditions by preventing anguished exporters from weakening prices."[20]

One aspect of the oil companies' behaviour at this juncture continues to be puzzling, even in retrospect. It is known that there were wide differences of opinion between individual companies as to the wisdom of a further cut in posted prices. And even within the inner sanctum of the price-cut leader, Exxon, the more politically sophisticated board members correctly warned their colleagues that "all hell would break loose" if such cuts were carried out.[21] But no-one at all in any company seems to have even considered the possibility of prior consultations with the host governments concerned. It seems that the companies were so wedded to their contractual right to make price changes unilaterally that they could not even conceive of an imaginative overture to the oil exporting governments in the direction of prior price consultations — which, if held, might have somewhat defused the head of steam which led to the creation of OPEC.

In one vital aspect the lack of consultation was crucial, namely in pushing Iran to join the other producers in OPEC — without which the Organization would have been gravely, perhaps fatally, weakened. The fact is that the Shah was a reluctant convert to the idea of OPEC. He was politically dependent on the United States (which had been responsible for maintaining him on the throne in 1953); he was relying on the oil companies to boost Iran's production so as to restore the Middle East leadership it lost in 1951; he was opposed to the Venezuelan-Saudi prorationing scheme; and his political relations with his Arab neighbours were decidedly shaky. What, above all, persuaded him finally to enter the OPEC fold was his fury at the failure of the oil companies to consult him before making the August 1960 price cuts. On this point he expressed himself forcefully at the time: "If the companies which produce our oil do not come and discuss the market situation with us, but cut our revenues without opening their books to us, what are we to think? The question is that we should not be left with the feeling that everything is being hidden from us. This is important for two reasons. First, the government has to know what revenues it can count on for its budgetary and economic development planning. Second, as owners of the oil, we must be treated as equal partners. The companies must realize that this is for their own good."[22]

The Baghdad Resolutions

Iraq's offer of Baghdad as the venue for the September 1960 conference of the five major oil exporting nations — Venezuela, Saudi Arabia, Iran, Iraq and Kuwait — was itself significant. For one thing, it made it clear that the inter-hemispheric oil entente was not confined to Venezuela and Saudi Arabia. For another, Iraq was at the time very much in need of a show of solidarity from its fellow oil exporters for reasons which were not solely attributable to the price question. Ever since the July 1958 revolution, relations between the new Iraqi Government and its oil concessionaries, the IPC Group (BP, Shell, CFP, Exxon, Mobil and Partex) had been distinctly uneasy, and a renewed series of acrimonious and ultimately ill-fated negotiations — in which the government's demand included a higher share of profits, state equity participation in the oil producing ventures and extensive relinquishment of concession acreage — had begun in Baghdad a month before the historic meeting of oil exporting countries.

After five days of deliberations, the delegates of the five nations* decided to form a permanent organization to be called the Organization of the Petroleum Exporting Countries (OPEC) whose function would be to institute regular consultations among the Member States with a view to "co-ordinating and unifying" their policies.

On the price issue the Conference passed the following seminal resolutions, calling for a rollback of posted prices to previous levels and

* *The signatories of this foundation document were: Perez Alfonzo for Venezuela; Abdullah Al-Tariki for Saudi Arabia; Fuad Rouhani (later to become OPEC's first Secretary General) for Iran; Tala'at al-Shaibani (Minister of Planning and Acting Oil Minister) for Iraq; and Ahmed Sayed Omar (Deputy Director of the Finance Department) for Kuwait. Hassan Kamel of Qatar attended as an observer, and Qatar joined as a full member at the next Conference in Caracas in January 1961.*

mandatory consultations on future price movements, and including a solidarity clause against divisive inducements by the oil companies:

— That Members can no longer remain indifferent to the attitude heretofore adopted by the oil companies in effecting price modifications.
— That Members shall demand that oil companies maintain their prices steady and free from all unnecessary fluctuations; that Members shall endeavour, by all means available to them, to restore present prices to the levels prevailing before the reductions; that they shall ensure that if any new circumstances arise which in the estimation of the oil companies necessitate price modifications, the said companies shall enter into consultation with the Member or Members affected in order fully to explain the circumstances.
— That Members shall study and formulate a system to ensure the stabilization of prices by, among other things, the regulation of production, with due regard to the interests of the producing and of the consuming nations, and to the necessity of securing a steady income to the producing countries, an efficient, economic and regular supply of this source of energy to consuming nations, and a fair return on their capital to those investing in the petroleum industry.
— That if as a result of the application of any unanimous decision of this Conference any sanctions are employed, directly or indirectly, by any interested company against one or more of the Member Countries, no other Member shall accept any offer of a beneficial treatment, whether in the form of an increase in exports or an improvement in prices, which may be made to it by any such company or companies with the intention of discouraging the application of the unanimous decision reached by the Conference.

OPEC was thus ushered on to the world stage on a note of moderation and sweet reason. There was nothing particularly inflammatory about the foundation resolutions, this rather downbeat note being no doubt necessary in order to ensure Iran's adherence to the new Organization. A suggestion by Tariki to the effect that the Middle East exporters should move immediately to a 60-40 profit split was reportedly turned down as being overly punitive at this stage. The controversial prorationing scheme was, moreover, placed in the context of a study regarding a price stabilization system.

Nevertheless, these initial resolutions can well be regarded a sort of "charter for change" in the world oil industry, giving notice that the exclusive right granted to the oil companies in Middle East concession agreements to monopolize all decision making on prices and production levels could no longer be tolerated. From now on the producer governments would have to have an equal, if not a decisive voice in such decisions.

Not surprisingly, there was jubilation in the producers' camp. "We have formed a very exclusive club," Perez Alfonzo told Fuad Itayim, the Editor and Publisher of Middle East Economic Survey (MEES) who was one of the few journalists to cover the meeting on the spot. "Between us we control 90% of crude exports to world markets, and we are now united. We are making history."[23]

On the companies' side the reaction was muted, but the cementing of the Baghdad entente had two immediate effects. The first was that those companies which had lowered their Middle East postings by 14 cents a barrel in August (Exxon, Shell, Texaco and Standard Oil of California) proceeded to raise them again by 4 cents in order to bring them into line with the 10-cent cut made by the other companies. Secondly, the companies let it be known informally during the Arab Petroleum Congress in Beirut in October 1960 — via Muhammed Salman, the Iraqi Director of the Arab League Petroleum Department — that in future they would make no move on posted prices before consulting and obtaining the approval of the oil exporting countries.[24] Of course, such an anonymous and informal assurance carried no legal weight. But the fact was that no oil company ever again attempted to lower posted prices, with or without the approval of the host governments.

For some years to come, however, the major companies maintained a formal refusal to recognize OPEC as a central body to represent Member Countries in collective negotiations with the companies. They continued to insist, at least for form's sake, that each company or group of companies could only deal with the individual government with which it had concluded a concession agreement. Yet within little more than a decade the companies found themselves in the position of actually pleading for collective bargaining with OPEC. The tables had turned with a vengeance!

CHAPTER III

ROYALTY EXPENSING — DEFENCE AND IMPROVEMENT OF UNIT REVENUES IN A SOFT MARKET

After the elan of the Baghdad Conference, OPEC's next two years were spent largely on consolidation: setting up a permanent Secretariat in Geneva with Fuad Rouhani of Iran as the Organization's first Secretary General; and commissioning studies, mainly on the financial aspects of integrated oil operations on an international scale, to provide the data back-up for future plans of action. But the main debate revolved around the general line of approach to be taken in the battle to stabilize and improve prices and the governments' unit revenue from oil.

The Evolution of Policy

Shortly after the September 1960 creation of OPEC, both Perez Alfonzo and Tariki made it clear that the kind of price stabilization system they would ideally like to have seen was one that would have re-established the point of equalization between the c.i.f. prices of Caribbean and Middle East crudes at London (rather than the US East Coast as under the 1950s formula). Had it been a practical possibility, this would have entailed an increase of no less than 68 cents/barrel in (post-August 1960) Middle East postings. At the same time, in a longer-range perspective Perez emphasized that in his opinion the only sound yardstick for determining oil prices would be the cost of alternative fuels. Therefore, the correct price for oil would be at a level cheaper, but only slightly cheaper than the cost of alternatives; and viewed in this light the price of oil in 1960 was absurdly, not to say dangerously, cheap.[1]

However appropriate in the longer term, these ideas were not susceptible to practical implementation in the politico-economic conditions of the 1960s. For some time to come, OPEC's efforts on the price front would have to be essentially defensive, concentrating on maintaining the status quo as far as posted prices (upon which government tax and royalty income was calculated) were concerned, while actual realized prices for crude oil remained weak in a buyers' market.

In this situation OPEC had two main options. Either it could take action on the supply side — as envisaged by the prorationing scheme —

to divide up demand growth between Member States and eliminate the competitive pressures arising from the existence of surplus export capacity, and the desire of individual governments (and oil companies for that matter) for higher revenues. Or it could concentrate on consolidating, and progressively raising, a price floor below which, for purely financial reasons, the companies would be unable to sell. Given that posted/tax reference prices would remain at least frozen on the downward side, such a floor would be formed at the level of the tax-paid cost (that is to say the cost of production plus statutory payments to the host governments by the oil producing companies) plus whatever profit margin on the production phase might be deemed as the essential minimum by the oil companies concerned. The level of this basic floor below market prices could then be progressively raised through improvements in the financial terms of the producing concessions — with the obvious emphasis, in the first place, on the correction of the fiscal imbalance between the Middle East and Venezuela described in the previous chapter.

These two options — prorationing of production and the floor price concept — were not, of course, mutually exclusive. But the practical exigencies of the time did make it advisable to concentrate on one rather than the other.

In fact, it became evident during and after the Baghdad Conference that solid backing for any formal proration plan was very thin on the ground among the Middle Eastern founder members of OPEC. Iran, in particular, was eager for a dramatic increase in its export volume and revenue position, and was usually sensitive to the arguments of the oil companies which were implacably opposed to any attempts on the part of the OPEC Governments to control production or export volumes. In a widely publicized press interview in December 1960, the Shah dismissed the idea of international oil prorationing as "impractical", and insisted that Iran must receive "at least one-half of each year's growth in total Middle East production, and be restored as fast as possible to its "historical position as No. 1 Middle East oil producer" which it had lost during the 1951-54 shudown*. "What interest", the Shah observed,

* In 1960 Iran (with 1,060,000 b/d) ranked third in the Middle East behind Kuwait (1,692,000 b/d) and Saudi Arabia (1,315,000 b/d), and slightly ahead of Iraq (955,000 b/d). Iran's output growth consistently outpaced that of the area as a whole during the 1960s. By 1967 Iran had overtaken Kuwait, and in 1969 and 1970 it produced marginally more than Saudi Arabia to regain the Middle East leadership for a brief period before being overtaken once again by Saudi Arabia in 1971.

40

"do we have in restricting exports? Many other ways can be found to hold our posted prices or compensate us for losses in revenues."[2]

In Kuwait, too, oil officials were quoted as expressing doubts regarding the practical problems involved in implementing any international proration plan.[3]

In Iraq, the authorities were becoming increasingly preoccupied with the impasse in their negotiations with the IPC Group, which in December 1961 culminated in the issue of the celebrated Law No. 80 under which the government took over 99.5% of the companies' concession areas (i.e. the portion that the companies had thus far failed to develop) leaving them with only the producing oilfields. At the same time, Iraq's participation in OPEC activities suffered a temporary hiatus owing to the claim to Kuwait, laid by the then Iraqi leader, General Qasim, in mid-1961. From that time until Qasim's overthrow early in 1963, Iraq sent no representatives to OPEC meetings.

In Saudi Arabia also, backing for prorationing was more of a personal advocacy on the part of Abdullah Al-Tariki, rather than a firm plank in the government's policy. And after Tariki was replaced as Oil Minister early in 1962 by Sheikh Ahmed Zaki Yamani, Saudi enthusiasm for the idea cooled considerably.

In the resolutions of OPEC's Second Conference in Caracas, in January 1961, prorationing was accorded only a rather perfunctory reference — in the context of a detailed study which was to be carried out "in order to arrive at a just pricing formula supported by a study of international proration, should that prove essential" — and then dropped out of sight in OPEC Resolutions for several years.

What apparently took place behind the scenes was an informal deal between the Middle East exporting countries and Venezuela. This was to the effect that OPEC should accord priority to the improvement of posted prices and financial terms in the Middle East to bring them more in line with prevailing conditions in Venezuela — on the understanding that, once this target had been achieved, OPEC should redirect its attention to the question of prorationing or regulation of production. In fact, as we shall see in Chapter IX, OPEC did take up the subject of prorationing (or production programming as it had by then come to be called) once again in 1965, with rather unsuccessful results.

Though obviously not as satisfactory to Caracas as a proration compact, the stabilization of postings and improvement of government unit oil revenue in the Middle East also stood to benefit Venezuela in the sense that any evening out of the disparity between crude oil costs in the two areas would serve to lessen the danger of any large-scale invasion of

Venezuelan markets by cheaper Middle Eastern oil, as well as firming up the underlying floor beneath world market prices in general.

An improvement in Middle East concession terms was also easily justified on a number of grounds, quite apart from the correction of the already mentioned disparity with Venezuela and the enormous returns on production investment earned by the majors. Ever since 1957 independent newcomers — such as Italy's ENI, Amoco (Standard Oil of Indiana) of the US, and the Arabian Oil Company of Japan — had been entering the Middle Eastern oil scene in exploration/production ventures which accorded the governments more attractive terms than the traditional major concessions, including a higher share of profits and government equity participation of up to 50% in the event of commercial oil discovery.

None of these ventures was yet producing oil in any significant quantities; yet the very fact of their existence stimulated a groundswell of public and governmental opinion in the oil exporting countries, both individually and collectively within OPEC, in favour of a change in the system of the majors.

Royalty Expensing Explained

The method finally chosen by OPEC, after much deliberation, as the means for achieving the desired increase in the unit oil revenue of Middle East governments was to demand that royalty payments (generally 12.5% of the posted price value of oil produced) should in future be "expensed" — that is to say treated as a cost item, rather than being fully credited against income tax liability as was then the prevailing practice in the Middle East.

The Middle East system of dealing with royalty payments was absolutely at variance with the general practice in other old-established oil producing countries, such as the United States, Canada and Venezuela. Conceptually, the royalty is payable by the lessee or concessionaire to the landowner of the petroleum deposit under production (be he a private individual or the government itself), regardless as to whether or not any profit is made from the oil produced. It may variously be categorized as rent, as compensation for using up a wasting asset placed at the concessionaire's disposal, or as a payment for the intrinsic value of the raw material produced. It is therefore quite distinct from income tax, which is a liability due to the government of a country in respect of profits earned.

In oil producing areas outside the Middle East this distinction was maintained and the royalty was treated as an operating cost deductible from gross income in determining taxable income. In the Middle East, on the other hand, the royalty was fully credited against and thus totally absorbed in the 50% income tax liability, so that the aggregate of all payments – including both taxes and royalties – would not exceed 50% of gross income. In other words, in effect the royalty, or compensation for the intrinsic value of the oil, simply did not exist.

In cash terms, the proposed change over to the expensing of royalties in the Middle East entailed an increase of about 11 cents a barrel in the total government take from the companies' operations. For purposes of illustration, the calculations would work out as follows:

Royalty Credited Against Tax

	$/Barrel
Posted Price	1.800
Royalty (12.5% of Posted Price)	0.225
Cost of Production	0.250
Income Tax Receipts (50% of gross income, i.e. Posted Price minus Production Cost)	0.775
Total Government Take (with Royalty credited against tax)	0.775

Royalty Expensed

	$/Barrel
Posted Price	1.800
Royalty (12.5% of Posted Price)	0.225
Cost of Production	0.250
Taxable Income (Posted Price minus Production Cost and Royalty)	1.325
Tax Receipts (50% of Taxable Income)	0.6625
Total Government Take (Tax plus Royalty)	0.8875

The June 1962 Resolutions

OPEC's demands on the oil companies were set out in a series of

Resolutions adopted at the Fourth Conference in Geneva in June 1962. In particular, they dealt with the following.

(a) Prices

The Conference called upon Member Countries to negotiate with the oil companies concerned "with a view to ensuring that oil produced in Member Countries shall be paid for on the basis of posted prices not lower than these which applied prior to August 1960." It also called upon Member States to formulate a "rational price structure to guide their long-term price policy", an important element of which would be "the linking of crude oil prices to an index of prices of goods which the Member Countries need to import."[4]

(b) Royalties

Noting that in the Middle East in general, unlike other parts of the world, "no compensation is paid for the intrinsic value of petroleum, royalty or stated payment commitments being treated as credits against income tax liabilities", the Conference recommended the Member Countries concerned to approach their concessionaires "with a view to working out a formula where under royalty payments shall be fixed at a uniform rate which Members consider equitable, and shall not be treated as a credit against income tax liability".

(c) Marketing Allowances

The Conference called upon Member Countries "to take measures to eliminate any contribution to the marketing expenses of the oil companies." (At the time the major concessionaires in the Middle East were allowed to deduct a certain percentage of the posted price from gross income before calculation of taxable income to compensate for expenses incurred in marketing operations. These "marketing allowances" — which, as OPEC pointed out, could hardly be justified as a true deductible expense against the producing operation, since most of the transactions concerned were inter-affiliate transfers — were generally fixed at 1% of the posted price, or about 1.6 to 1.8 cents a barrel. Saudi Arabia, however, had for some years been allowing deductions on the basis of actual audited expenses incurred in marketing, which worked out at about 4.2 cents a barrel.)

The Resolution on marketing allowances dealt with a relatively minor issue which was settled when the companies agreed to reduce such allowances to half a cent a barrel, and the demand for the restoration of posted prices to their pre-August 1960 level gradually faded out of the agenda. The focus was then concentrated on the issue of royalty expensing which was worth 11 cents/barrel in revenue to OPEC's Middle East Members.

The Royalty Expensing Negotiations

The royalty expensing negotiations provided OPEC's baptism of fire in the field of collective confrontation with the oil companies. It was a long hard slog which put a very heavy strain — probably the heaviest — on inter-OPEC solidarity. On paper, in terms of sovereign power and barrels of oil production, OPEC bargaining power looked impressive indeed. But at that time the oil market was still in substantial over-supply, the economic power of the oil companies was still formidable, and the underlying political muscle was on the side of the parent governments of the oil companies.

As might have been expected, the negotiating tactics of the companies were rough and tough. Maximum efforts were made to split the OPEC front, usually focusing on Iran as the potential weakest link; meaningful offers were withheld until the very last moment before OPEC Conferences, and were only made at all if it really seemed that the threat of legislative action by the OPEC Countries could not otherwise be averted. Above all, the offers were always booby-trapped with a battery of extremely problematical conditions.[5]

In the beginning the OPEC Countries delegated Iran and Saudi Arabia to conduct the necessary negotiations with the oil companies because the shareholders of their respective concessionaires (the Consortium and Aramco) included all the major companies. This was one way of getting over the problem posed by the fact that the majors would not (or perhaps genuinely could not owing to anti-trust complications) recognize OPEC as a collective negotiating body.

This early stage of the negotiations was characterized by a battle of memoranda. In August 1962 OPEC issued a memorandum containing a comprehensive exposition of its case concerning the three Resolutions. Particular emphasis was laid on the fact that crude oil prices had declined by 7.5% between 1953 and 1960, whereas the index of prices of manufactured goods had risen by 9%.

Both the Consortium and Aramco submitted counter-memoranda to their host governments vigorously attacking the OPEC presentation on points of fact and interpretation. In particular, they emphasized the current soft market conditions and the widening gap between the prices actually realized in world markets and the posted prices on which taxes and royalties were calculated, as well as urging that the two governments in question (Iran and Saudi Arabia) would do better — given the current competition from other oil suppliers* and the potential competition from alternative sources of energy — to show more concern for export volumes than for prices. At this stage, apart from an expression of willingness to consider minimum guarantees for the governments' per-barrel revenues, the companies' reaction to OPEC's June 1962 Resolutions was wholly negative.

Moreover, a whole year of rather desultory talks conducted by Iran and Saudi Arabia with their respective oil groups produced no progress beyond a minor concession on the part of the companies offering to reduce their marketing allowances to half a cent per barrel.

Not surprisingly, in view of this dearth of results, pressure was building up within OPEC for more concrete action. And in July 1963 a consultative meeting initiated a detailed examination of measures which might be taken in retaliation against the companies' obdurate attitude. Some were advocating a straightforward unilateral legislation of the royalty expensing demand which, in the event of a refusal to comply on the part of the companies (or retaliation in the form of another re-duction in posted prices), would be followed by further measures, possibly including various forms of controls on oil production, exports and prices, or even partial nationalization. Another possibility under serious consideration was one that would not have infringed the existing concession agreements. This was a proposal for a 10% tax on the gross earnings of all tankers calling at the ports of the Member Countries concerned — a measure which would have increased the government's take by around 7-8 cents a barrel. In the first place, this would have been implemented by Saudi Arabia, Iraq, Kuwait and Qatar, since Iran's 1954 agreement with the consortium specifically prohibited a tanker tax; but the plan was that Iran would follow suit later by claiming 'most-favoured-nation' treatment.[6]

Early in August 1963 came a new OPEC initiative which was to prove a turning point in the royalty battle. All OPEC Member States delegated authority to Secretary General Fuad Rouhani to negotiate on their behalf with the oil companies. After some initial hesitation among

* On a visit to Tehran in October 1962, Exxon's Howard Page did his best to convince the Iranians that the Soviet Union, Venezuela and Libya were dangerous direct competitors to Middle East oil — see MEES, October 26, 1962.

46

the companies, the Iranian Consortium reacted by appointing a three-man team — J.M. Pattinson of BP, H.W. Page of Exxon and G.L. Parkthurst of Standard Oil of California — to meet Rouhani. In a statement, the consortium emphasized that the team was (a) representing only the consortium, (b) empowered to deal with Iranian matters only, and (c) negotiating with Rouhani purely in his capacity as a representative of the Iranian Government. However, as the Middle East Economic Survey pointed out at the time: "if the form of collective bargaining was precluded by legal obstacles, the substance was certainly there."[7]

The companies' first offer was a manifest absurdity, consisting of a forumula under which royalty payments would have been expensed, but whereby any financial gain to the governments concerned would have been effectively nullified by an accompanying 12.5% discount off posted prices for tax purposes. Subsequently, early in November, the companies presented another and supposedly "final" offer. This was that royalty payments should be expensed, but this time with an 8.5% discount allowance off posted prices for tax purpose — the net result being an increase in government oil income of about 3.5 cents a barrel, as compared with OPEC's original demand for 11 cents.

Quite apart from its insufficiency in cash terms, the offer was made dependent upon the acceptance of a variety of restrictive conditions, notably:
(1) that the offer should be recognized as bringing complete satisfaction for all claims under the OPEC Resolutions;
(2) that the oil companies should be given the final tax quittance which had been withheld since 1960;
(3) that the OPEC Countries concerned should impose no restrictions on the production or movement of oil;
(4) that a formula for equal treatment should be worked out and applied to the other non-major oil companies (i.e. what amounted to a most-favoured-company clause).*

After being predictably turned down by Rouhani in his capacity as negotiator, the offer was formally rejected by the OPEC Goverments concerned at a special consultative meeting in Beirut early in December. At this meeting there was general unanimity in favour of legislative measures to implement OPEC's demands, and it was agreed that such measures

*   This fourth condition was, as it turned out, of some benefit to OPEC since it provided the stimulus for the 1965 changeover from realized prices to posted prices as the basis for tax calculation in Libya. Libya and Indonesia had been admitted as full members of OPEC in June 1962.

should be proposed to the full Ministerial Conference which was due to meet in the Saudi capital of Riyadh towards the end of the month.

Thoroughly alarmed by the news from the Beirut meeting, the companies resorted to the technique of the last-minute offer. On the eve of the Riyadh Conference, the Iranian Consortium and Aramco informed Iran and Saudi Arabia respectively that the companies might be prepared to eliminate some of the objectionable conditions attached to the previous offer and to consider reducing the 8.5% allowance in the future, depending on market conditions.

In the event, a decision in favour of unilateral action was averted in Riyadh — a key factor (in addition to the companies' last-minute offer) being a very significant softening in the attitude of Iran in the period since the Beirut consultative meeting.* Venezuela and Iraq still argued vehemently for legislation, but the soft-liners led by Iran carried the day. The revised offer was regarded, in the Conference Resolutions, as "conducive to an advancement in the direction of the Organization's objectives", as a result of which "resort by Member Countries to unilateral action is not called for." The Conference further decided to delegate a three-man committee, composed of Fuad Rouhani of Iran (outgoing OPEC Secretary General), Abdul Rahman Bazzaz of Iraq (OPEC Secretary General elect) and Hisham Nazer of Saudi Arabia, to continue negotiations with the companies.

Further negotiations in March 1964 failed to bring about any substantive change in the companies' offer. There was even a step backwards when the oil companies operating in Iraq made it clear that the implementation of their offer to Iraq would be contingent upon the settlement of all the outstanding issues between the government and the companies which had accumulated over the years, and particularly since the promulgation of Law No. 80 of 1961. Moreover, an OPEC counter-proposal to the effect that half the royalty (5.5 cents/barrel) should be expensed immediately and the rest over a specific period of years, was turned down by the companies' team.

Once again OPEC impatience mounted and once again, shortly before the next full OPEC Conference scheduled for July 1964, the companies came up with a last-minute offer designed to avert the threat of

* *The year 1963 witnessed a good deal of political turbulence in Iran. There is good evidence to suggest that in the interval between the Beirut and Riyadh Meetings, the Shah was subjected to economic and perhaps political pressure from western oil companies and governments to go easy on the OPEC front.*

48

OPEC measures. The new offer was first communicated, significantly enough, to Reza Fallah, Deputy Managing Director of Iran's NIOC, during a visit to London about the middle of June. Basically the formula was much the same: expensing of royalties with an 8.5% allowance off posted prices for tax purposes, giving the Middle East Governments an extra 3.5 cents/barrel from January 1, 1964. However, the allowance off posted prices would be reduced to 7.5% in 1965 and 6.5% in 1966 (subject to a gravity adjustment in favour of the heavier crudes) which would increase government take by an additional half to three-quarters of a cent per barrel in each of these years. The overall three-year package was therefore worth 4.5 to 5.0 cents a barrel, yielding OPEC's Middle East Members an additional income of $100 million in 1964, $135 million in 1965 and $170 million in 1966. Any further change in the tax allowance after 1966 would be subject to review according to market conditions at the time.

In the Resolutions of OPEC's Sixth Conference held in Geneva in July, this revised offer was described as "a suitable basis for the full implementation" of the royalty expensing resolution "subject to certain improvements and amendment." The Member Countries concerned were therefore called upon to "make new approach to the oil companies operating in their territories to explore the possibility of reaching a final agreement."

It soon became apparent that the companies' latest offer, apart from some last-minute problems with the conditions which were finally ironed out in November, was broadly speaking regarded as satisfactory by most of OPEC's Middle East Members, namely, Iran, Saudi Arabia, Kuwait, Libya and Qatar. Iraq, however, rejected it.

Explaining Iraq's position, the then Iraqi Minister of Oil, Abdul-Aziz Al-Wattari, said that for the sake of OPEC solidarity Iraq had gone along with the other Member Countries as far as the financial provisions of the offer were concerned, but was not prepared to accept the conditions attached to the implementation of this offer.[8] The companies, he said, had dropped their original insistence on making the royalty offer conditional upon the settlement of all other outstanding issues arising from Law No. 80. However, there remained several highly objectionable conditions, some of them general and some applicable only to Iraq:

— The 'most-favoured-company' clause. Thought it was not conceivable that the government would grant new concessions on easier terms than the current agreements with the majors, it was intolerable that the companies should set themselves up as arbiters over the state in this matter.

— In the current agreements the royalty on Iraq's Mediterranean exports was calculated on the Mediterranean posted price (then $2.21/barrel). However, for the purposes of royalty expensing the companies were proposing to calculate the royalty on the Iraqi-Syrian border value which was 35 cents/barrel lower, thus causing a loss of over 1 cent a barrel to Iraq (and 2.5 cents on full royalty expensing).
— The companies were insisting that a prior Iraqi claim for 5 cents a barrel on Basrah crude should be considered as settled, although that had nothing to do with the royalty issue.
— A clause for compulsory international arbitration of disputes had been slipped in at the last moment.

The Djakarta Conference

Predictably, with the royalty expensing settlement at the top of the agenda, OPEC's Seventh Conference in the Indonesian capital of Djakarta in late-November 1964 was a stormy meeting. More than at any other point in the Organization's history, it was here in Djakarta in November 1964 that OPEC came closest to breaking up or at least being consigned to the deep freeze. In the event, however, the OPEC Members had the good sense to evolve a formula which has stood them in good stead whenever internal conflicts threaten to get out of hand: simply to agree to disagree, and to keep the Organization in working order pending the inevitable emergence of another unifying issue. This particular brand of ultra-flexible pragmatism has contributed greatly to OPEC's strength and durability over the years.

The disagreement between the Members is set forth frankly in Resolution 49 of the Djakarta Conference. The delegates of Iran, Kuwait, Libya, Qatar and Saudi Arabia considered that the companies' latest offers on November 16 "met the minimum requirements" laid down by previous OPEC Meetings. Iraq on the other hand — supported by Venezuela and Indonesia, although these two Members were not directly involved in the royalty issue — rejected the offer on the grounds that it did not meet the said minimum requirements, and because its non-financial provisions "constitute a clear infringement on its sovereignty and restrict its freedom of action in the achievement of higher common objectives of the Organization."

The solution adopted at Djakarta was simply to delete the royalty issue from the Conference's agenda, leaving each Member State free to proceed as it deemed fit.

Although full of valuable lessons for the future, the royalty expensing negotiations were an exhausting test of OPEC's endurance. An OPEC paper summed up the Organization's experience in this respect as follows: "The case study showed that the major oil companies, by their own behaviour, have made the principle of negotiations, which OPEC generally endorses, increasingly hard to apply. This is a tax on OPEC's time and effort that it obviously cannot afford to pay forever."[9]

The Aftermath of Royalty Expensing

Three countries — Iran, Saudi Arabia and Qatar — promptly signed and ratified their royalty expensing agreement. In Kuwait, ratification of the agreement, which had been signed by the government, was blocked by the fiercely independent National Assembly which, apart from specific objections particularly directed at the agreement's restrictive non-financial clauses, made use of the occasion for a general critique of the government's oil policy. Finally, after cosmetic changes to some of the non-financial clauses, the agreement was ratified in May 1967, with its financial effect retroactive to January 1, 1964.

In Libya, too, the royalty settlement was delayed until January 1966 pending resolution of a dramatic dispute with the independent concessionaires which had been calculating their taxes on realized prices rather than posted prices.

In Iraq, the royalty expensing issue merely joined the log-jam of other unresolved disputes with the oil companies. Royalties in Iraq were, of course, fully expensed as a result of the 1971 Tehran agreement, and there had been the equivalent of a partial expensing on Mediterranean exports since 1967. But the arrears for 1964-71 were not finally liquidated until the post-nationalization settlement of March 1973.

When the time came in 1966-67 to pressure the oil companies into committing themselves to a schedule for the elimination of the tax allowances in order to bring about the full expensing of royalties, the OPEC Governments found themselves faced with yet another gruelling round of protracted negotiations lasting 18 months, and yet again the threat of unilateral action was required in order to extract an acceptable offer. Finally, in January 1968, a schedule was agreed upon whereby the percentage allowance would be phased out by 1972 and the gravity allowance on lighter crudes by 1975.[10] However, this long-delayed phase-out was curtailed by the 1971 Tehran price agreement under whch all such allowances were eliminated.

Meanwhile, in 1967 following the June war and the closure of the Suez Canal, the tax discount allowances were fully eliminated on Mediterranean crude exports, which yielded a "Suez premium" of some 7-8 cents/barrel in additional government take for Libya and on Mediterranean exports by Saudi Arabia and Iraq. However, Algeria (which joined OPEC in July 1969) was at that time bound by the 1965-69 oil agreement with France and was not accorded this Suez premium — a cause of considerable Algerian resentment which contributed to the souring of its oil relations with France.

Consolidation of the Posted Price Tax Base

The royalty expensing settlement also had a very useful side-effect in that it helped to stimulate the closing of those gaps in OPEC's front where taxes were still calculated on realized rather than posted prices, namely:
- In Libya, where oil exports had begun in 1961, the authorities had been convinced that price incentives were needed in order to maximize the country's exports and revenues. And so a special regulation (No. 6) was issued in December 1961 which interpreted the petroleum law in such a way as to allow taxes to be calculated on the basis of prices actually realized in the market.
- In Saudi Arabia, as a result of a verbal agreement made in 1958 by the then Director General of Petroleum and Mineral Affairs, Aramco had been permitted to calculate its taxes on realized prices in respect of third-party sales of crude and products to non-affiliates.
- In Venezuela, taxes had traditionally been based on realized prices, though the Coordinating Commission had since 1962 been calling into question discounts in excess of 10%.

In Libya, the change over from realized to posted prices as the tax base was truly dramatic. By 1964 the situation had become intolerable. Making full use of the realized price tax concession to open up European markets for their oil, the independent operators were paying the Libyan Government only 30-45 cents a barrel, as against payments of around 90 cents by the majors.[11] Moreover, any implementation of the royalty expensing settlement offered by the majors entailed a shift to a posted price tax base. For once the interests of the government and the majors coincided. After an initial show of resistance, the independents gave way after the Libyan Parliament in December 1965 had issued a decree

52

empowering the Council of Ministers to stop production and exports and expropriate the assets of companies which did not comply with the new legislation stipulating that taxes be based on posted prices, and royalties expensed in line with the majors' offer. At the same time, the Tenth OPEC Conference Meeting in Vienna in December 1965 issued a Resolution (No. 63) recommending Member Governments not to grant any new oil rights to companies which failed to comply with the new oil legislation in Libya.

For its part, Saudi Arabia signed an agreement with Aramco in September 1966 providing that tax returns for all sales of crude and products, including those to non-affiliates, should be filed on the basis of the full posted prices, with retroactive effect to 1961 for crude and 1963 for products.

Meanwhile, after a lengthy wrangle with its oil concessionaires over back taxes, Venezuela, in September 1966, reached a settlement with the companies providing for the calculation of taxes on the basis of fixed tax reference prices, with an increase in the basic rate of income tax from 47.5 to 52%.

OPEC and Prices in the 1960s: A Summing Up

OPEC clearly moved with great caution in the 1960s, being prepared for interminable bargaining about what now look to be insignificant sums and showing great reluctance to use sovereign powers of legislation. However, the OPEC Members were at that time still labouring under difficult political and economic conditions. Politically, there was a lack of self-confidence and the memory of Iran's agony during the 1951-53 crisis was still fresh. Economically, it was a period of widespread surplus export capacity and declining prices which − from the standpoint of the 1960s − looked almost as though it might never end.

But despite these adverse circumstances, OPEC in the 1960s did register some significant achievements which served as a foundation for the more spectacular successes of the 1970s.

Firstly, by insisting on the generalization of the principle that taxes and royalties should be calculated on posted rather than realized prices, and by ensuring that postings could no longer be lowered unilaterally by the companies, OPEC in effect set a firm floor under oil prices at the level of the tax-paid cost, below which market prices simply could not fall, whatever the extent of surplus crude oil availability. By the late 1960s this tax-paid cost floor had reached about $1.00 per barrel.

Secondly, OPEC did succeed in adverse soft market conditions, in pushing up its unit revenue and ensuring that it was the companies that bore the brunt of the decline in realized market prices. With the fall in realized prices to something like $1.30-1.40/barrel during the sixties, company margins on production fell to around 30-40 cents a barrel. However, the companies were, of course, compensated to a large extent for this erosion of their margins on production by the enormous increases registered in their sales volumes. For example, the volume of crude and products sales by the eight majors (Exxon, Shell, Texaco, Socal, Gulf, Mobil, BP and CFP) nearly doubled during the eight years 1962-70 from 14.6 million b/d in 1962 to 27.2 million b/d in 1970, while the aggregate net income of the group rose from $3 billion to $4.8 billion over the same period.

The OPEC Countries, too, depended a great deal on growth in production volumes to generate revenue increases in the 1960s, and rivalry on this score — particularly between Iran and its Gulf neighbours — was quite intense at times. Overall, in the decade that followed the creation of OPEC, crude production by the 11 Members that had joined the Organization by 1971 — Iran, Iraq, Saudi Arabia, Venezuela, Kuwait, Indonesia, Libya, Algeria, Nigeria, Abu Dhabi and Qatar — more than doubled from 8.7 million b/d in 1960 to 23.2 million b/d in 1970, while total OPEC oil revenues during the same period grew from $2.5 billion to $7.8 billion .

CHAPTER IV

THE TURN OF THE TIDE: TRIPOLI—TEHRAN—TRIPOLI

By and large, the 1960s had been a time of uphill struggle for OPEC in its effort to establish a floor to crude oil prices in a weak market where key decisions were still mainly in the hands of the international oil companies. Around 1970, however, the tide began to turn and by the end of the decade not only had the levers of decision-making for supply and prices been fully taken over by the exporting governments, but also the price problem itself had become more a matter of finding a ceiling than a floor.

The dramatic change in the oil scene, which began in 1970 on the Mediterranean, had its origins in a powerful combination of political and economic forces. In particular, in 1970 two OPEC Member Governments on the Mediterranean — Algeria, soured by the disappointing results of the past five years of the oil co-operation pact with France, and Libya, with its new revolutionary government anxious to remedy the oversights of the deposed monarchy — manifested both individually and in co-ordination on the price issue, the necessary degree of tough political will to mount a successful challenge to their concessionaire oil companies.

In this they were aided by various developments on the economic front. The market for short-haul crude (i.e. closer to the markets of Europe and America than Gulf crude) from Mediterranean terminals had tightened considerably after the closure of the Suez Canal in mid-1957; and probably in 1967-69 Mediterranean crude could have merited a substantially higher increase in government take than the 7-8 cents/barrel "Suez premium" resulting from the elimination of the royalty expensing discount allowances on short-haul oil. This already tight situation with regard to Mediterranean short-haul crude was exacerbated firstly by the shut-off of 500,000 b/d of Saudi crude deliveries to the Mediterranean after the rupture of the Trans-Arabian pipeline (Tapline) in Syria, and secondly by output cutbacks for conservation reasons totalling some 800,000 b/d in Libya itself. Though adequately justifiable on technical grounds, these cutbacks did, of course, also serve to strengthen the government's position on price issues. Furthermore, Libya found itself in an advantageous position in that many of its concessionaires were independent companies whose newly established international operations were almost entirely dependent on the continuity of their crude oil supplies from Libya.

Playing these trump cards with considerably skill, Libya in September 1970 prevailed upon first the independents and then the majors to accept a 30-40 cent increase in postings, plus a 5% increase in the tax rate (in lieu of past arrears on account of previous under-posting).

This achievement galvanized the rest of OPEC to score its first major collective success vis-à-vis the oil industry in the five-year Tehran and Tripoli agreements, the story of which will be related in detail in this chapter. Again this success — on the way to which oil company efforts to set up a credible counterforce against OPEC were completely out-manoeuvred — was attributable to a favourable combination of economic and political developments.

In 1970-71 the cushion of spare crude oil output capacity in the producing countries was still quite substantial — about 4 million b/d (as compared with a total non-Communist world production of 38 million b/d) according to Exxon figures. But whereas at the time of the 1967 June war there was still some 2-3 million b/d of surplus capacity in the United States which could be, and was, utilized in the event of an inter-national emergency, by 1971 this supplementary oil availability in the US had just about dried up and virtually all the immediately available spare capacity was concentrated in the OPEC area. No wonder Sheikh Yamani felt confident in warning George Piercy of Exxon in January 1971 just before the conclusion of the Tehran agreement with regard to the possibility of a shutdown in Libya: "George, you know the supply situation better than I. You know you cannot take a shutdown."[1]

Politically, even before the Tehran negotiations began it became evident that the main consumer governments were more interested in ensuring the continuity of the flow of OPEC oil than in providing political backing for the oil companies on the price front. By con-trast, the collective political muscle of the OPEC Governments was very much in evidence in their ultimatum to the companies that if agreement were not reached by a certain deadline, the Gulf OPEC exporters would legislate new prices and any company which refused to pay such prices would not be permitted to lift crude oil — though such embargo would not have applied to those consumers who were willing to pay the new prices. Needless to say, in the event no such measures were necessary.

After Tehran, once again the more militant Mediterranean exporters, aided by the continuing shortage of short-haul crude and vulnerability of the Libyan operators, went ahead of the field and outpaced the parameters of the Tehran agreement.

Political and Economic Background in 1970

On the political front, the year 1970 saw the Arab world as a whole still smarting from the effects of the June 1967 war, which tended to engender a climate of opinion hostile to the West in general and to the oil companies in particular. Despite the inconvenience to the West of the closure of the Suez Canal, the Arab cause had not derived any significant political benefit from what had been a rather half-hearted use of the oil weapon in 1967. True, the Arab oil exporters did apply a destination embargo against western states accused of having aided the Israeli agression, namely the United States, Britain and (in some cases) West Germany; but its effectiveness was minimal. For one thing the embargo was short-lived, lasting no more than a couple of months. For another, the embargo was not accompanied by any overall limitation of export volumes. And most important of all, whatever shortfall there was (brought about mainly by the transport bottleneck arising from the closure of the canal, and by the temporary shutdown of some export facilities due to popular indignation in the Arab countries and Israeli bombardment of Mediterranean oil export installations in Syria) was made up without too much difficulty by supplemental production from available spare capacity in the United States, Iran and Venezuela.

However, the lingering fallout from the 1967 war definitely did have a significant effect on the oil market, and consequently on the bargaining power of the exporting countries in the longer run. Despite the growing entry into service of a new generation of very large crude carriers (VLCCs) designed to operate round the Cape, the Suez Canal shutdown had left the European market in a perilous state of dependence on short-haul crude from the Mediterranean, where by early 1970 the export volume had risen to over 6 million b/d as against 3.5 million b/d in 1967. (During the same period Gulf production rose rather more slowly from 9 million b/d in 1967 to 12 million b/d in 1970.) And it was, of course, the 1970 cutbacks in Mediterranean crude availability in Syria and Libya which to a large extent set the scene for the 1970-71 crude price increases.

The 500,000 b/d Tapline, which transported Saudi crude across Jordan and Syria to the Mediterranean export terminal at Siden in South Lebanon, had already been shut down for 112 days from May 30 to September 18, 1969, after its sabotage in the Golan Heights area (Syrian territory under Israeli occupation) by units of the Popular Front for the Liberation of Palestine (PFLP). On May 3, 1970, according to official Syrian accounts, Tapline was accidentally ruptured near Deraa, in Syria, by a bulldozer working on a telephone cable. However, the Syrian authorities refused to allow the line to be repaired. This prompted a vigorous protest by Saudi Arabia, which retaliated by barring the entry of Syrian goods into the country. Finally, in January 1971, Syria permitted the repair and reopening of the line after the conclusion of an agreement providing for the doubling of transit fees and a lump-sum payment to Syria of $9 million for spillage damage and other claims. Whereas the 1969 sabotage was clearly a political move, Syria's action in keeping the line closed in 1970 was probably motivated partly by a desire to demonstrate hostility to the US (Tapline being owned by the same four US parents as Aramco) and partly by a determination to boost Syrian transit receipts.

At the same time, the three OPEC Members which accounted for the bulk of Meditteranean oil exports — Libya, Algeria and Iraq with 1970 Mediterranean outputs of around 3.5 million b/d, 1 million b/d and 1 million b/d respectively — were all in their various ways in a state of ferment.

In Libya, the new revolutionary regime of youthful army officers under Colonel Mu'ammar Al-Gaddafi, which had swept the enfeebled monarchy of King Idris from power in September 1969, set as its priority the evacuation of the US and British military bases in the country. This was achieved through agreement by the end of 1969, and the government then turned its attention to gaining better price terms from the oil companies.

In Algeria, the government of President Houari Boumedienne was engaged in a reappraisal of its ultra-close economic relations with France, the former colonial power. The Algerians were particularly disappointed with the results of the 1965 oil and gas co-operative association ASCOOP) with France, complaining on the one hand that French invest-ment in exploration in Algeria had been woefully insufficient, and on the other that the fiscal terms applicable to Algerian oil lifted by French companies had fallen way behind those in other areas, particularly Libya, in terms of comparative government take per barrel. Failure to resolve this dispute by negotiations was to lead to the nationalization measures of February 1971.

Iraq, too, was still engaged in its protracted dispute with the oil companies, which had been in progress on and off throughout the sixties since the breakdown of the Qasim negotiations and the passing of Law

No. 80 of 1961. However, in July 1968, the indecisive regime of General 'Abd Al-Rahman Arif was overthrown by a movement of the Ba'th (Arab socialist) party under General Ahmad Hasan Al-Baker. The new regime was in the process of evolving a harder line towards the companies which culminated in the nationalization of IPC in June 1972.

In the summer of 1970 the Iraqis were concentrating on two main grievances, one being the still unsettled question of royalty expensing (the arrears for which, with other financial claims, had reached over $200 million), the other being the slow growth in Iraqi production which had averaged only 5% from 1960 to 1969 as against 13.6% for the Middle East/Africa as a whole and 13.7% for Iran. In fact, through the surplus-ridden sixties, the dispute with Iraq had given the companies a convenient rationale for holding back Iraqi production, both as means of penalizing Iraq and, at the same time, permitting the satisfaction of demands for increased production elsewhere. In 1970, although (as might have been expected in the prevailing market circumstances) exports via Mediterranean terminals were running at a near-capacity level of 1.1 million b/d, shipments of Iraqi oil from Gulf terminals at Basrah were averaging only 320,000 b/d, or less than half the rated capacity of 720,000 b/d. In July, the government warned the companies that if they did not use the spare capacity at Basrah Iraq would do so itself. (The following year — 1971 — output from the Basrah field rose sharply to over 600,000 b/d.)

These three radically minded governments — Libya, Algeria and Iraq — got together in May 1970 to form a common front of Mediterranean oil exporters to do battle with the oil companies. After a meeting in Algiers on May 23, the Oil Ministers of the three countries announced their determination to (a) "set a limit to the lengthy and fruitless negotiations" currently in progress with the oil companies in each of the three countries, (b) implement their demands and plans by means of unilateral legislation if necessary, and (c) set up a "joint co-operative fund" for reciprocal financial support in the event of economic damage resulting from any confrontation with the companies.[2]

In addition to this broad three-nation front, a closer and more intimate oil collaboration had been cemented between the two North African neighbours, Algeria and Libya. These two countries co-ordinated their price demands and held regular consultations of an advisory and supportive nature all the way through the price negotiations of 1970-71.

Meanwhile, the development of another valuable source of short-haul crude from West Africa, i.e. Nigeria, had been held up owing to the war of the Biafran succession in 1967-68. However, exports regained their pre-war level of 500,000 b/d in 1969, and by May 1970 had topped the 1 million b/d mark, with projected expansion to 2 million b/d by 1972-73.

While the political climate was becoming more radical, the oil market was showing the first signs of a significant tightening for more than a decade. The previous year — 1969 — had been a dismal time for the oil industry. Product prices in the main markets were generally depressed and spot prices for crude oil reached almost record low levels — $1.25-1.30/barrel for Arabian or Iranian Light in the Gulf, $1.70-1.75 for Libyan crude (Sider-Brega) at the Mediterranean. And despite a healthy increase in sale volumes, net profits of the five US majors as a group had fallen by 2% in 1969.

However, the underlying indicators were showing a rather different picture. In the second half of the 1960s world demand for crude oil, with demand for crude from the OPEC area, had been growing at a rate of 10-11% annually, which meant that by the end of the decade the required annual increase in OPEC production was over 2 million b/d in volume terms. From 8.67 million b/d in 1960 (40% of world total including Communist countries), OPEC area production rose to 14.03 million b/d in 1965 (46.4% of world total) and 23.21 million b/d in 1970 (51% of world total).

Although the oil market had been generally weak in 1969, it was clear that the very high increase in demand, coupled with the continued closure of the Suez Canal, was putting a mounting strain on the world's transportation system which could only be surmounted by boosting the availability of short-haul (African/Mediterranean) crudes to the maximum. In other words, though the bulk of crude availability and spare capacity was concentrated in the Gulf, far from the European and US markets, the strategic pivot of the supply/demand balance had temporarily shifted to the Mediterranean owing to the tanker shortage.

During 1969 the system held up without too much trouble. Even the four-month shutdown of Tapline from May to September of that year did not have any startling effect on freight rates. However, when the second closure of Tapline occurred in May 1970, closely followed by the Libyan cutbacks, tanker freights — which had already begun climbing steadily through the winter of 1969-70 — went through the roof, substantially exceeding even the 1967 post-Suez high. Spot rates for the Gulf-Northwest Europe run, which had been around 80-90 cents a barrel in mid-1969, rose to $2.40/barrel in June 1970 and hit nearly $3.50/barrel at times later in the year. For deliveries of Middle East Gulf crude to the US East Coast, spot freight rates rose to $3.30/barrel in July

1970, as against something like 90 cents a year earlier. Thus, the delivered price of Middle East crude to refineries on the US East Coast at spot rates jumped to about $4.75/barrel, which was some 75 cents above the comparable price of US domestic crude shipped from the Gulf of Mexico. Customarily, the c.i.f. US East Coast price of Middle East crude was around $1.50/barrel less than that of US crude.

The strengthening of the market first reflected itself in a worldwide shortage of fuel oil, which emerged during the winter of 1969-70 and intensified, almost to the point of crisis, throughout 1970 as the supply of short-haul crude became tighter. Apart from the basic crude supply problem, a number of other complex factors had combined to aggravate the 1970 fuel oil shortage, notably: the high freight rates which stimulated processing in European refineries of light short-haul crudes with their lower yields of fuel oil; the failure of nuclear power coal and hydro-electric power to meet their anticipated shares of the energy market — particularly coal in Germany and the United States, and hydro-electric power in Scandinavia and Switzerland; a bottleneck in US refining capacity and consequent drainage to the US of fuel oil from elsewhere, especially low-sulphur fuel oil from Europe's traditional Mediterranean refining sources; and finally absorption by Japan of Middle East fuel oil from Gulf export refineries which, with the prevailing high freight rates, prevented Europe from tapping that source of supply.

Not surprisingly, the price of fuel oil rocketed. From around $9.00-9.50/ton in mid-1969, the spot price for fuel oil at Rotterdam more than doubled to $17/ton in June 1970, and over $20/ton by the end of the year.

Other products were by no means so spectacular in their performance, but they nevertheless also registered respectable price gains on the Rotterdam market. Gas oil advanced from about $19.50-20.00/ton in autumn 1969, to $21/ton in June 1970, $30/ton in August and $33/ton by October-November. Naphtha, after remaining steady at around $18/ton through the June 1969-June 1970 period, moved up to around $20.50/ton by October; premium gasoline was being quoted at $31/ ton in October 1970 as against $24/ton a year earlier.

In the spot market for crude the reaction to the new situation was mixed. Open market prices for Middle East Gulf crudes, burdened as they were by sharply higher freight rates, showed little movement with Iranian Light still quoted at $1.28/barrel in the third quarter of 1970 — roughly the same low level as in 1969. Predictably, however, realized prices for Mediterranean crudes rose steeply. In August 1970, after the production cutbacks had begun to bite, the Libyan Government sold

300,000 tons of Sider crude to Austria's OeMV at $2.19/barrel — 44-49 cents above the previously current market price of $1.70-1.75 and actually 2 cents above the posted price of $2.17. This was the first time that any crude oil had been sold above the posted price since the 1950s.

In the background to this sudden transformation of the oil market, in which temporary factors had played a significant role, there emerged the first signs of other, more profound developments which were to bring about a permanent structural change in the supply/demand equation and the balance of power in the world oil business.

As was already mentioned, the cushion of spare capacity in the United States — which had been as high as 4 million b/d at its peak in the late fifties and early sixties (equivalent to over 20% of non-Communist world production and more than 40% of OPEC output at that time) — had virtually evaporated by 1970-71 (the state of Texas actually went to 100% production in April 1972). There was still in 1970 substantial spare capacity in the Gulf — probably in the region of 2-3 million b/d — but this too was being eroded and was destined to be almost totally mopped up in the boom of 1973, before the picture was altered by the embargo measures and price explosion of 1973-74.

The availability of whatever spare capacity existed was also to be curtailed through producer government action. During the sixties, despite their collective efforts via OPEC to stabilize and marginally increase unit oil revenue, the oil exporters had remained extremely volume conscious. The great bulk of their additional revenue in this period had come from increases in export volumes, not unit income; and, notwithstanding sporadic abortive attempts at production programming and controls, the competition for the lion's share of the growth cake became quite intense at times. By 1970, after the huge volume gains of the previous decade during which OPEC output tripled, the producers began to look with an uneasy eye on the future of their depleting resources, highlighted by the fall in the reserves to production ratio for the OPEC area as a whole from 68:1 in 1960 to 48:1 in 1970.

In Libya the desire of investors — particularly the independent newcomers — to maximize financial benefits from their jackpot discoveries, coupled with Europe's thirst for short-haul crude, had clearly led to overproduction against which the govermental reaction, starting in 1970, was only to be expected. Then, in April 1972 (the very month in which Kuwaiti production reached an all-time peak of 3.86 million b/d), the Kuwait Government gave orders to the Kuwait Oil Company (owned by BP and Gulf Oil) to cancel a major oil export expansion scheme and to limit its output to a maximum of 3 million b/d, as a national interest measure with a view to prolonging the life span of the country's oil reserves. Subsequently, at various times all the leading OPEC producers followed suit by adopting more conservationist production profiles than those previously envisaged by the oil companies, as long-term considerations of national interest began to assert themselves over mere subservience to projected consumer requirements.

The year 1970 definitely marked a turning point in the switch from the earlier volume consciousness towards a philosophy based on output conservation and a consequent optimization of prices. As late as June 1970 — only a few days before Libya's first cutback order against Occidental Petroleum shook the oil world — the Shah of Iran could confidently assert in an interview with French radio and television: "Our aim is not to get a higher price for Iranian oil; rather we are trying to increase our revenues through more production of crude oil."[3] This was the last time that any statement of this sort was to be heard from the lips of an OPEC leader.

Conservation and the Declaratory Statement

Of course, well before 1970 some OPEC planners in the Secretariat and Member Governments had been turning their attention to the subject of resource conservation, and this matter was included in a wide-ranging declaration of OPEC policy objectives issued in June 1968.

This influential document — known as the "Declaratory Statement of Petroleum Policy in Member Countries" (Resolution XVI. 90) — listed the following principal goals with a view to ensuring "the exercise of permanent sovereignty over hydrocarbon resources" by OPEC Governments:

Mode of Development
The statement urged that Member Governments should endeavour, as far as feasible, to explore and develop their hydrocarbon resources directly, obtaining any necessary capital or expertise from outside on a commercial basis. However, in cases where governments lacked the capability for direct development, they should enter into contracts with outside operators "for a reasonable remuneration taking into account the degree of risk involved," subject to maximum government participation in and control over operations. Such contracts should be "open to revision at predetermined intervals as justified by changing circumstances," and "such changing circumstances should call for the revision

of existing concession agreements."

Participation
The statement called for acquisition by OPEC Governments of a "reasonable participation" in the ownership of the concession-holding companies.

Relinquishment
The statement stressed the need for "progressive and more accelerated relinquishment of acreage of present contract areas," including government participation in choosing the acreage to be relinquished.

Pricing
The statement stressed that taxes and other oil payments to the governments must be assessed on the basis of a posted or tax reference price, which "shall be determined by the government and shall move in such a manner as to prevent any deterioration in its relationship to the prices of manufactured goods traded internationally."

Fiscal Stability and Renegotiation
The statement declared that the government may, at its discretion, give a guarantee of fiscal stability to operators for a reasonable period of time; but it emphasized that, this notwithstanding, operators "shall not have the right to obtain excessively high net earnings after taxes." Thus "financial provisions of contracts which actually result in such excessively high net earnings shall be open to renegotiation."

Conservation
In this connection the statement stipulated: "Operators shall be required to conduct their operations in accordance with the best conservation practices, bearing in mind the long-term interests of the country. To this end, the government shall draw up written instructions detailing the conservation rules to be followed generally by all contractors within its territory."

Settlement of Disputes
The statement also insisted that all disputes arising between the governments and the operators should (instead of being subject to international arbitration as provided for in the traditional concession agreements) "fall exclusively within the jurisdiction of the competent national courts or the specialized regional courts, as and when established."

This document amounted, in fact, to a comprehensive programme for a takeover of all the effective levers of power on the crude production side of the oil industry by the governments concerned. And the remarkable thing is that, unlike most policy declarations or plans of action put out by international agencies, it was virtually 100% implemented within five or six years of its appearance.

At the time, world attention focussed mainly on the more immediately dramatic features of the OPEC's Declaratory Statement – pricing, participation, direct development, renegotiation of agreements, etc.; but the passage which called for "best conservation practices bearing in mind the long-term interests of the country" – conveniently blurring as it did (and as Texas and other US states had done before it) any distinction between the concepts of conservation for technical reasons related to reservoir performance and conservation for broader economic purposes – was an important straw in the wind.

Later in the same year, the OPEC Secretariat followed up the conservation provision of the Declaratory Statement of Policy by drafting a "Pro-Forma Regulation for the Conservation of Petroleum Resources", based on rules already applied in the United States, Canada (Alberta) and Venezuela. This Pro-Forma Regulation was approved by the XVII OPEC Conference, held in Baghdad in November 1968, as a suitable model for governmental conservation regulations to be implemented by Member Countries with appropriate modifications in each case. The first Member Country to implement the regulation was, significantly enough, Libya.

Breakthrough in Tripoli

Even before the revolutionary government of Col. Mu'ammar Al-Gaddafi took over power in Libya, in September 1969, there had been a long-standing dispute between the authorities and the operating companies over the posting of prices for Libyan oil. The dispute dated back to August 1961 when, prior to the export of the first shipments of Libyan crude, Exxon (then called Esso) had posted a price of $2.21/barrel for 39° API Zelten crude (later $2.23/barrel for 40° API crude) f.o.b. Brega terminal. The government protested against this posting as being unduly low and failing to give Libyan oil full credit for quality advantages, notably higher gravity and lower sulphur content, relative to existing crude export streams. At the very least, the government reckoned the Brega posting to be 10 cents undervalued as compared with the posting for 36° API Iraqi crude at the East Mediterranean ($2.21/barrel) on the basis of gravity (6 cents in favour of Brega given the traditional escalation of 2 cents per API degree) and freight (4 cents in favour of Brega) alone.[4] Although in the early years, taxes were calculated on realized rather than posted prices, the posted price was confirmed as the basis for tax calculation in the royalty expensing settlement of 1965.

Other companies followed Exxon's lead in posting a price of $2.23/ barrel for 40° API crude, and later — again in the teeth of government opposition — introduced a 5-cent penalty on a new blend of waxy high-pour crudes. The government routinely protested against all these postings, but to no practical effect whatever. On the legal side the companies' right to set postings unilaterally was covered by Petroleum Regulation No. 6 of 1961, which effectively nullified a provision in an earlier Petroleum Law amendment requiring that such prices should be set in agreement with the government.[5] This was further reinforced by the tax and price quit-claim for 1961-64 contained in the 1965 royalty expensing settlement.

Towards the end of the 1960s the evidence of price discrimination against Libya was growing. The freight advantage enjoyed by Libyan oil after the closure of the Suez Canal had not been adequately compensated for by the agreement to eliminate the royalty expensing discounts, which yielded a "Suez premium" of 7-8 cents/barrel in additional government take (equivalent to around 14-15 cents on postings). Nor was there yet any price recognition for the low-sulphur content of Libyan crude, despite growing international attention to the problem of sulphur pollution and the adoption in some major markets, notably the US East Coast, of stringent limitations on the sulphur content of fuel oil. However, no such regulations had yet manifested themselves in Europe, which provided the biggest market for Libyan oil.

Shortly before the Libyan revolution of September 1969, the monarchical regime was itself gearing up to tackle the price problem with a demand for an increase of at least 10 cents in postings.[6] But before the scheduled negotiations could begin the revolution intervened.

Thus, the revolutionary authorities had at their disposal a ready-made issue on the question of oil prices — one on which the government had a strong case, but which the previous regime had manifestly failed to press home.

The price negotiations with the companies were launched towards the end of January by the Libyan leader, Col. Gaddafi, who advised the assembled representatives of 21 oil companies operating in Libya to accept his government's demands with good grace, at the same time warning them that "people who lived without oil for 5,000 years can live without it again for a few years in order to attain their legitimate rights."

Based on detailed studies, the Libyan position was that the current freight and quality (i.e. gravity and low sulphur content) advantages enjoyed by Libyan crude would justify an increase in the posted price of between 40 and 50 cents a barrel – 44 cents/barrel being the most commonly quoted figure. Even at the level of average (AFRA) freight rates prevailing early in 1970 (that is before the mid-year take-off in freight rates widened the differential between short and long-haul crudes still further), this was an eminently justifiable stand, as was later acknowledged by no less a personage than James Akins, who was then head of the Office of Fuels and Energy in the US Department of State. In his 1973 testimony to the US Senate hearings on multinational corporations and foreign policy, Akins described the Libyan demand as "quite reasonable" and noted that his department had come up with much the same figures as the Libyans themselves when calculating the prevailing quality/freight differential between Gulf and Libyan crudes.[7]

As time went on the Libyans also made it clear that, in order to correct the past injustice, any price settlement must be retroactive to January 1, 1965, or to the start of exports if that came later.

The talks, however, proceeded slowly, with the companies initially contending that there was no justification for any rise in postings at all. By April the government's price committee had narrowed its negotiating sights down to two companies – Exxon as the leading major, and Occidental Petroleum as representing the independents. Occidental came up with an offer of a low-sulphur credit of 6 cents spread over 5 years at a rate of 1.2 cents a year, while Exxon proposed a minor increase related to the OPEC 1967 gravity discount allowances. Both were rejected out of hand by the government.

In May, the situation began to heat up with the initiation by the government of a series of restrictions on production allowables in various oilfields, which in successive steps reduced Libya's total output by around 800,000 b/d by early September – down to 2.9 million b/d from its all-time peak of 3.67 million b/d in April 1970. The cuts bore heaviest on Occidental, whose 800,000 b/d output was reduced to 680,000 b/d in May, 485,000 b/d in June and 425,000 b/d in August. Other cuts were imposed on Amoseas (120,000 b/d) in June, the Oasis group (150,000 b/d) in September. The cuts were made for technical reasons under Petroleum Regulation No. 8 (itself based on the earlier mentioned OPEC Pro-Forma Regulation for the Conservation of Petroleum Resources), and no doubt represented a genuine effort to rectify overproduction, which would inevitably have been carried out sooner or later. The basic technical motivation for the cuts was evidenced by the fact that, except partially in the case of Occidental, none of them were later rescinded when price settlements were reached. However, coming as they did on top of the shutdown of Tapline in May, the cutback measure obviously greatly strengthened the government's hand in the price negotiations.

In the meantime, the climate of government-company tension was heightened by various other developments. A dispute over gas pricing between the government and Esso blocked the start of exports from the latter's new LNG plant in June, and in July the government nationalized the local product marketing operations in Libya of Esso, Shell and Agip. Contacts were initiated with the Soviet Union, Hungary and other Eastern Bloc states with a view to developing co-operation on oil matters. On the political front, Col. Gaddafi warned that US interests in the Arab world were "balanced on a razor's edge" owing to American support for Israel.

In July, another price pressure point on the Mediterranean erupted when Algeria, after months of fruitless negotiations, unilaterally raised the tax-reference price applicable to French oil companies from $2.08/barrel to $2.85/barrel, with retroactive effect to January 1, 1969 (the date on which the fiscal terms applicable to French companies under the ASCOOP agreement were subject to revision). The Algerians had long complained that their fiscal terms under ASCOOP (tax of 53% in 1965-67, 54% in 1968 and 55% subsequently, based on a reference price of $2.08/barrel with no royalty expensing) were inferior to those of Libya (50% tax based on posed price − then $2.23/barrel − with full royalty expensing), particularly after Libya obtained its "Suez premium" of 7-8 cents in extra government take in 1967 − a benefit which the French refused to extent to Algeria. In 1970, on the basis of the ASCOOP terms (before the rise in reference prices), Algeria's average take per barrel amounted to 79 cents as against $1.10 in Libya − a gap too large to be accounted for merely by the difference in production costs (65 cents in Algeria as against 30 cents in Libya).

In the negotiations which started in November 1969, the Algerians were demanding that the ASCOOP fiscal terms as from January 1, 1969, should be revised to comprise 55% tax calculated on the posted prices (which Algeria had recently restored to the pre-1963 level of $2.65/barrel, as against $2.35/barrel posted by the French) with royalty expensing on OPEC lines. By June 1970, the only French response had been an offer to raise the tax-reference price to $2.18/barrel, escalating to $2.30/barrel by 1975 − a proposal which the Algerians described as an "insult".

Hence the unilateral increase to $2.85/barrel in July, which was rationalized by the Algerians as comprising the $2.65 posting plus 20 cents for unexpensed royalty and the added value of Mediterranean crude with Suez, closed. Negotiations on this issue with the French were later resumed, but the Algerian action certainly made an impression on the Libyan scene.

In Libya, meanwhile, the companies had during June-July raised their offers to allow for an increase of 10 cents a barrel in the posted price, which still fell far short of the government's expectations. Then, in August, matters came to a crunch when responsibility for the negotiations was removed from the Libyan Pricing Committee and directly taken over by the Revolutionary Command Council (RCC) represented by the Deputy Prime Minister, Major Abdesselam Jallud. Both then in 1970 and later in the post-Tehran round of Libya-company price bargaining in the spring of 1971, Major Jallud was to prove himself a formidable negotiator. Psychologically, he was adroit at unsettling his opponents with skillful changes of mood between sweet reason and full-blooded anger. He also proved himself adept at identifying the strengths and weaknesses of the various individual companies, playing them off against one another and exploiting the bitter differences that had grown up between the majors and the independents (and to some extent between the majors themselves) as a result of their fierce competition for the European market. At the beginning of August Jallud called for final offers from Exxon and Occidental.

By this time — with an already tight world oil situation exacerbated by a growing shortage of short-haul crude, transport bottlenecks and a consequent upsurge in freight rates — Exxon had become convinced of the necessity to make a further effort to satisfy Libya's aspirations. However, it was afraid that too large a permanent increase in Libyan postings, reflecting temporarily high freight rates, would prove impossible to reverse once freight rates fell, and give rise to reactive claims from the Gulf producing countries wherein lay the bulk of the oil interests of Exxon and the other majors. With an eye to balancing these factors the Exxon chief negotiator, George Piercy, made an offer that split the proposed price adjustments of 21 cents a barrel into a fixed amount of 10 cents and a variable freight premium of 11 cents which would fluctuate as freight rates went up or down. The Libyan side rejected this offer as being too low on the fixed element, but indicated that there might be some interest if Exxon was to make the 21 cents a fixed portion and add a further variable freight element. However, at this point the Libyan team broke off negotiations with Exxon and concentrated its attention on the more vulnerable Occidental.[8]

Like the other independents operating in Libya — Continental Oil, Marathon Petroleum, Amerada-Hess and Bunker Hunt — Occidental was massively dependent on its newly-won Libyan crude oil supplies, and deeply vulnerable to the squeeze of successive government-ordered production cutbacks with the threat of a total takeover looming in the background. Nor had the Libyan independents any big interests in the Gulf to worry about which might deter them from acceding to Libya's demands.

Well aware of the extreme weakness of his position, the President of Occidental, Dr. Armand Hammer, went to New York on July 10, 1970, to see the Chairman of Exxon. Kenneth Jamieson, with the general message that Occidental could not be expected to stand up to the Libyan pressure unless it were assured of an alternative source of crude oil. Hammer therefore proposed that Exxon should supply Occidental with replacement oil at little more than cost, to make up for Libyan production lost by the latter through government measures designed to force compliance with Libya's price demands. Two weeks later Exxon turned down Hammer's request, offering Occidental only back-up oil at the regular market price applicable to third-party sales.[9] Thus, left with no negotiating leverage and faced with yet another output cut of 60,000 b/d in mid-August — bringing Occidental's allowable down to 425,000 b/d, or nearly half its April peak of 800,000 b/d — Hammer had no alternative but to strike the best deal he could manage with the Libyan Government.

After a week of hectic exchanges, with Hammer commuting daily between Paris and Tripoli, an agreement was reached on September 2, of whch the main features were as follows:

— A 30 cent increase in the posted price effective September 1, raising the posting for 40° API Libyan crude from $2.23 to $2.53 a barrel.
— Annual posted price escalation of 2 cents a barrel for the 5 years 1971 through 1975, to bring the 40° API posting to $2.63 on January 1, 1975. Though it was not specified at the time, this escalation was understood to be in the nature of a premium for low-sulphur content.
— Increase in the rate of income tax from 50% to 58%. Of the extra 8%, 3% was attributable to retroactivity of the new posting (back to 1965 in theory, but for Occidental back to the start of exports in 1968) and 5% in lieu of Occidental's contractual contribution to the Kufra Oasis agriculture project which was now taken over by the government.
— Most crucial of all for Occidental, its allowable production rate was

raised to 700,000 b/d.

This, by and large, was the shape of the settlement eventually accepted by all the Libyan operators, although no other company secured any restoration of its output cutback. The price increase was taken as a package deal, without going too deeply into the question of the breakdown of its elements. Later it became apparent that the companies were interpreting most if not all of the increment as being attributable to freight adjustment, whereas the Libyans reckoned that part of the initial 30 cent increase, as well as the 10 cent escalation over 5 years, should be considered as a low-sulphur premium. This confusion was to be the cause of problems later on.

As for retroactivity, the companies were given the option of settling their arrears back to 1965 either in cash or in the form of an increase in the tax rate such as would pay off the debt, within around five to seven years (and in effect remain in perpetuity thereafter). With the exception of a few minor producers which elected to pay their very small arrears in cash and keep their tax rate at 50%, most chose the tax route resulting in (apart from Occidental's 3%) an extra 4 to 5.5%. This no doubt made it easier for the companies to pass on the resulting cost increases for Libyan crude; but the very fact of having achieved this by means of a permanent rise in the tax rate made it inevitable that the other OPEC Countries would demand similar treatment.

But the five weeks that elapsed between the Occidental settlement and the final surrender of the majors witnessed a touch of drama behind the scenes. After Occidental, the government shifted its attention to the Oasis group which was the country's largest producer with an output of 900,000 b/d after having been ordered to cut back from 1,050,000 b/d in July. The largest shareholders in the group – three US independents, namely Continental, Marathon and Amerada-Hess – quickly came to terms on September 21 with a price settlement similar to that of Occidental, except for the retroactivity buy-out back to January 1, 1965 which entailed a 4% rise in the tax rate to 54%. However, the fourth partner in the group (with a one-sixth share) was one of the major international companies – Shell – which refused to sign for the Libyan terms, in fear that such capitulation, involving not only a large future increase in government take but also an "admission of past guilt" involving a higher tax rate on account of retroactive underposting, would, in the words of the then Chief Executive, Sir David Barran, "undermine the whole nexus of relationships between producing government, oil company and consumer."[10]

In retaliation, the government promptly prohibited Shell from lifting its share of the Oasis group's exports (around 150,000 b/d) as from September 22. On the same day, representatives of two major companies (Texaco and Standard Oil of California), with most of the remaining independents (Bunker-Hunt, Atlantic/Richfield and Grace Petroleum of the US and West Germany's Gelsenberg), were summoned to the Oil Ministry and given until September 27 to accede to Libya's terms on pain of the same shutdown as Shell.

For a moment it looked as though the majors might organize a resistance front. That at least was in the minds of Sir David Barran of Shell and Sir Eric Drake of BP when they travelled to the US towards the end of September for a consultative meeting between oil company chiefs and State Department officials. On September 24, Barran and Drake tried to convince the then British Foreign Secretary, Sir Alec Douglas-Home, of the need to stand firm against the Libyan demands even at the risk of a shutdown. However, Sir Alec, having consulted his European colleagues at the UN reported that they were far from enthusiastic at the prospect of any reduction in Europe's oil supplies.[11]

The next day, September 25, representatives of the American oil companies operating in Libya, plus BP and Shell, gathered for a meeting at the State Department in Washington with Under Secretary of State, U. Alexis Johnson, and other officials. Barran reiterated his tough line arguing that "sooner or later we, both oil company and consumer, would have to face an avalanche of escalating demands from the producer governments and that we should at least try to stem the avalanche," and even suggested that the American companies should dare the Libyans to nationalize. This thesis apparently drew a measure of support from representatives of BP and Mobil. Others, however, remained distinctly unconvinced.[12]

James Akins of the State Department's Office of Fuels and Energy — who, it will be recalled, had found the Libyan price demands "quite reasonable" — was adamantly opposed to the employment of confrontation tactics, deeming it to be in the US interest for the companies to maintain a "reasonable working relationship" with the Libyans and the other producers. In any case, he argued, the companies could not succeed in blocking the sale of Libyan oil to Europe in the event of a takeover by Libya; and any effort to do so would be liable to provoke counter-measures, even nationalization, by European countries which were on no account prepared to do without Libyan oil.[13] For his part, Under Secretary Johnson held out little hope of any US government backing for a tough stand by the oil companies in Libya, since the US had scant influence with the Libyan Government and any US intervention would therefore be ineffective at best.[14] Nor was there much enthusiasm for the fray amongst the rest of the majors. Two of them — Texaco and Socal — being under the threat of a Libyan embargo deadline two days later, were in no mood to face up to the consequences of confrontation.

Divided and bereft of any meaningful backing from the consumer governments in general, or even from their own home governments in particular, the majors had no real alternative but to settle with Libya on the same terms as the independents. The first of them to do so were Texaco and Socal on September 30 — thereby giving rise to the persistent jibe in oil company circles about the "great Caltex cave-in". Other majors — Exxon, Mobil and BP — followed suit on October 8 (after a forlorn attempt to hold the line by posting new prices "voluntarily" while still declining to admit liability for retroactivity). Finally, Shell brought up the rear with a similar aquiescence to the government terms on October 16; exports were restored and no further retaliation was forthcoming in respect of the company's earlier resistance.

By the standards of the time, Libya had indeed done well for itself. As a result of the increase in the posted price and the higher tax rates (now generally averaging 54-55% instead of the previous 50%), the government's take per barrel rose by around 25 cents from $1.10 to $1.35, with annual oil income (at a production rate of 3 million b/d) rising by $330 million to $1,420 million. Recuperation of arrears through the retroactivity tax buy-out was estimated at about $785 million.

But that, of course, was far from being the whole story. For the first time the international majors had suffered what amounted to a public humiliation at the hands of a producer government. The rest of the OPEC Countries were quick to size up the situation, and the resulting wind of change that blew through the oil industry in the coming years more than confirmed the apprehensions of the oil company Cassandras in September 1970. But it is highly improbable that they could have done anything to alter the eventual outcome.

The Libyan triumph did indeed prove to be a watershed for international oil — one which washed away so many of the ideas of former times, including the complacent predictions of a number of western petroleum economists that oil abundance was a permanent fixture and that prices had nowhere to go but down. What was actually happening was that the era of ultra-cheap energy — where in certain societies fuel and power were regarded almost as free goods like air and water — was drawing to a close. The point was brutally rammed home at the time by Hollis Dole, US Assistant Secretary of the Interior, who warned in October 1970 that consumers "aren't going back to the bargain basement prices we have so long been accustomed to paying for energy. Not this year or next. Not ever."[15]

Repercussions of the Libyan Terms

It was not long before the impact of the Libyan settlement made itself felt elsewhere in the OPEC area. In the Gulf the first to react was Iran, not surprisingly in view of the fact that the Shah was in the midst of his annual hassle with the Consortium about raising production projections in order to meet Iran's revenue needs for the coming year. In addition to extra volume of exports (the Consortium agreed to raise its offtake by 200,000 b/d) the Shah now insisted on an increase in government take per barrel in the light of Libya's achievement. Specifically, the Iranians demanded: a general increase in Gulf postings on the grounds that the Libyan settlement had left Gulf crudes underposted by at least 16 cents; a 5% increase in the rate of income tax to match the new situation in Libya; and an upward adjustment in heavy crude prices in response to the surge in fuel oil prices.

Under pressure (the Shah had threatened to expropriate some of the Consortium's oil-bearing acreage if his demands were not met) the Consortium agreed to raise its tax rate to 55% and raise the posted price of heavy crude by 9 cents a barrel. The same terms were rapidly offered to the other Gulf states, in some cases being accepted on account and in others (like Saudi Arabia) left outstanding pending a more general settlement. However, the Gulf states in general were definitely not at all satisfied with what they considered to be a mere technical adjustment of heavy crude postings. They wanted a substantial general increase in the level of Gulf postings for light and heavy crudes alike, and planned to co-ordinate their strategy in this direction at the next OPEC Conference due to be held in Caracas, Venezuela, in mid-December.

There was also dissatisfaction on the Mediterranean. Iraq contested the IPC companies' decision to raise postings for Iraqi crude by only 20 cents instead of 30 cents as in Libya. However, this problem was to a certain extent defused by the achievement in October of a partial settlement between the government and the companies on outstanding financial issues, notably royalty expensing. In Algeria, where negotiations with France — which had been broadened to encompass the whole spectrum of economic and political relations between the two countries – were still grinding along, it was held that the new Libyan posting would justify an Algerian reference price of $3.24/barrel as against the $2.85 which had previously been demanded.

In Venezuela, as on earlier occasions, legislation not negotiation was the order of the day. Early in December, just as the OPEC Conference was beginning, legislation was passed raising the rate of income tax to a flat 60% as compared with the previous graduated scale with a maximum of 52%, retroactive to January 1, 1970. This raised the effective profit split between governments and companies from around 70-30 to nearly 80-20. The legislation also empowered the chief executive of the government to set tax reference prices for crude oil and products unilaterally.

Caracas: Unified Price Strategy for OPEC

In Caracas, that December of 1970, the atmosphere was electric. For the first time the OPEC oil exporters really felt that the tide of world market and power realities was turning decisively in their favour. Though opinions differed on just how far to go, there was nevertheless unanimous agreement between the Member States that a substantial minimum boost in posted prices and government take was an absolute necessity.

Most important of all, for the first time the OPEC leaders – including those of the two biggest producers, King Faisal of Saudi Arabia and the Shah of Iran – had agreed in advance on concrete measures to be taken against the oil companies if OPEC's minimum price demands were not met. In such a case the OPEC Members concerned would post the new prices themselves, and any companies which refused to pay their taxes and royalties on that basis would be denied access to oil supplies.

Broadly speaking, the strategy envisaged in the Caracas Resolutions provided for the following:
– Establishment of 55% as the minimum rate of income tax.
– Introduction of a "uniform general increase" in posted or tax reference prices in all Member Countries "to reflect the general improvement in the conditions of the international petroleum market."
– Elimination of the remaining discounts allowed to the companies under the royalty expensing schedule.
– Introduction of a new system for the adjustment of gravity differentials (on the basis of 1.5 cents per degree API below 40°, as had been adopted in Libya in the September/October settlements, instead of the prevailing 2 cents), and elimination of disparities between posted/

tax reference prices in the Member Countries, taking into consideration the quality/freight differentials.

The provisions of the above Resolution (No. 120), though of general application were designed first and foremost to lay the foundation for a negotiating effort by the Gulf states. Another Resolution (No. 124), however, supported any appropriate measures which Libya or any other short-haul producer might take to obtain a premium reflecting their comparative freight advantage in view of "the excessive and windfall profits accruing to the concessionaires as a result of the closure of the Suez Canal and the extraordinary circumstances prevailing in the tanker market." Furthermore, Libyan efforts to step up exploration and development activities by oil companies received OPEC backing in Resolution 123.

The key to the new pricing strategy was the concept of "regionalization" through which the price objectives of each particular region within the OPEC area were to be negotiated separately under a loose overall OPEC coordination. The idea was that the OPEC area should basically be divided into three regions:

— Firstly, the six Gulf countries — Iran, Iraq, Saudi Arabia, Kuwait, Abu Dhabi and Qatar. It was agreed that a committee composed of the representatives of Iran, Iraq and Saudi Arabia would negotiate on behalf of the six with the oil companies concerned. A very tight timetable for the negotiations in question was set in Resolution XXI 120. The talks were to start in Tehran within a month of the conclusion of the Caracas Conference (i.e. by January 12) and an Extraordinary Conference would be convened to evaluate the results not more than three weeks later. In the event of the failure of the negotiations, the OPEC objectives were to be achieved through "concerted and simultaneous action by all Member Countries."
— Secondly, a Mediterranean region composed of Libya, Algeria, Iraq and Saudi Arabia (in as much as the last two countries exported part of their crude from Mediterranean terminals). However, each of these governments retained the right to negotiate separately.
— The original plan envisaged a third region composed of the remaining two Member States — Venezuela and Indonesia — but, in fact, each of these two countries went their separate ways.

As explained by Dr. Amouzegar of Iran, the regionalization approach was an idea promoted by Iran and other OPEC moderates in order to ensure that the Gulf producers could negotiate as they wished without being stampeded by the more hawkish Members elsewhere. He also said that, at Caracas, Iran had taken the lead in eliminating some of the more extreme demands from Resolution 120, namely, further escalation of the tax rate beyond 55%, retroactivity and obligatory reinvestment.[16]

Overall, however, OPEC was going into its big test with the oil companies in a buoyant mood. In January 1971, the market both for crude and products was still tight. Freight rates, though showing some signs of easing, were still at very high levels. Short-haul crude was fetching record prices, and Libya was selling spot cargoes of its royalty crude for something like $2.90/barrel, or 35 cents more than the new posted price. Spot product prices had been showing continued strength, while between August and the end of 1970 product prices in domestic European markets had been raised by between 60 and 90 cents a barrel.

As yet OPEC had not officially declared its hand as to the size of its projected price increases. But whereas the Gulf states were reported to be aiming at a general increase of 30-35 cents a barrel, the Libyans were setting their sights way beyond that.

Libya Sets the Pace

The first shots in the 1971 campaign were fired not, as had been expected, in Tehran but in Tripoli, Libya. On January 3, Major Jallud summoned representatives of the operating oil companies and presented them with a list of Libya's demands under the Caracas Resolutions: (1) As regards the call in Resolution 120 for a minimum tax rate of 55% (already implemented in most OPEC Countries since the September 1970 settlements in Libya), it was noted that this must be treated separately from the 3-5.5% increases in tax rates agreed to by the Libyan companies in September 1970 in lieu of retroactive arrears. It was therefore proposed that the basic rate of tax should be raised by 5% to 55%, and the companies would once again be given three options for settling their 1965-70 retroactivity: cash down with 10% discount; installments over 5 years with interest at current market rates; or an increase in the tax rate above the 55% OPEC minimum.
(2) It was made clear that Libya would also claim whatever uniform general increase was achieved by the Gulf states under Resolution 120.
(3) In relation to Resolution 124 (OPEC support for short-haul premium to eliminate the companies' excessive windfall profits), Libya was demanding an increase of 69 cents a barrel in postings – 39 cents in permanent increase retroactive to June 1967 when the Suez Canal closed, plus 30 cents in temporary variable freight premium retroactive to May 1970 when freight rates began to soar following the closure of

Tapline. The Libyan rationale for this increase was that the 30 cent rise in September 1970 had been merely a correction of past underposting in respect of gravity/freight vis-à-vis the Eastern Mediterranean (10 cents) and low-sulphur premium (20 cents). Therefore no allowance had yet been made for Suez and short-haul premiums.

(4) In addition, in relation to Resolution 123 (OPEC support for stepped-up exploration and development activity), Libya was demanding that the companies reinvest in Libya, in oil or non-oil projects, 25 cents of their profits on each barrel of crude oil exported.

The Companies Band Together

The Libyan demands sent shock waves coursing through the head offices of the international oil companies, majors and independents alike. Whatever their differences, all now felt that they must form a unified front if they were not, as in Libya the previous year, to be outmanoeuvred and dismembered piecemeal in their negotiatons with the various OPEC groups, with each set of demands "leapfrogging" its predecessor. As Sir David Barran of Shell put it: "At this time our Shell view was that the avalanche had begun and that our best hope of withstanding the pressures being exerted by the Members of OPEC would lie in the companies refusing to be picked off one by one in any country and by declining the deal with the producers except on a global basis."[17]

A series of meetings was arranged in New York early in January attended by representatives of 24 oil companies — the eight majors (with France's CFP), all the leading US independents, and a number of independents of other nationalities such as the Arabian Oil Company of Japan, Spain's Hispanoil, Belgium's Petrofina and Gelsenburg of West Germany* — to set about putting together a common front, with the necessary liason with the Departments of State and Justice being assured by the companies' attorney, John J. McCloy. By January 16, within a week or so of the initial meetings, just about everything was in place.

First of all, the companies drafted a joint letter to OPEC proclaiming their common front. Then, in order to avoid a repeat of the 1970 debacle when Occidental was obliged to cave in to Libyan pressure owing to lack of replacement crude, the companies with interests in Libya entered into an oil sharing agreement — known as the Libyan Producers'

* *Two big state-owned European oil companies, ENI of Italy and Elf/ERAP of France, declined to join the group.*

Agreement (or safety net agreement) of January 15, 1971 — whereby if any one company was forced to cut back its production by Libyan Government action, the others would replace such lost production with crude from Libya or the Gulf at tax-paid cost. Finally, again through John J. McCloy, they succeeded in getting the necessary clearance from the Department of Justice that neither the message to OPEC nor the safety net agreement would render them liable to anti-trust proceedings.

The message to OPEC, delivered on January 16, injected a touch of irony into the proceedings. Ten years before the companies had refused to recognize OPEC as a collective negotiating body; now they were insisting on an "all-embracing negotiation" with OPEC. "We have concluded," the message said, "that we cannot further negotiate the development of claims by Member Countries of OPEC on any other basis than one which reaches a settlement with all producing governments concerned. It is therefore our proposal that an all-embracing negotiation should be commenced between representatives of ourselves .... on the one hand, and OPEC as representing all its Member Countries on the other hand, under which an overall and durable settlement would be achieved."

The message proposed a five-year price settlement involving a general increase in the posted prices of all OPEC crudes with a moderate annual adjustment for worldwide inflation. Also envisaged was a further temporary freight premium for Libyan and other short-haul crudes, variable up and down by reference to a freight escalator. However, the message insisted that there must be "no further increase in the tax rate percentage beyond current rates, no retroactive payments, and no new obligatory reinvestment" (these three elements being all included in the latest package of demands in Libya).

On the organizational side, the companies set up a joint task force, known as the London Policy Group (LPG), composed of senior executives of all the participating firms, with its headquarters in the main offices of British Petroleum. Its principal function was to establish, and modify as necessary, the terms of reference for the negotiating teams in Tehran and Libya. A corresponding group of company representatives was formed in New York, whose job was to review and comment on the policy decisions proposed in London and to provide technical expertise and information to London for use in connection with the negotiations.

Chosen to lead the negotiations in the field were Lord Strathalmond of British Petroleum (formerly the Hon. William Fraser, son of a former Chairman of BP) and George Piercy of Exxon, who had recently taken over from the redoubtable Howard Page as director concerned with the Middle East.

Finally, the companies felt that it would be wise to enlist the assistance of the US Government via the State Department. In the words of John J. McCloy, the objective was to induce the US Government to "enter into this thing and get the heads of the countries involved to moderate their demands, to persuade them at least to engage in fair bargaining practices."[18] The man chosen for this mission was Under Secretary of State John Irwin who, with the personal authorization of President Nixon, set off on January 17 on a four-day trip to Iran, Saudi Arabia and Kuwait. However, this part of the companies' strategy was destined to misfire in a rather crucial fashion.

Procedural Snags in Tehran

Meanwhile, in Tehran the Gulf OPEC States had named a formidable team to lead their side of the negotiations: Sheikh Ahmed Zaki Yamani, Oil Minister of Saudi Arabia; Dr. Jamshid Amouzegar, Iran's Minister of Finance; and Dr. Saadoun Hamadi, Oil Minister of Iraq. All three were men of exceptional calibre. Although only just 40 years old, Yamani had already been nine years in office as Saudi Oil Minister and ranked as OPEC's longest serving elder statesman. A lawyer by training, Yamani had in the course of many a contest with the oil companies over the years proved himself to be a superb negotiator, possessed of a profound grasp of the oil business as well as a subtle and sophisticated turn of mind. Amouzegar, who had been responsible for Iran's OPEC policy since 1965, was a multilingual cosmopolitan diplomat with a keen mind and a persuasive manner. Hamadi, a respected economist, had recently taken over as Oil Minister in Iraq and was to show himself as a shrewd and effective protagonist on the OPEC scene over the next few crucial years (he is now Foreign Minister of Iraq). From time to time these three were joined by Kuwait's experienced and forceful Minister of Finance and Oil, Mr. Abdulrehman Salim Al-Ateeqy.

In order to give themselves time to consolidate their common front, the companies had resorted to stalling tactics with regard to the start of substantive negotiations in Tehran, which according to the OPEC timetable had been scheduled to begin on January 12. It was in an atmosphere of general OPEC impatience, therefore, that the companies' message to OPEC was delivered on January 16.

For their part, Libya and Algeria issued a joint statement denouncing the companies' message, but the reaction in Tehran was less hostile.

Amouzegar welcomed the positive points in the message – the offer of a five-year price settlement involving a general increase in postings with escalation for inflation – but categorically rejected the idea of an OPEC-wide all-embracing negotiation.

On January 17, Under Secretary Irwin arrived in Tehran on the first leg of his Gulf tour as the special envoy of President Nixon. As Irwin understood it the general objectives of his mission were : "(a) to prevent an imminent impasse in discussions between the oil producing countries and oil companies from resulting in an interruption of oil supplies; (b) to explain the reasons why the US Government had taken steps to make it possible under American anti-trust laws for the oil companies to negotiate jointly; and (c) to seek assurances from the Gulf producers to continue to supply oil at reasonable prices to the free world." It became clear that the US Government was less concerned about the details of any price agreement that might be reached than about the continuity of oil supplies; in other words supply rather than price was the main consideration. In his testimony to the Senate Hearings in 1974, Irwin himself described his basic mission as being concerned not so much with the form of the negotiations, global or otherwise, but rather "to stress the importance to the United States and really to the free world, of which they were a part, of not halting production or cutting production."[19]

In Tehran by the Shah and Amouzegar – and later in Riyadh and Kuwait by King Faisal and the Ruler of Kuwait – the Gulf states' case for the regionalization of negotiations was put to Irwin in the following terms:

– The Gulf states would welcome a reasonable five-year price settlement along the lines described in the companies' message to OPEC. They believed that the increase in government take they were considering was modest enough to be absorbed within the increases in product prices already made by the companies in Europe over the past few months, and therefore there would be no reason for the companies to pass on any further increase to the consumers.

– However, the idea of an OPEC-wide negotiation leading to an overall settlement was impractical and unrealistic – a "most monumental error," in the words of the Shah – and would in fact be against the companies' own best interests and those of the consuming countries. It was the moderate Gulf states themselves which had insisted on the regionalization concept in Caracas, in order to allow them to conduct their own negotiations in a businesslike fashion without being stampeded by the hawks.

– But the Gulf producers could not impose their will on Venezuela,

Libya or Algeria. And if the companies were stubborn enough to continue insisting on the global approach — i.e. that no agreement with the Gulf group could be signed in advance of an overall settlement with all OPEC Members — this would lead to the imposition of a settlement, by legislation if necessary, on the basis of the "highest common denominator"; in other words probably something like Venezuelan terms (60% tax, 16.67% royalty and tax-reference prices set unilaterally). On no account would the Gulf producers be prepared to compromise on the question of OPEC solidarity, and the companies should not hope "that insistence on OPEC-wide negotiations would cause the dissolution of OPEC in disagreement over extremist demands. This would not happen and OPEC would stay firmly together even to the point of cutting off production."[20]

— If, on the other hand, the companies were to deal with the Gulf producers as a separate group, the latter would be prepared to sign an agreement and stick to it without "leapfrogging" in the event other OPEC producers obtained better terms. The Gulf producers were not interested in demands which went beyond the scope of Resolution 120, like increase of the tax rate above 55%, retroactivity and obligatory reinvestment; nor would they afford embargo support to other producers for demands which went beyond the compass of the Gulf deal.

Irwin and the US Ambassador to Iran, Douglas MacArthur, were convinced by the Gulf leaders' case, and the former cabled back promptly with a recommendation to the State Department to "encourage the companies to negotiate with the Gulf countries separately unless the companies had good reasons to the contrary." Irwin's recommendation was endorsed by Secretary of State William Rogers, and the Department told the companies that "they would be well-advised to open negotiations with the Gulf producers and conduct parallel negotiations with Libya."

Despite all the criticism that was later directed at Irwin by hard-nosed US oilmen and politicians, there can be little doubt that he was absolutely correct in his assessment of the situation. To have gone on blindly insisting on OPEC-wide negotiations with countries so diverse in their conditions and outlooks would only have been asking for big trouble; and it is difficult to understand how the companies could ever have thought otherwise. In fact, the proof of the pudding was in the eating. The companies and the Gulf producers did negotiate separately and did reach a reasonable agreement, and the latter did keep their word and refrain from leapfrogging even though Libya achieved better terms.

Nevertheless, it came as a severe psychological shock to the companies to discover, when their negotiating team arrived in Tehran on January 19, that one of the main planks in their common front strategy had already been jettisoned by the US Government.

In the circumstances, the companies had no alternative but to abandon the strict global approach towards OPEC-wide negotiations. But, in an effort to hold on to at least a remnant of their position, they put forward on January 21 a "separate but necessarily connected" formula for negotiations, under which "discussions could be held initially with groups comprising fewer than all OPEC Members" but on the understanding that "any negotiated settlement must be acceptable overall and would not lead to further leapfrogging." On this basis, the industry team was split in two parts — one under Strathalmond in Tehran and the other under Piercy in Tripoli — with a view to tabling a single comprehensive proposal in the two separate places.

This approach still meant, in effect, that even if an acceptable deal were to be reached with the Gulf countries, it could not be signed unless and until the same settlement had been agreed to in Libya, Algeria and elsewhere in OPEC. Amouzegar described the companies' letter outlining the "separate but necessarily connected" formula as a "poor lawyer's effort," and even Strathalmond confessed that he too was "a bit lost on it."[21] On January 22, the Gulf negotiators formally replied with an ultimatum to the effect that the companies must start substantive negotiations with the Gulf Committee by January 28 and reach a settlement by February 1, failing which an extraordinary OPEC Conference would be convened on February 3. Such a settlement "should not be delayed if the negotiations elsewhere are not yet concluded, neither should it be dependent upon settlement with any other country." To ram the point home, the Shah gave a combative press conference on January 24 at which he described the companies' proposal for an OPEC-wide settlement as "either a mere joke or an attempt to waste time," and threatened the imposition of "Venezuelan terms" if the companies refused to deal with the Gulf countries separately.

Under pressure, the companies finally agreed to scrap the "separate but necessarily connected" approach — much to the disgust of some of the hard-line Libyan independents, one of whose representatives (Norman Rooney of Bunker Hunt) accused the other companies of "selling us down the river" — and on January 28 embarked on substantive negotiations with the Gulf group. An attempt by the Piercy team to start parallel discussions in Tripoli was rebuffed by the Libyans who made it clear that they were not now prepared to negotiate until the Tehran talks had been concluded.

Even after the start of substantive talks in Tehran, however, questions relating to assurances regarding leapfrogging or embargo action in respect of Mediterranean demands continued to play a major role. First, the companies tried to gain what they called a "hinge" between the Gulf and Mediterranean settlements, by urging that those Gulf producers which also possessed some export outlets on the Mediterranean (i.e. Iraq and Saudi Arabia) should agree on their East Mediterranean postings as part of, or at least simultaneously with the Gulf deal. This would then provide some general limitation on what could reasonably be demanded by Libya. This idea was, however, turned down flat by Hammadi and Yamani who — while willing to give all necessary assurances against leapfrogging claims on Gulf exports as a result of future better terms for Mediterranean oil — refused in any way to commit themselves on East Mediterranean postings for Iraqi and Saudi crudes in advance of whatever might be agreed upon in Libya.

Another problem was the so-called "reverse hinge". The Gulf negotiators agreed to give an unconditional assurance against leapfrogging on Gulf exports, except in the hypothetical case where a variable short-haul premium obtained by Libya did not for one reason or another (i.e. government refusal) move downwards in accordance with the stipulated formula when freight rates fell. In such a case, the Gulf states would expect some compensation from those major companies which had production both in Libya and the Gulf. The question was: should such compensation be on an equivalent cents per barrel basis, in which case the majors would be liable to an enormous financial loss since their aggregate Gulf production was ten times greater than their output in Libya, or should it be limited to a total sum to be determined pro rata according to the ratio between the production volumes of the majors in Libya and the Gulf?

After much intricate bargaining the assurances which were finally offered by the Gulf Committee and accepted, with not a few misgivings, by the companies amounted to the following:

— Firm assurances against embargo or other action by the Gulf states in respect of Gulf exports to support demands by any OPEC Member for increases in government take beyond the terms agreed upon in the Gulf settlement, i.e. the general price increase applicable in the Gulf plus what was agreed to be a reasonably justified short-haul freight advantage for Mediterranean crude.

— Firm assurances against leapfrogging by the Gulf states in respect of Gulf exports as a result of better terms achieved in the Mediterranean or elsewhere. At the same time the "reverse hinge" compensation to the Gulf states by major companies with production in both Libya and the Gulf would be limited to a pro rata supplemental payment related to the total monetary cost of any failure of the Libyan variable freight premium to fall in line with the formula.

— No commitment whatever by Iraq or Saudi Arabia on East Mediterranean exports, either with regard to government take leapfrogging or embargo action.

OPEC Threatens Embargo Measures

Meanwhile, bargaining was also under way on the cash terms. On January 28, the companies submitted their first offer which proposed a general posted price increase of 15 cents/barrel with annual escalation for inflation, as well as a variable short-haul premium of 18 cents/barrel for Mediterranean crudes. This was rejected by the Gulf Committee which counter-proposed a posted price rise of 54 cents/barrel to be split in any way convenient as between the "general increase" and "elimination of disparities" provisions of Resolution 120. In addition to the inflation escalator, they also demanded that provision should be made for some increase in crude prices to reflect any rise in refined product prices during the five-year term of the agreement.

On January 31, the companies raised their general increase offer to 20 cents/barrel, and proposed an annual posted price rise of 2% to cover all types of escalation. This was again turned down by the Gulf negotiators who put forward their final rock-bottom demands for alternative five-year and one-year deals. For a five-year deal they demanded: 35 cents/barrel general posted price increase on 40° API crude*; annual escalation of 3% for inflation, plus a flat five cents/barrel to cover any rise in refined product prices; settlement of minor issues such as readjustment of the gravity escalation system, removal of posted price disparities on Gulf crudes and elimination of remaining OPEC royalty expensing allowances; effective date, January 1, 1971. For a one-year deal the Gulf Committee stipulated a 40 cents/barrel general increase.

Despite pleas from Strathalmond's team in Tehran for further

* *The increase agreed upon by the Gulf producers between themselves in a secret memorandum as being the minimum requirement necessary to avert legislation and embargo measures was actually 30 cents. As it turned out, they got the 35 cents in any case.*

authority so as to avoid legislation, even to the extent of suggesting acceptance of a one-year deal on the understanding that negotiations for a five-year agreement should begin no later than April 1, 1971, for completion before the end of the year, the oil company "chiefs" in London and New York instructed their negotiators on February 2 to inform the Gulf Committee that the latter's terms for both the one-year and the five-year deals were unacceptable. It was not so much the financial terms which caused the oil company chiefs to dig in their heels. They still felt the assurances being offered against Mediterranean leap-frogging were inadequate, and once again vainly urged that Iraq and Saudi Arabia should commit themselves on East Mediterranean postings.

After the talks had broken down, OPEC swung into action very rapidly. The very next day, February 3, an extraordinary OPEC Conference met in the Iranian capital and adopted a Resolution (No. 131) under which the six Gulf states − Saudi Arabia, Iran, Iraq, Kuwait, Abu Dhabi and Qatar − resolved to impose their price and revenue demands under the Caracas Resolution 120 by means of unilateral legis-lation, unless the companies agreed to accept them voluntarily by February 15. In the event that any oil company should fail to comply with these legislative measures within one week of their issue, nine OPEC Members − the six Gulf states plus Libya, Algeria and Venezuela (that is to say all OPEC Members with the exception of Indonesia) − would "take appropriate measures including total embargo on the shipment of crude oil and petroleum products by such a company".

Also, at their own convenience, Libya and Algeria would legislate the implementation of their objectives under Resolution 120. In the event of non-compliance by any company "with the same minimum requirements agreed upon by the Member Countries bordering the Gulf plus an additional premium reflecting a reasonably justified short-haul freight advantage," the nine OPEC Members would also place a total embargo on oil shipments by the company in question.

It was, however, made clear by Sheikh Yamani at the time that even if the OPEC Countries did find themselves obliged to embargo oil deliveries to the international companies as a result of the pricing dis-pute, consuming nations would still be able to maintain their oil supplies provided that they were prepared to buy the oil directly from the national companies of the producing countries at the new prices.[22]

Concern about consumer countries' reactions to the OPEC moves was also evident in the opening declaration made by the Shah at the Tehran extraordinary Conference. He pointed out that the Gulf states' demands represented less than half of the increases than had been imposed on refined product prices in major market areas since mid-1970. He also noted that the Gulf demands would raise average government take by about 25-30 cents to $1.25/barrel, still a very small proportion of the $12-14/barrel realized on the sale of refined products to the ultimate consumers.

Agreement in Tehran

This credible threat of imminent legislation served to concentrate the companies' minds wonderfully. For most of the time in Tehran they had been chasing shadows — all the myriad assurances and safeguards which were simply never on the cards from the start. Now they were faced with two clear-cut alternatives: a five-year price agreement with a group of the world's leading oil producing nations, collectively representing the centre of gravity of the world oil industry, complete with good-faith assurances of stability; or a chain reaction of unilateral legislation which would have rapidly undermined their position as arbiters of the world oil business. Both would signify a loss of power for the companies, but the latter route was clearly swifter and more lethal.

With only a few hard-liners still dissenting, the companies decided to make do with the embargo and leapfrogging assurances offered by the Gulf negotiators, and to press ahead for an agreement as best they could. Only a few more meetings, in Paris with Amouzegar and in Tehran with the Gulf Committee, were necessary to clinch the deal which was signed on February 14, a few hours before the February 15 deadline.*

* *A last minute threat to the conclusion of the settlement arose from the ever-problematical relations between Iraq and IPC. The companies were seeking some sort of quit-claim from Iraq with regard to various long outstanding disputes (among them Law No. 80, royalty expensing, cost determination and a six-cent underposting of Basrah crude dating back to the 1950s) which the Iraqis refused point blank to accept. Hammadi declined to sign the main agreement until the matter was clarified. In the end, the IPC companies addressed a side letter to Iraq confirming that the implementation of the Tehran agreement "will not be wholly or partially dependent on the settlement of any outstanding claim or dispute between the Iraqi Government and any of the said companies," and that the agreement applied only to Iraqi exports from Gulf terminals and not to Mediterranean exports. In the Tehran agreement the posting for Basrah crude was adjusted upwards by an extra six cents, but the question of retroactivity was left open.*

The terms of the five-year agreement were more or less in line with the rock-bottom demands submitted by the Gulf negotiators on February 2 before the OPEC embargo threat. The main financial features were as follows:

— General increase of 35 cents/barrel in Gulf posted prices (including 2 cents labelled under the heading of correction of freight disparities) for 40° API crudes. Heavier crudes were to be increased by up to 5 cents/barrel more, owing to a lowering of the previous 2 cents/barrel per degree gravity differential to 1.5 cents. Thus the increase in the key 34° API crudes came to 38 cents/barrel.
— Annual escalation of 2.5% for inflation plus 5 cents in respect of refined product price increases. The first such increment was advanced to June 1, 1971 to compensate for lack of retroactivity of the overall agreement to January 1, 1971.
— Stabilization of the income tax rate at 55%.
— Elimination of the OPEC allowances, resulting in an extra 3-4 cents/ barrel in government take for 1971.
— Reference was made to 21.5 cents as being "agreed with the Gulf states to be the short-haul premium".
— The no-leapfrogging and no-embargo provisions followed the lines of the assurances proposed during the negotiations.

The terms (including the effects of the increase in tax rate from 50% to 55% in November 1970 and the first escalation increment on June 1, 1971) boosted the 1971 per barrel oil revenue of the Gulf governments on 34° API crude, by 35 cents/barrel or 39% from $0.91/barrel to $1.26/barrel. The total 1971 revenue increase for the six governments was estimated at something like $1.5 billion — rising 40% from $3.7 billion under the previous conditions to $5.2 billion under the new terms. The original five-year schedule for the Tehran (later, of course, modified by the Geneva I and II currency agreements and finally abandoned in October 1973) was as follows for the key 34^O API Arabian Light crude ($/barrel):

		1971		1973	1974	1975
	Previous	Feb. 15	June 1	Jan. 1	Jan. 1	Jan. 1
Posted Price	1.800	2.180	2.285	2.392	2.502	2.615
Govt. Take	0.908	1.261	1.321	1.390	1.456	1.525

(Previous government take calculated on 50% tax, 12.5% royalty expensed with 1970 allowances; subsequently 55% tax, 12.5% royalty expensed with no allowances.)

Libya Scores Again

After the conclusion of the Tehran agreement, attention once more switched back to Tripoli where the Mediterranean round of negotiations was about to begin. From the start, the Libyans made it clear that they planned to surpass the Tehran terms and take the toughest possible line against the companies. Commenting on the Tehran agreement, Libya's Deputy Primer Major Jallud declared: "The Tehran agreement did not fulfill the aspirations of the Gulf peoples. Nevertheless, it did represent the first successful effort at unity by the various governments to restore the people's rights, and to that extent the joint stand of the producing countries against the industrialized countries and their monopolistic companies was a victory...... The Tehran agreement will allow us to increase our income considerably, but we shall not be satisfied with what was obtained in that agreement." A simple projection of the Tehran terms would have allowed for an increase of 56.5 cents (35 cents general increase and 21.5 cents temporary short-haul freight premium), raising the Libyan posted price from $2.55/barrel to $3.115/barrel; but the Libyans were evidently shooting for a lot more than that.

In general, Libya's position in market terms was still a very strong one, though perhaps marginally weakened by the reopening of Tapline at the end of January. On the other hand, Algeria's decision on February 24 to nationalize 51% of French oil interests in Algeria provided a reminder of the general climate in the area.

Apart from the battle regarding the overall size of the Libyan price increase and its relation to the Tehran terms, other important aims of the Libyan negotiators — mainly Jallud supported by Oil Minister Ezzedin Mabruk — were to ensure that the previous gains of 1970 were preserved intact as the base point for addition of the post-Tehran increases, and to get the largest possible part of the new increment in the form of a permanent increase, rather than of a temporary freight premium. Conversely, the companies were greatly concerned to erode the government's 1970 gains, which they regarded as excessive and having been imposed under duress, and to try to put the greatest possible part of the new increase under the heading of temporary freight for fear of establishing an inordinate permanent differential with the Gulf which might prove unrealistic when freight rates fell.

To start the ball rolling, the Oil Ministers of the four OPEC Countries with exports on the Mediterranean — Libya, Algeria, Iraq and Saudi Arabia — met in Tripoli on February 23 and delegated Libya to negotiate prices on their behalf and report back on the results within two weeks.

If by that time the companies had failed to accept the minimum terms agreed upon between the Member Countries, the Ministers concerned would meet again in Tripoli "to take decisions concerning the necessary measures to be applied, including a stoppage in the flow of oil." Evidently, the East Mediterranean exporters — Iraq and Saudi Arabia, both of whom signed the Tehran agreement in respect of their oil exports in the Gulf — were leaving the ball with Libya on the basis of "get what you can and we will follow suit." However, it was not yet clear how far Iraq and Saudi Arabia were prepared to go in committing their Mediterranean exports (which were not bound by the no-embargo provisions of the Tehran agreement relating to Gulf exports) to embargo support for Libyan demands over and above the routine projection of the financial terms of the Gulf settlement on to the Mediterranean.

The following day, February 24, representatives of all the main operating oil companies were summoned to a meeting with Major Jallud at which they were handed a list of Libya's demands. These called for a permanent increase of $1.20/barrel in the Libyan posting, from $2.55 to $3.75. The proposed increase comprised 50 cents general increase (the rationale being that since 35 cents represented 19.5% of the previous Gulf posting, a rise of 50 cents would be required to yield an equivalent proportion of the higher Libyan posting), 40 cents freight allowance (retroactive, after offset for earlier Suez premium, to July 1, 1967), 20 cents sulphur premium, and 10 cents security allowance (i.e. no transit pipeline risk). Other demands included: compensation for the 1970 retroactivity buy-out either by means of supplemental payments or though a further increase in the tax rate above the new OPEC minimum of 55%; 5% annual escalation factor; and a 25 cent per barrel reinvestment undertaking based on 1970 production volumes.

The companies' offers in the early part of March amounted to barely half of Libya's initial demand. The first, on March 2, proposed a posting of $2.985/barrel (an increase of 43.5 cents of which 22 cents would be permanent and 21.5 cents temporary); this was raised to $3.15/barrel (an increase of 60 cents, of which 22 cents would be permanent and 38 cents temporary) on March 7 and to $3.19/barrel (an increase of 64 cents, of which 28 cents would be permanent and 36 cents temporary) on March 13. Added to each of the latter two offers was 12 cents in accelerated first-year escalation applicable as of the effective date of the agreement in lieu of retroactivity to January 1, 1971. The companies also proposed to pay off their 1970 arrears by means of a government take surcharge of 5 cents/ barrel, which was substantially less than the 9 cents they were already paying under this heading in the form of extra tax.

All these offers were angrily rejected by Major Jallud, not only because they fell so far short of the Libyan target, but also because the offers were so structured (being built up element by element from the pre-Tehran Gulf posting, rather than the Libyan posting of $2.55) as to cause maximum erosion of Libya's 1970 gains. The March 7 and 13 offers were so put together as to reduce the basic freight differential between Libyan and Gulf postings from the 63 cents built into the Libyan posted price structure in September 1970 to 40-46 cents, which the companies considered to be more representative of the actual difference in long-term freight as between Gulf/Rotterdam and Libya/Rotterdam. On the other hand, they were prepared to offer as much as 38 cents for short-haul premium as long as it was temporary and not part of the basic posted price structure. From Libya's point of view this was unsatisfactory since it meant a much lower base level of permanent posting — only $2.83/ barrel under the March 13 offer.

Matters came to a head with the rejection of the March 13 offer. Jallud countered with a rock-bottom demand for a $3.41/barrel posting, plus 5% escalation factor, plus full buy-out for the 1970 arrears, and threatened not only embargo action but nationalization on the Algerian pattern, with compensation to be offset against retroactive claims, if the companies did not rapidly improve their offers to the desired level.

Meanwhile, on March 15, the Oil Ministers of OPEC's four Mediterranean exporters met again in Tripoli where, according to their communique, they "agreed on the minimums for the posted prices of crude oil produced from their territories, the flow of which will be halted if the companies fail to agree to and apply such minimum prices by a date to be fixed by the Libyan Government." The agreed minimum was never revealed, but was understood to have comprised $3.05/barrel as the base permanent posting plus accelerated escalation and short-haul freight premium.

Once again a credible threat of concerted action paved the way for a speedy settlement. The companies were in no mood for a fight and, with one exception (Bunker Hunt, the smallest of the independents in Libya), voted to pursue the settlement path. The company team flew to London on March 16 to obtain new terms of reference, and upon its return to Tripoli basic agreement was hammered out at a crucial seven-hour meeting on March 20 between Jallud and Mabruk on the one side, and the representatives of Mobil and Gelsenberg (Andrew Ensor and Enno Schubert respectively) on the other.[23] Negotiations on details dragged on for another 10 days — Libya gaining an extra 2 cents on permanent freight in the process, in return for confirmation of a five-year term for the deal and no Suez retroactivity — before the agreements were finally signed on April 2, with validity set from March 20, 1971, through to December 31, 1975.

The result in posted price terms fell somewhere in between the positions of the two sides before the March 15 ultimatum. The new posting was set at $3.32/barrel ($3.07 permanent base and $0.25 in temporary freight), to which was added 12.7 cents as accelerated first-year escalation to make a total of $3.447/barrel (for breakdown see Table 1). Other relevant terms were:

- Annual escalation of 2.5% of the permanent posting plus 5 cents/barrel in 1973, 1974 and 1975. In addition, the annual escalation of 2 cents/barrel for low sulphur specified in the September 1970 agreements was maintained.
- Tax rate standardized at 55% (except for Occidental which was liable to an extra 5% on account of the Kufra agricultural project), with buy-out for the 1970 retroactivity assured by means of a supplemental payment to the government averaging around 9 cents/barrel.
- The demand for a 25-cent/barrel reinvestment obligation was dropped, but the companies undertook to maintain active exploration programmes.

Including the accelerated first-year escalation, Libya boosted its posted price by 35% and its government take by 46% under the Tripoli agreement: the posting by 90 cents a barrel to $3.45, government take by 64 cents to $2.02, and 1971 total oil income by $700 million to $2.3 billion (see Table 2).

On a comparative basis, the Libyans obtained about 20 cents/barrel more than would have been axiomatic under a straight projection of the Tehran terms; this was on top of the September 1970 gains which remained intact. Though silent in public, the Shah was reportedly furious about the Tripoli agreement. However, the Gulf states kept their word and there was no leapfrogging.

For their part, the companies conspicuously failed in one of their main objectives, which was to hold down the permanent differential between the Gulf and the Mediterranean. In fact, the March 1971 agreement actually raised the gravity-adjusted permanent differential between Libyan and Gulf postings (mainly freight but

92

including 10 cents for low sulphur after March 1971) to 82 cents a barrel, as compared with 63 cents under the September 1970 deal and 31 cents previously.

Other Countries Follow Tripoli Terms

After some argument about quality premiums between the Iraqi Government and IPC, the problem of East Mediterranean postings was settled in June 1971 on the basis of $3.21/barrel for 36° API Iraqi crude and $3.18/barrel for 34° API Saudi Arabian crude, which with adjustments for quality and freight matched the new Libyan price of $3.447/barrel. Other East Mediterranean terms were also in line with the Tripoli agreement.

In Algeria the situation was quite different. After more than a year of fruitless negotiations over prices and government take back to the beginning of 1969, during which the French companies never really even began to approach the level of the Algerian demands, Algeria nationalized 51% of French oil interests on February 24, 1971.* In April, the government unilaterally assessed compensation to the French firms at $100 million and decreed a new schedule for tax reference prices both in respect of the 1969-71 arrears and for future periods taking into account the March 20, 1971, Libyan settlement: $2.77/barrel (f.o.b. Bejaia) from January 1, 1969, to December 31, 1970, on ASCOOP fiscal terms (55% tax, no expensed royalty); $2.70/barrel from January 1 to March 19, 1971, on OPEC fiscal terms (55% tax, 12.5% expensed royalty); rising to $3.60/barrel on March 20, 1971 (including 25 cents adjustable short-haul freight premium) and escalating thereafter in line with the Tripoli terms. The $3.60 price for Algeria's 44° API crude equated with Libya's $3.45 for 40° API crude allowing for gravity and freight differentials. It was also demanded that French companies should retain in Algeria

* *At the final round of negotiations in December 1970 (i.e. before the Tehran/Tripoli agreements) the French offered a tax reference price of $2.65/barrel for 1969 and 1970 (as against the previous $2.08/ barrel) and $2.75/barrel thereafter, with the transfer of one-third of the French companies' oil production to Algeria's Sonatrach. Algeria rock-bottom demand was for a 1969-70 tax reference price of $2.85/ barrel rising to $2.92/barrel in January 1971 pending a new price settlement in Libya, plus Algeria 51% majority control of all French production operations in Algeria.*

$2.95 for each barrel supplied in order to cover the cost of production, transport fees, taxes and back payments.

Table 1

Breakdown of March 20, 1971, Libyan Posting

	$/Barrel
Posted Price for 40° API Libyan Crude	
(Prior to 20/3/71)	2.550
General Price Increase (1)	0.350
Low-Sulphur Premium (2)	0.100
Fixed Freight Premium	0.050
Increase Agreed on April 2, 1971	0.020
Base Posted Price	3.070
Temporary Elements:	
— Suez Canal Allowance (3)	0.120
— Temporary Freight Premium (4)	0.130
March 20, 1971, Posted Price	3.320
First Escalation Increment	
(Effective March 20, 1971) (5)	0.127
Total New Libyan Posting for 40° API crude	
(Effective March 20, 1971)	3.447
Increase Over Previous Posting ($2.55)	0.897
Of which:	
— Permanent	0.647
— Temporary	0.250

(1) In line with the general increase obtained by 40° API crude in the Gulf under the Tehran agreement of February 14, 1971.
(2) Applicable to crude oils with 0.5 weight per cent sulphur content or less.
(3) To be reduced to 4 cents as soon as the Suez Canal was open for the passage of vessels to a draft of 37 feet, and to be eliminated entirely

when the Canal was open for the passage of vessels to a draft of 38 feet. However, if the Canal opened and the Suez Canal Authority formally announced that it would not be deepened to a draft of 38 feet, then the allowance would terminate forthwith.

(4) To remain unchanged until June 30, 1971. Subsequently, this premium would vary on a quarterly basis in accordance with the prevailing AFRA assessement for Large Range 2 tankers (80,000-159,999 dwt). In each three-month period, the premium would be calculated at 0.058 cents per barrel for each 0.1% point of Worldscale by which LR2 AFRA exceeded Worldscale 72, rounded to the nearest tenth of a cent per barrel. The premium was thus not applicable unless the assessed LR2 AFRA was greater than Worldscale 72.

(5) 2.5% of the base posting of $3.07 (rounded to the nearest tenth of a cent), plus 5 cents/barrel.

Table 2

Increases in Libyan Prices and Revenues Under
New March 20, 1971, Agreement

	Posted Price 40° API Crude ($/Barrel)	Govt. Unit Revenue ($/Barrel)	Tax-Paid Cost to Oil Cos. ($/Barrel)	Annual Govt. Inc. at 3.1 m. b/d ($ Million)
Pre-March 20, 1971*	2.550	1.381	1.681	1,563
March 20, 1971**	3.447	2.015	2.315	2,280
Increase	0.897	0.634	0.634	717

* 30 cents/barrel production cost; 55% tax; 12.5% expensed royalty.
** 30 cents/barrel production cost; 55% tax; 12.5% expensed royalty; "tax buy-back" surcharge averaging 9 cents/barrel.

The French companies thereupon mounted a fierce but short-lived show of resistance to the Algerian measures, mainly on account of the Algerian assessment of compensation, which amounted to about one-seventh of the French evaluation, and the demand for retention in Algeria of $2.95/barrel which was roughly equivalent to the realized market price at the time. Among the measures resorted to by the companies were withdrawal of technical personnel from Algeria, stoppage of oil liftings and the address of formal warnings to international companies and banks not to purchase oil or gas from the nationalized fields. However, negotiations were soon resumed and agreements reached with CFP in May and Elf/ERAP in December 1971 on Algeria's terms as regards compensation, tax-reference prices and investment commitments. The retention obligation was, however, eased slightly to $2.75/barrel for 1971 and 1972.

In May 1971, Nigeria (which was to join OPEC formally in July 1971) and its operating oil companies signed a five-year price agreement patterned on the Libyan settlement, with the posting for 34° API crude being raised effective from March 20, from $2.42/barrel to $3.21/barrel (including 21 cents temporary freight premium).

In its reaction to the Tehran agreement, Venezuela on March 18 raised its tax-reference prices by an average of 58 cents with the price of 35° API Oficina moving to $2.73/barrel.

For its part, Indonesia (whose oil revenues were calculated on actual sales prices rather than posted/tax-reference prices) raised its base selling price from $1.63/barrel in the first-quarter of 1972 to $2.21/barrel in May and $2.60/barrel in October.

Compensation for Dollar Depreciation

A new situation was created in August 1971 with the floating of the US dollar and the subsequent realignment of currency parities and formal devaluation of the dollar against gold by 7.89% in December of that year. Although some escalation on account of inflation (2.5%), inadequate though it later proved to be, had been provided for in the Tehran and related agreements, there had been no such safeguard against any depreciation in the value of the US dollar, the currency in which crude oil prices were expressed and revenues calculated. At the same time, OPEC's Caracas Resolution 122 of December 1970 had stipulated that "in case of changes in the parity of monies of major industrialized countries which would have an adverse effect in the purchasing power of Member Countries' oil revenues, posted or tax-reference prices should be adjusted so as to reflect such changes."

Negotiations between the six Gulf Member States of OPEC and the same Tehran group of 24 oil companies were held in Geneva in January 1972, and resulted in an agreement (supplemental to the Tehran accord) under which posted prices were raised by 8.49% with effect from January 20 — this being the amount necessary to raise government take by 8.57%, which corresponded to the rise in the price of gold vis-à-vis the US dollar. In future, postings were to be adjusted upwards or downwards on a quarterly basis in line with an index based on the movement of the currencies of nine major industrialized countries (Britain, France, West Germany, Italy, Japan, Belgium, Holland, Sweden and Switzerland) vis-à-vis the US dollar. Similar arrangements were subsequently implemented in other OPEC Countries.

The parity problem raised its head again in February 1973 when the US officially devalued the dollar by 10%. However, the Geneva I formula comprised a number of features which tended to blunt and retard the impact of exchange rate changes in crude oil prices, with the result that the scheduled April 1 price rise under this formula would have been only 5.8% — far below the 11.1% needed to offset the 10% devaluation. After protracted negotiations, another supplemental agreement (Geneva II) was signed between the six Gulf Members of OPEC plus Libya and Nigeria with the oil companies in June 1973. It provided for an increase of 11.9% in postings over the pre-devaluation prices and a revision of the adjustment formula to make it more responsive to future exchange rate movements, including monthly rather than quarterly operation.

However, the Geneva formula for automatic price adjustment in response to exchange rate movements was abandoned altogether in the aftermath of the October 1973 price upheaval and has never been revived since.

The Tehran Agreements — An Interregnum

The Tehran and related price agreements, which boosted government take by a salutary and much overdue 40-45% in 1971 after so many years of stagnation, remained valid for roughly two and a half years from early in 1971 until October 1973. This period may be regarded as a sort of interregnum between company control and OPEC Government control over crude oil pricing — a relatively short in-between time when prices were set by agreement between the two sides.

Criticism, particularly from consumer interests, is often levelled at the Tehran agreements because they failed to maintain their validity for the full five-year term. But, in fact, the really surprising thing is that they lasted as long as they did, given the inadequate protection they afforded against loss of purchasing power through inflation, to say nothing of the general turbulence affecting the oil scene at the time. Rather against the odds, the Tehran/Tripoli accords lingered on until they were literally blown apart by an exceptionally powerful politico-economic explosion.

CHAPTER V

THE 1973-74 BREAKTHROUGH — OPEC TAKES CONTROL

Like the 1970-71 turning point in OPEC's fortunes exemplified by the Tehran, Tripoli and related agreements, the 1973-74 oil price explosion had its roots in a complex interplay of economic and political forces — but on a significantly magnified scale. This time the gathering intimations of war were for real; and for the first time the Arab oil producers made systematic and effective use of their oil resources as an international political weapon.

In the public mind the 1973-74 oil price rise has become inextricably entangled with the oil cutback and embargo measures imposed by the Arab producers in the aftermath of the October 1973 war. There is no doubt of course that the extent of the jump in prices was greatly influenced by the cutback/embargo; but the etiology of the two events is nevertheless quite distinct since the move by the six Gulf Members of OPEC to revise the Tehran price agreement was underway well before the outbreak of the October war. On the whole, it would probably be true to say that the October 1973 price increase (when the marker crude posting was raised from $3.011/barrel to $5.119/barrel) was a result of the OPEC drive, whereas the January 1974 rise (to $11.651/barrel on the marker crude posting) stemmed mainly from the sudden surge in market prices brought about by supply fears arising from the Arab oil measures.

The various strands forming the causal background to the breakdown of the Tehran agreement and the ensuing quantum leap in oil prices can be grouped under four headings: the fall-out from world economic and monetary instability in the form of currency fluctuations and mounting inflation; demand pressure on OPEC oil as a result of the 1971-73 economic boom and delays in the development of other sources of oil and alternative energy, combined with production restrictions in some OPEC Member Countries; the drive for greater control over oil production operations by OPEC Governments; and mounting Arab frustration at the complete lack of progress towards securing Israeli withdrawal from the Arab territories occupied in 1967.

As far as the OPEC Countries were concerned the Tehran and related price agreements rested on two basic assumptions: a stable dollar and an annual inflation rate of no more than 2.5% in the industrialized world. Both of these assumptions turned out to be very wide of the mark. As regards the dollar, it did prove possible to patch up the Tehran formula to take account of the 1971-73 dollar depreciation by means of the Geneva I (January 1972) and Geneva II (June 1973) currency agreements. The problem of inflation, however, was another matter. The figure of 2.5% for the inflation escalation factor in the Tehran accord was agreed upon on the basis of studies of price movements of imports by the Gulf producing countries during the Sixties when inflation was comparatively modest. But in the early Seventies inflation had begun to take off with export prices of OECD manufactured goods rising at 6 to 8% annually (6.3% in 1970, 5.9% in 1971 and 8% in 1972), and this in itself was regarded by OPEC as a sufficient justification for renegotiation of the Tehran formula.

Another powerful source of strain on the Tehran agreement stemmed from the dramatic tightening of the oil market and the consequent surge in market prices which began in the fourth quarter of 1972 and continued with increasing velocity in 1973.

The Tehran and Tripoli agreements in early 1971 had been followed by a period of comparative calm in the world oil market as far as supply/demand and price conditions were concerned. The tanker shortage which had put such a premium on short-haul crude in 1970-71 had largely evaporated by the second half of 1971 and freight rates remained generally low through most of 1972 (until the last quarter when they began to rise again quite steeply). During this period the realized market prices for crude oil rose by roughly the same amount as the extra government take arising from the Tehran and related agreements, but no more than that; apart from some improvement in gasoline values, refined product prices in Europe remained at relatively depressed levels until the third quarter of 1972.

However, this comparative and deceptive calm masked the underlying precariousness of the supply/demand balance. World economic growth and growth in demand for energy in the early 1970s had outstripped the forecasts of the planners in the major oil companies.[1] Moreover, contributions from non-oil energy sources — notably coal and nuclear — had not matched up to expectations, owing to cost problems, long lead times for projects, environmental resistance and other factors.

Also, anticipated supplies of oil from various OPEC and non-OPEC sources were not forthcoming. The flow of some 2 million b/d of Alaskan oil to the market, originally scheduled for 1972-73, was blocked for over five years by environmental protests and not finally given the go-ahead until 1974 under the impact of the energy crisis. At the same time, crude production in the lower 48 states of the United States itself had peaked in 1970 at 9.6 million b/d and had started to fall; at 9.2 million b/d in 1973 US crude output was some 900,000 b/d below forecasts a few years before. And then there were the production restrictions introduced for conservation reasons in some OPEC Countries, such as Libya, Kuwait and Venezuela, which had collectively rendered unavailable over 2 million b/d of installed capacity.

All this meant that additions to capacity had to concentrate mainly on two Middle Eastern OPEC Countries – Iran and Saudi Arabia. The extent of the world's growing reliance on these two countries may be deduced from the following table showing percentage increases in production during the period 1970-73 up to the time of the Arab embargo measures (with volume figures in million b/d for the first nine months of 1973 in brackets):

	1970	1971	1972	Jan-Sept 1973
World	10	6	5	12 (56.0)
OPEC	12	8	7	17 (30.9)
Middle East	12	18	11	23 (22.6)
Saudi Arabia	18	26	26	35 (7.8)
Iran	13	19	11	19 (5.8)

Traditionally the Aramco partners had endeavoured to maintain spare capacity in Saudi Arabia equal to 20% or more of anticipated needs.[2] Capacity had been increased from around 4 million b/d in 1968-69 (when production was running at about 3 million b/d) to 6.5 million at the end of 1972, and was programmed to reach 9.1 million b/d by the end of 1973.[3] However, even this was not enough when it came to the crunch in 1973. By September-October of that year, just before the embargo both Saudi Arabia and Iran had reached just about their maximum sustainable output at the time of roughly 8.5 million b/d and 6 million b/d respectively. And, in fact, at that time – before the embargo measures and price explosion changed the picture entirely – it was true to say that, in the basis of the then projected forecasts for the winters of 1973-74 and 1974-75 there would have been virtually no spare producing capacity available anywhere in the world. Quite a difference from the mid-1960s when spare oil producing capacity amounted to 6 to 7 million b/d (3 to 4 million b/d of it in the US), or 24 to 28% of the then prevailing non-communist world demand!

Europe and Japan had long been dependent on OPEC and were fully accustomed to that fact of life. But now the US itself — traditionally impregnable in its energy self sufficiency* — was becoming more and more reliant on imported oil. By 1973 imports of crude oil and refined products had reached 6.2 million b/d, or roughly 35% of total US oil demand. The implications of this basic change of strategic status took a long time to sink into the consciousness of the United States, and one wonders whether they have truly done so, even in 1980.

Given this general outlook, it was obvious that something had to give in the market — and so it did. In late 1972 all the main market indicators — tanker freight rates, refined product prices and spot crude prices — began taking off all at once and continued their upward climb through 1973.

In addition to the market take-off, the situation was also hotting up in another part of the oil scene, namely the drive by the producer governments for control over the running of their own oil operations. The story of this campaign will be related in Chapter X. Here it is relevant to mention that the producers' push towards operational control, through participation or nationalization, had been gathering momentum since mid-1971. A moderate group, headed by Saudi Arabia and including Kuwait, Abu Dhabi and Qatar, took the route of negotiations with the concessionaires for a participation deal; while others — notably Algeria, Libya and Iraq — went ahead with outright nationalization measures, usually on a piecemeal basis.

After more than a year of arduous negotiations, conducted mainly by Sheikh Yamani of Saudi Arabia, the moderate group succeeded in reaching agreement with their operating companies for a 25% equity share in the producing ventures, rising in stages to 51% by 1982.

The more radically minded producers, meanwhile, were proceeding unilaterally. Algeria, it will be recalled, was the first to move with its 51% takeover of French oil-producing interests in the Sahara in February 1971. Libya began its drive with a politically inspired nationalization of British Petroleum in December 1971 after Britain (the departing pro-

* *Up to 1948 the US had been a net exporter, and in the 1950s and 1960s oil imports had been counterbalanced by spare crude producing capacity which evaporated entirely by 1972.*

101

tecting power) had failed to prevent an Iranian takeover of three Arab islands in the Gulf, and followed this with the takeover of Bunker Hunt (BP's former partner in the Sarir oilfield) in June 1973. In August of that year the main Libyan independents – Occidental, Continental, Marathon and Amerada-Hess – agreed under pressure to Libya's terms for a 51% government participation deal. The majors – Texaco, Socal, Exxon, Mobil and Shell – resisted and 51% of their assets were nationalized on September 1. Early in 1974 Libya took over 100% of the holdings of Texaco, Socal and Shell; while, shortly afterwards, Exxon and Mobil came to terms with the government on a 51-49 joint-venture arrangement.

For its part Iraq – weighed down by the accumulated burdens of its 12 years of dispute with the Iraq Petroleum Company (IPC) group and infuriated by the company's abrupt cutback in liftings of Iraqi crude exports from Mediterranean terminals in the early months of 1972 – nationalized the northern oilfields operated by the IPC on June 1, 1972. For the time being, the southern oilfields operated by the Basrah Petroleum Company were left untouched, though the US and Dutch (Exxon, Mobil and Shell) shares in these fields were nationalized in October 1973, as a reaction against the anti-Arab stance of those governments in the October war. However, a compensation settlement on the northern fields between Iraq and IPC was reached in March 1973.

By mid-1973 it became evident that the 1972 Gulf deal, with its delay of majority control by the host governments until 1982, had been overtaken by events and could not hold much longer (in Kuwait the National Assembly even refused to ratify the agreement). So it was no surprise when early in 1974 the Gulf group assumed an immediate 60% majority interest in the producing ventures; and some of them were already planning for a 100% takeover in the near future.

On the political front, meanwhile, the storm clouds were darkening. After six years of impasse following the 1967 war, the Arabs were desperate for some movement towards recovery of the Israeli-occupied territories. Both President Sadat of Egypt and King Faisal of Saudi Arabia were convinced that the key to a breakthrough lay with the US. Sadat was already convinced that only a successful military move could give him the necessary bargaining power with the US, as well as with Israel. And by the spring of 1973 King Faisal had for the first time come round to the idea of using the oil weapon as a means of exerting international political pressure. But the Nixon administration was unresponsive in those crucial spring and summer months of 1973, preferring to believe that both Sadat and Faisal were bluffing.

Clearly, as the year 1973 progressed all the economic and political signposts began to point towards an upheaval on the oil scene. But the magnitude of the impending change was still by no means fully appreciated — even by those most closely involved.

The Market Tightens

The first signs that the oil market was on the upturn came during the final stages of the 1972 negotiations on the Gulf participation deal. The agreement provided that in the early years the bulk of the host governments' 25% equity entitlement of crude oil production should be sold back to the foreign partners. Part of this recycled crude (known as "bridging crude") was to be priced approximately at realized market levels, and the remainder (known as "phase-in crude") at a few cents less than the market price. So it proved necessary for the governments and companies concerned to hold discussions about the prevailing level of market realizations for crude oil in order to arrive at an agreed price for the participation "buy-back" oil.

In September 1972, on the basis of the market price information then available, Saudi Arabia and the Aramco partners had reached an understanding in principle that the 1973 buy-back price for Arabian Light bridging crude should be $1.95/barrel. However, by December the market had strengthened to such an extent that the deal had to be renegotiated, and the 1973 bridging price for Arabian Light was pushed up to $2.05/barrel; higher-quality crudes such as Abu Dhabi Murban and Qatar Dukhan were fixed at $2.25 and $2.17 respectively, while the heavier high-sulphur Kuwait crude was set at $1.95. The formula on which these prices were set allowed for escalation in line with increases in posted prices and tax-paid costs.

These buy-back prices to the major concessionaire companies were soon surpassed when the producer governments came to sell those comparatively small volumes of participation crude which were earmarked for direct marketing (around 2.5% of production for 1973). Such sales naturally aroused great interest at the time among independent firms and national companies in the consuming countries, which were largely dependent upon the international majors for their crude supplies. Crude oil availability was already getting tighter on a worldwide basis; and the advent of the participation deals and nationalization takeovers in OPEC

Countries meant that, as time went on, the majors would have less oil to sell to third parties and more would inevitably be marketed directly by OPEC Government suppliers. Awareness of this likely trend served to intensify the scramble for participation crude by crude-short companies desirous of establishing a long-term direct supply relationship with the producer governments.

The first of these new-style crude sales took place in Abu Dhabi early in February 1973. The winner in a pretty brisk round of bidding was the Japanese shipping and trading firm Japan Line, which contracted for the bulk of the Abu Dhabi Government's availability of participation crude for several years (30,000 b/d in 1973) with the 1973 price pegged on the basis of \$2.38/barrel for 39° API Murban — some 13 cents higher than the buy-back "market" price agreed upon with the majors six weeks previously. But, though it caused quite a stir at the time, this price for Abu Dhabi participation oil was itself rapidly overtaken.

The next significant development with regard to the marketing of participation crude took place in Saudi Arabia, when in May the state agency Petromin concluded three-year contracts covering the sale of 200,000 b/d to a widely diversified list of 23 independent or national companies from Japan, the US, Europe and the Third World. But far more important than the comparatively trivial volume of oil involved was the formula used by the Saudis in setting the prices for these contracts. This was to have a major and lasting impact on the whole of the world oil price scene.

As might have been expected, customer competition for the Saudi sale had been intense, and there is no doubt that the Saudis could, had they so wished, have set their selling prices at or even above the prevailing level of posted prices. But this would have entailed the immediate collapse of the already embattled five-year Tehran price agreement — which was something for which the Saudis were not yet ready. The solution, as conceived by Sheikh Yamani, was to peg the price somewhat below the level of postings — the figure finally decided upon being that the selling price should be maintained at 93% of the posted price. This meant that the initial selling price for Arabian Light worked out at \$2.55/barrel (93% of the May 1973 posting of \$2.742/barrel), or some 40 cents above the 1973 "bridging" buy-back price agreed with the Aramco partners the previous December (this having escalated in the meantime from \$2.05 to \$2.15 under the impact of an increased posted price in line with the Geneva currency agreement).

Moreover — and this was the really crucial factor — the Petromin contracts contained an escalation formula which provided for continuous maintenance of the selling price at 93% of the prevailing posted price (whatever that might be), with a cent-per-cent escalation with posted price increases effected under the Geneva currency agreements. This marked a notable departure from the usual escalation clause in crude oil contracts with company sellers at that time, under which the pass-through was limited to increases in government take or tax-paid costs, these being equivalent to roughly 60% of posted price rises. However, as the market hardened in 1973, refiners came under mounting pressure from their crude suppliers (i.e. the international majors) to accept voluntary increases in contract prices more in line with the market.

Some months later, in August 1973, when the by now absurdly low buy-back prices to Aramco were being renegotiated, Yamani shrewdly insisted that the Aramco partners should accept the Petromin price for actual sales to third parties as the price yardstick for all sales of the government's participation crude to the companies. No doubt scenting a dangerous precedent, the companies at first resisted, proposing instead that the yardstick should be the weighted average of third-party sales by all shareholders (i.e. Petromin and the four US companies); but eventually, in mid-September, they gave way under heavy pressure including the threat of a production cutback to 7 million b/d.

At the time the Saudi motive for this move was probably no more than to ensure that Saudi Arabia would get the best possible price deal for its participation crude and not fall behind other OPEC Countries in this respect. But the eventual result, probably more by accident than by design, was that the Petromin price became the linch pin of the world-wide crude oil pricing system. After the big increases in posted prices in October 1973 and January 1974, it was by and large the Petromin price to third-party customers, automatically raised to 93% of the new posting, which provided the signpost at a time of great uncertainty as to what the market price should actually be; and in time, by 1975, the official OPEC Government sales price (based on the 93% of postings formula in the Gulf) took over from the posted price as the operative price for the world oil trade. From then on the posted price was used only to calculate tax and royalty obligations in those countries where the oil companies still preserved some equity interest in the producing ventures.

But in the summer of 1973 such developments were still in the future. In the meantime crude prices, particularly for government participation crude, continued to strengthen. In June and July the National

Iranian Oil Company (NIOC)* sold around 300,000 b/d for the second half of 1973 at posted prices minus 12 cents/barrel, or roughly 96% of postings; and in June Qatar sold its high-quality participation crude to the US firm Koch Oil at $3.15/barrel or 4% above the then posted price. Meanwhile, Abu Dhabi renegotiated its base price for the Japan Line deal to 93% of postings.

In general, by September 1973 Arabian and Iranian Light crudes in the Gulf were fetching not far off the posted price of around $3/barrel**, as compared with $1.90/barrel or 24% below the posted price 12 months previously. In the Mediterranean, prices for short-haul crude were once again showing the effects of soaring tanker freight rates. From an average of Worldscale 80 (roughly $1.05/barrel on the Gulf-Northwest Europe run) in 1972, spot freight rates had risen to over Worldscale 300 (about $4.05/barrel from the Gulf to Northwest Europe) by September 1973. As a result, realized prices for short-haul Libyan crude started to rocket. In August, Libya fixed the price of buy-back participation crude to equity-holding companies at $4.90/barrel or 7% above the then posting of $4.58/barrel, and by the end of September spot prices had reached over $5.50/barrel or 20% above postings. Twelve months earlier the realized market price for Libyan crude had been in the region of $2.80/barrel, or 23% below postings.

During the same period spot product prices also reflected the growing tightness in the market, with spot quotations for light products and middle distillates almost trebling. Spot product prices at Rotterdam, for example, showed the following increases as between the 1972 averages and the third quarter of 1973: 91/92 gasoline from $30/ton to

* In July 1973 Iran concluded its own version of the participation deal with the Consortium, based on 100% NIOC ownership. The Consortium undertook to provide operational services and to offtake the bulk of the crude in return for payments equalled pro rata with these in other Gulf states under the participation arrangements. NIOC's crude availability for export was set at 200,000 b/d for 1973 rising by stages to 1.5 million b/d by 1981.

** Under the impact of the Geneva II currency agreement (concluded in June 1973 in revision of the January 1972 Geneva I formula) reflecting the currency fluctuations which followed the 10% dollar devaluation in February, the posted price of Arabian Light had reached $3.011/barrel by October 1, 1973 as against $2.591/barrel early in the year. Under the Geneva II agreement, changes in postings due to currency fluctuations were calculated on a monthly basis rather than quarterly as under Geneva I.

106

$80 to 90/ton; kerosene from $30/ton to $70 to 80/ton; gas oil from $26/ton to $75/ ton; and heavy fuel oil (3.5% sulphur) from $13.70/ton to $16 to 18/ton.

Calls for a revision of the Tehran agreement had been forthcoming from some OPEC Members – notably Algeria, Iraq and Libya – since March 1973, and at the June OPEC Conference in Vienna, Iraq proposed that the agreement should be scrapped altogether and that tax reference prices should henceforth be set unilaterally by the OPEC countries themselves. This was resisted by the majority – with Iran and Saudi Arabia still notably reluctant to dismantle the Tehran framework completely – but there was general agreement that the oil companies should be approached with a view to updating the inflation factor. And although the Iraqi proposal for setting tax reference prices unilaterally was not carried at the June Conference, the idea was definitely gathering strength. A few weeks earlier, after the conclusion of the Geneva II currency agreement, Sheikh Yamani speculated at an off-the-record briefing to a few correspondents (among them the present writer) that this might be the last time that OPEC would negotiate the determination of tax reference prices with the oil companies.

By August, the case for a total overhaul of the Tehran agreement had become overwhelming. Not only was world inflation, at 7 to 8% or so, far outstripping the 2.5% oil price escalation factor, but also the firming up of the market had resulted in a substantial increase in oil company profit margins way beyond the underlying assumptions of the Tehran deal. In 1972, with a realized market price of $1.90/barrel for Arabian Light, the companies' profit margin on crude sales (i.e. the difference between the tax-paid cost and the realized price) stood at approximately 35 cents a barrel. By September 1973, when the market price had risen more or less to the posted price level of $3/barrel, this company margin had escalated to around a dollar per barrel, even after taking into account the added cost of participation crude. In Libya the margin on equity crude had escalated from 35 cents a barrel or so in 1972 to something in the region of two dollars a barrel by September 1973 (though on total production this margin was roughly halved as a result of the government's assumption of 51% participation in August-September 1973).

After intensive consultations with the other Arab producers of the Gulf region (particularly Iraq, which sent a special mission to Saudi Arabia towards the end of August), Saudi Arabia too became convinced that the Tehran agreement had outlived its usefulness. This left only Iran as the remaining hold-out. The Shah's reluctance to abandon the Tehran accord — rather ironic in view of this hard-line posture on prices a few month later — was no doubt largely attributable to the agreement's close identification with Iran and the Iranian capital. However, early in September, Yamani visited Iran and succeeded in persuading the Shah and Amouzegar that the time had come to jettison the Tehran five-year price deal and replace it with something more appropriate to prevailing conditions. Shortly afterwards, Yamani publicly declared that the Tehran agreement "is either dead or dying and is in need of extensive revision," and warned that if the oil companies refused to co-operate OPEC would act unilaterally in line with the June 1968 OPEC Declaratory Statement of Petroleum Policy which gave Member Governments "an unequivocal right to determine posted or tax reference prices in such a manner as to prevent any deterioration in their relationship to the prices of manufactured goods traded internationally." What was needed, according to Yamani, was in the first place "a sizeable lump-sum increase" in posted prices to restore them to their traditional level above realized market prices together with a mechanism for maintaining the differential relationship between posted/tax reference and market prices in the future, and in the second place an ungrading of the escalation factor in the Tehran agreement in order to reflect more realistically the prevailing rate of worldwide inflation.[4]

A few days later, at an extraordinary Ministerial Conference in Vienna on September 15-16, the OPEC Members as a whole met to decide how to set about overhauling the Tehran/Tripoli/Lagos agreements. Everyone was agreed that a substantial increase in OPEC Government take, with more realistic future escalation, was in order. It was also recognized that the recent strengthening of market prices for crude oil had led to an unwarranted windfall boost in the profit margins of the oil companies, as well as a distortion in the previously prevailing differential relationship between posted/tax reference prices and market realizations. Theoretically, there were two alternative (though not necessarily mutually exclusive) solutions to the problem of readjusting the companies' margin: on the one hand to increase the tax and/or royalty rates; or on the other to increase the posted/tax reference price to a point where the traditional relationship between it and the market price was restored.

At the Vienna Meeting there emerged a difference of opinion as to which approach to adopt. Iraq espoused the former, calling for an increase in the income tax rate from 55 to 75%. Saudi Arabia, on the other hand, opted for the latter method with a proposal that tax rates should remain unchanged but postings should be maintained permanently at a level 40% above market realizations. This was intended to re-establish the same relationship between posted/tax reference and realized prices as existed in 1970-71 before the Tehran agreement and, by extension, roughly the same profit-sharing ratio as well.* The Saudi proposal for maintaining the 1:1.4 ratio as between realizations and postings was the methodology adopted by the OPEC Gulf States in September-October 1973. However, as we shall see, this approach ran into severe conceptual and practical difficulties in the confused market situation which followed the October war and had to be abandoned shortly afterwards.

Meanwhile, in Vienna in September 1973, the OPEC Ministers decided that the governments concerned with the five-year price agreements — essentially the six Gulf exporters, Libya and Nigeria — would negotiate individually or collectively with the companies for their revision. Talks between the Gulf group and the companies were set to open in Vienna on October 8.

Oil and Politics: The Road to War

Meanwhile, on the political front of the Arab-Israeli conflict, a combination of Israeli intransigence and American indifference as regards any meaningful move towards an acceptable settlement had led to an impasse of complete stagnation — a situation of "no war, no peace" which had brought Arab frustrations to boiling point.

For his part, President Sadat of Egypt had reached certain broad conclusions about how to proceed in order to break the Middle East deadlock. Firstly, Sadat believed that the United States held just about all the cards necessary to bring about a Middle East settlement, since it alone — as Israel's number one backer and provider of aid and

* According to figures put forward by the companies to OPEC in the negotiations leading up to the Tehran agreement, the realized price for Arabian Light at that time was around $1.28 to $1.29/barrel as compared with the posting of $1.80/barrel. This indicated a ratio of 1:1.4 as between realized and posted prices (or alternatively that realized prices were at a 28.6% discount off postings). At this ratio the government-company profit split on realized prices worked out at about 80 to 20 in the government's favour. With the increase in realized prices to about the level of postings by September 1973, the government's share of profits on realizations fell to around 64% while that of the companies rose to 36%.

armaments — could exercise the required leverage over the Jewish state. Having distanced himself from the Russians in July 1972 with the expulsion of the 15,000-strong Soviet military mission to Egypt, Sadat in 1973 initiated contacts with the newly re-elected Nixon administration. However, the problem was that the US at that time refused to take Egypt seriously; and Sadat realized that he would have no bargaining weight with the US unless and until he launched a successful military initiative against Israel. This conclusion emerged inescapably from a meeting which Egypt's National Security Adviser, Hafiz Ismail, had with Henry Kissinger in Paris in February 1973, about which Sadat wrote in his autobiography: "Hafiz Ismail's meeting with Kissinger ...... failed to produce any results. It was impossible for the United States to make a move if we ourselves didn't take military action to break the deadlock. The drift of what Kissinger said to Ismail was that the United States regrettably could do nothing to help so long as we were the defeated party and Israel maintained her superiority."[5]

In order to ensure the success of any military action against Israel Sadat needed backing from two quarters in addition to Egypt's own role: firstly from Syria in order to open a simultaneous second front against Israel, and secondly from the Arab oil producers — Saudi Arabia in particular — with a view to bringing the oil weapon into play. A joint war plan was duly worked out with President Hafiz al-Asad of Syria, and when Sadat visited Saudi Arabia at the end of August 1973, King Faisal assured him that this time the oil weapon could be used.[6]

Faisal's conversion to the idea of using oil as a weapon, or even as an instrument of pressure, had been a lengthy and problematical process. In fact, up to the end of 1972, the Saudi monarch had been firmly convinced that oil and politics should be kept absolutely separate. As late as July 1972, in a statement to a Cairo magazine, Faisal had categorically rejected Egyptian calls for the use of the oil weapon against the US in the following terms: "I recall that such a suggestion was made by some at the Rabat (Arab Summit) Conference, but it was opposed by Gamal Abdel-Nasser on the grounds that it would affect the economies of the Arab countries and interfere with their ability to support Arab staying power; at the same time such a measure would not affect America because America does not need any of our oil or other Arab Gulf oil before 1985. Therefore my opinion is that this proposal should be ruled out, and I see no benefit in reviving its discussions at this time."[7]

In September 1972, in a speech in Washington, Sheikh Yamani proposed an exclusive Saudi-US commercial oil agreement under which the US would remove its tariffs and quotas for Saudi oil and permit the

Saudis to invest in the American oil market in return for a long-term Saudi guarantee of an uninterrupted oil supply. At the same time, he mooted the possibility of a future expansion of Saudi production capacity to 20 million b/d.[8] However, this never-to-be-repeated offer met with a surprisingly lukewarm reception in Washington, where officials made it clear that such a deal would be politically unacceptable in the form proposed, and the matter was never followed up.

But by early 1973 the atmosphere in Saudi Arabia had changed. King Faisal was by then in no doubt about the potential effectiveness of the oil weapon; he was fully aware of the extent of America's growing dependence on imported oil and of Saudi Arabia's crucial position in the future world oil supply picture. He was, at the same time, coming under constant pressure from Arab public opinion and other Arab leaders, particularly Sadat, to use the oil lever to bring about a change in US policy on the Middle East. The King therefore took the momentous decision to play the oil card. The plan, as conceived by the Saudis in those pre-war days of 1973, was to apply increasing pressure on the US for an appropriate initiative on the Arab-Israeli front, failing which Saudi Arabia would cut back its output expansion programme and eventually freeze production at the prevailing (early 1973) level of 7 million b/d.

From then on the Saudis sent out a battery of signals to Washington to underline their seriousness of purpose. In April, Yamani visited Washington with the message that Saudi Arabia would not significantly expand its oil production unless the US changed its pro-Israeli stance in the Middle East.[9] Some officials in Washington apparently took this to be an expression of personal opinion rather than state policy, whereas nothing could have been further from the truth.

Shortly afterwards the King himself, who had been under considerable pressure from Sadat to make use of his influence with the Americans, entered the scene. On May 23, 1973, in Geneva — where he was resting after official visits to Cairo and Paris — Faisal received a group of top executives from the Aramco parent companies, cautioning them in no uncertain terms that time was running out for US interests in the Arab world in general and Saudi Arabia in particular as a result of unequivocal American backing for Israel. Unless there was a change in the direction of US policy, Saudi Arabia would risk increasing isolation in the Arab world owing to its traditional friendship with the US — which was something the Saudis could not permit. Action must be taken urgently, "otherwise you may lose everything," the King warned.[10] In later interviews with US publications, King Faisal further

111

stressed the problem for Saudi Arabia of maintaining close co-operation with a pro-Israeli United States, and indicated the possibility of a freeze or cutback in Saudi oil production unless a more even-handed US policy emerged.[11]

None of these warnings, however, appeared to disturb the complacent slumber in Washington. The King's Geneva message was duly passed on to the White House and the State and Defence Departments by the oil executives concerned, but the response was minimal. This is how an Aramco executive, Joe Johnston, described the Washington reception of King Faisal's warning in a cable dated June 1, 1973, from New York to the company's President, Frank Jungers, in Dhahran: "The general atmosphere encountered was attentiveness to the message and acknowledgment by all that a problem did exist, but a large degree of disbelief that any drastic action was imminent or that any measures other than those already underway were needed to prevent such from happening. It was pointed out by several from the government that Saudi Arabia had faced much greater pressure from Nasser than they apparently face now and had handled such successfully then and should be equally successful now. The impression was given that some believe that His Majesty is calling wolf when no such wolf exists except in his imagination. Also there is little or nothing the US Government can do or will do on an urgent basis to affect the Arab-Israeli issue."[12]

In retrospect, the lethargic insouciance manifested by the powers that be in Washington in those summer days of 1973 with regard to the problems both of the Middle East and of energy appears truly astonishing. On the Middle East, the received wisdom was that Israel was still unchallengeably powerful, and that Sadat and Faisal were bluffing. As regards oil and the impending energy squeeze for the US and the West, the Nixon/Kissinger administration simply failed to focus on the problem at all – despite energetic lobbying by the oil companies, and despite the clear-sighted warnings delivered by the Director of the Fuels and Energy Office in the State Department, James Akins.[13] As late in the day as September 1973, Nixon publicly reminded Arab leaders, with particular reference to Libya, of the fate of Dr. Mossadegh 20 years previously, warning them that they would lose their markets if they continued to raise prices and expropriate without fair compensation.[14] The reaction to such outdated bluster in the Arab world was certainly not one of alarm but rather of simple incredulity that – in the words of one commentator at the time (as it happens the present author): "the President of the United States had not yet grasped the predominant fact of life in the energy picture over the coming decade, that the problem is not whether oil will find markets but whether markets will find oil."[15]

However, Washington and the West were brought face to face with the realities of the twin problems of the Middle East and oil when, on October 6, 1973, Egypt and Syria moved into military action in a bid to dislodge Israel from at least some of the Arab territory it had captured in 1967 and occupied uncompromisingly ever since.

October 1973: Prices

When, as scheduled, the Oil Ministers of the six Gulf Members of OPEC met with oil company representatives in Vienna on October 8, the war had already started and the atmosphere among the Arab participants was appropriately electric. However, at this stage the war did not exert any direct influence on the price issue. The Gulf group had already laid down the broad lines of its price plans in prior consultations, and one of the key participants − Iran − was a non-Arab state with no involvement in the October war (though the Shah had lately come round to a pro-Sadat position, in contrast to his earlier covert tolerance of Israel). Nevertheless, it may well have been that the fact of war did stiffen the resolve of the Gulf team not to bargain overmuch with the companies, and to proceed swiftly to unilateral determination of prices.

It soon transpired that the gap between the two sides was far too wide to be bridged in any conventional process of negotiations. Initially, on October 8, the company negotiations offered merely to modify the Tehran agreement with an inflation "catch-up" involving an 8% increase in the posted price of the marker crude from $3.011/barrel to $3.25/barrel. This having being firmly rejected, the companies came up with a new proposal for an immediate 15% increase in the posted price (i.e. by around 45 cents to $3.46/barrel for the marker crude), with an adjustment of the inflation factor in line with an appropriate index.

This too was turned down flat by the OPEC Gulf team, which countered with a proposal for an immediate 100% increase in postings (i.e. to $6.02/barrel), coupled with a mechanism for keeping posted prices 40% above realization at all times (i.e. the 1:1.4 ratio between realizations and postings described earlier). As regards escalation for inflation, it was proposed that postings should be adjusted quarterly on the basis of the IMF's wholesale price index for 12 industrialized countries (this had moved by 8.9% in first-quarter 1973 as against first-quarter 1972, and by 6.3% between first-quarter 1971 and first-quarter 1972), with the Tehran 2.5% annual escalator being retained as a minimum

113

floor increment should the IMF index drop below the level. Although the demand for 100% increase was no doubt in the nature of a bargaining position, the OPEC team made it crisply clear that it was aiming at a substantial boost in postings – in any case not less than 70% – and was perfectly prepared to implement this unilaterally if the companies did not care to go along.

The Gulf States' demand for a 100% rise in posted prices was based on a prior study by an OPEC working group which found that product prices in the inland markets of seven selected West European consumer countries (Britain, Belgium, France, Italy, Holland, Sweden and Switzerland) had risen by $2.44/barrel since January 1971, the last month prior to the Tehran agreement. It also calculated that world average realized prices for crude had risen by some $2/barrel during the 12-month period preceding September 1973. Because product price increases were close in magnitude to those in the crude oil market, the study group recommended that the best way to set new posted prices would be (assuming constant freight rates) to add all of the net increase in product prices to the OPEC Government take and leave the companies with the same margin of profit as at the time of the Tehran agreement. Given that since the Tehran agreement government take had increased by 53.7 cents to $1.804/barrel, this meant that a further $1.903/barrel should be added to adjust the government take to $3.707 – which would in turn entail raising the posted price of Arabian Light crude to $6.205/barrel f.o.b. Ras Tanura.[16]

The companies did in fact have a little leeway still left in their original negotiating brief, under which they had been authorized to offer an immediate posted price increase of up to 25%, but this was clearly a long way below the minimum requirement of the Gulf States. The company negotiators then consulted their boards as to whether they should raise their offer to a point where it might stand a reasonable chance of acceptance, the reply being that the companies could go no further without consultation with the consumer governments. Having been granted a two-day recess by the OPEC team, from October 10 to 12, the companies canvassed a number of leading oil consuming governments and organizations – notably Britain, the Netherlands, Germany, Italy, Belgium, France, Spain, Japan, the USA, the EEC and the OECD – as to whether they should improve their price after to the point of potential acceptance by OPEC. However, the "virtually unanimous" reaction of the governments contacted was negative.[17]

The company negotiators in Vienna then, on October 12, asked the OPEC team for a two-week adjournment for further consultations with the consumer governments in view of the serious implications of the OPEC price proposal for the world economy. The Gulf Ministers replied that they were not prepared to wait that long. The negotiations were then broken off with a warning to the companies that unilateral action was now inevitable — and so it proved to be.

Meeting at the Sheraton Hotel in Kuwait on October 16, the six Gulf Ministers of OPEC announced the raising of the posted price of the Arabian Light marker crude by 70% to $5.119/barrel. This posting was arrived at in order to establish the posted price at a level 40% above the realized market price of $3.65/barrel — which was the figure the Gulf Ministers had selected after reviewing various actual market prices for sales of government crude in the Gulf and other areas such as the Mediterranean, Venezuela and Indonesia (netted back to the Gulf). The OPEC communique noted that this new market price was in fact only 17% above prices realized in recent sales of the same crude. It was also specified that henceforth actual market prices would determine the level of posted/tax reference prices "keeping the same relationship between the two prices as existed in 1971 before the Tehran agreement" (i.e. 1:1.4), such market price to be adjusted from time to time in the light of producer government sales to third parties whenever it rose above or dropped below the previously announced price by 1% or more.

Finally, the Gulf Ministers declared that in the event the oil companies refused to accept the new prices, the producer governments would "make available to any buyer the various crudes at prices computed on the basis of Arabian Light at $3.65/barrel f.o.b. Ras Tanura." In the event, of course, the new prices were accepted by the companies without undue fuss.

At the same time, the producers of low-sulphur crudes adopted a new formula for setting low-sulphur premiums, roughly on the basis of between 7 and 8 cents a barrel for each 0.1% of sulphur below the benchmark Arabian Light's sulphur content of about 1.7%. In the Gulf, premiums on the lower-sulphur crudes thus ranged between 25 cents/barrel for 1.4% sulphur crudes (Iranian Light, Qatar Marine and Abu Dhabi Umm Shaif) and 70 cents/barrel for Abu Dhabi Murban (0.75% sulphur). For African crudes (Libya, Algeria and Nigeria) the low-sulphur premium was set at around $1.30-1.40/barrel.

Other OPEC Countries swiftly followed the Gulf countries' lead by raising posted/tax-reference prices by varying percentages. Venezuela increased its average tax reference price for crude by 50% to $7.12/barrel. In Africa the percentage increases were higher owing to sharply boosted sulphur and freight premiums. Algeria raised its posted/tax reference price by 108% to $9.250/barrel (44⁰ API), and Libya and Nigeria by 94% to $8.925/barrel (40⁰ API) and $8.310/barrel (34⁰ API) respectively.

On the October 16, 1973, marker posting of $5.119/barrel, the government take rose by $1.28 to $3.04/barrel. On the basis of the new deemed market price of $3.65, the companies' margin on equity crude was trimmed to 50 cents a barrel (i.e. the difference between the $3.65 market price and the tax-paid cost of $3.15), but the over-all margin on all crude would have worked out at about half that amount when the extra cost of buy-back of participation oil was averaged in.

October 1973: Embargo

Considerable though the worldwide interest in the price decision had been, even greater international attention was focused on the oil meeting which was held in Kuwait on October 17, the day after OPEC's Gulf Ministerial Committee had raised posted prices by 70%. This was the Conference of the Oil Ministers of Ten Arab Countries – Saudi Arabia, Kuwait, Iraq, Libya, Algeria, Egypt, Syria, Abu Dhabi, Bahrain and Qatar – convened in order to decide on means of employing the oil weapon in support of the Arab war effort.*

It will be recalled that King Faisal of Saudi Arabia had already promised Egypt's President Sadat that in the event of hostilities against Israel the oil weapon would be brought to bear in an effective manner. And prior to the Kuwait meeting, Oil Minister Yamani had devoted a great deal of thought to the question of how the oil instrument might best be employed in the prevailing circumstances when, by shattering the Bar-Lev line and recapturing the eastern shore of the Suez Canal as well as penetrating the Golan defences, the Arab armies had succeeded in giving the Israelis and their American backers a severe jolt.

*   *The 10 Arab countries represented at the meeting comprised the membership of the Organization of Arab Petroleum Exporting Countries (OAPEC), an organization set up in 1965 with headquarters in Kuwait to promote co-operation and commercial ventures between the Arab oil producing countries. However, when assuming their political role in respect of the oil weapon, the delegates met under the title of Conference of Arab Oil Ministers rather than the regular OAPEC Council of Ministers.*

116

Obviously, the use of the oil weapon would have to make itself felt sufficiently to galvanize the West into a more pro-Arab posture as regards the Arab-Israeli conflict, without at the same time totally undermining the western economy upon which the well-being of the Arab world was itself dependent. Again, the oil measures would have to be sufficiently sophisticated and capable of fine tuning to enable the Arabs to reward their friends and punish their enemies within the western camp. For Saudi Arabia the option of nationalization of US oil interests as a means of retaliation against US support for Israel was not really a practical proposition, given the degree of Saudi reliance on Aramco (besides, the object of the exercise was to change American policy, not to break with the US altogether). This really meant that the Arab oil measures would have to concentrate on a combination of flexible production cutbacks with discriminatory treatment of destinations according to the attitude manifested towards the Arab cause.

The main lines of the Saudi-sponsored plan, as adopted at the October 17 meeting and elaborated at subsequent conferences, can be summarized as follows:[18]

— On October 17, the 10 countries (except Iraq whose special position is dealt with below) each agreed to cut their production by a minimum of 5% forthwith, using the September 1973 level as a base, and thereafter by a similar percentage each month, using the previous month's figure as a base, until such time as "total evacuation of Israeli forces from all Arab territory occupied during the June 1967 war is completed and the legitimate rights of the Palestinian people are restored." At another meeting in Kuwait on November 4, the minimum initial output cut was raised to 25% below the September 1973 level, to be followed by a further cutback of 5% (on the November output level) in December. The actual extent of the cutback by Saudi Arabia and Kuwait in fact approximated to 30% in November.

— Notwithstanding the above, any state designated as "friendly" in that it "has extended or may in the future extend effective concrete assistance to the Arabs" would continue to be supplied with the same volume of oil it was receiving before the cutback, which meant that the other less-favoured customers would have to suffer correspondingly larger supply cuts. In the end the oil consuming countries were divided into four categories:

(1) Most Favoured

This category was introduced in December 1973, comprising countries

which would be allowed to import their full current demand requirements for Arab oil. Among those placed in this category were France,
Britain and various Arab, Islamic and African countries.

(2) Preferred

Comprising countries which were allowed to import the equivalent
of their average imports of Arab oil during the first nine months of
1973 or during the month of September 1973, whichever was the
greater. Included (before some were translated to the most-favoured
category) were: all Arab countries, Islamic oil-importing countries,
African states that had broken off relations with Israel, France, Spain,
Britain, India and Brazil.

(3) Neutral

Comprising other non-embargoed countries whose imports of Arab oil
were reduced by the amount of the across-the-board cutbacks, as well
as by the extra volumes supplied to the two above categories. Japan
and Belgium were originally placed in this category before being promoted to the preferred list in January 1974.

(4) Embargoed

Comprising countries whose supplies of Arab oil were cut off completely. The list consisted of the USA (and all locations trans-shipping
oil to or processing oil for the US or the US military overseas), the
Netherlands, Portugal and South Africa.

Although the October 17, 1973 communique condemns America's
hostility towards Arab interests in no uncertain terms — the Arab oil
cutback, it said, would let the US know "the heavy price which the
big industrial countries are having to pay as a result of America's blind
and unlimited support for Israel" — it did not specifically impose a
formal embargo on oil exports to the US. The chosen wording represented a compromise between the majority of delegates, who wanted
an immediate ban on all Arab oil exports to the US, and Saudi Arabia
which favoured giving Washington a little more time in the hope of a
policy change before imposing a formal oil embargo. However, three
days later on October 20, as a reaction against President Nixon's
announcement of a $2.2 billion military aid resupply package for Israel,
Saudi Arabia itself joined the other Arab producers in declaring an oil
embargo against the US. The Netherlands was put on the blacklist
following the pro-Israeli and anti-Arab stand adopted by the Dutch
Foreign Minister at a meeting with Arab ambassadors at the Hague.

For its part, Portugal was later added to the embargoed list after it became known that it had allowed its airports to be used as staging posts in the US military resupply operation for Israel.

However, the Arab oil plan did not achieve full unanimity. One major producer — Iraq — dissociated itself from that part of the scheme which called for graduated cutbacks in oil production. Iraq publicly declared its opposition to an across-the-board reduction in production which, whatever its motives and however administered, would tend to hurt the potentially friendly countries of Europe, Japan and other areas as much as, or even more than, the principal enemy, the United States. Instead, at the first meeting of Arab Oil Ministers (from which the Iraqi delegate withdrew without signing the communique), Iraq had advocated using the oil weapon by nationalizing oil and economic interests in the Arab world belonging to the US and other hostile powers, as well as breaking off diplomatic relations with embargoing oil supplies to, and withdrawing Arab funds deposited in such states; at the same time, friendly and neutral states should continue to be supplied with their full oil requirements.[19] However, although declining to cut production, the Iraqis did go along with the destination embargo against the US and the Netherlands. Also, in line with its nationalization prescription, Iraq promptly nationalized the remaining US and Dutch equity holdings in the Basrah Petroleum Company.

At its peak, in November and December 1973, the Arab oil cutback removed about 4.5 million b/d from the market, equivalent to about 14% of OPEC production and 10% of non-Communist world oil supply at the time (for details see table overleaf). And owing to the fact that the whole OPEC production was virtually at full capacity by September 1973, the non-Arab Members of OPEC were unable to inject any significant additional volumes of oil into the system after October 17. Also the Saudi cutback — 27% in November as compared with September — was even more considerable (33%) when compared with the originally programmed Aramco output of 9.1 million b/d in November.

The Arab measures began to be relaxed towards the end of December, and largely evaporated by the end of March 1974 when the embargo on oil exports to the US was lifted (though the embargo on the Netherlands lasted a few more months). By this time, Egypt itself was urgently pressing for a removal of the ban on the supply of oil to the US, since the latter had made it clear that this would be a precondition for any serious US effort to bring about a political solution in the area. However, the decision to lift the oil ban against the US met with vigorous opposition from various Arab quarters, and some of the producers – Iraq (which had earlier withdrawn from the group), Libya and Syria – carried on with the US embargo for a while after it had been lifted by the majority.

OPEC Crude Production: November vs. September 1973
(Thousand Barrels Daily)

| | 1973 | | Change | |
	Sept.	Nov.	Vol.	%
Arab OPEC				
Saudi Arabia	8,570	6,268	-2,302	-27
– Aramco	8,291	6,055	-2,236	-27
– Neutral Zone	279	213	-66	-24
Kuwait	3,526	2,470	-1,056	-30
– KOC	3,237	2,250	-987	-30
– Neutral Zone	289	220	-69	-24
Libya	2,286	1,766	-520	-23
Iraq	2,112	2,148	+36	+2
UAE	1,671	1,308	-363	-22
Algeria	1,100	900	-200	-18
Qatar	609	474	-135	-22
Total	**19,874**	**15,333**	**-4,541**	**-23**
Rest of OPEC				
Iran	5,828	6,046	+218	+4
Venezuela	3,387	3,380	-7	–
Nigeria	2,138	2,238	+100	+5
Indonesia	1,420	1,450	+30	+1
Total	**12,773**	**13,114**	**+341**	**+3**
Total All OPEC	**32,647**	**28,447**	**-4,200**	**-13**

Nevertheless, even after the disappearance of the cutback measures, some ceilings on production were retained in place – for example 8.5 million b/d for Aramco in Saudi Arabia, and 2.5 million b/d for KOC in Kuwait (later reduced to 2 million b/d and finally to 1.5 million b/d in April 1980). Owing to the slackening of oil demand after the 1973-74 crisis, such production ceilings were of no great practical significance during the next few years, but their longer-term importance was nonetheless considerable.

Despite the more flamboyant manifestions of the oil crisis during the winter of 1973-74 — queues for petrol, driving restrictions, dimmed lighting, the three-day working week in Britain (which had more to do with the coal miners' strike than with any lack of oil supplies), etc. — the Arab oil measures operated for too short a time to wreak any real damage on the western economies. That indeed was not the purpose of the exercise — the objective being to bring home to western governments and peoples the seriousness of the Middle East problem and the potential strength of the Arab oil producers. And in this a good measure of success was achieved.

However, the really dramatic impact of the Arab oil measures made itself felt not so much on the political scene as on prices.

Panic in the Market

The interaction between the price and cutback measures of October 1973 predictably left the world oil market in a state of some confusion. Within the next few weeks there emerged in fact several different price levels at which oil was changing hands.

First of all there was the market price of $3.65/barrel for the marker Arabian Light crude as specified at the Kuwait meeting of the six Gulf Members of OPEC on October 16. Insofar as it is available, the evidence shows that by and large the major oil companies observed this price level in their inter-affiliate transactions in the October-December 1973 period. Arms-length crude sales by the majors, however, indicated a somewhat higher price bracket, say around $4 to 4.25/barrel for Arabian or Iranian Light.

The problem, of course, with the market price concept as laid down at the Kuwait meeting — that the ratio of 1:1.4 should at all times be maintained between market realizations and posted prices — was that it amounted essentially to a self-propelling ratchet. Any increase in market realizations would entail a rise in postings, and that same rise in postings would itself bring about a further increase in market prices, and so on. In a tight market the price progression could have been unmanagably precipitous, so the Gulf Ministers themselves decided to abandon the 1:1.4 concept at their Tehran meeting in December 1973.

A second tier of market prices was formed by sales of participation crude by producer governments at 93% of the posted price which, as we have seen, had become the touchstone of government crude transactions since the Petromin sales in May and its recognition in September as the yardstick for Aramco buy-back price. After the October posted price rise, the Petromin price automatically escalated to 93% of the new posting, that is to say $4.76/barrel for Arabian Light.

But naturally it was in the open market that the full force of the October cutback made itself felt. In the crude market, with little or no oil available for normal trading, it was the auction sales by producer governments that set the general line. By early December, sales of Gulf and African crude were being made in the $12-16/barrel bracket. And in mid-December a key auction of 475,000 b/d of Iranian crude for delivery during the first six months of 1974 yielded a price of $17.04/ barrel. This large-volume term sale could not be dismissed as a mere spot deal, though part of the price was no doubt attributable to a premium for crude with no destination embargo attached to it. A subsequent government auction of Nigerian crude, on the eve of the OPEC Gulf price-fixing meeting in Tehran on December 22, reportedly elicited some bids of over $22/barrel, though it appears that nobody actually paid this price for delivered crude when the time came.

The spot markets for refined products told a similar story — rocketing prices in a situation of very thin trading and availability, particularly at Rotterdam where activity was hit by the Arab embargo against Holland. Spot prices in Europe (Rotterdam and Italy) more than doubled for most products between September and December 1973, while heavy fuel oil (3.5% sulphur) registered a truly spectacular seven-fold rise from $15/ton to $112/ton. Needless to say spot product prices far outpaced those of the domestic markets in Europe; in December, Rotterdam prices were running at around double average domestic market prices at European refineries.[20] All in all, the value of a barrel of Arabian Light crude f.o.b. Ras Tanura, netted back from Rotterdam spot product prices, reached $17.60/barrel in December 1973 as against $3.90/barrel the previous June.

On the other hand, as might have been expected with the sudden decrease in volume after the October cutback, tanker freight rates plummeted by 75% between September and December 1973, with the rate for the Gulf-Northwest Europe run falling from $4.25/barrel to $1.20/barrel.

In short, the market was exhibiting all the signs of an unprecedented panic, and these were the price indications which presented themselves to the OPEC Gulf Ministers when they convened in Tehran on December 22-23, 1973, for the meeting which was to prove a crucial landmark in the history of world economic relations.

Bombshell in Tehran

Towards the end of November, in response to a request from the companies for "clarification" of OPEC pricing policies, a consultation session — it was stressed that this was in no way to be construed as negotiations in any sense of the term — was held in Vienna between OPEC experts and oil company representatives on current price problems. It was, however, more like a dialogue of the deaf. The companies' team argued strongly for longish-term predictability of oil prices within the framework of some sort of agreement between producers, consumers and companies, though conceding the legitimacy of the producers' anxiety to protect the value of their oil revenue in real terms.

To the OPEC experts, this approach smacked too much of an attempt to re-imprison the oil producers in the straightjacket of a Tehran-type agreement from which they had only too recently released themselves. To OPEC at that time one thing was absolutely incontestable — namely that whatever the future crude oil price structure was to be, it would be decided upon by OPEC and nobody else.

But there was, nevertheless, a significant divergence of opinion between the leading OPEC exporters as to where the new price yardstick should be pitched. It was precisely on this point that a rift developed between the two principal producers — Saudi Arabia and Iran — and the new line-up manifested more than a touch of irony.

Although the Shah of Iran had been the last hold-out in defence of the Tehran agreement a few months earlier, in fact, if logic were to be the only criterion, he should have been the leading price hawk. In the face of burgeoning state expenditure and an ever-mounting burden of foreign debt incurred by this most heavily populated of the Gulf oil producers, the Shah had, for year after year in the late Sixties and early Seventies, battled with the western oil consortium to boost production sufficiently to cover Iran's revenue requirements, and as the year 1973 drew to a close Iran had run up a dangerously inflated foreign debt and was at the same time drafting an ambitious new five-year development programme. Iran's need for cash was therefore prodigious, and at the same time during the early winter of 1973 the Shah had evidently recognized that the upheaval in the oil market resulting from the Arab measures represented a golden opportunity to solve Iran's financial problems — both accumulated debt and future expenditure requirements — at a stroke.

For Saudi Arabia, on the other hand, which did not suffer from the same pressing financial difficulties as Iran, the problem was somewhat different. Saudi Arabia had itself spearheaded the Arab oil measures to serve a specific political purpose and was now very anxious to limit the potentially explosive economic side-effects of these moves. Shortly before the Tehran meeting, Yamani was at pains to stress that the $17/barrel price bid for Iranian crude at the December auction should not be taken as a basis for determining the new posted prices of Gulf crudes. Such prices, he said, "reflect to a large extent the effects of the oil embargo and cutback measures taken by the Arab oil producing countries, and since these measures are of a political nature, they should not have an economic effect."[21]

However, the use of the auction prices of $17 to 20/barrel as a yardstick for fixing the new postings was precisely what the Shah had in mind; and, as the host of the gathering in Tehran, the Shah had a certain built-in advantage in pressing home his own point of view. This approach also had the backing of OPEC's expert body, the Economic Commission Board (ECB), which in its report to the Ministers proposed, on the basis of a netback formula, that a government take of $14/barrel, entailing a posted price of $23/barrel, would have being justified. After arguing in favour of this sort of elevated price level in the early stages of the meeting, Iran later came down to a firm position calling for a government take figure of $8 a barrel which would have entailed a posted price of $13.30/barrel. For its part, Saudi Arabia counter-proposed a government take of $5/barrel on a posted price of some $8/barrel. But then the Shah made it abundantly clear that he would in no case settle for anything less than a government take of $7/barrel – this being a popular figure in circulation at the time as an estimate of the cost of alternative sources of energy such as shale oil and coal gasification or liquefaction – for which a posting of around $12 would be required; and the Shah had a majority of the six Gulf producers on his side.

With grave misgivings – and, as it turned out, to the subsequent displeasure of King Faisal[22] – Yamani decided to accept the majority verdict. "In our opinion," he said, "a lower posted price would have been more equitable and reasonable. However, we went along with the majority."[23] Thus emerged the first beginnings of a crucial divergence of view between Saudi Arabia and the rest of OPEC on the optimum level for crude oil prices – a split that persists unabated to the present day.

So, in Tehran, the new posted price was set at $11.651/barrel for the 34° API Arabian Light marker crude with effect from January 1, 1974, an increase of around 130% over the previous level, yielding a government take on equity crude of roughly $7/barrel. However, these new prices exhibited a grave structural imbalance, in that it left the oil companies with a potential margin of over $3/barrel between their tax-paid cost (including participation cost at the 25% level) and the government sales price of $10.84/barrel (93% of postings). Through 1974 this was adjusted in stages — by increasing the percentage participation to 60% on the one hand, and raising income tax and royalty rates on the other — to the point where by the end of the year average government take had reached $10.12/barrel, and the company margin had been whittled down to about 22 cents a barrel.

The Levers of Power

By early 1974, therefore, the OPEC Members had taken into their own hands all the effective levers of power at the crude oil producing end of the oil industry: control over operations (through majority interest in the producing ventures), control over prices, and control over production volumes. No longer could the oil producing areas be treated as a mere cog in the machine of the international economic order created by the industrialized nations and their major multinational oil companies. This was the first time that any grouping of raw material producers in the Third World had taken their own destinies so decisively in hand.

But now that they were in charge, the OPEC Governments themselves had to grapple with some of the perennial problems of the industry previously handled by the majors, as well as a number of new ones arising from the radically changed structural alignment of the oil business. Among these, to be analyzed in the next chapter, were the determination of a market price structure to replace the now outmoded posted/tax reference price system; a decision on how much of a margin to leave for the oil companies in return for the services they still provided in some OPEC Countries; and the establishment of a workable system for fixing relative value differentials between the various OPEC crudes.

CHAPTER VI

SOME PROBLEMS OF CONTROL

Although by 1974 the OPEC Governments had taken over the effective levers of power in the upstream segment of the oil industry, there was still some time to go before the exercise of this power would translate itself into direct operational involvement at all levels — and then there were wide differences in the takeover experiences of the various individual OPEC Governments. For the time being most of the OPEC Countries continued to channel the bulk of their crude oil exports via the major international companies. But, particularly in the wake of the price increases of October 1973 and January 1974, one question loomed very large: what sort of a profit margin should be left for the concessionaire companies which still retained equity holdings in the OPEC producing countries? This was a problem which it took the whole of the year 1974 to solve.

Paring Down the Companies' Margin

The increase in the posted price of the marker crude by 130% to $11.651/barrel effective January 1, 1974, added further complications to an already confused price structure. Basically, this confusion stemmed from the fact that the posted or tax reference price was still being used as the operative value, whereas what was really needed, now that the OPEC Governments had taken full control of crude oil pricing, was a definite market sale price fixed by the exporter governments themselves; and it was some time before this concept actually took root. In January 1974, therefore, there were several levels of price and cost influencing the overall market situation, notably:

- The tax-paid cost (government take plus cost of production on equity crude) of $7.11/barrel. However, the tax-paid cost on equity crude could no longer be considered as the average cost of crude to the major companies, since this had been boosted by the extra cost of participation oil bought back from the governments.
- The average cost of crude to the equity-holding major companies, including the cost of participation oil. However, in January 1974 it was still uncertain what this would be. For one thing, although

the level of government participation under the original Gulf agreement still stood at 25%, several Gulf governments had made it clear that they were not prepared to accept less than 60% for 1974. For another thing, it was not yet clear what the level of buy-back prices for participation crude would be.

— Then, most crucially, there was the level of prices for the sale of government crude both to third parties and in the form of buy-back to the concessionaire companies. The idea of the 1:1.4 ratio between market and posted prices having been abandoned, this left the government sales price in the region of 93% of postings which had been initiated by Saudi Arabia's Petromin in 1973.

Taking 93% of postings as the generally operative market price for sales by both governments and companies (in fact it did not establish itself as such until later in the year) the spread of the potential company margin between the market price and the average cost to the companies presented itself as follows in January 1974: around $3.70/barrel on equity crude; $2.80/barrel on the basis of 25% government participation; and $1.50/barrel on the basis of 60% government participation. In the end the size of the companies' margin — and indeed the whole world crude oil price structure — would be decided by the determination of three elements: the extent of government participation; the government price for buy-back by the companies and sales to third parties; and the applicable tax and royalty rates. At the beginning of January 1974 all these elements were still uncertain.

Towards the end of January, the participation issue clarified itself somewhat when Kuwait signed an agreement with its concessionaires (BP and Gulf Oil) providing for 60% government participation in the producing venture; and this example was later followed by most of the other Gulf producers — Saudi Arabia, Qatar and Abu Dhabi (Iran having its own agreement with the Consortium for income equation with Saudi Arabia, and Iraq well on the way to full nationalization) — with all the agreements backdated to January 1, 1974.

After a prolonged period of uncertainty — during which Kuwait, in May, threatened to sell its entire 60% entitlement of participation crude to third parties following a breakdown of buy-back prices talks with BP and Gulf — the buy-back price pattern for 1974 was set at 94% of postings for January-May, 94.846% of postings for June-September, and 93% of postings for the fourth quarter. This pattern, too, was initiated by Kuwait in its agreements with BP and Gulf Oil and subsequently adopted by the rest of the Gulf producers.

Given this level of government participation and buy-back price, the major companies' notional profit margin between their average cost of crude (assuming full buy-back) and the government-set market price worked out at somewhere around $1.50/barrel, given the then prevailing royalty and tax rates (12.5% and 55% respectively). Such a margin — some four times greater than the 35 cents/barrel registered in 1972 — was regarded by OPEC as far too large and something which it was essential to cut down to a more appropriate size in the new price structure that OPEC was in the process of elaborating.

The desirability of paring down the company margin was not just a question of recuperating that part of the economic rent for the owner of the oil, that is the producer governments. It was also a pressing commercial question. With such a large margin to play with, the majors could well afford to undercut, and did in fact undercut, the prices charged by the OPEC Governments themselves in their direct sales to third parties, especially since the governments had a gentlemen's agreement between themselves not to sell at less than 93% of postings. Countries which had retained the majors as minority equity holders in the producing operations were protected by their high-priced large-volume buy-back sales to the majors. But those who had nationalized large segments of their operations — like Iraq, Algeria and Libya — were, in the soft market that developed once the Arab production cutbacks were eased in early 1974, quite hard hit by price competition from the majors.

Another cause of price confusion during most of 1974 stemmed on the one hand from repeated assertions by Saudi Arabia that the posted price increase decided upon in Tehran was too high for the health of the world economy and should be brought down by some $2/barrel, and on the other hand from a growing anti-OPEC clamour on the side of the consumers, orchestrated by the United States, that the market price of crude oil should be rolled back to somewhere in the region of $7/barrel.

Towards a New Price Structure

At its first full Conference after the big price rise, in Geneva early in January 1974, OPEC instructed its expert body, the Economic Commission Board (ECB) to conduct urgent studies with a view to establishing a long-run crude oil pricing system, taking into account the following factors as its terms of reference: competitive price levels of other sources of energy; protection of the purchasing power of the oil barrel; the intrinsic value of petroleum as a natural non-renewable resource; the advantages enjoyed by petroleum over other fuels, such as ease of handling, petrochemical derivatives, etc.; the impact of oil prices on world balances of payment; the effects of supply and demand considerations, i.e. maintaining equilibrium through production programming.

In the shorter run there were the pressing problems firstly of converting the basis of the OPEC price system from the posted/tax reference price to the market sale price and determining what that market price should be; and secondly of reducing the companies' margin and increasing average government take, either by raising tax and royalty rates or by abolishing the posted price mechanism altogether and establishing instead a certain fixed margin between the average cost of crude lifted by the equity-holding companies and the government sale price.

There was also the puzzle as to what to do about the 1973 Geneva II currency agreement, basically a leftover from the days of the Tehran accord. Owing to the strengthening of the dollar in late-1973 and early-1974, the operation of Geneva II (which had continued up to December 1973) would have resulted in a significant decrease in posted prices — probably in the region of 6% — in February 1974. Nevertheless, since a number of OPEC Members — Iraq and Libya in particular — were dead set against this, Geneva II was quietly, but permanently placed on the shelf. Not surprisingly, however, the problem of the fluctuating dollar was destined to raise its head on a number of occasions in the coming years.

At that time, early in 1974, there was still a fairly strong current in OPEC which favoured a further increase in prices, the market at that time continuing to hold fairly strong under the influence of the still-operative Arab cutback and embargo measures. At the next OPEC Conference, in Vienna in March 1974, the ECB proposed, on the basis of its netback formula, a posted price increase of between $1.40/barrel and $2.60/barrel. This recommendation met with the open or tacit backing of the majority of Member States, but was effectively vetoed by Saudi Arabia, which threatened to post a lower price unilaterally if the others went ahead with the proposed increase. The result was a freeze in postings for the second quarter and an agreement that an extraordinary Conference could be convened at any time at the request of any Member Government, with a view to revising posted prices in the light of changing market conditions. By these means Saudi Arabia, which was reckoning on a further softening of the market in response to the easing of the Arab oil measures (decided upon by the Arab Oil

Ministers at a meeting in Vienna on March 18, the day after the OPEC Conference) and slackening demand for oil as a result of the price increase and the deepening worldwide economic recession, hoped to press home its case for a price reduction.

In fact, the market did soften significantly over the coming months, but the evidence was never quite conclusive enough to necessitate any substantial reduction in crude prices and Saudi Arabia itself did not in the end have the political will to force the issue against its OPEC partners. In terms of refined product prices, the value of a barrel of Arabian Light crude f.o.b. Ras Tanura netted back from Rotterdam spot prices, which had reached a peak of $17.60/barrel at the height of the crisis in December 1973, dropped to $10.50/barrel in May 1974 and to $9/barrel in September, recovering somewhat to $9.80/barrel by the end of the year. On the other hand, the prices of the bulk of Gulf crude moving in world oil trade actually rose during the period under the impact of increased government take from participation and higher tax/ royalty rates. In January, the major companies' transfer prices to affiliates for Arabian or Iranian Light-type crudes were generally in the $8.40 to $9/barrel range, rising to $9.50 to $9.75 in the second quarter and to $10.20 to $10.35 in October. Contract sales to non-affiliates in January-October generally ranged between $10.20 and $11. After the big tax and royalty increase in government take in November 1974 and the consequent compression of company margins, the majors' crude prices tended to approximate to those of the official OPEC Government sale prices (from November 1, 1974, $10.46/barrel for the Arabian Light marker, equivalent to 93% of postings). What this proved was that, given the necessary cohesion, OPEC Governments were perfectly capable of raising and maintaining effective price levels even in a soft market. In other words, provided the governments themselves abstained from price competition in their own sales, the level of average government take (plus production cost and a minimum company margin) provided an unbreachable floor to crude oil prices whatever the state of the market might be.

Meanwhile, for the majority of the OPEC Membership, who believed that the world economy could well absorb a fully justified rise in the price of a strategic raw material whose value had been artificially held down at an absurdly low level for so many years, there were two outstanding priorities early in 1974: firstly, to defend the new Tehran price level and improve it at least to the extent of maintaining the price in real terms; and secondly, to consolidate the market price by increasing the government take element, and consequently cutting down the company margin to an acceptable figure, as quickly as possible.

The position of Saudi Arabia was more complicated. On the one hand, it felt that the big jump in prices decided upon in Tehran was a threat to world economic stability, and had been made possible only by the artificial supply and price climate created by the Arab oil measures which themselves had been undertaken for a specific political purpose and not for economic reasons. Therefore, it believed a posted price reduction of around $2/barrel would be in order. On the other hand, the Saudis were in fully agreement with the rest of OPEC that the potential margin of profit to the major companies was far too high under the prevailing conditions.

At the same time, the Saudis had a particular individual problem with regard to the latter point. Even before October 1973, Yamani had realized that it would be extremely difficult to maintain the participation framework for very long in the face of the effervescent climate of national aspirations. He had, therefore, started negotiations with Aramco for a 100% government takeover of the producing venture. The ex-owners of Aramco (Exxon, Texaco, Socal and Mobil) would continue to offtake the bulk of the crude oil exported and would provide all necessary technical and managerial services to the new Saudi operating company in return for an agreed fee per barrel of production. Since the fee in question would be roughly the conceptual equivalent of the company margin under the prevailing system, Yamani did not want to get boxed into anything irreversible on the OPEC front before reaching agreement with Aramco.

Also, as OPEC's biggest actual and potential producer and a country enjoying a close relationship with the United States and the West in general, Saudi Arabia bore the brunt of the political pressure from the industrialized consumers in favour of lower oil prices. Particularly active in this field were US Secretary of State Henry Kissinger and Secretary of the Treasury William Simon. However, in the case of Kissinger at least, the Saudis detected a marked ambiguity in the US position on oil prices. Had the Americans really wanted to bring down oil prices, they should have directed the main thrust of their pressure not towards the Saudis, who were already convinced that the Tehran price jump had been too steep, but towards the Shah of Iran who, though a staunch regional ally of the US with pretensions of becoming the military protector of the Gulf, remained a convinced hard-liner on the subject of oil prices. Clearly the key to the whole situation lay in Iran. If the US had succeeded in convincing the Shah of the desirability of a lower oil price, nothing could have prevented a combined effort by Iran and Saudi Arabia to bring this about. In fact, no such US pressure on Iran was forthcoming at this stage. When Kissinger visited Tehran in 1974, the Saudis confidently expected that he would remonstrate with the Shah on the question of oil prices. Not only did the US Secretary of State fail to do anything of the kind, but — so the Iranians informed the Saudis afterwards — he expressed general satisfaction with the prevailing oil price level. Naturally enough, in Saudi eyes, all this cast grave doubts on the seriousness of the US administration's commitment to bring down oil prices.[1]

One obvious reason for the American ambivalence on this subject lay in the fact that the US was still a very substantial oil producer in its own right (second in the world after the USSR in fact) and, despite rising imports, would be less hurt by higher oil prices than other western industrial powers, and indeed stood to benefit from the potential boost to US energy production as a result of higher prices. But a further cause of confusion was that Kissinger was in fact pursuing two contradictory objectives. One, as much political as economic, was to force a collapse of oil prices (among other things, through a combination of political pressure and consumer action on the demand side by way of consumption restraint and development of new energy sources) and thereby break the power of OPEC which was regarded as a challenge to the dominance of the western industrial powers.[2] The other was to set a floor price for oil which would be high enough to encourage investment in new oil and alternative sources of energy. But whereas the price of $7 to $8/barrel which the US was proposing to the International Energy Agency (IEA) — the Paris-based oil consumers' organization composed of most OECD countries (with the notable exception of France), which was set up on Kissinger's initiative in November 1974 — might have been just about adequate to cover (on current 1974 estimates at least) North Sea and Alaskan oil, as well as nuclear power and a good deal of coal, it was not nearly enough to provide any incentive for the development of other energy alternatives such as tar sands or shale oil. For that (again on 1974 reckoning) a price of at least $12/barrel, already more than the existing OPEC price, would have been necessary.[3] Not surprisingly, none of these objectives were attained: oil prices were not rolled back; OPEC was not broken; and the IEA completely failed to agree on a floor price. For their part, Europe and Japan backed away from the confrontation approach against OPEC initially favoured by Kissinger, while the IEA lost whatever teeth may once have been planned for it and settled down into a mere consultation and data-collection agency whose single potential weapon — an oil-sharing plan in the event of a 7% shortfall in supplies — remained unused even in the 1979 emergency.

But from early 1975 onwards — by which time it had become clear beyond question that the new price level had come stay — the strategy of the industrialized consumers oriented itself towards an erosion of the real price of oil through inflation and dollar depreciation. This approach seemed to be working efficiently enough until 1978, but it was a very short-sighted policy. Inevitably, as with all such endeavours, the oil price freeze and erosion in real terms was followed by yet another price explosion in 1979-80.

Meanwhile, on the OPEC front in the summer of 1974, a number of developments took place which were to have a decisive influence on the future determination of oil prices.

In June, in Quito, Ecuador, at the Organization's Fortieth Conference, the tussle over prices and government take between Saudi Arabia and the rest of OPEC resumed, with the former threatening to go its own way on prices and production if the ECB's proposals for substantial increases in postings and government take were implemented. Once again the outcome was a stand-off, with the only concrete result being a 2% rise in the royalty rate from 12.5% to 14.5%, yielding a mere 10 to 11 cents a barrel in additional government take.[4] Saudi Arabia, for its part, dissociated itself from the implementation of this measure "for the time being" pending the conclusion of its new arrangement with Aramco.

A month later, towards the end of July 1974, Saudi Arabia indicated that it was planning a drastic solution to the price problem. Sheikh Yamani told a press conference on July 21 that Petromin would hold a major auction sale of crude oil early in August. The Saudi national company would, he said, accept the best bids in line with whatever price was set by market forces without imposing any minimum. (In earlier government crude auctions in Kuwait, Iran and Abu Dhabi, the auctioned supplies had been withdrawn from sale when the bids received did not measure up to the government's ideas on appropriate minimum prices.)

Yamani did not at the time publicly disclose how much oil the government intended to put up for auction, but reliable reports indicated that the planned sale volume was in the region of 1.5 million b/d — roughly 18% of Aramco's then prevailing production allowable of 8.5 million b/d — to be lifted over the 16-month period September 1974 to December 1975.[5] Since the market was weak at the time, it was confidently expected that bids would be well below the government sale prices (93 to 95% of postings). Recent unsuccessful crude auctions in Iran and Kuwait had yielded top bids of only 89% of postings; and the general level of spot market prices for Arabian Light was in the region of $10.10 to 10.25/barrel, as compared with the prevailing Petromin contract prices of $10.835/barrel (93% of posting). Thus if the resulting auction price did demonstrate a significant weakening in the market price, Saudi Arabia would have been able to present the evidence to OPEC to support its case for a reduction in posted prices. Also, the auction price could have served as the market price basis for sales to the Aramco participants under the projected 100% takeover deal.

Not surprisingly, the prospect of a large-scale auction in Saudi Arabia with no minimum limit on prices sparked off a furore of alarm among the other OPEC Countries, particularly as (much to the embarrassment of the Saudis) the publicity surrounding the affair was intensified by the US Secretary of the Treasury, William Simon, who at various press conferences heralded the projected Saudi auction as a harbinger of lower oil prices.

In the Gulf, urgent consultations were held between Iran, Iraq, Kuwait, the UAE and Qatar on the subject of the impending Saudi auction, and on July 25 the UAE Oil Minister, Dr. Mana Saeed Otaiba, visited Saudi Arabia to express the deep concern of the Gulf producers directly to King Faisal. As a counter to any Saudi move to weaken prices, the other Gulf producers were seriously discussing a co-ordinated plan to reduce their own output. Iran's Finance Minister Hushang Ansary warned publicly that "if Saudi Arabia decides to increase oil production in order to lower oil prices, Iran and other oil producers will reduce their production accordingly."[6]

Another important visitor to Saudi Arabia on the same errand towards the end of July was Algeria's powerful Minister of Industry and Energy, Belaid Abdesselam. Although in terms of volume Algeria was a relatively small producer of oil (1 million b/d as against 8.5 million b/d in Saudi Arabia), it was a big developing country with a leading role in the councils of the Arab region and the Third World in general. Moreover, Minister Abdesselam was a political and intellectual heavyweight, at that time at the height of his power as the architect of his country's all-out industrialization drive based on oil and gas. Also, he and Yamani had formed a good working relationship when the two of them made a joint tour of Europe and the US in November-December 1973 to explain and defend the Arab oil measures. Abdesselam was thus very well placed to bring home to the Saudis the extent of OPEC anxiety about the Kingdom's price and production policy.

134

Finally, the OPEC pressure had the desired effect and the Saudi Government cancelled the auction plan. Out of the various consultations leading to this outcome, a rather shadow unwritten bargain emerged: Saudi Arabia, for its part, would not take any action to undermine the prevailing level of prices, while in return the other OPEC Members would show more understanding for Saudi Arabia's policy of price restraint in the future and agree to keep prices frozen for a while.

Between Saudi Arabia and Algeria the understanding over prices was even more explicit. Abdesselam's trip to Saudi Arabia was quickly followed up by a return visit to Algeria by Prince Sa'ud al-Faisal, son of King Faisal and at that time Deputy Oil Minister (he later became Foreign Minister). The result of these consultations was a public disclosure of the Saudi-Algerian entente which the Saudi newspaper al-Madinah described as the adoption of a common position by the two countries "whereby Saudi Arabia agreed to drop its demand for reducing prices on condition that prices should be frozen at their current levels for a reasonable period of time pending the stabilization of the oil market."[7]

In mid-August, there intervened another OPEC Meeting which, though not in the mainstream of Ministerial Conferences, did nevertheless bring some long-term influence to bear on the price scene. This was an ad hoc meeting of representatives of national oil companies of OPEC Member States held in London to discuss price and market developments. The meeting came out with wide-ranging proposals for regular co-ordination between OPEC National Oil Companies, as well as for regulation of production in line with market demand. These proposals failed to gain the necessary endorsement of the Oil Ministers and so remained a dead letter. But there was one recommendation which, though never formally ratified (Saudi Arabia and the UAE did not attend the meeting or accept its recommendations), did form the basis of a gentlemen's agreement which was eventually recognized and observed by all Member Countries. This was that OPEC Governments and their national oil companies should undertake not to sell crude oil at prices below certain minimum levels, namely, 93% of postings in respect of Gulf crudes, with crudes in other locations being priced according to the following formula: marker crude (Arabian Light) price at 93% of posting with appropriate adjustment for freight (using AFRA Long-Range 2 for Gulf crudes and Long-Range 1 for Mediterranean crudes) and quality factors (gravity and sulphur).[8]

In view of the prior consultations that had taken place, a decision to continue with the freeze on posted prices was reached without too much difficulty at the OPEC Ministerial Conference in mid-September 1974. At the same time, the Conference decided on a further increase in royalty and income tax rates with a view to narrowing the gap between government sale prices and the average cost of crude to major companies. The royalty rate was raised from 14.5% to 16.67% and the tax rate from 55% to 65.75%, effective October 1. The result was an increase of 33 cents, or 3.5%, in average government take (on a 40% companies' equity and 60% government participation basis) from $9.40/barrel to $9.73/barrel, which was justified in the Conference communique as compensation for inflation in the industrialized countries. Once again, Saudi Arabia dissociated itself from the application of this tax/royalty boost on the grounds that it was "awaiting the outcome of its new arrangements with the foreign owners of Aramco." It also noted that it believed that "the increase in the average government take is justified only on the basis of excess profits realized by the international oil companies," and that "therefore the increase in the rate of tax and royalty should be coupled with a reduction in the posted price." However, privately the Saudis made it clear that they would eventually apply the new tax and royalty rates or their equivalent.

Another idea mooted at the September Conference is worthy of mention, though it never reached the implementation stage. At the time there was a strong current of OPEC opinion, of course excluding Saudi Arabia, which favoured a speedy adoption of a price indexation formula to compensate for inflation. As discussed by a working group of OPEC experts meeting in Vienna in October 1974, the plan envisaged that starting January 1, 1975, a base price reflecting average government take on the 60-40 mix would be set for a period of one year ahead subject to quarterly adjustments for inflation in accordance with a suitable index. (The 3.5% increase in government take for the fourth quarter of 1974 was equivalent to an annual rate of 14% – more or less in line with the average OECD inflation rate at the time). However, the plan sunk without trace in the aftermath of the subsequent Ministerial decisions on prices and government take.

It was recognized, of course, that the September increase in tax and royalty rates was still only a step in the direction of a comprehensive solution to the problem of the new market price structure incorporating an appropriate margin for the equity-holding companies. Even at the new level of government take, the difference between the government sale price and the average cost of crude to the companies was still in the region of $1/barrel, while the margin on equity crude stood at around $2.50/barrel – far too high by OPEC reckoning. Pressure for action on this front was particularly strong from countries like Iraq, Algeria and Libya whose sales of nationalized crude at government prices were liable, in a softening market, to be undercut by the majors with their ample margins on lower crude costs.

Various proposals were put forward at the September Conference for a definitive solution to this imbalance. The ECB wanted simply to raise the average cost of crude to the companies by 14% to $10.68/barrel and the tax-paid cost on equity crude to $10.46/barrel (as against $9.85/barrel and $8.37/barrel respectively under the actual September 1974 decisions) — which on the basis of a government sales price of $10.84/barrel would have yielded company margins on equity crude and average crude cost of 38 cents and 16 cents respectively. Iran advocated the scrapping of the posted price system altogether and the adoption of a single government market price, at $10.35/barrel for the marker crude, with the interest-holding companies being accorded a specified discount which would be equated to a margin of 50 cents a barrel on 40% of the output, that is to say the equity share under the Gulf 60-40 participation arrangements.

For its part, Saudi Arabia proposed a scheme which, though having much the same practical effect as the Iranian idea, would have retained the tax/royalty and posted price mechanism in being for the purpose of calculating the companies' equity margin. The Saudi proposal envisaged that the targeted increase in government take, designed to mop up excess company profits, should be combined with a modest reduction in the posted price, and therefore in the government market price fixed at 93% of the posting, in order to give some relief to the consuming countries. Although the Saudi scheme met with a sympathetic hearing in some OPEC quarters, it was greeted with deep suspicion by others; and its non-adoption by the Conference was the cause of some bitterness in the Saudi camp. After the meeting a prominent Saudi source commented sourly: "Saudi Arabia has done its best in recent months to co-operate to the full with its OPEC partners, notably by putting off the auction sale it originally intended to hold in August and by not increasing production. However, OPEC has not reciprocated by taking Saudi Arabia's views into consideration in its decisions. Saudi Arabia may therefore be obliged to reconsider its attitude towards OPEC."[9]

However, the Saudi plan was nonetheless implemented before very long in a rather dramatic fashion, when in November 1974 the Kingdom took the initiative to convene in Abu Dhabi a meeting not of the full OPEC Conference but of the Committee of Oil Ministers of the Six Gulf Member States of OPEC — Saudi Arabia, Iran, Iraq, Kuwait, the

UAE and Qatar. What, in fact, had galvanized Saudi Arabia into action on this front was not anything to do with OPEC as such, but rather the stalemate which had developed in the Saudi-Aramco negotiations for a 100% government takeover. And it was in expectation of this new arrangement, it will be recalled, that the Saudi Government had kept all tax and royalty changes in a state of suspension throughout 1974.

The crux of the matter was that the four foreign partners in Aramco had been fighting the proposed 100% government takeover tooth and nail, both in principle and in detail, to a point where it seemed to the Saudis that further negotiations in this spirit would be pointless. As far as the terms were concerned, the going was tough enough: Aramco was demanding a fee for services under the new arrangement, which was to take the place of the equity margin under the prevailing system, of some 60 cents/barrel, whereas the most the Saudis could contemplate at that time was 35 cents/barrel (Saudi ideas hardened as time went on and the eventual settlement was for about half that amount). But the matter was not just a question of hard bargaining over terms. To combat the whole idea of the Saudi takeover the companies brought their political influence into play, enlisting the aid of the US State Department – everyone concerned from Kissinger downwards – as well as local personalities in Saudi Arabia, in an effort to undermine Yamani's position. Moreover, the Saudi oilmen also suspected that the Aramco companies were behind a media compaign, the thrust of whose message was that, despite the public espousal of price moderation, the Saudis were using the 100% takeover as a covert means of raising prices.

The companies' campaign came to nothing, principally because King Faisal remained steadfastly behind the takover policy and so the whole move was very much a matter of state policy, not just the inspiration of an individual. However, Yamani felt that, by employing political pressure tactics, the companies had gone beyond the normal framework of commercial bargaining; and by October 1974 he had come to the conclusion that the only way out of the impasse was to bring the Aramco majors to their senses by means of a sharp lesson which would put them face to face with the imminent threat of a massive loss of profit and world position. Finally awake to the danger, the companies dispatched a delegation to Saudi Arabia in a last-minute effort to avert the Abu Dhabi decision. But Yamani replied that it was too late, since he was now irrevocably committed to the Abu Dhabi meeting and what it entailed.

In the event, what the Abu Dhabi Meeting entailed was a sharp cut in the companies' margin of profit – to 54 cents a barrel (from $2.50)

138

on equity crude and to 22 cents a barrel (from $1) on the average cost of crude calculated on the basis of a 60-40 participation-equity mix. This was brought about by an increase in the rates of royalty and income tax to 20% and 85% respectively with effect from November 1, 1974, as compared with the 16.67% and 65.75% rates adopted at the Vienna OPEC Conference in September. At the same time, the posted price for the marker (Arabian Light) crude was reduced by 40 cents a barrel from $11.651 to $11.251 — which in turn, on the principle of 93% of posting, made for a parallel decrease in the government sale price from $10.835 to $10.463. The net effect of the overall package was to make crude slightly cheaper, i.e. by about 37 cents a barrel, for those independent and national companies in the consuming countries which were buying at the government sale price, and more expensive for the international majors whose average cost of crude on the 60-40 mix rose by 40 cents a barrel from $9.85 to $10.25. At the same time average government take also rose by 40 cents, or roughly 4%, from $9.728 to $10.125 per barrel.[10]

For Saudi Arabia, the Abu Dhabi package accomplished a threefold objective: firstly to give Aramco a severe jolt designed to set it on the path of a more realistic negotiating stance on the Saudi takeover, while at the same time establishing an interim fiscal regime pending the completion of the new arrangement (in addition to the new November 1 rates, the OPEC tax and royalty increase of July 1 and October 1, 1974 were applied to Aramco retroactively); secondly to mend Saudi Arabia's fences with OPEC regarding the proposed new price and tax structure; and thirdly to make some goodwill gesture to the consumers in the form of a small reduction in posted prices and government market prices.

But the Abu Dhabi decision was not the only card up Yamani's sleeve in his battle of wills with Aramco. If the Aramco majors had persisted with their hard line over the government takeover scheme, the Saudis planned to pile on the pressure still further with a double blow: firstly to fix the buy-back price to Aramco at 94.8% of postings rather than the 93% of postings which had become the general level elsewhere in the Gulf in the fourth quarter; and secondly to sell 40% of Saudi Arabia's production on the world market directly to independent and national companies (i.e. excluding the international majors) at a price even lower than 93% of postings. The result would have been a catastrophe for the big four US majors involved in Aramco — Exxon, Texaco, Socal and Mobil — both in terms of profitability vis-à-vis their competitors and of loss of crude oil volume at their disposal.

Faced with such a grim prospect, the Aramco companies threw in the towel and moved quickly to restore good relations with the government. They submitted a written offer to the government accepting the principle of the 100% takeover and agreeing to negotiate the deal within a framework which satisfied Saudi Arabia's requirements. In return, the government cancelled its plan for raising the buy-back price to Aramco to 94.8% of postings (it was set at 93%) and selling 40% of production at a lower price to customers outside the Aramco circle.

Meanwhile, at the Abu Dhabi Meeting, not all the Gulf producers had emerged as immediate converts to the Saudi scheme. Only three countries — Saudi Arabia, the UAE and Qatar — opted for prompt adoption of the new prices and tax/royalty rates as from November 1. Kuwait declared itself in favour of the Saudi plan in principle, but preferred not to take any implementation step before the proposal had been discussed and endorsed by the whole of OPEC at the forthcoming full Conference in December. Iran, whose representation at the Meeting had been only at low level, reserved its position in the belief that the question of prices should be dealt with at the December Conference. Finally, Iraq declared itself opposed to the Saudi proposal on the grounds that: any decision on prices should be taken by the full OPEC Conference; though the increase in tax and royalty rates would be a positive step, Iraq was against any reduction in the posted price which could only tend to depress the whole structure; the Saudi scheme did nothing to strengthen the position of the OPEC National Oil Companies which should be one of the main aims of any new pricing structure.

Despite these reservations, the price mechanism and financial effects of the Abu Dhabi decision were endorsed by the full OPEC Conference in Vienna in December. The figure actually specified in the Conference communique was the new average government take figure of $10.12/barrel for the marker crude, rather than the posted price which was now finally phased out as the OPEC operative price, being retained only for tax reference purposes where applicable. From 1975 onwards the official government sale price, which had evolved from the 93% of posting principle, became the operative price for OPEC.

Another part of the December 1974 OPEC agreement was a decision to freeze the average government take figure for nine months until the end of September 1975, thereby effectively freezing all levels of price and government take. The most significant consequence of this decision, both immediately and in the years to come, was the abandonment of the plan to index oil prices against inflation.

For OPEC as a whole the Abu Dhabi/Vienna package did at least provide a definitive solution to the problem of the company margin and the OPEC-determined market price, as well as laying a pragmatic basis for a workable, though by no means perfect model for a pricing structure. And since the decision was a unanimous one inspired by the leading price moderate, Saudi Arabia, this meant that the 1973-74 price increase was now fully legitimized and safeguarded from possible attack from any quarter — though not of course from erosion in real terms by inflation and dollar depreciation, which was to be the nub of the oil price argument over the next four years.

To put the matter another way: given the enormous potential gap at the beginning of 1974 between the posted price and its related government sale price at the top end and the average cost of crude to the major companies at the bottom end, the effective market price could theoretically have settled anywhere between these two poles. In the event, actions by the OPEC Members through the year, both individual and collective, ensured that the point of effective price stabilization was closer to the top end of the scale.

The evolution of the key price indicators for the Arabian Light marker crude during the relevant period of 1973-74 is shown in the table on page 142. An estimation of the companies' notional profit margins on equity crude and the average cost of crude is given in the table on page 143; but it should be noted that these are theoretical estimates for illustrative purposes, since the prices and costs from which the margins were derived do not necessarily correspond to the actual prices charged or costs incurred by individual major companies.

But the system, as devised in Abu Dhabi and Vienna, did have its share of anomalies, quirks and differences of interpretation, particularly in relation to the company margin. One interpretation, implemented by Iran and Kuwait, was that the company margin should be held at a flat 22 cents a barrel below the government sale price regardless of the quantity of participation buy-back crude lifted by the companies. Saudi Arabia and the UAE, on the other hand, allowed the company margin to vary according to the amount of participation crude lifted, with 22 cents as the theoretical minimum in the event of full buy-back of the government's 60% share. Thus the less the quantity of participation crude lifted the higher the company's unit margin of profit, subject to a maximum of 54 cents a barrel if offtake was limited to equity crude.

Actually, December 1974 marked the last occasion for collective OPEC involvement in the company margin issue. From then it became a matter for individual governments. In some OPEC Countries where 100% nationalization is not counterbalanced by the provision of any production

OPEC Marker Crude (Arabian Light) Calculations 1973-74
($/Barrel)

	1973		1974				% Increase
	Oct. 1	Oct. 16	Jan. 1	July 1	Oct. 1	Nov. 1	Nov. 1, '74/Oct. 1, '73
Posted Price	3.011	5.119	11.651	11.651	11.651	11.251	274
Govt. Take on Equity Crude	1.759	3.037	6.997	7.102	8.247	9.799	457
Tax-Paid Cost on Equity Crude	1.879	3.157	7.117	7.222	8.367	9.919	427
Govt. Sale/Buy Back Price	2.800	4.761	10.952	11.051	10.835	10.463	274
Average Govt. Take	1.989	3.438	9.298	9.400	9.728	10.125	409
Average Cost to Companies	2.109	3.558	9.418	9.520	9.848	10.245	386

Assumptions:

— Government Participation: 25% in 1973 and 60% in 1974; and assuming full buy-back government share by concessionaire companies.

— Government Take: 12.5% royalty, 55% tax up to June 30, 1974; 14.5% royalty, 55% tax effective July 1, 1974; 16.67% royalty, 65.75% tax effective Oct. 1, 1974; 20% royalty, 85% tax effective Nov. 1, 1974.

— Buy-back Price: 93% of posting in 1973; 94% of posting effective Jan. 1, 1974; 94.846% posting effective July 1, 1974; 93% of posting effective Oct. 1, 1974.

— Production Cost: 12 cents/barrel.

Estimated Evolution of Company Crude Margin 1972-74
($/Barrel)

	Mid-1972	1973 Oct. 1	1973 Oct. 16(A)	Oct. 16(B)	Jan. 1	1974 July 1	1974 Oct. 1	Nov. 1
Companies' Margin on Equity Crude Cost	0.35	0.92	0.49	1.60	3.84	3.82	2.47	0.54
Companies' Margin on Average Crude Cost	0.35	0.69	0.09	1.20	1.53	1.53	0.99	0.22

Notes:
— Margin is calculated on the difference between equity crude/average crude cost on the one hand, and on the other estimated realized market price in mid-1972; government sale price (93% of posting) on Oct. 1, 1973; deemed OPEC market price of $3.65/barrel for Oct. 16(A), 1973; government sale price (93% of posting) for Oct. 16(B), 1973; government sale price (94% of posting effective Jan. 1, 94.846% effective July 1 and 93% effective Oct. 1) in 1974.
— Assumes full buy-back of government participation share of crude by equity-holding companies, which was not generally the case in fact.

143

services by the companies (i.e. Iraq, Algeria, Venezuela, Kuwait, Iran), the company margin has been phased out entirely. In Saudi Arabia and Qatar it has been replaced by a fixed service fee per barrel; while in those countries where equity involvement by the companies persists (the UAE, Libya and Nigeria notably) the margin is still calculated on a tax/royalty basis.

Another consequence of the OPEC price takeover of 1973-74 was the emergence of OPEC areas outside the Gulf as semi-autonomous price regions, relating to the marker crude according to their own estimation of market conditions. In OPEC Conferences the focus has always been on the determination of the price for the marker Arabian Light crude, this being the linchpin for the whole system. The prices of other Gulf crudes have tended, at least until the extraordinary circumstances of 1979-80, to be grouped around the marker crude in a fairly tight pattern of differentials. However, despite some generally unavailing OPEC attempts to arrive at a worldwide structure for differentials between the prices of the various OPEC crudes, Member Countries outside the Gulf usually set their own prices periodically (mostly quarterly) according to what they reckon the market will bear, above or below the marker crude as the case may be, taking into account the quality and location of each crude. Between the main African exporters — Algeria, Libya and Nigeria — there is a substantial degree of price co-ordination, whereas Venezuela and Indonesia — with their widely differing circumstances, one in South America and the other in South East Asia — tend to go their own separate ways.

The Problem of Differentials

It is one thing to set a price for a yardstick or marker crude oil to serve as the anchor for the whole price structure. But it is quite another matter to devise a system to cover the pricing of all the 130-odd different types of crude oil produced in the OPEC area. The determination of the values of the various OPEC crudes in relation to the marker crude — relative values or differentials as they are generally called — has posed a perennial problem for OPEC which is unlikely ever to find a definitive solution.

To state the issue in its simplest possible terms, the various types of crude oil are priced differentially above or below the marker crude in accordance with the quality characteristics of each and its geographical location in relation to the principal markets. The combination of quality and freight premiums, or penalties as the case may be, comprises the differential vis-à-vis the marker crude. The more valuable "light" crudes are those with a greater refinery yield of the higher-priced light products such as gasoline, kerosine and gas oil, while the "heavy" crudes which yield a higher proportion of lower-priced fuel oil are correspondingly penalized in price terms. Though the relationship to ultimate product yield is by no means uniform, the "lightness" or "heaviness" of a crude oil is expressed in terms of gravity, measured in degrees according to a scale devised by the American Petroleum Institute (API). In general, OPEC crudes range from 44° API Algerian Saharan Blend at the light end of the scale to 10° API Venezuelan Boscan at the heavy end, with the marker Arabian Light rated at 34° API. Other important quality plus points are low sulphur content (usually but not exclusively associated with the lighter crudes) and low metal content.

Before the 1979 price explosion – i.e. in 1975-78 – the premium enjoyed by the most expensive crude (Saharan Blend) over the marker level was in the region of $1.40 to $1.50/barrel, while the cheapest (Venezuelan Boscan) bore a penalty of about $3/barrel. However, owing to the market turbulence, the range of differentials widened very considerably in 1979-80. The premium for light African crudes hit $8 to $9/barrel at times and in mid-1980 was set by OPEC at $5/barrel; but it is generally considered that the pattern of differentials will return to a more normal level when the market settles down again after the 1979-80 shakeup.

While the pricing system was still under the control of the major companies, the problem of differentials, though by no means uncommon as a bone of contention between governments and companies, never assumed too acute a form. Each major company owned and lifted a wide range of crudes from the areas in which it had producing interests, so that any minor price anomalies there may have been between the crudes tended to get ironed out without too much difficulty in the overall package.

But, with some exceptions, the production of individual OPEC Countries tend to be concentrated on a fairly narrow range of crudes, with the result that, when OPEC took over control of production and marketing and the major companies developed into buyers rather than owners of crude, fine tuning of differentials became much more important if each OPEC Member was to maintain its proper competitive position in the market. In other words, the differential fixed by the seller for a specific crude should conform fairly closely to its relative value to the refiners vis-à-vis other crudes in terms of product yield.

Such fine tuning is, of course, essential only when the market is soft.

In a tight market — like that of 1973-74 or 1979-80 — anything goes; and the normal differential patterns tend to become disturbed and inflated by what is, in essence, a scarcity premium on all crudes. But it is a different matter when the market weakens. The country whose crude is overpriced in relative terms will be the first to feel the pressure of disgruntled customers and loss of export volume.

A classic example of this process took place in 1975 when the producers of light crudes (notably Abu Dhabi and the African exporters) were caught short by the demand slow-down occasioned by the post-1973 recession. At the end of 1973, at the height of the supply crisis and seemingly in response to the demand pattern at the time, OPEC raised the differential per degree of API gravity above 34° API to 6 cents a barrel, as compared with the previous 1.5 cents, and set a low-sulphur premium of roughly 7 cents per 0.1% of sulphur content below the marker crude level of 1.7%. This formula proved to be too high for the post-crisis market and the producers concerned were faced with quite a severe loss of export volume until the price imbalance was rectified by reducing the gravity differential to 3 cents per API degree and the sulphur premium to 3 cents for each 0.1% of sulphur content below 1.7%.

The OPEC decision to choose 34° API Saudi Arabian Light as the marker crude was a logical one. It was, and still is, by far the largest-volume single crude moving in the world oil trade; and its characteristics as a middle-of-the-road, medium-sulphur crude between the light and heavy extremes also made it eminently suitable for the marker role. However, difficulties arose when, in 1977 and 1979-80, Saudi Arabia's price policy diverged from that of the rest of OPEC to the extent of a split in actual pricing. At such times, while Saudi Arabia priced its actual Arabian Light crude at a lower level, the other OPEC Countries aligned their prices on a higher level for the marker crude which was purely notional and did not correspond to the price of any actual crude (in the multi-tier price confusion of 1979-80, it would be more appropriate to speak of a plurality of notional marker levels). In practice, the use of a purely notional marker crude with the hypothetical characteristics of Arabian Light proved to be a workable, if not ideal expedient, at least in the short term and in a fairly tight market. But in the longer term, the maintenance of such a system would tend to complicate the problem of differentials to an intolerable degree.

Of course, it is by no means mandatory that the marker crude should permanently be identified with Arabian Light. In theory (and this has been suggested within OPEC) it would be feasible, for example, to take the highest-priced crude in the Gulf or the OPEC area in general and work backwards for the pricing of other crudes, or alternatively to take the lowest-priced crude and work upwards.

Any system for determining differentials also has to be flexible enough to cope with short-term and long-term shifts in the pattern of demand for various types of crude. Around 1977-78 it became clear that whereas demand for lighter products was increasing as a proportion of the total requirement, the average gravity of anticipated future crude supply was getting heavier — a trend which was underscored when Saudi Arabia started placing limitations on the production of its lighter oils in order to brings its light-heavy output ratio more into line with the pattern of its reserves. This meant that refiners, particularly in Europe and Japan, would be obliged to invest in more sophisticated processing equipment to increase the yield of light products from heavier crudes.

Producers of heavy crudes were thus faced with the problem of whether to give some price incentive to refiners, in the form of a wider differential, to encourage them to make the necessary investment in equipment to handle the heavier crude stream. In 1978, it was generally agreed between the heavy crude producers in the Gulf — notably Saudi Arabia and Kuwait — that differentials should gradually be widened for this purpose. However, in the changed market climate of 1980, the Kuwait Oil Minister, Sheikh Ali Khalifa Al-Sabah, made it clear that he was no longer prepared to countenance any differential penalty on Kuwait crude below the Arabian Light marker of anything more than the traditional 50 cents a barrel, and that given the limited future supply of Kuwait crude price incentives to refiners would be out of the question.[11]

To cope with the complexity of the differentials problem OPEC has developed a number of useful computerized tools on the technical level, with calculations including the "replacement value method" which works out the values of the crudes concerned relative to Arabian Light based on spot product values in the Rotterdam, Caribbean and Singapore markets, and the crude-by-crude netback method which determines the differentials on the basis of f.o.b. crude netbacks from refined product values in European markets. The trouble is that even if the results are clear and consistent on the technical level (which is by no means always the case), the Oil Ministers are quite liable to dispute the verdict of the computer when it comes to their own crudes.

1975-78: THE EROSION OF REAL PRICES

The majority of OPEC Countries, whatever their public posture may have been, were prepared for at least some degree of inflationary erosion of the real price level decided upon in Tehran at the end of 1973. The question was: how far, how fast, and where to draw the line? After the 1974 shakedown of government take, the whole of OPEC had agreed to a price freeze until the end of September 1975. This was as far as most of OPEC was prepared to go as regards the reduction of purchasing power, but Saudi Arabia wanted to see it stretched still further.

The Saudis, as we have seen, were extremely worried about the possible effects of the oil price increase on the economic and, indeed, political stability of the West, upon which in the final analysis their own prospects for harmonious development also depended. King Faisal, for example, is known to have been profoundly concerned that the 1974-75 recession might so seriously destabilize the western economy as to pave the way for a Communist takeover in certain European countries like Italy and France, and as regards the Third World the Saudi prognosis was even more gloomy. Saudi Arabia, therefore, was ready to see the attenuation of the 1974 price go quite a long way, and this policy maintained its continuity after the tragic assassination of King Faisal in March 1975.

The Saudis were also wont to emphasize the difficulty and inadvisability of trying to raise oil prices while the market remained potentially in surplus: when demand picked up again, so would prices – and OPEC (and Saudi Arabia) would be back in the driver's seat, both politically and economically. The Saudis, it should be noted, were particularly sensitive to the lessening of the political impact of their oil power as a result of the 1974-75 slump in demand, and were anxious to see this restored.

It would be wrong to try and group all the other OPEC Members together in one camp on the pricing issue. "Other OPEC" covered a wide spectrum of views and shifting alliances during this period of real price erosion in a soft market situation. The UAE, for example, usually sided with Saudi Arabia when the chips where down. By and large it would be fair to say that the hard line was generally represented by Iran, Iraq, Libya, Nigeria and sometimes Algeria (though the latter did show some understanding for the Saudi position up until mid-1976), whereas such countries as Kuwait, Venezuela and Indonesia tended towards a more middle-of-the-road position. But all of them regarded the accelerating diminution of the purchasing power of their oil barrel through inflation and dollar depreciation with growing dismay and resentment. Unlike Saudi Arabia with its enormous oil potential and financial ease, many of them were populous countries with limited oil reserves, whose production had already peaked but whose development prospects were dependent on an immediate return from that dwindling natural resource. Such countries — one could count among them Algeria, Indonesia, Nigeria, Iran, Venezuela and Ecuador — could ill afford the luxury of extended patience and the long-term view.

Although these OPEC Countries also appreciated the importance of a healthy world economy, they were much more sanguine than the Saudis about the ability of the industrialized West to absorb the shock of the 1973-74 oil price increase. Furthermore, they saw OPEC as a sort of advance guard of the Third World which, with the bargaining power of oil, could change the whole world economic order in favour of the developing countries, whose problems with the higher oil prices could in the meantime be alleviated by a generous programme of OPEC aid, both bilateral and collective.

As far as the difficulty of raising prices in a surplus-ridden market was concerned, the OPEC mainstream view was that this could be accomplished provided the oil exporters strictly adhered to their no-price-competition compact with the backing, if necessary, of a formal or informal understanding on the regulation of production in line with market demand. In the event, no such programming of production proved possible since Saudi Arabia always adamantly refused to discuss production levels in OPEC Conferences. Nevertheless, some price increases were put through during the 1974-78 period; and, on the whole, serious competition between the OPEC Members on prices and/or export volumes was avoided.

In discussing the differences of outlook which arose between Saudi Arabia and some of the other leading OPEC Countries during this period, it should be emphasized that the argument, however bitter it became at times, was nevertheless kept within the OPEC family. Saudi Arabia never lent itself to western efforts to "break OPEC", and in case of emergency (such as the 1975 drop in demand when Saudi Arabia bore the brunt of the decline in OPEC output), it could be relied upon to close ranks with its OPEC partners. For example, in early 1977, at the height of the row over the two-tier price split — the most serious internal crisis that OPEC

149

had ever known – Sheikh Yamani stressed Saudi Arabia's fundamental commitment to OPEC in the following terms:[1]

"We do not worry about these differences. They are only natural ...... The secret of OPEC's strength is that no matter how much we differ in our meetings, we all realize the importance and the imperative need for that Organization. We would not operate without it, or deal with the outside world except through it. Therefore, we have drawn a line beyond which our differences should not go. This defines the extent of our co-operation and our differences. Beyond these lines, no OPEC Member should trespass."

The Algerian Proposal: A Lost Opportunity

After the reorganization of the price structure in 1974, OPEC's next move was to convene, in Algeria at the beginning of March 1975, a Summit Conference of Sovereigns and Heads of State of Member Countries to tackle the broad issues of OPEC policy, including international relations with the industrialized nations on the one hand and the non-oil exporting countries of the Third World on the other. In the run-up to the Summit – at a joint Conference of OPEC Ministers of Oil, Foreign Affairs and Finance in Algiers in January 1975 – Algeria unveiled an overall plan for the regulation of international economic relations, which would have involved OPEC guarantees to the industrialized world as regards the supply and pricing of oil and recycling of petrodollars, in return for a wide-ranging commitment by the governments of the industrialized nations to intensified development of the Third World, including opening up of their markets to the products of the Third World industries, transfer of technology, pricing schemes for raw materials other than oil and reform of the international monetary and economic system. This, it was stressed, was a package deal which would have to be accepted in toto by the industrialized world, not just in part.[2]

The part of the overall proposal dealing with oil prices envisaged a six-year "transitional" period to give the industrialized countries time to redress their balances of trade and phase in new sources of energy. The first three years of this period would have allowed for some fall in the value of oil in real terms, to be followed by three years of full indexation for inflation, as follows:

- For the year 1975 crude oil prices would be frozen at their January 1, 1975, level.
- For 1976 and 1977, oil prices would be adjusted to reflect a partial

compensation for inflation in accordance with an agreed index of goods and services imported by OPEC, with the percentage for 1977 being higher than in 1976. (In his presentation to the Conference, Algerian Industry and Energy Minister Belaid Abdesselam suggested that the percentage for these years might be in the region of 80 to 90%).

— For the last three years of the transitional period, 1978, 1979 and 1980, the price adjustment would reflect full compensation for inflation in line with the agreed index.

— After the transitional period, oil prices would again be permitted to rise in real terms in the light of the prospects for alternative sources of energy and the financial needs of the OPEC Countries.

Although quite a few of the ideas contained in the overall plan put forward in the Algerian working paper were taken up later at the OPEC Summit and the subsequent 1975-77 North-South Dialogue in Paris, the price proposal was not among them. There was no concrete follow-up either on the part of the OPEC Governments or of the consumers – the former were in no shape to agree on a specific formula for oil pricing, while the latter were dead set against the principle of indexation in any form in case it should spread to commodities other than oil – and the idea simply sunk without trace.

Possibly this was inevitable since – apart from the 1971-73 application of the Tehran agreement, which was in any case before OPEC took over sole responsibility for prices – forward-planned formula pricing has not so far stood much of a chance of practical application by OPEC; the surrounding political and economic climate has been too volatile for that. One can nevertheless speculate about what might have happened had the Algerian price proposal been implemented. The price of oil might have been not so very far from where it is now in 1980, but at least it would have been phased in gradually and the world – producers and consumers alike – would have been spared the relentless erosion of 1974-78 followed by the second great leap forward of 1979-80.

The Market Slackens

While OPEC as a whole was busy in 1974-75 with problems related to the new price structure and the broad policy issues dealt with at the Summit Conference, market demand for OPEC crude was slackening off to a very considerable degree. As compared with average annual growth

151

rates of 10 to 11% in the late 1960s and early 1970s, OPEC crude production actually fell by 0.8% in 1974 (to 30.73 million b/d from 30.99 million b/d in 1973) and by 11.6% in 1975 (to 27.16 million b/d). From this low point output recovered with a 13.2% rise to 30.74 million b/d in 1976 and an increase of 1.8% to 31.29 million b/d in 1977, before falling back by 4.7% to 29.81 million b/d in 1978.

The causes of this fairly dramatic levelling off of demand for OPEC between 1974 and 1978 were threefold: the sharp world economic recession of 1974-75; a degree of energy conservation attributable to the 1973-74 price rise; and the phasing in of new energy production, particularly non-OPEC oil from the North Sea and Alaska.

The oil price rise did, of course, contribute to the severity of the recession, but it was not the cause of that recession. In fact the boom peaked in the first half of 1973, and the slowdown was already well underway by the second half of that year — before the big jump in oil prices had taken effect. In the first half of 1973, growth in the seven major OECD countries had been at an annual rate of 8.6%, and this throttled back to 2.3% in the second half of the year in response to contractionary policies introduced in a number of countries to combat the sharp acceleration in inflation. For the OECD area as a whole growth of real GNP/GDP — after averaging a little over 5% through most of the 1960s, and declining to 3.2% in 1970 and 3.6% in 1971 — accelerated to 5.5% in 1972 and 6.3% in 1973 before crashing to 0.6% in 1974 and minus 0.5% (minus 1.3% in the US and minus 1.4% in the EEC) in 1975. Recovery, though accompanied by continued high inflation and unemployment, got underway in 1976 with OECD real growth of 5.3%, followed by 3.8% in 1977, 3.9% in 1978, 3.4% in 1979 and 1.25% in 1980.[3]

Nor, incidentally, can it be claimed (as anti-OPEC propagandists have been wont to do) that the oil price increase was largely responsible for the 1973-75 spurt in inflation. Again, the inflationary trend preceded, and to a certain extent prompted, the oil price rise; and, on OECD's own figures, the contribution of higher energy prices to inflation during this period did not, at its peak, exceed more than two percentage points of the 1974 14% increase in consumer prices in the major industrial countries (the contribution of higher food prices was substantially greater).

Although both the supply and demand for energy (and particularly oil) are relatively inelastic to price changes in the short run — which also means that it takes only a small increase in demand or reduction in supply to produce a big rise in prices — some elasticity does nevertheless exist and the cumulative effect can be quite significant in the longer term. The OECD estimates, on the basis of research since 1960, that the price elasticity of demand for final energy might be around minus 0.15 in the first year, about minus 0.3 after two years, eventually rising to around minus 0.5 after six years. Substantial energy saving is evidenced by the fact that energy consumption has grown proportionately much less than OECD-area GNP in the period since 1973. From 1960 to the early 1970s, energy use in the OECD area grew at about the same rate as real OECD GNP. Since 1973, however, OECD's primary energy requirements have increased by about 7% (1973-79), while real OECD GNP has grown by about 17% over the same period, implying a reduction of energy use per unit of GNP of about 9%.[4] The major reason for this saving, according to OECD, almost certainly lies in the reaction of energy users to increased prices.*

Demand for OPEC oil was also mitigated by the arrival on the market of new oil from the North Sea and Alaska's North Slope in substantial quantities from 1976 onwards. From virtually zero in 1974, North Sea output climbed to 500,000 b/d in 1976, 1 million b/d in 1977, 1.5 million b/d in 1978 and 2 million b/d in 1979; while production from Alaska (which was able to do little more than offset declining output in the lower 48 states of the US) built up from 170,000 b/d in 1976 to 460,000 b/d in 1977 and 1.3 million b/d in 1978-79. Production in Mexico also rose steadily from 640,000 b/d in 1974 to 1.62 million b/d in 1979.

As a long-term phenomenon, the slackening of demand for OPEC oil could be nothing but welcome to the Member Governments, whose general philosophy was becoming more and more oriented towards maximum conservation of resources. The problem was that action on the consumers' side had not gone far enough. Apart from some well-intentioned but not really extensive moves towards a less wasteful use

---

* *It should be noted that the final price of oil products — particularly gasoline and diesel oil — have risen far less than the crude price, especially in real terms, mainly owing to the fact that the excise tax component on these products has not been adjusted proportionately. Also rises in the prices of other forms of energy after 1973 lagged behind those of oil. OECD's Economic Outlook for July 1980 estimates that over the period 1973-79 the rise in the real price of energy to final users has been roughly 40%, and it may increase by a further 15% in 1980. However, in most major industrial countries real energy prices to final users were by 1978 still far below the levels prevailing in 1960.*

of energy, relief of the demand pressure on OPEC oil had come from essentially transitory phenomena: low economic growth and the entry of new non-OPEC oil supplies into the market. As soon as sustained economic growth resumed and the new oil sources plateaued, the pressure would resume on OPEC to supply more than it would rationally wish.

Meanwhile, lip-service apart, very little had been accomplished in the consuming countries to increase the supply of energy other than oil. In the US, promised investment programmes in alternatives such as tar sands, shale oil and coal gasification failed to materialize, while coal and nuclear development plans persistently fell foul of environmental protest.* Elsewhere also (except perhaps in France and the Soviet bloc) activism by environmentalist lobbies succeeded in halting or slowing down the expansion of nuclear power. Between 1973 and 1978 the percentage shares of the various fuels in the overall energy supply of the OECD area altered hardly at all, except for a minor (in volume terms) boost in nuclear power, as can be seen in the following table:[4]

OECD Energy Supplies: 1974 and 1978
(Million Tons Oil Equivalent)

	1973		1978	
	Supply	% Share	Supply	% Share
Coal	687	19.5	712	19.1
Oil	1,865	52.9	1,945	52.0
Gas	712	20.2	703	18.8
Nuclear	45	1.3	132	3.5
Hydro	214	6.1	248	6.6
Total	**3,523**	**100.0**	**3,740**	**100.0**

So it is clear that, despite all the rhetoric and bluster on the subject of energy emanating from the major industrial powers, the 1973-74 price shock did nothing to change the overwhelming dependence

* *Coal production in the US has, however, been on the upturn since 1977, growing by almost 500,000 b/d of oil equivalent annually from 1977 to 1979, with the prospect of double that in 1980. Coal production in Western Europe, meanwhile, has remained stagnant.*

154

of the West on oil in general and OPEC oil in particular.* Lead times for energy projects are, of course, notoriously long — 10 years or more — and one would not have expected any programme started after 1973 to have made any contribution by 1978. But the point is that — apart from the new oil from the North Sea, Alaska and Mexico, and perhaps the French nuclear programme — no major new energy effort was either started or finished during the 1974-78 period.

From the perspective of 1978, therefore, it looked to OPEC experts as if the consumers had learnt nothing from the 1973-74 crisis. Alternative energy supplies were not being developed, and could not be developed economically so long as the real price of oil was being eroded so relentlessly. The falling real price for oil was lulling the consumers into a renewed sense of complacency over oil and energy, thereby discouraging any serious and sustained energy conservation effort. Another round of boom and bust, oil shortage and price explosion thus looked to be unavoidable. But most forecasters saw it coming sometime later on in the 1980s. Naturally, it could not be foreseen at the time just how soon and in what manner the crunch would arrive.

Saudi Arabia: The Swing Producer

In spite of their long-term commitment to production restraint and conservation of oil resources, the 1974-75 dip in demand did pose a short-term price and production management problem for the OPEC Governments.

Not surprisingly, the first to be affected were the African producers of light low-sulphur crudes which had priced their oil in line with what the market would bear during the 1973-74 crisis period. As the market slackened and freight rates fell dramatically, the high differentials charged for African crudes over and above the Arabian Light marker became way out of line, and the African exporters suffered quite substantial volume losses before they eventually reduced their sale prices to bring the differential down to a more realistic level.

Libya was particularly hard hit in this respect since, in late 1974, not only was its oil overpriced in relation to Gulf crude but it was also still burdened by a destination embargo to the US, which offered a big

---

* *There was a minor increase in domestic OECD oil production from 652 million tons in 1973 to 681 million tons in 1978. Nevertheless, net oil imports increased from 1,233 million tons to 1,249 million tons.*

potential market for Libyan-type oil (most of the other Arab producers had lifted their ban on oil shipments to the US the previous March). Libyan output consequently plunged, falling to under 1 million b/d in December 1974, as compared with about 2 million b/d at the beginning of the year. However, after the lifting of the US embargo in late-December 1974 and a series of market-related price cuts, Libya succeeded in restoring the balance and by July 1975 production was back up over the 2 million b/d mark. Between the first quarter of 1974 and June 1975 Libya cut its official sale price by nearly $5/barrel, from $16/barrel (over $5 above Arabian Light) to $11.20/barrel (only 74 cents above Arabian Light). However, these price cuts by Libya, as well as comparable reductions by Iraq on its Mediterranean crude sales, were regarded as excessive by some of the other OPEC exporters and were protested by Algeria (which kept its second and third quarter 1975 price for Saharan Blend at $11.75/barrel) and Saudi Arabia in particular.

Nor was market pressure on overpriced crudes confined to Africa. In the Gulf Abu Dhabi, which it will be recalled, in the heady winter days of 1973-74 had augmented the price of its light (39° API) Murban crude with a low-sulphur premium of 70 cents/barrel and an added gravity uplift (6 cents/barrel per API degree above 34° instead of 3 cents) was also in trouble. The resulting premium was too much for market conditions in the post-crisis shakedown, and in January-February 1975 output slipped to around 750,000 b/d as compared with the 1974 average of 1.4 million b/d before a cut in the low-sulphur premium (to 30 cents/barrel) and the gravity allowance (back to 3 cents per API degree above 34°) restored the situation.

In the second half of 1975, partly due to the price adjustments and partly to the fact that the recession had hit demand for heavy fuel oil, the principal product for industrial use, more than for lighter products, demand for lighter crudes picked up markedly.

However, despite these temporary perturbations and given the absence of any formal agreement on, or even meaningful discussion of, regulation of production within OPEC, the 12% fall in 1975 demand for OPEC oil was handled remarkably smoothly by the individual Member Countries, with the drop being on the whole fairly evenly distributed between those major producers who could best afford it. As a result, the price pressure was confined to differentials at the margin, while the base price for the marker crude itself remained pretty much rock-solid. Thus, with no serious price competition between the producers, the steady base price for crude oil was in turn capable of maintaining a floor under refined product prices. And although spot product markets

156

were weak in relation to crude prices in 1975 (i.e. with an estimated average f.o.b. crude netback somewhat lower than the government sale price), realizations and margins on product sales in European domestic markets were generally rather better, except in markets totally free of government control, like that of West Germany, which tend to parallel the spot markets.[6]

Writing in April 1975, one trade journal neatly summed up the situation at the time as follows: "Crude oil prices have been faltering at the margin under the twin pressures of surplus producing capacity and shrinking demand. In a competitive setting they would already have collapsed. That they are merely fraying at the edges is a measure of the extent to which political considerations rather than the desire to maximize revenues are for the present dominant. OPEC's cohesion on the central issue of price has thus far survived the economic strains largely because of the internal political compromise between the hawks that initially wanted to raise prices on the one hand and, on the other Saudi Arabia with the reserves and productive capacity sufficient to impose virtually any price level by putting forward or withholding incremental supplies."[7]

Altogether, in 1975 OPEC took an output drop of 3.6 million b/d from 30.7 million b/d to 27.1 million b/d. Of this the major portion — 1.4 million b/d or nearly 40% (considerably more proportionately than Saudi Arabia's 28% share in 1974 OPEC production) — was borne by Saudi Arabia, with Iran, Venezuela, Nigeria and Kuwait accounting for most of the rest (for details see table overleaf).

It was, of course, only fitting that Saudi Arabia should have borne the brunt of the 1975 dip in demand, being both by far and away the largest OPEC exporter and the one with the biggest financial surplus. Publicly, the Saudis always emphasized that they were by no means cutting production deliberately as part of any preconceived plan, but only allowing it to fall in response to the natural trend of market forces. This was certainly true as far as it went, but the very fact that Saudi Arabia allowed and perhaps encouraged such a steep drop in export liftings by the Aramco companies — "taking the swing" as it is called in oil jargon — was in itself tantamount to a very positive action in support of OPEC.

Of the other producers who took a major share of the 1975 OPEC output decline, all were in a reasonably comfortable financial situation at the time, with the possible exception of Nigeria, whose 1975 international payments ended up just about in balance. In percentage terms Venezuela took the biggest drop of all, but this happened to be entirely consistent with the government's conservation policy to cut back output to a ceiling of 2.3 million b/d in anticipation of the nationalization of the Venezuelan oil industry on January 1, 1976.

OPEC Crude Oil Production Change 1974-75
(Thousand Barrels Daily)

	1974	1975	Volume Change	% Change
Saudi Arabia	8,480	7,075	-1,405	-16.6
Iran	6,022	5,350	-672	-11.2
Venezuela	2,976	2,346	-630	-21.2
Kuwait	2,546	2,084	-462	-18.1
Nigeria	2,255	1,783	-472	-20.9
Iraq	1,971	2,262	+291	+14.8
UAE	1,679	1,664	-15	-0.9
Libya	1,521	1,480	-41	-2.7
Indonesia	1,375	1,307	-68	-4.9
Algeria	1,007	983	-24	-2.4
Qatar	518	438	-80	-15.4
Gabon	202	223	+21	+10.4
Ecuador	177	161	-16	-9.0
Total	**30,729**	**27,156**	**-3,573**	**-11.6**

On the face of it, it looks as though Libya and the UAE got off rather lightly. However, in the case of the former, the 1974 level of output had been substantially depressed on account of overpricing and the prolongation of the ban on deliveries to the US. The only OPEC Countries which could have been described as genuinely short of money in 1975 — Indonesia, Algeria and Ecuador — did not suffer very greatly in volume terms; while Iraq, the sole member to have increased production to any significant extent during that year, could argue that its output had been kept artificially low in previous years due to its protracted conflict with the oil companies. Nevertheless accusations of covert price cutting were levelled at Iraq in OPEC Meetings. The Iraqis hotly denied these changes, while pointing out that Iraq needed some leeway in pricing in order to be able to meet competition from the major companies, which still enjoyed their producers' margins of 22 cents/barrel or more in most other OPEC Countries.

All in all, therefore, given the particular circumstances of each of the

Member Countries concerned, the 1975 cuts seem to have distributed themselves pretty evenly and fairly. In fact, it is difficult to see how the whole business could have been managed better even if it had been planned in advance — which it assuredly was not.

Much expert attention has been focused on Saudi Arabia's role as the "swing" producer during the 1974-78 period. The idea was that Saudi Arabia, given its high level of surplus producing capacity and the relatively low level of output needed to meet its financial requirements at that time, could be relied upon to bear the main burden of any reduction in demand while remaining a potential source of incremental supplies when demand resumed an upward trend. Something of this sort certainly did take place. In 1975, as we have seen, Saudi output dropped to nearly 7 million b/d from 8.5 million b/d the year before, then recovered sharply to 8.6 million b/d in 1976 and 9.2 million b/d in 1977, before moving back to 8.3 million b/d in 1978 — a far wider fluctuation than experienced by any other producer during that period.

At the time it was generally reckoned in oil circles that Saudi Arabia had the capability of raising or lowering production by some 2 to 3 million b/d above or below its preferred ceiling (for Aramco) of 8.5 million b/d. Perhaps this was somewhat of an exaggeration — on the downward side the Kingdom's financial needs were rising fast, and on the upward side production capacity, which was often loosely rated at over 11 million b/d, was probably in actual fact closer to 10 million b/d on a sustained basis. Nevertheless, it remains true that Saudi Arabia's 1974-78 swing potential was considerable by any standards.

By rights, such swing potential in the slack market conditions of the time should have invested Saudi Arabia with price leadership within OPEC. And to a considerable extent it did so. Throughout these years Saudi Arabia exercised a moderating influence on prices — mitigating those increases that did occur and an occasions effectively vetoing rises which would otherwise have taken place.

But this leadership was by no means absolute. For one thing political considerations put certain limits on Saudi Arabia's exercise of oil power within OPEC. For another, even Saudi Arabia's spare capacity could not really outgun the rest of OPEC in terms of barrels if the latter were really determined and united. When the trial of strength came with the 1977 two-tier price split, the Saudis proved unable to expand production far enough, fast enough, to enforce a quick solution on Saudi terms; so the obvious way out was a sensible compromise before inter-OPEC antagonism got out of hand.

In 1979, Saudi Arabia's swing capacity on the upside, and

consequently any pretention to control or leadership over prices, evaporated (albeit temporarily perhaps) under the impact of the Iranian supply crisis. All the Kingdom could do was to produce an extra one million barrels a day (above its traditional 8.5 million b/d ceiling) in the hope of alleviating the force of the new price explosion, pending the return of more normal conditions.

September 1975: Agreement on 10% Rise

Meanwhile, by mid-1975, OPEC's attention had returned to the recurring problem of the weak dollar. The US dollar had been falling since September 1974, and by May 1975, in terms of strong currencies like the German mark and the French franc, the dollar's decline had reached 12% and 16% respectively. In terms of the Special Drawing Rights (SDR) basket of the International Monetary Fund, with its heavy dollar weighting of about one-third, the fall in the dollar's value had been a little over 5%.

At the regular mid-year OPEC Ministerial Conference in Libreville, Gabon, in June 1975, it was agreed in principle, as a means of protecting the purchasing power of oil revenues against the depreciation of the dollar, to adopt the SDR as the unit of account in which crude oil prices would be expressed (though payments would, as before, continue to be settled mainly in dollars). However, owing to the Conference's inability to agree on what point in time to use as the base for the new system — crude oil prices in dollar terms would have risen by anywhere between 11 cents and 47 cents a barrel depending on which month was taken as the base — it was decided to postpone the application of the scheme until October 1, 1975, after the scheduled price-fixing Conference in September.[8]

However, already by June 1975 the dollar had begun to recover and continued its improvement through the remainder of 1975 and in 1976. As a result, the Libreville plan to adopt the SDR as the price unit of account was dropped.

By now price positions were starting to be delineated in preparation for the September Conference which was to herald the end of the nine-month price freeze decided upon the previous December. In the event, it turned out to be a tough battle, involving a sharp clash of wills between the two largest producers, Iran and Saudi Arabia, before a compromise was reached on a price increase of 10%. Real policy differences as regards oil prices and global outlook, with less tangible considerations of national prestige and rivalry for the leadership of OPEC, combined to produce the worst bout of internal tension the Organization had experienced since the royalty expensing drama of 1964.

In pre-Conference consultations, the Shah of Iran made it clear to a visiting Saudi delegation headed by Sheikh Yamani that, given the prevailing rates of inflation, he would be in no way prepared to settle for an increase of less than 15%.

The Saudis argued that, particularly with the prevailing soft oil market, the best course would be to continue the oil price freeze at least until the end of 1975 in order to assist the emerging signs of recovery in some of the major western economies. However, according to Saudi Arabia's own studies, a price rise of up to 10% could be absorbed by the West without undue hardship, but anything above that could inflict positive harm. Also to be taken into consideration was the plight of the developing countries which could not absorb another price hike without compensating aid.

Although it looked as though a numerical majority of the Members would probably side with Iran, the pre-Conference consultations showed that an influential minority — among them Algeria, Venezuela, Kuwait and the UAE — would be prepared to compromise on a 10% increase if Saudi Arabia would go along with that. Algeria, which was particularly anxious that Saudi Arabia should not be forced into a position where it might break with OPEC, suggested splitting the 10% into a 5% increase in October 1975 to be followed by another 5% in January 1976. The Saudis indicated that they would agree to this provided it gained unanimous OPEC acceptance and that the January 1976 price should be frozen until the end of the year.

At the Conference itself, which convened in Vienna on September 24-27, Saudi Arabia indicated its acceptance of the Algerian formula provided unanimity could be achieved, while the group led by Iran countered with a proposal for a 15% increase — 10% in October 1975 and a further 5% in January 1976, but with no commitment to any period of freeze thereafter. The difference between the two positions was only 5% plus the freeze period, but the whole atmosphere was sharpened by the evident contest between Iran and Saudi Arabia for the leadership of OPEC.

Iran then called for a vote on the proposal for the two-stage increase of 10% immediately and a further 5% in January, and 9 of the 13 Member Countries voted in favour — Iran, Iraq, Nigeria, Venezuela, Libya, Indonesia, Qatar, Ecuador and Gabon.

Saudi Arabia, however, dug in its heels, making it clear that it could on no account accept such an increase; and if the others went ahead without Saudi Arabia, then the Kingdom would keep its prices frozen at current levels and let its production rise to wherever the market might take it within the limits of Saudi surplus capacity.

In the highly depressed state of 1975 market demand, this was not a threat to be dismissed lightly and, although Iran indicated that it would be prepared to hold to the 15% and let Saudi Arabia go its own way, most of the others had no desire for such a showdown. Finally, a compromise proposed by Kuwait with the backing of Algeria and Venezuela, calling for a 10% increase as from October 1, 1975, with a nine-month freeze until the end of June 1976, gained majority backing and eventually the grudging assent of Iran and Libya as well. Saudi Arabia agreed to the compromise, while noting that ideally it would favour an extension of the freeze beyond June 1976.[9]

The compromise nevertheless left an aftermath of bitterness, and Iran's Chief Delegate, Dr. Amouzegar, publicly castigated what he described as an "unholy alliance" between Saudi Arabia and Algeria.

As a result of the Vienna decision, the official government sale price for the Arabian Light marker crude rose with effect from October 1, 1975, by $1.047/barrel, or 10%, from $10.463/barrel to $11.510/barrel.

This increase still left OPEC's January 1974 price trailing quite a long way behind in the inflation stakes. OECD export prices rose by 27% in 1974 and a further 10% in 1975, to reach an index figure of 139 (1973=100) by the end of 1975. As for the index, compiled by OPEC itself, of the prices of goods imported by the OPEC states from the industrialized countries, this rose by 32.6% in 1974 and a further 27.5% in 1975, to reach an index figure of 169 (1973=100) by the end of 1975.

The September 1975 Conference also laid the groundwork for a new system of differentials between the various Gulf crudes which incorporated the earlier reductions in gravity and low-sulphur premiums on the ligher crudes above 34° API which had already been implemented in Abu Dhabi earlier in the year, and introduced a sulphur penalty on crudes with more than 1.7% sulphur content. This did have the effect of bringing down the prices of the heavier Gulf crudes somewhat relative to the marker crude, but failed to deal with the salient fact that the problem with heavy crude pricing was related more to the yield of low-priced fuel than to sulphur content. And in the opinion of most experts the new system left the lighter crudes (for which demand was on the upswing) underpriced and the heavier crudes overpriced in market terms.

Efforts to rectify the evident disparities between various crudes at the December 1975 OPEC Conference in Vienna were unfortunately cut short by the kidnapping of the 13 Ministers and their delegations by an international terrorist gang led by the notorious "Carlos". From then on Conferences of OPEC Oil Ministers were held at venues other than Vienna, although the Organization's Secretariat continued to be located in the Austrian capital. However, OPEC Finance Ministers, who started holding regular Conferences in November 1975 in connection with the setting up of the OPEC Special Fund for aid to the Third World, continued to meet in Vienna.

Doha: The Two-Tier Price Split

With the bottoming out of the 1974-75 recession and the resumption of OECD economic growth at a healthy rate of 5.3%, demand for OPEC crude perked up considerably in 1976 with output registering a gain of 13% from the depressed level of 1975 (30.74 million b/d as against 27.16 million b/d).

Demand for light crudes was especially buoyant, with Libya, Algeria and Nigeria registering impressive volume gains; and by mid-year spot market prices for light African crudes had overtaken official sale prices by a substantial margin. In the Gulf, on the other hand, spot realizations for 34^0 API crudes remained roughly in line with official prices, while for heavier crudes spot prices were somewhat below official levels.

Against this background the OPEC Oil Ministers met in Bali, Indonesia, at the end of May 1976 to decide on prices as from July 1. At what was described at the time as a "strenuous and sometimes stormy session,"[10] the various OPEC schools of thought on prices resumed their by now familiar contest. A majority of eight Members – Nigeria, Indonesia, Iran, Iraq, Libya, Qatar, Gabon and Ecuador – argued in favour of an increase in the region of 20%, which had been the Economic Commission's estimate for inflation in the prices of goods imported by the OPEC Countries in the nine-month period since October 1975. Algeria, Venezuela and Kuwait declared themselves in support of a more modest increase; while Saudi Arabia, backed by the UAE, stood firm against any increase at all, arguing that a continued freeze till the end of the year would be in OPEC's best interests since it would serve to nurture the emerging world economic recovery and thus the recovery in demand for OPEC oil (thereby relieving the competitive strains on production and differentials which had developed within the Organization during the slump), as well as strengthening the OPEC and Third World position in the North-South Dialogue which was then in progress in Paris.

After heated debate — including some sharp words from Iraq in condemnation of the Saudi position — the Saudis had their way and the price of the marker crude was left unchanged. However, the way was paved for some further readjustment of differentials, involving a 5 to 10 cents/barrel decrease in heavy and medium crude prices in the Gulf, and a 30 cents/barrel increase in Libyan crudes which had been regarded as markedly underpriced in relation to similar Algerian and Nigerian oils.

It was clear that some price increase would have to be decided upon at the year-end 1976 Conference in Doha, Qatar; the only question was how much? The impatience of the OPEC majority with the Saudi-inspired price freeze since October 1975 was becoming too explosive to contain further. Moreover, surging demand in the fourth quarter of 1976 — the normal seasonal rise having been compounded by a certain amount of speculative pre-lift in advance of the anticipated year-end price increase — had taken spot prices for all crudes, light, medium and heavy, well above official levels.

The run-up to the December 1976 Doha Conference was accompanied by an even more than usually confusing battery of signals from various quarters. But it was generally anticipated at the time that Saudi Arabia would, after the customary round of inter-OPEC bargaining, agree to accept a 10% increase for the whole year 1977 as part of a general compromise which would rally the support of middle-of-the-roaders, such as the UAE, Kuwait, Venezuela and Indonesia, and outflank those OPEC hawks still pressing for a rise of 15% or more — in other words, a sort of re-run of the September 1975 scenario. This, of course, did not happen in Doha because the Saudi maximum position failed to reach the 10% minimum necessary to attract compromise support from the majority camp. The indications are that a 10% maximum did in fact represent the thrust of Saudi policy until a comparatively short time before the Doha Meeting when, faced with disturbing evidence of a possible hiatus in the world economic recovery, the Saudi leadership under Crown Prince Fahd decided to stick at 5%.[11]

At Doha, after the preliminaries, the line-up established itself somewhat as follows:

- A majority of eight countries — Iran, Iraq, Nigeria, Libya, Algeria, Qatar, Gabon and Ecuador — favoured an increase of 15% or more. (The Economic Commission Board, in its report to the Conference, had estimated the inflation in the prices of goods imported by OPEC — i.e. on the basis of the OPEC import price index — at 26% since the last oil price increase in October 1975).

- Kuwait, Indonesia and Venezuela supported a 10% increase.
- Saudi Arabia advocated a continued freeze for a further six months, but indicated that it might be prepared to accept a maximum 5% rise. The UAE said it would follow Saudi Arabia.

At that point (it being midday Thursday, December 16) there was still some hope in Conference circles that a compromise on 10% might be arranged if Saudi Arabia could be so persuaded. Then, on Thursday afternoon, Sheikh Yamani flew off to Jeddah for consultations with Crown Prince Fahd, and the big question in the corridors of Doha's Gulf Hotel was: would Yamani come back with the required manadate for 10%? Anything under that would be no good since even the middle-of-the-roaders had no brief from their governments to go below 10%.

By the time Yamani returned to Doha late on Thursday evening, excitement had reached fever pitch; and, despite the tight security, the Saudi Oil Minister was mobbed and buffeted by a pack of news-hungry pressmen in the lobby of the Gulf Hotel. In fact, Yamani had come back with only a minor extension to his original mandate. The official position was still a 5% increase for the year 1977; but he was authorized to go up to 7% provided that OPEC unanimity could be reached on that level for the whole of 1977. However, the extra 2% was never used or even put to the test since the Ministers of 11 countries (i.e. all except Saudi Arabia and the UAE) met in the early hours of Friday morning and agreed to implement their own price plan whatever Saudi Arabia might do.

The 11 decided to increase the official sale price of their version of the marker crude (by now theoretical, since the actual marker crude, Saudi Arabia's 34° API Arabian Light, was to be assigned lower price) by 15% split into two tranches — 10% from \$11.51/barrel to \$12.70/ barrel with effect from January 1, 1977, and a further 5% to \$13.30/ barrel as of July 1, 1977. After the night meeting of the eleven, the Venezuelan Oil Minister, Dr. Valentin Hernandez-Acosta, strolled down to the lobby of the Gulf Hotel around 3 or 4 a.m. on Friday where he came upon a lonely Reuter man keeping vigil after most of the press corps had retired to their own separate hotel nearby. Hernandez-Acosta passed the information and the news of the price split was out.

In the morning, Saudi Arabia and the UAE announced that they, for their part, would increase their marker crude price by only 5% with effect from January 1, 1977, raising the price of 34° API Arabian Light from \$11.51/barrel to \$12.09/barrel. Thus emerged a two-tier price structure with a gap of 61 cents a barrel between the upper and lower bounds.

In addition, Saudi Arabia increased its prices for medium and heavy crudes by only around 3%, thereby widening the differentials between these crudes and the marker to 47 cents on medium and 72 cents on heavy, as against 23 cents and 47 cents previously.

The UAE's unquestioning support for Saudi Arabia was a matter of state policy, carried out on the explicit instructions of the UAE President and Ruler of Abu Dhabi, Sheikh Zayid Ibn Sultan Al Nahayyan. But when the UAE Oil Minister, Dr. Mana Saeed Otaiba, returned to Abu Dhabi after the Doha Conference, he found that a certain amount of domestic grass-roots criticism had developed regarding the UAE's acceptance of the lower price. It was therefore proposed in oil circles that, as well as raising its basic price by 5%, Abu Dhabi should also make an upward adjustment in its differentials (its light crude being in any case relatively underpriced at the time) to make for a higher effective price rise. However, Sheikh Zayid intervened to make it clear that when he spoke of 5%, he meant 5% and not 5% plus. Thus the prices of Abu Dhabi crudes were raised by exactly 5%, and the adjustment of differentials had to await the healing of the price split six months later.

However, although standing four-square with Saudi Arabia on the price issue, the UAE nevertheless resisted Saudi pressure to allow a temporary increase in production above its prevailing level of around 2 million b/d.

Among the eleven-Member majority there was a feeling of confidence that they were in a sufficiently strong position to ride out the storm until Saudi Arabia rejoined the fold. There was, nevertheless, a fear of the consequences of a dramatic increase in production by the Saudis and an overt antagonism against Saudi Arabia on this account.

For example, on his return to Baghdad after the Conference, the Iraqi Oil Minister, Mr. Tayeh Abdul-Karim, injected a political note of warning into his reply to a press question as to whether he was afraid of an output increase by Saudi Arabia. "We believe," he said, " that Saudi Arabia will not be able to maintain an isolated stand on prices and production. Oil and energy are hot issues in the Arab world, and Arab public opinion will not allow any one Arab oil producing country to undermine the price structure and violate OPEC solidarity."[12]

The Algerian Energy Minister, Mr. Belaid Abdesselam, was even more blunt in his assessment. "I think OPEC can absorb the 5% difference," he said. "There will be no real distortion — unless Saudi Arabia raises production. That would be an act of direct aggression against OPEC."[13]

In Iran, the Saudi Oil Minister was personally singled out as the principal target for criticism by both the Shah and the Tehran media, and the Shah also warned that overproduction by Saudi Arabia would constitute an "act of aggression" against Iran.[14]

Unabashed by these warnings, Saudi Arabia announced that it was lifting its 8.5 million b/d ceiling on Aramco production and was planning on a target output of 10 million b/d for the first quarter of 1977 (as against 8.3 million b/d for the year 1976 and nearly 9 million b/d in the fourth quarter), and possibly more later in the year. It was evident that a trial of strength was in the offing.

Meanwhile, Crown Prince Fahd defended Saudi oil policy as "an effective instrument for the promotion of stability and economic development throughout the world and for the fight against inflation which is a worldwide problem." In the past, he went on to say, "we used to go along with positions that we were not altogether convinced of. Now, we will do what we consider to be appropriate for our own interests and the interests of the world economy."[15]

The basic divergence of views on prices between Saudi Arabia and the majority of its OPEC partners had been much in evidence at every Conference since the December 1973 "watershed" meeting in Tehran. Hitherto, some way had always been found to paper over the cracks and maintain uniformity of prices; and there seemed no real reason why this somewhat precarious cohesion should not be kept up indefinitely. But, at Doha, it looked as though OPEC, usually so adept at brinkmanship, had finally missed its footing and tumbled over the edge. The majority had finally got fed up with the perpetual tug-of-war on prices and decided to cut themselves loose from Saudi tutelage, while Saudi Arabia was now determined to demonstrate that its views could not go thus unheeded with impunity.

But it is in the nature of intra-OPEC dynamics that a compromise should always be lurking not too far from the surface, even when things are looking at their blackest. And the seeds of a possible future compromise could already be discerned in the majority decision to withhold part of its increase until July 1, 1977. Obviously the extra 5% could serve as a bargaining card to be discarded if Saudi Arabia were to rejoin the others at the 10% mark by mid-year.

That, in fact, was what actually happened in the end; but not before the production contest had run its course.

Together Again in Stockholm

Apart from concern for the world economy, the motivation for Saudi

Arabia's price stand at Doha also contained a political element, as was made clear by Oil Minister Yamani at the time. In particular, the Saudis were anxious to see the incoming Carter administration show its appreciation for Saudi Arabia's moderation on oil prices by (a) initiating concrete steps for progress towards a settlement of the Arab-Israeli conflict acceptable to the Arabs, and (b) deblocking the North-South Dialogue in Paris.[16] Progress towards peace in the Middle East was clearly a matter for the longer term*; but Saudi hopes for a fruitful conclusion of the North-South Dialogue in Paris were dashed when, after 18 months' work, the Dialogue collapsed in general disarray in June 1977, and this was one of the reasons behind the Saudi price rise at mid-year.

In the bitter aftermath of the Doha Meeting, the Saudi plan was to administer a short, sharp shock in the form of a rapid boost in production, as a consequence of which other OPEC producers would (a) be unable to sustain the higher price level (spot prices would gravitate towards the lower tier), (b) lose export volume, and (c) be obliged to seek a compromise with Saudi Arabia on a reunified price closer to the Saudi tier than their own. Those most likely to be hit by the incremental Saudi output were the other Gulf producers, such as Iran, Iraq and Kuwait, which exported crudes similar to those of Saudi Arabia.

The plan did not work to anything like its full extent because, owing to a series of mishaps and accidents, the projected production expansion fell far short of its target.

In this situation spot market prices for Gulf crudes floated uneasily between the two price tiers, tending towards the upper end rather than the lower. Since the Saudi Government had expressly forbidden the sale of lower-priced Saudi crudes at anything above the official levels, Saudi oil could not be freely and openly traded on the spot markets at higher than the Saudi official price. But it was frequently traded as part of a package on exchange deals with other crudes, which made the actual price of any of the crudes involved difficult to determine.

At the time, the installed "facility" capacity of the Aramco system was rated at 11.8 million b/d. However, the facility capacity rating does not mean that such a volume can be produced and exported on a

---

* In the event, Carter's main initiative in the Middle East, namely his sponsorship of the Camp David agreement between Egypt and Israel, amounting to a separate Egyptian-Israeli peace with no solution to the key problem of Palestine, was not at all to the liking of Saudi Arabia. But all that came later.

sustained basis. There is always a gap between facility capacity and maximum sustainable capacity, with the latter usually running at about 90% of the former; but one never knows exactly how much the system can handle on a sustained basis until it has been fully tested. As earlier indicated, Aramco was given the go-ahead for 10 million b/d in the first quarter, and the Saudis were looking to the possibility of going higher, perhaps to 10.5 million b/d or more, as the year progressed. But, even making full allowance for bad luck and accidental factors, it soon became clear that the Aramco system was having trouble building up to and sustaining an output of much more than 10 million b/d.[17]

In January and February, in addition to technical bottlenecks of one kind and another, Aramco's production surge was held back by a spell of unusually bad weather in the Gulf, which meant that the loading terminals had to close down for several days and work well below full capacity for extended periods. As a result, crude production averaged only 8.35 million b/d in January, but built up gradually to 9.45 million b/d in February and 9.68 million b/d in March. However, the first-quarter average was only 9.15 million b/d, hardly more than in the fourth quarter of 1976.

In April, Aramco output rose to an average of 10 million b/d, and it really looked as though the Saudi production steamroller was on the move. Peace feelers were being put out by various Members of the OPEC majority, and consultations were afoot regarding a possible price compromise at the level of 8% above December 1976 — i.e. Saudi Arabia up 3% and the rest down 2%. However, most of the OPEC majority were still resolutely opposed to any backing down on their part from the 10% mark, though there was general acceptance of the idea of foregoing the additional 5% scheduled for July. In this connection, President Carlos Andres Perez and the Shah of Iran sent amicable messages to Saudi Arabia early in May to notify the Saudis of their decision to renounce the 5% price increase in July, while emphasizing their concern about the production issue. Iran's message stressed that this gesture on prices was being made not with a view to pressuring Saudi Arabia to put up its prices — the Kingdom being free to make its own decisions on price policy — but to narrow the price gap in the hope that Saudi Arabia would not increase production in such a way as to damage the interests of its OPEC partners. The conciliatory tone of the Iranian message was much appreciated by the Saudi leadership, which thereupon resolved to modify its production policy appropriately from mid-year onwards.[18]

At this point fate took a hand in the form of a serious fire in the Saudi oilfield area at the Abqaiq gathering centre, which on May 11 destroyed a pump station and ancillary gas/oil separating and pipeline facilities. (A subsequent investigation established that the cause of the blaze was accidental, being traceable to a pipeline rupture due to corrosion.) Although the damage was repaired with astonishing rapidity considering the extent of the disruption, output in May fell some 2 million b/d below target, ending up at 8.27 million b/d before rising again to 9.37 million b/d in June.

The Abqaiq fire removed some of the pressure on the rest of OPEC, and stiffened their resolve not to compromise at anything below their prevailing price level, namely 10% above December 1976. Saudi Arabia meanwhile, was still prepared to go no further than 8% — which seemed to indicate that a narrowing of the price gap to 2% of the January 1977 increase was all that could be expected when the OPEC Ministers met for their mid-year Conference, this time to be held in Stockholm, Sweden.

However, early in June the North-South Dialogue foundered under the weight of what, in Third World eyes, was the intransigence of the West on virtually every major issue between the two groups. Almost immediately afterwards Saudi official circles let it be known that, as a direct reaction to the failure of the Dialogue, Saudi Arabia would raise its oil prices at mid-year by an extra 2% above what had been previously planned, and the OPEC price would thus be reunified at 10% above December 1976.[19] The formal realignment of Saudi and Abu Dhabi crude price on a marker (Arabian Light) level of $12.70/barrel (along with some adjustment of the light/heavy differentials) was finalized in advance of the Stockholm Conference which convened on July 13.

From July onwards, Saudi Arabia limited its production projection to embrace only the 8.5 million b/d traditional ceiling plus any unavoidable extra volume resulting from year-long commitments entered into at the beginning of 1977. In practice this meant an Aramco output average of 8.85 million b/d for the second half of 1977, and the ceiling of 8.5 million b/d was reimposed for 1978.

In retrospect it appears that, despite all the sound and fury at the time, neither OPEC nor any of its individual Members were noticeably harmed by the 1977 two-tier price conflict. The producers of light crude were not hurt since demand for this type of oil remained very strong in the early part of the year. The Gulf producers most affected — Iran, Iraq and Kuwait — undoubtedly did lose volume, but their performance over the period in question (except when compared with the artificially inflated demand in the fourth quarter of 1976) was really not too bad, and their volume losses to Saudi Arabia were certainly counterbalanced

170

by the higher prices they received. Their relatively poor showing in the second half of the year was due more to the growing influx of new non-OPEC oil than to Saudi production. The following table gives an idea of the relative production performances of the four countries concerned in 1977 (volumes in thousand barrels daily):

	1977 1Q	% Change vs. 1Q'76	% Change vs. 4Q'76	1977 1H	% vs. 1H'76	1977 Year	% vs. Year'76
Saudi Arabia—							
Aramco	9,150	+18.5	+2.0	9,178	+15.2	9,017	+8.1
Iran	5,787	+10.5	-12.4	5,604	+2.1	5,663	-3.7
Iraq	2,293	+14.7	-19.9	2,214	+22.6	2,348	-2.8
Kuwait—KOC	1,589	-3.6	-38.8	1,628	+0.2	1,784	-6.7
All OPEC	31,367	+11.6	-6.5	31,193	+8.7	31,278	+1.8

On the other hand, there can be no doubt that the two-tier price episode was extremely profitable for the four Aramco majors. Although strict control by the Saudi Government precluded them from selling Saudi crude oil at anything above the flat official price, they naturally benefited greatly by obtaining crude oil supplies for their own refineries at substantially cheaper prices than their competitors.

Shah Concurs with Caracas Freeze

A growing infusion of non-OPEC crude into the market in the second half of 1977 contributed to an overhang of surplus oil availability in the market which was estimated to be in the region of 2 million b/d, with the result that spot market prices for all crudes plunged quite substantially below official price levels.

Despite the soft market, some OPEC pressure was nevertheless building up for a January 1978 price increase, in anticipation of the year-end price-fixing Conference scheduled to convene in Caracas, Venezuela, on December 20, 1977. However, any prospect of such a price rise was effectively ruled out in mid-November when, after a meeting with President Carter in Washington, the Shah of Iran declared that he would support moves for a price freeze at the Caracas Conference, to continue until the end of 1978. The Shah explained his policy shift in terms of a willingness to show new "sympathy and comprehension" for the US view that any oil price rise would damage

171

the world economy. Though it was never explicitly acknowledged, there appeared to be the hint of a trade-off in the air — US readiness to meet Iran's defence needs in return for Iran's moderation on oil prices.[20]

The Shah's sudden conversion to a price-freeze posture made the position of the price doves virtually impregnable at Caracas. All the Gulf producers with the exception of Iraq — that is to say Saudi Arabia, Iran, Kuwait, the UAE and Qatar, together representing nearly two-thirds of OPEC's production — lined up solidly in favour of a 1978 price freeze. This meant the advocates of a price hike of 5 to 10% — notably Iraq, Libya, Nigeria, Venezuela and Algeria — did not stand a chance of prevailing; and so the 1978 marker price remained unchanged.

The Spirit of Taif

The weak market which had plagued OPEC in the second half of 1977 continued well into 1978 under the impact of generally low world demand for oil, reflecting the fruits of conservation efforts on the part of the consumers and the relatively poor state of the economies of the major industrialized countries, combined with the continued build-up of new supplies from Alaska, the North Sea and Mexico. In the first quarter of 1978, OPEC output crashed to 28 million b/d — some 3.3 million b/d less than the fourth quarter of 1977 — and was only marginally better, at 28.6 million b/d, in the second quarter. However, this was not all due to falling demand; a much greater than usual draw-down of consumer stocks also played a big part. Normally there is a seasonal draw-down of perhaps as much as 2 million b/d in the first quarter of any year. But in the first quarter of 1978 the rate of de-stocking was estimated to have reached something like 4 million b/d. This being so, it was not surprising that OPEC should have been convinced that the consuming countries and the oil companies were deliberately using the stock weapon in order to put pressure on prices. (If so, the move was a very shortsighted one since it resulted in stock levels being much lower than normal later on in 1978, just when the Iranian supply crisis hit the world.)

And pressure on prices there certainly was. The African producers were obliged to cut their official prices by 35 to 37 cents a barrel in the first half of the year; and Gulf crudes, while maintaining their official price levels, were being heavily discounted on the spot market.

One interesting aspect of the first-half 1978 slump in demand for OPEC crude was that a major part of the drop was again shouldered by

172

Saudi Arabia where output declined by 17% or 1.6 million b/d, to 7.8 million b/d in first-half 1978 as compared with the corresponding period of 1977 — thus amply confirming Saudi Arabia's position as the principal swing supplier at that time. But there was another highly significant factor which was tending to depress Saudi production in 1978. In February of that year, the government had given orders to limit output of the most popular and prolific Saudi crude — 34° API Arabian Light — to 65% of total production, as compared with 70 to 80% previously. This was part of a long-term effort (a) to curb overproduction from some of the Arabian Light reservoirs, (b) to bring production of Arabian Light more into line with its percentage of total reserves (this being about 50%), and (c) to boost exports of the Kingdom's heavier crudes which would provide the bulk of incremental availability in the future.

The supply/demand situation in the first half of 1978 was so alarming, and indeed puzzling, that at their June Conference in Geneva under the presidency of Kuwait's newly appointed Minister of Oil, Sheikh Ali Khalifa Al-Sabah*, the OPEC Ministers held their first meaningful discussion of the production issue for many years, moreover with the participation of Saudi Arabia. The session was strictly informal and discursive; no firm commitments were entered into, and the while affair was (successfully) kept secret to avoid embarrassment for any of the more reluctant participants. What the Ministers did, in effect, was to swap and analyse figures of their respective projected outputs for the second half of 1978, basically to see whether there was any danger of a serious surplus situation. Adding up the tentative numbers emanating from these projections, the OPEC total for the second half of 1978 came to a maximum of 30.2 million b/d. And since this figure was, in fact, rather lower than anticipated demand for the second half, there was a feeling of general reassurance that no big problem was in view on the production side (actual OPEC production in this period, even with the effect of the Iranian crisis in the fourth quarter, averaged 30.94 million b/d). Overall, the Ministers were confident that the days of oversupply were drawing to a close.

* *A young and exceptionally able technocrat with wide experience in oil and finance, Sheikh Ali Khalifa was no stranger to OPEC. As a senior official in Kuwait's Oil Ministry, he took part in all the crucial OPEC negotiations and meetings from 1970 to 1976. In Kuwait also, he had for a number of years been playing a leading role in formulating oil and financial policy. Before being appointed Minister of Oil, he served for three years as Under Secretary of the Ministry of Finance.*

This confidence was not misplaced. Well before the upheaval in Iran began its momentous course in late October, the market had turned around as crude customers boosted their liftings both in response to normal seasonal demand increase and to rebuild stock levels which had been so brutally depleted earlier in the year. By September-October spot prices had once again overtaken official levels across the board; and from there on it was a case of upwards ever upwards as booming demand collided head-on with the loss of supply from Iran.

Mid-1978 also saw a resurgence of OPEC concern regarding the US dollar which, after a period of relative stability in 1975-77, began another prolonged slide in 1977 under the impact of massive US trade deficits, and registered a trade-weighted decline against major currencies (with appropriate weight to the US dollar itself) of some 11% in 1978. By the end of July the majority of OPEC had more or less agreed on a formula for indexing the dollar price of oil against a basket of 11 currencies (the Geneva II basket) plus the US dollar. However, the plan came up against the veto of Saudi Arabia which was anxious to avoid any OPEC action which might even further exacerbate the plight of the dollar, this being the currency in which the bulk of the Kingdom's enormous financial reserves were held. But, like everything else, worry about the dollar was soon to be submerged by events in Iran.

Meanwhile, a few months earlier, OPEC had taken a significant step to get away from the hurly-burly of current events for a moment and take a strategic look at the future. On the initiative of Saudi Arabia and Oil Minister Yamani, the OPEC Ministers were invited to a special meeting early in May 1978, at the Saudi summer capital of Taif, for an informal exchange of ideas about a long-term price and production strategy for OPEC.[21]

Broadly speaking, the thesis put forward by Yamani was this: When at some time in the 1980s (as it was then thought) the market moved towards balance and then probably shortage, the price issue would be dominated by considerations of supply and demand. These would then be responsible for determining the price rather than OPEC. It was therefore essential, if OPEC wished to maintain a viable raison d'etre in the 1980s, that it should draw up a long-term strategy for the coming decade.

By and large, this idea was accepted at the Taif Meeting, and it was decided to set up a Ministerial Committee drawn from six Member Countries — Saudi Arabia, Iran, Iraq, Kuwait, Venezuela and Algeria (i.e. the five founder Members plus Algeria) — to carry out an exhaustive study of the issues involved, under the chairmanship of Sheikh Yamani.

174

The six Ministers later set up an expert study group to assist it in its work. This working group completed its report early in 1980, which was then accepted by the six-man Ministerial Committee in February of that year and finally endorsed, with reservations by some Member States – by the full OPEC Conference meeting, again in Taif, in May. The Long-Term Strategy Committee's report will serve as a basis for policy recommendations to be forwarded to the second OPEC Summit Conference scheduled to convene in Baghdad early in November 1980.

The Taif Meeting was thus a resounding success – Minister Ali Khalifa of Kuwait declared that it was the most productive OPEC Meeting he had ever attended. Not only did it launch OPEC into a vital new perspective of long-term strategic planning, but it also helped a great deal to relax the strains that had been accumulating between the Member Countries down the years, and particularly since the two-tier price showdown.

Price Erosion: How Far Did It Go?

Precise determination of the 1974-78 erosion of OPEC oil prices in real terms is a tricky matter. It all depends, of course, among other things, on the type of index one employs and exactly which of the variety of 1974 prices one uses as a base.

As far as indices are concerned, the table overleaf gives a selection of those that could legitimately be used. As regards inflation, indices A, B and C (OECD export prices in national currency terms, OECD export prices in dollar terms, and OECD domestic inflation, respectively) give roughly the same result. Index B naturally reflects the US dollar depreciation in 1978-79, but this is offset if indices A and C are aggregated with the currency index to make a composite. On this basis, for indices A and C one reaches composite index numbers (1973=100) in the range of 180 for 1978 and 208 to 210 for 1979.

Using $10.84/barrel as the government sale price for the marker crude (93% of posting) at the start of 1974, one arrives at an indexed price of $19.51/barrel as against an actual price of $12.70/barrel at the end of 1978, indicating a decline of some 45% in real terms to a deflated price of $7.05/barrel.

On the same basis, the average actual price for 1979 ($17.28/barrel) is still some 24% below the indexed price for that year ($22.65/barrel). But by the end of the year the actual price of the marker crude ($24/barrel for Saudi Arabia and $26/barrel for most of the rest of the Gulf producers) had overtaken the indexed price, and this process was carried further in 1980 as the marker price rose to $28/barrel for Saudi Arabia and $32/barrel for most of the others.

Various Inflation and Currency Indices
(1973 = 100)

Year	Inflation				Currency
	A	B	C	D	
1974	127	126	113	133	99
1975	139	140	126	169	102
1976	148	141	137	221	97
1977	157	153	149	262	100
1978	162	172	162	324	111
1979	180	199	178	400	117

Inflation:

A— Export price index of OECD countries in national currency terms (source OECD)

B— Export price index of major industrial countries in US dollar terms (source IMF)

C— Index of OECD domestic inflation calculated on the basis of consumer price indices of 23 OECD countries weighted according to private final consumption (source OECD)

D— Index of the prices of goods imported by OPEC Members from the industrial countries (source OPEC)

Currency:

Index of exchange rate changes of US dollar in relation to the nine currencies of the OPEC Geneva I basket (those of Belgium, France, West Germany, Italy, Japan, the Netherlands, Sweden, Britain and Switzerland) plus the US dollar, export trade weighted.

In a recent book, the Deputy Secretary General of OPEC, Dr. Fadhil Al-Chalabi, comes to similar conclusions as regards price erosion by 1978-79. Using what he describes as a "conservative" measurement — i.e. composite index for inflation (OECD export price index in national currency terms) and currency (US dollar movement against trade-weighted basket of nine Geneva I currencies plus US dollar) — Chalabi makes the following calculations:[22]

Year	Inflation Index	Currency Index	Aggregate Index	Indexed Price ($/b)	OPEC Price ($/b)*
1974	127.00	99.60	126.49	13.64	10.78
1975	139.07	103.02	143.27	15.44	10.72
1976	147.76	97.53	144.11	15.54	11.51
1977	157.00	100.79	158.24	17.06	12.39
1978	162.10	112.89	182.99	19.73	12.70
1979	177.50	117.83	209.15	22.55	17.28

*   *Yearly average of marker crude (Arabian Light)*

But, as Chalabi points out, these estimations really are conservative when contrasted with the loss of purchasing power of the oil barrel as measured by the index, kept by OPEC itself, of the prices of goods imported by OPEC Members from the industrialized countries (index D) which by 1978-79 had reached about double the OECD export and domestic inflation indices. On the 1978 price, this would mean an erosion of something like 65% in real terms, with a deflation to around $4.50/barrel — not very much more than the actual price before the 1973-74 rise.

Of course, the two sets of indices — OECD export and OPEC import — are in no way directly comparable. The former is on an f.o.b. basis and the latter c.i.f.; about 80% of the export trade of the industrialized countries is within the OECD area itself; and the types of goods and commodities traded between the industrialized countries are different from these imported by OPEC.

The implications of these OPEC import indices, anomalous though they may seem, cannot lightly be dismissed. Even making all possible allowances for factors which might raise the cost of OPEC imports (port congestion, quality of merchandise, etc.), it is difficult to avoid the suspicion of price discrimination against OPEC. Above all, it would mean that the massive transfer of resources from the West to OPEC, which was forecast as a consequence of the 1973-74 oil price jump, did not take place — or at least not on anything like the scale originally predicted.

The Head of OPEC's Economics and Finance Department, Mr. Adnan Al-Janabi, put the point forcefully in a recent paper on trade between the industrialized world and OPEC: "If we deflate OPEC imports by the OPEC Import Price Index, we will come to the conclusion that by far the biggest portion of OPEC revenues have been recycled to the industrialized countries through the new instrument of international income redistribution, i.e. inflation. The $93.6 billion of OPEC imports from the industrialized countries (in 1978) were worth only $25.2 billion in 1973 money. This means that the merchandise bought by the OPEC Countries did not increase materially in a manner commensurate with what is expected by them for the sale of their increasingly scarce oil. It means that the attempt by the OPEC Countries to effect a real transfer of resources through adjustments in the oil price has been only marginally successful. The material goods obtained by OPEC through spending nearly four times as much money in imports were only 70% more in quantity between 1973 and 1978."[23]

Some Misconceptions Examined

For the OPEC Countries the great upheaval of 1973-76 served to consolidate the process of change which finally put them in undisputed charge of their own economic destinies. But, on the other side of the coin, it also served to catapult OPEC into the forefront of public awareness on the world stage. Hitherto, OPEC's doings had been of interest mainly to oilmen and related specialists. Now, given OPEC's high profile, the tendency in the West was to blame OPEC for all the world's economic ills.

It is not within the scope of this work to examine all the manifold global effects of OPEC's price moves in any detail. But it would be worthwhile just to recapitulate some of the doomsday predictions which were constantly repeated in the West at the time of the 1973-74 crisis, and to see how these corresponded with reality up to 1978. Briefly, these may be summarized as follows:

— The oil price increase which raised the OECD net oil import bill from $35 billion in 1973 to $100 billion in 1974, or by roughly 2% of GNP, was the main cause of the 1974-75 recession and inflation.

— The oil price increase would undermine the entire world monetary system owing to the insuperable problem of recycling the financial surpluses of the so-called "low-absorbing" OPEC producers.

— The oil price increase would entail a massive transfer of real resources from the West to the OPEC oil producers.

— The oil price increase would deal a death-blow to the development prospects of the non-oil producing countries of the Third World, whose oil bill rose from $8 billion in 1973 to $24 billion in 1974, or by roughly 2.5% of GNP.

- By raising the price of oil so far so fast, the OPEC Countries would be cutting their own throats, since the new oil price level would stimulate the development of an avalanche of competing energy sources.

As was previously noted, it cannot logically be maintained that all the economic ills of 1974-75 were attributable to higher oil prices. For one thing the recessionary trend was already well under way before the oil price rise, due to contractionary measures initiated in some industrialized countries as a reaction to the already rampant inflation, which was in itself one of the causes of the OPEC drive towards a higher price for oil. Also, it is established that the oil price increase in itself made only a fairly modest contribution to subsequent inflation.

On the monetary side, the recycling of the cash surpluses of the oil producers proved to be no real problem, being handled quite adequately through conventional channels. Moreover, the import absorption capacity of the oil producers proved to be much higher than expected, with the value of total imports of the OPEC oil exporters rising from $21 billion in 1973 to $104 billion in 1978 and the overall current surplus, which had been as high as $59 billion in 1974, dropped to only $5 billion in 1978 (see table on page 181).

Also, as we have seen, the transfer of real resources from the industrialized world to OPEC was very much less than had originally been anticipated, owing to the loss of oil purchasing power through the ravages of inflation.

As far as the non-oil producing developing countries are concerned, they were at least reasonably well catered for by a combination of recycling of petrodollars via loans from commercial banks and an extensive programme of OPEC aid, both collective and by individual Member States, the flow of which totalled over $30 billion in the 1973-79 period (for details see Chapter XI). OPEC's record in this respect has been incomparably better than that of the industrialized world, with the major OPEC donors providing an average of 4 to 6% of their GNP in aid to the Third World, against around 0.3% for the industrialized countries. At the same time, some of the more advanced developing countries — Brazil, India, Pakistan, South Korea and Taiwan, for example — have benefited greatly from a major expansion of their exports of goods and services to the Middle East.

Despite the forecast of those like The Economist magazine of London, which in 1974 predicted that the world would be "glutted with energy" by 1980,[24] the 1973-74 oil price rise did not stimulate a bonanza flow of alternative sources of energy. Even the new price was not really high enough for this purpose and there was uncertainty (understandable enough) about the extent to which it would be maintained in real terms. (Luckily, though, the new price was high enough to bail out some of the North Sea oilfields where development would not otherwise have been economic.) In any case, quite apart from the long lead times involved, there is a tendency for the cost of alternatives simply to move on ahead of the price of oil, whatever it may be, particularly since many of the projects concerned (tar sands and shale especially) are themselves highly energy intensive. And those energy sources which are potentially competitive with oil, in electricity generation at any rate – coal and nuclear power, for example – are beset with environmental problems and other obstacles not always directly related to cost.* Natural gas, immense reserves of which are lying untapped in OPEC Countries, is undoubtedly a fuel of the future, but the problems involved in its pricing and transportation to market have to be solved first. Development of new energy and conservation in the use of energy are vital both for the consumers and the producers of oil, but it is not a matter of economics alone; both require a degree of political will which is often lacking.

For their part, the OPEC producers have also learned a number of lessons from the 1974-78 experience. One is that oil in the ground is a better investment than cash above ground, since the accumulated reserves of those oil producers which are in financial surplus have also been subject to erosion in real terms through the depredations of inflation and the depreciating dollar. The fact that some countries – Saudi Arabia in particular – continue to produce oil at rates far above what is necessary to meet their financial requirements is a function of their concern for the world economy rather than their own individual interests – a recognition also that they themselves cannot develop properly except within the context of a healthy world economy. But that does not make the financial sacrifice any less impalatable to public opinion in the countries concerned.

Another perhaps even more important lesson learned by the oil producers is that the pace of development should not be accelerated beyond the capacity of the country to absorb it in a meaningful way – economically, politically and socially. As the experience of Iran amply

* In this connection it is rather difficult to put much faith in the pledge, however praiseworthy, of the western leaders at the June 1980 Venice Summit to increase the supply of energy other than oil by 15 to 20 million b/d of oil equivalent over the next 10 years, mainly through expanded production of coal and nuclear power.

demonstrates, crash programmes for development are likely to be unproductive and dangerous for the very fabric of society. The oil producers, particularly these of the Gulf, are coming to feel that their developmental transformation should proceed at a more measured pace, and cannot possibly be completed in the span of a few five-year plans. One highly influental voice in the Gulf today — Kuwaiti Oil Minister Ali Khalifa Al-Sabah — believes that the process will occupy the better part of a century at the very least.[25] And the corollary of this is that the producers will need to spin out their oil reserves for longer than is suggested by the current reserves-to-production ratios (the 1979 average being around 40:1 for OPEC as a whole, with 50:1 in Saudi Arabia and 76:1 in Kuwait).

Both these lessons, it will be noted, tend to reinforce the OPEC trend towards oil production restraint and conservation of resources.

OPEC Revenues and Cash Surpluses 1973-80
($ Billion)

	1973	1974	1975	1976	1977	1978	1979[a]	1980[b]
Exports	42	116	107	132	145	146	212	306
Imports	21	39	58	68	84	104	102	138
Net services & transfers	-14	-17	-22	-28	-32	-37	-43	-54
Current surplus	8	59	27	36	29	5	67	114
Cumulative surplus		67	94	130	159	164	231	345
Estimated cash surplus invested in:		57.0	35.2	37.2	33.5	13.4	53.8	
United States		11.6	9.5	12.0	9.1	1.3	8.9	
United Kingdom		21.0	4.3	4.5	3.8	-1.8	17.2	
Other Countries		20.9	17.4	18.7	20.3	13.8	28.1	
International Organizations		3.5	4.0	2.0	0.3	0.1	-0.4	

a) *Estimates*
b) *Forecasts*
Source: *OECD Economic Outlook, July 1980*

CHAPTER VIII

THE IRANIAN CRISIS AND THE SECOND OIL PRICE EXPLOSION

In normal circumstances, given the strength of demand in the last quarter of 1978, crude oil production from Iran might have been expected to maintain its September near-capacity level of 6 million b/d through the fourth quarter. Instead, under the impact of oil workers' strike action against the Shah's regime, it declined to 5.5 million b/d in October, 3.5 million b/d in November and 2.3 million b/d in December. Towards the end of December oil exports were suspended, with only some 700,000 b/d being produced for local consumption. After the deposition of the Shah and the triumph of Ayatollah Khomeini, Iranian crude exports were resumed at the beginning of March 1979; production built up to a rhythm of around 4 million b/d, falling towards 3 million b/d in the last quarter of the year to make an overall 1979 average of 3.1 million b/d.

Part of the shortfall was offset by higher production elsewhere — notably Saudi Arabia whose output rose to over 10 million b/d in November and December (1 million b/d above October and 2 million b/d above September). No special government decision was necessary for this since, owing to the low output in the first half of the year, Aramco could maintain this high rate in the last quarter and remain well within the 8.5 million b/d average ceiling for the whole of the year 1978. However, in January 1979, the Saudi Government decided specifically to raise the allowable output to 9.5 million b/d for the first quarter of the year. Some further incremental production came from other OPEC Countries — particularly Iraq whose output rose by 1 million b/d from 2.5 million b/d in 1978 to 3.5 million b/d in 1979 — as well as non-OPEC sources, such as the North Sea, Mexico and Alaska. But this still left a substantial shortfall. In early January, US Energy Secretary James Schlesinger was estimating the non-Communist world's stock draw-down at some 2 million b/d out of total stocks of 3.8 billion barrels plus 700 million barrels in transit.

Although the supply situation overall was by no means catastrophic, it was bad enough to leave the consumers, the oil companies and the oil markets in general in a highly nervous condition. There was the fear that supplies from Iran might be further disrupted by political upheavals at any time. There was also uncertainty about how much

Iran's Revolutionary Government would want to produce for export, as well as forebodings about the technical maintenance of the oilfield production and export systems. All in all, the gut reaction of consumer governments and companies was to rebuild stocks at any cost and keep them replenished at the highest possible level.

It was basically this panic syndrome — the wages of fear one might say, fear of being caught without inventory and, above all, fear of losing contractual supply connections — which kept spot prices way up high for 18 months (even way into 1980 when all vestiges of physical shortage had evaporated and — irony of ironies — US, European and Japanese companies were, in effect, actually boycotting contractual crude supplies from Iran) and ensured that official prices would in the end climb up most of the way to meet them. And finally, in August 1980, they did so, with the declining spot price for Arabian Light meeting the ascending (mainstream OPEC, not Saudi) official price for the marker crude at the $32/barrel mark. Spot values for African crudes, meanwhile, had already plunged below official levels by around $2.50 per barrel (for comparison of spot and official prices 1978-80, see table on page 192).

In retrospect, it is possible to identify one crucial point of departure in the whole 1979-80 price explosion. This was in May 1979. By February, under the impact of the Iranian shutdown, the spot price for Arabian Light had risen to $23 per barrel (nearly $10 above the official price). Then, in March-April as Iranian exports resumed and production went back up to 4 million b/d, the market seemed to be cooling off a bit and the spot price went down to $21 per barrel. At this point, at the end of the first quarter, Saudi Arabia felt it safe to revert to its traditional ceiling of 8.5 million b/d as from April 1.

There was no immediate reaction in the market, but it soon became evident that some fundamental change in the logistics of the world oil supply system, for so long managed primarily by the major oil companies, had been set in motion. In the past, through their blanket arrangements with the producing countries, some of the majors had had access to large volumes of crude oil which were surplus to the requirements of their own integrated refining and marketing systems, and these supplies they resold to third parties mainly under term contracts. But the massive loss of automatic oil availability from Iran, in combination with other supply limitations elsewhere, had left the majors short of crude, even in some cases for their own requirements. The first thing the majors did was to try to cut back their deliveries to third parties as soon as possible, which was not always easy, particularly since OPEC Governments had directed the companies to continue supplying Third

World customers with the same volumes as previously.

On top of this came the loss to the majors' systems of a further 1 million b/d of Saudi crude in April. Whatever the exact motivation may have been, the fact is that the majors, which had hitherto generally lept aloof from spot crude purchases, entered the market in force as spot buyers in mid-May. The result was explosive indeed. Within a couple of weeks the Arabian Light spot price had shot up by an amazing $13/barrel to reach nearly $35/barrel, some $20 above Saudi Arabia's official price at that time. From then on the market never really looked back, and even Saudi Arabia's decision to let its production revert to 9.5 million b/d as from July 1, had little impact. Being already so close to its capacity output (perhaps 10 to 10.5 million b/d), Saudi Arabia did not have much leverage to control or even influence the lumbering advance of prices, as one OPEC producer after another, sometimes in co-ordination, sometimes not, moved its effectively realized prices forwards step by step towards the goal of the spot market level.

For any kind of understanding of what was actually happening in OPEC during the rather chaotic period of 1979-80, it is necessary to recognize the key role of the spot market. Often castigated by consumers as unrepresentative (but only when it is on the upswing), the spot market covers perhaps no more than 5 to 10% of the oil trade depending on circumstances. But it does provide a vital indicator as to the price that the oil barrel will fetch at the margin at any given time.

For the producing countries, any substantial gap between spot prices and official prices simply means a potential profit to other people at the producers' expense. There is really no way of avoiding this. In cases where sellers are charging different price levels for their crudes, refined product prices will inevitably tend to move to cover the cost of the highest priced crude whose supply is necessary to meet market demand. Therefore, the benefit of the cheaper crude price goes not to the ultimate consumer — and certainly not, of course, to the seller of the first resort, the producing country — but to the man in the middle, be he the oil company that refines and markets the oil, or perhaps, in some cases, the trader or broker who manages to get access to some of the cheaper crude on the ground floor and to resell it at the open market price. (Officially, OPEC Governments frown on selling crude to anyone who is not an end user, that is to say a refiner/marketer, in his own right, but somehow the enterprising traders and brokers always seem to muscle in on the act.)

This, incidentally, is where the Saudis find themselves in a most uncomfortable dilemma. If, out of a desire to put a brake on headlong crude price surges, they keep their official crude price below that of the other OPEC Countries, there is no way they can channel this differential to benefit the consumer rather than the Aramco companies. The Saudis can, and do, oblige the Aramco companies to sell the crude (which mostly goes to their own affiliates) at the cheaper Saudi official price; and they can police these transactions right up the entrance to the refinery. But once the oil is processed and marketed as products, the profit to be gained from having access to cheaper crude supplies than one's competitors will end up in the pockets of the US majors which participate in Aramco, and there is nothing Saudi Arabia can do about it.

Of course, product prices in the inland domestic markets of the big consuming areas tend to lag behind the spot market, both on the upside and the downside. But they are undoubtedly influenced by strong and persistent trends on the open market, just as they are influenced by increases in the cost of crude. A PIW analysis of domestic market prices in six key European countries (Britain, France, Germany, Italy, Belgium and the Netherlands) in 1979-80 shows that in the fourth-quarter of 1979 the netback from product values for a barrel of Arabian Light crude was very much higher when calculated on the basis of spot prices than in inland market prices ($36.47/barrel spot Rotterdam, $26.06/ barrel inland). But by July 1980, the position had entirely turned around, with the inland value having risen to $32.66/barrel and the spot net-back having fallen to $31.59/barrel.[1]

A prolonged and overwhelming ascendancy of the spot market over official prices for crude such as occurred in 1979-80 naturally presents an almost irresistable challenge to the astute marketing chiefs of the OPEC Countries. If, for any reason, it is inappropriate to raise official prices all the way up, then other ways must be found of closing the price gap: imposing covert or overt premiums above the official price; selling on the spot market oneself; or entering into so-called processing deals whereby the producing country either refines crude on its own account or shares the extra profit from the refined barrel with the crude off-taker. All these means were employed, with no small measure of success, during the crisis of 1979-80.

Abu Dhabi Deal Falls Apart

In December 1978, against a background of tightening supplies and soaring spot prices for crude — to say nothing of the political fall-out emanating from the general Arab disenchantment over the Camp David agreements — it was hardly surprising that Saudi Arabia was neither able nor willing to engage in price polemics with its OPEC partners at th price-fixing Conference in Abu Dhabi.

The indications are that Saudi Arabia had originally hoped to contain the 1979 price increase within the 5 to 10% bracket, with the emphasis on the lower end. However, with the advent of the revolution in Iran, the initiative passed to the OPEC mainstream which was looking towards 15% or more. After a series of OPEC-wide consultations, the decisive bargain was struck early in December during a visit to Saudi Arabia by the Kuwaiti Prime Minister, Sheikh Saad al-Abdullah Al-Sabah, and his Minister of Oil, Sheikh Ali Khalifa Al-Sabah, who was well briefed to represent the OPEC mainstream. It was there that the basic understanding was reached on the average 10% price increase for 1979, to be carried out in stages starting at 5% in the first quarter and ending up with 14.5% in the last quarter. All that really remained to be done at the Abu Dhabi Conference was to choose the precise pattern for the quarterly increments. The compromise had something for everyone: the doves could stress the containment within the 10% average for the year, while the hawks could emphasize the 14.5% culmination.

For the record, the Abu Dhabi formula — neat and elegant, but doomed to be overtaken by events before very long — would have brought about the following result over the year 1979:

		Increase	
Date	Govt. Sale Price	%	$/b
Dec. 1978	12.700		
Jan. 1, 1979	13.335	5.000	0.635
April 1, 1979	13.843	3.809	0.508
July 1, 1979	14.161	2.294	0.318
Oct. 1, 1979	14.542	2.691	0.381

Average Increase Year 1979/Year 1978 — 10%
% Increase Oct. 1, 1979/Dec. 1978   — 14.5%
$/b Increase Oct. 1, 1979/Dec. 1978   — $1.842

By February 1979, with exports from Iran shut down and spot prices nearly $10 above official levels, the Abu Dhabi deal began to split at the seams. First Abu Dhabi and Qatar ($1), then Libya ($0.68), then Kuwait and Iraq ($1.20) and finally Libya again ($0.70) slapped market premiums and/or surcharges on their crude prices.

At the next OPEC Conference in Geneva at the end of March, ideas on prices were so divergent that any attempt at unification was clearly hopeless. In the end an agree-to-disagree compromise was reached, which in effect, simply resulted in a multi-tier price structure. At the level of the lowest common denominator, Saudi Arabia agreed to go along as far as advancing to the originally scheduled fourth-quarter price with effect from April 1, which meant an Arabian Light marker crude price of $14.456/barrel. On top of that, however, everyone else was left perfectly free to load on top whatever surcharge or premium he chose. At first there was a plan to standardize the surcharges at $1.20 per barrel (over the original fourth-quarter prices) but this soon broke down, as first the UAE and Qatar, and then Iran and Kuwait set the surcharge level at $1.80/barrel. For their part, the African producers raised their differential premium over the Arabian Light marker to $4/barrel, as against the previous $1.50/barrel, to reach price levels in the $18.50/barrel area.

In mid-May, as we noted earlier, spot prices crashed through the $30 barrier and up to nearly $35 after crude-hungry major oil companies entered the market in force. Not surprisingly, premiums and surcharges flew thick and fast. In the Gulf, Iran escalated the surcharge to $3.80 for an Iranian Light price of $18.47 per barrel. Not to be outdone, the African producers reacted by pushing out ahead to prices beyond the $21 mark — $6.50 above Arabian Light.

In June, some of the Gulf oil exporters, notably Iraq and Kuwait — irked by the African leap forward, produced the ultimate in anti-leapfrog measures: the introduction of a most-favoured-seller clause into their crude sales contracts, on the basis of which the two governments announced that they would bill customers for June liftings on the basis of the highest premium charged by any other OPEC producer above the original fourth-quarter price — in the event the $5.31/barrel clocked up by Libya.

Floor and Ceiling in Geneva

When the OPEC Oil Ministers met again in Geneva at the end of June 1979, there was a general recognition that something ought to be done to stem the price disorder, but no consensus on how to go about it. The compromise agreement cobbled together with considerable difficulty did have the merit of clamping a ceiling of $23.50/barrel on the official prices of all OPEC crudes. It also limited market premiums or surcharges to $2 per barrel, but this limit was rather easily evaded by some countries which simply increased their differentials to unrealistic levels instead. For its part, Saudi Arabia agreed to increase the price of the Arabian Light marker to $18 per barrel.

The trouble was that between the two price poles — Saudi Arabia's $18 and the $23.50 ceiling for light African crudes — all was confusion. Traditional differential alignments between the various crudes had simply been thrown out of the window. In the Gulf it was possible to distinguish three different effective marker price levels — $18 employed by Saudi Arabia, $20 used by Iraq, Kuwait, the UAE and Qatar, and $22 practised by Iran. However, these differences scarcely mattered so long as there was no problem in selling crude at any price in the prevailing tight market.

Confusion in Caracas

The OPEC June agreement on a ceiling price was at best a threadbare compromise. Nobody expected it to last very long, particularly if spot prices remained high thereby exerting the usual magnetic upward pull on official prices. In the event, the spot market not only held firm, but, after slipping a little to $32/barrel for Arabian Light in July, rose strongly through the second half of 1979 to end the year around the $40/barrel mark — an all-time record.

Statistics show that crude oil supplies during the last three quarters of 1979 were more than adequate to meet basic consumer demand. (Non-Communist world oil demand rose by 850,000 b/d or 1.7% from 51.08 million b/d in 1978 to 51.93 million b/d in 1979; while OPEC production increased by 1,035,000 b/d, or 3.5%, from 29.805 million b/d in 1978 to 30.840 million b/d in 1979). There was thus quite a substantial build-up of stocks during the last part of the year, partly to make up for the first-quarter draw-down and partly to keep overall stock levels abnormally high in view of the disturbing uncertainty factors. These included the risk of a further disruption of supplies as a result of political upheaval in Iran or elsewhere; the breaking up of normal supply channels owing to the widespread displacement of the major international companies as bulk crude offtakers from the producing countries; the fact that long-term crude supply contracts were up for renewal at the end of 1979 in a number of OPEC Countries; and the prevalent warnings of 1980 crude oil supply cuts by several OPEC

Members. Fear rather than shortage was, therefore, the dominant force behind the buoyant market in the second half of 1979.

The OPEC ceiling held for a few months but broke up in mid-October when the Iranians put up the price of Iranian Light to the ceiling level of $23.50/barrel. This meant that there was no differential premium left for African crude above Iranian Light in the Gulf. Libya, followed by Nigeria and Algeria, promptly riposted by jettisoning the ceiling and raising their official prices to $26.27/barrel.

In mid-December, came an abortive Saudi-inspired bid to reunify prices. In a co-ordinated move a few days before the OPEC Conference was due to convene in Caracas, Venezuela, three Gulf producers — Saudi Arabia, the United Arab Emirates and Qatar — raised their official prices by $6/barrel and Venezuela joined them the same day with a matching increase of $4 (taking into consideration Venezuela's existing $2 surcharge). They evidently hoped that by raising prices before the Caracas Conference, they would be able to muster enough middle-of-th road support for the new marker price of $24/barrel to achieve a general price reunification at this level, thereby, in the words of the Venezuelan Oil Minister, Dr. Humberto Calderon-Berti, "clipping the wings of the price hawks".

However, the plan misfired. The hawks — mainly the African producers and Iran — refused to have their wings clipped or even trimmed and pressed for a higher marker price. There was also renewed controversy over differentials, with the heavier crude producers in the Gulf objecting to the differential premiums claimed by the producers of light crude, which they argued were not true differentials at all but scarcity premiums made possible by the distorted market, and which would have to be restored to normal if a proper price structure was to be re-established.

There was thus no price decision at all at Caracas, and multi-tier pricing continued to be the order of the day, with individual producers going their own separate ways. After Caracas, some of the Gulf states aligned on a $26/barrel marker, while the Africans, led by Libya, pushed on ahead to $35/barrel. Iran, for its part, adopted an individual stand at $30/barrel in January rising to $32.50 in February.

At Caracas there had been speculation about a deal between Saudi Arabia and the middle-of-the-road group — Iran, Kuwait, the United Arab Emirates, Qatar, Venezuela and Indonesia — that if Saudi Arabia were to go up to $26/barrel within a few weeks, the others would stay at that level and so some degree of price reunification would be achieved. At the end of January 1980 Saudi Arabia did raise the price of Arabian

Light to $26/barrel, but all that happened was that the others moved on ahead by a further $2.

However, there were definite signs that the hectic days of the price explosion were numbered. In April, when Iran put up its price to $35/barrel in a move not followed by any other OPEC Country, its main European and Japanese customers stopped lifting Iranian crude (thus doing for price reasons what they were in any case being urged by their governments to do for political reasons to support the US over the hostage issue).

In May, Saudi Arabia raised the price of Arabian Light by $2/barrel in order to narrow the price gap with the rest of OPEC and to mop up some of the excess profits being amassed by the Aramco companies as a result of their access to cheap Saudi crude. However, this step, too, was taken as a signal for another $2/barrel rise everywhere else.

By the time OPEC met again in Algiers in June 1980, the market atmosphere had calmed down a bit, but not yet enough to secure price reunification. However, certain price guidelines were established. A ceiling of $32/barrel was set for the marker crude, on which the OPEC majority aligned itself, leaving Saudi Arabia at $28/barrel and Iran still ahead of the field with an unchanged $35/barrel. A maximum differential of $5/barrel was fixed for premium crudes, which allowed for an African crude price of $37/barrel. At this level the Gulf marker price was still below the current spot level of $35/barrel, but the African price was roughly in line with the spot market.

By August, despite production cuts as from the second quarter by Kuwait (600,000 - 700,000 b/d), Libya (400,000 b/d) and perforce Iran (800,000 b/d), an oversupply situation was beginning to reassert itself, just as the Saudis (still producing at 9.5 million b/d) had predicted it would. Oil demand in the main industrial countries was down by 7.8% in the first four months of 1980, a fall of 2.9 million b/d, while non-OPEC oil production rose by 4% or 800,000 b/d. This was bound to have its effect on OPEC output, which dropped by 7.5% to 28.4 million b/d in the first half of the year with a further decline being forecast for the second half. Spot prices too had begun to come down, meeting the ceiling price for the marker at $32/barrel in the Gulf in August; while by that time the spot price for African crudes had fallen to $33.50/barrel — $3.50 below the official level of $37.

From the perspective of August 1980 the calming of the market augured well for a possible reunification of OPEC prices in September, as part of the run-up to the scheduled OPEC Summit Conference in Baghdad in November. If such reunification occurs, Saudi Arabia has pledged to cut production and go back to its traditional 8.5 million b/d ceiling.

In view of the 1980 demand weakness, some such production cutback moves on the part of those OPEC States which raised output during the crisis period — i.e. mainly Saudi Arabia and Iraq — will be required if Iran is even to restore its output to the 3 million b/d which is now held to be the preferred level by the Tehran authorities. Actual Iranian production had fallen as low as 1.5 million b/d (with an export volume of only 700,000 b/d) by mid-1980 after the suspension of liftings by major European and Japanese customers.

A Formula for the Future?

One of the ideas that OPEC's Long-Term Strategy Committee will be submitting to the Baghdad Summit in November 1980 is a formula for the future pricing of oil, which would also involve a degree of production management to help to keep the price steady in times of glut and shortage. Under the formula, there would be a floor price for crude which would be adjusted on a quarterly basis in line with the following:
(a) An index reflecting the impact of inflation on international trade composed roughly two-thirds of an OECD export price index (to reflect merchandise) and one-third of an OECD domestic consumer price index (to reflect services).
(b) An automatic exchange rate adjustment factor based on the basket of the nine Geneva I currencies plus the US dollar.
(c) In addition to the two above elements, which would serve to keep prices constant in real terms, there would also be a provision for increasing the floor prices in real terms proportionately to the growth in real GNP of the OECD countries.

The formula was accepted by nine out of the 12 OPEC Members present (Nigeria being absent) at the Conference held in Taif, Saudi Arabia, in May 1980. The other three — Iran, Algeria and Libya — expressed reservations, the main one being that the inflation index should be based on OPEC import inflation rather than OECD inflation.[2]

Formula pricing is a tricky business at the best of times, and previous attempts to work out something on these lines have not been very encouraging. In something so volatile and strategic as the oil business, price formulas are always in danger of being blown apart by one crisis or another. But both OPEC and the world as a whole would be better off if the recurring oil price cycle of erosion followed by explosion could be broken.

Comparison of Spot and Official Prices 1978-80
($/Barrel)

| | Gulf — Arabian Light (34°) | | | | | Libyan Zuetina (41°) | | |
	Spot	Off.(1)	Off.(2)	Diff.(1)	Diff.(2)	Spot	Off.	Diff.
1978								
Jan.	12.65	12.70	12.70	-0.05	-0.05	13.85	14.0	-0.20
Feb.	12.65	12.70	12.70	-0.05	-0.05	13.85	14.0	-0.20
March	12.65	12.70	12.70	-0.05	-0.05	13.75	14.0	-0.30
April	12.67	12.70	12.70	-0.03	-0.03	13.75	13.90	-0.15
May	12.72	12.70	12.70	+0.02	+0.02	13.75	13.90	-0.15
June	12.72	12.70	12.70	+0.02	+0.02	13.75	13.90	-0.15
July	12.77	12.70	12.70	+0.07	+0.07	13.75	13.90	-0.15
Aug.	12.79	12.70	12.70	+0.09	+0.09	13.85	13.90	0.05
Sept.	12.80	12.70	12.70	+0.10	+0.10	14.00	13.90	+0.10
Oct.	13.00	12.70	12.70	+0.30	+0.30	14.50	13.90	+0.60
Nov.	14.90	12.70	12.70	+2.20	+2.20	16.25	13.90	+2.35
Dec.	15.00	12.70	12.70	+2.30	+2.30	16.75	13.90	+2.85
1979								
Jan.	17.50	13.40	13.40	+4.10	+4.10	19.75	14.74	+5.01
Feb.	23.00	13.40	13.40	+9.60	+9.60	26.00	15.42	+10.58
March	21.00	13.40	13.40	+7.60	+7.60	24.00	16.12	+7.88
April	21.50	14.55	16.35	+6.95	+5.15	24.50	18.30	+6.20
May	34.50	14.55	16.95	+19.95	+17.55	36.00	21.31	+14.69
June	34.00	18.00	18.00	+16.00	+16.00	36.50	21.31	+15.19
July	32.00	18.00	20.00	+14.00	+12.00	36.00	23.50	+12.50
Aug.	34.00	18.00	20.00	+16.00	+14.00	36.00	23.50	+12.50
Sept.	35.00	18.00	20.00	+17.00	+15.00	37.00	23.50	+13.50
Oct.	38.00	18.00	22.00	+20.00	+16.00	40.50	26.27	+14.23
Nov.	40.00	24.00	26.00	+16.00	+14.00	43.00	26.27	+16.73
Dec.	39.00	24.00	26.00	+15.00	+13.00	41.50	30.00	+11.50
1980								
Jan.	38.00	26.00	28.00	+12.00	+10.00	41.00	34.72	+6.28
Feb.	36.00	26.00	28.00	+10.00	+8.00	38.50	34.72	+3.78
March	36.00	26.00	28.00	+10.00	+8.00	38.00	34.72	+3.28
April	35.00	28.00	28.00	+7.00	+7.00	37.50	34.72	+2.78
May	35.50	28.00	30.00	+7.50	+5.50	38.50	36.72	+1.78
June	36.00	28.00	30.00	+8.00	+6.00	37.50	36.72	+0.78

192

	Gulf — Arabian Light (34°)					Libyan Zuetina (41°)		
	Spot	Off.(1)	Off.(2)	Diff.(1)	Diff.(2)	Spot	Off.	Diff.
July	34.50	28.00	32.00	+6.50	+2.50	36.50	37.00	-0.50
Aug.	32.00	28.00	32.00	+4.00	—	33.50	37.00	-3.50

Off. (1) — Official sale price set by Saudi Arabia for Arabian Light marker crude.

Off. (2) — Theoretical official price for marker crude used by other Gulf producers.

Marker Crude Prices 1978-80
($/Barrel)

	1978	1979		1980		% Increase	
	Dec.	Jan.	Dec.	Jan.	July	July'80	Dec'78
Saudi Arabia	12.70	13.40	24.00	26.00	28.00	120.5	
Others	12.70	13.40	26.00	28.00	32.00	152.0	

CHAPTER IX

CONTROL OF PRODUCTION

In the original Middle East concession agreements, mainly concluded between the two world wars, oil companies were granted the "exclusive right to explore, prospect, drill for, extract, treat, manufacture, transport, deal with, carry away and export" petroleum and other hydrocarbons found within the area of the concession. This particular wording happens to come from the 1933 agreement between Saudi Arabia and the Standard Oil Company of California, but all the others are remarkably similar. More importantly they were all interpreted (by the companies at least) to mean that, subject to technical observance of what is known as "first-class oilfield practice" and in certain cases to stipulated minimum levels of production, the companies concerned were free to produce and export as much, or as little, as they wanted or were able to sell.

Particularly in the quarter of a century, which followed the Second World War, this freedom to decide upon output levels in the various producing countries was a source of enormous strength for the major multinational oil companies with their high degree of horizontal integration – which means to say that, severally and collectively, they owned and controlled a wide variety of crude oil sources across the globe. This, in conjunction with the interlocking pattern of ownership by the majors of the various operational consortia in the producing areas, conferred on the companies the means to co-ordinate and plan the bulk of non-Communist world oil supply entirely in relation to the market requirements of the industrialized West and the convenience (technical, financial and logistic) of their own integrated systems, without necessarily showing much regard for the particular needs of the countries where the oil was produced.

For the producer governments, on the other hand, the privation of the power of decision-making on oil production levels, as well as on pricing and management of operations, was tantamount to a loss of sovereignty in an extremely vital area of the life of their countries. It was as if an essential steering mechanism was missing from the ship of state. It was difficult, if not well-nigh impossible, to plan for the overall development of a country's economy so long as the massively dominant oil sector remained a self-contained enclave, a state within a state subservient to the dictates of international rather than national exigencies.

This does not mean to say that the companies always had an easy time in determining the production rates of individual areas or countries within the overall market requirement. They were, of course, constantly subject to more or less intense pressure from one producer government or another with a view to boosting production to meet revenue needs. This meant that a perpetual balancing act was required to keep the various countries satisfied. But, when all was said and done, it was the companies who were the arbiters of the final share-out of overall market growth among the producing countries. It was they, in effect, who served almost as a sort of global authority for the prorationing or programming of oil production, albeit with increasing difficulty as the years went by.

Also, in those days when many oil producing countries were still beset by financial problems, the companies could, and did, make use of their ultimate discretionary control over production rates in their various areas of operation as a highly effective bargaining counter in any disputes that arose between them and individual producer governments.

Naturally enough, the majors were jealous defenders of what they insisted on as their contractual right to determine production rates wherever they operated. (When, in 1965, there was a question of Saudi Arabia joining a tentative OPEC effort at oil production programming involving output quotas, Aramco protested and threatened to take the government to international arbitration on the matter. Similar protests were made by companies operating in Iran and Libya.) But it is difficult, with hindsight, to see how such an attitude could have persisted if a determined exercise of state sovereignty had been brought to bear. And, in the early 1970s when the governments began issuing orders that production levels should be cut back for technical, economic or political reasons, the companies had no alternative but to comply.

Probably it would be true to say that the roots of the problem were practical rather than legal. When it came to a question of cutting back an already established production level or future target, no private company could contest an unequivocal government order to this effect, whatever the contractual position. But if the government command envisaged an increase rather than a reduction in production, the situation became quite different. The company concerned could turn around to the government and argue that it could not comply for practical reasons — because, given the prevailing market, it could not boost its sales of that country's oil without aggressive price competition (which the government would be unlikely to endorse).

195

In such a case, the only course open to the government, if it insisted on raising output, would be to take some of the production and sell it itself. Here, there was a minefield of further snags, both practical and contractual. Under the old-style concession agreements, the governments had no right to take any part of the production for export on their own account, except for the so-called 12.5% royalty oil entitlement which the governments could take in cash or kind. But since this royalty crude was valued and invoiced at the full posted price — and during the late 1950s and 1960s crude oil was being sold at substantial discounts off posted prices — such sales would inevitably be a losing proposition for the governments, on a unit revenue basis anyway.

So whereas it was feasible, though prior to 1970 by no means easy, for a determined government, if it so wished, to order a reduction in or place a ceiling on its oil production, it was not at all a simple matter to pressure the operating companies into raising output beyond the level they had projected. Any increase in one country's rate of growth would have to be achieved at the expense of other areas; one could not sell more than the market, which throughout the Sixties was soft and competitive, could absorb; and, by and large, the market itself was dominated by the same major companies that operated the oil-fields in the producing countries. Increased output, therefore, was not something that could be effected by government fiat.

Up to around 1970 nobody (except to some extent Venezuela, which was in any case not bound by the same contractual limitations on its freedom of action as the Middle East producers) was thinking very seriously about limiting production; the tentative and abortive OPEC production programme of 1965-66 was conceived as a means for rational share-out of projected growth to alleviate pressure on prices, not as an attempt to cut back production. Although in the 1960s OPEC had succeeded arresting the decline of, and even slightly improving its members' unit oil revenue in current dollars, the unit revenue was still being subject to erosion in real terms through the decade and the producing countries were dependent on growth in export volumes to meet their increasing financial needs. This was particularly true of the high absorbers like Iran, but in the 1960s none of the major producers, with the possible exception of Kuwait, was in a position of really comfortable financial surplus.

Thus, from 1945 to 1970 the tendency was for individual producers to want to maximize output. Although this made for balancing head-aches for the companies, it also put them in the strong position of being able to play off one country against another.

196

From 1970 onwards, three converging currents rapidly demolished the major companies' control over crude production volumes. One was the trend towards conservation exemplified by the actions of Libya (1970) and Kuwait (1972) in reducing their long-term output targets; another was the exercise of sovereign power by the Arab governments in 1973 to impose production cutbacks and destination embargoes in support of the Arab war effort; and, finally, there was the takeover by the producer governments, via participation and/or nationalization, of majority control over the producing ventures. In addition to control over management of operations, this gave them access to large volumes of crude for direct government sale, while drastically curtailing the automatic availability of crude to the majors.

In the light of all this, it can be seen that a change of very considerable international significance has taken place. Until a few years ago, the OPEC producers had no choice but to allow their oil to be depleted at whatever rates appeared to be most convenient to the western industrial economy. Now, the industrialized world is having to get used to the prospects of adapting to rates of supply decided upon by the OPEC Countries. The latter have shown themselves to be responsive to the needs of the consumers, with Saudi Arabia and Iraq, for example, having raised output substantially to fill the gap during the Iranian crisis; but the national interests of the producers, individual and collective, can no longer be ignored as a major factor in determining the supply/demand balance.

The Volume-Conscious Sixties

Judging the relative performances of individual Middle East producers during the 1960s, one is struck by two things in particular: on the one hand, the poor showing of Iraq which throughout most of the decade was in constant dispute with its concessionaire companies; and on the other hand, the better than average results of Iran, where persistent pressure was applied by the Shah to get the Consortium to raise output. And in the background, there was the frenetic expansion in Libya, from zero in 1960 to 3.3 million b/d in 1970, which siphoned off a large part of the growth that would otherwise have gone to the Middle East. The comparison is shown in the table overleaf.

That Iraq was punished by the companies with loss of volume in terms of production growth relative to the rest of the Middle East and Africa during the 1960s is an established fact of history. Despite the fact that the dispute centred mainly on as yet underdeveloped areas of the concession (though including a northward extension of the Rumaila oilfield) which were repossessed by the state under Law No. 80 of 1961 after the failure of government-company negotiations on relinquishment of acreage, participation and other matters, output from the existing oil-fields was held down and expansion of capacity from these fields (for which there was plenty of scope particularly in the south) was more or less frozen for the decade. In this lay the roots of the anti-company bit-terness in Iraq which culminated in the nationalization of IPC in 1972.

OPEC Crude Output Increases 1960-70
(Thousand b/d)

| | Production | | Increase | | |
	1960	1970	Volume	%	% Annual Avge.
OPEC Middle East	5,221	13,309	8,088	155	9.8
— Saudi Arabia	1,314	3,799	2,485	189	11.3
— Iran	1,068	3,829	2,743	259	13.7
— Kuwait	1,692	2,990	1,298	77	5.9
— Iraq	972	1,549	577	59	3.4
OPEC Africa	200	5,539	5,339	2,670	41.7
— Libya	—	3,318	3,318	—	—
All OPEC	8,697	23,413	14,716	169	10.4

In the 1974 US Senate Hearings on multinational oil companies and US foreign policy, two senior officials of Exxon — George Piercy and Howard Page — admitted that no expansion had taken place in Iraq due to the government-company disputes dating back to the Qasim regime at the beginning of the 1960s. Page also acknowledged that the stagnation in Iraq had to a large extent let the companies off the hook in so far as expanding output in other countries was concerned. Questioned by Senator Charles Percy about this, Page came out with a revealing reply about the major companies' production predicament in the 1960s. The full exchange went as follows:

Percy:
"Given Libya's capture of most of the growth in Eastern Hemisphere production during the 1960s and the severe problems this created in Iran and Saudi Arabia, what would have happened if Iraqi production had also surged when there was a heavy glut of production facilities?"

198

Page:

"I admit we would have been in one tough problem, and we would have had to lower our liftings from the Consortium that we could possibly take there and meet the agreement. Remember we were taking more than the agreement called for out of Iran, you see, and we were taking an equal amount, though, from Saudi Arabia. We would have had to cut back on both of these, and we would have had to slow down our development of Libya, which nobody wanted to do. But this was discussed at a time when people came to me and said: 'Can you swallow this amount of oil?' And, of course, with Iraq down, the answer was: 'Yes, I am going to have a lot of problems and some tough problems, but I will undertake to do it'. And I was successful, that is all I can say. But if Iraq had come on, it would have been that much harder; but we would have done it, because we weren't going to lose any concessions because of this".[1]

Thus, as James Akins of the US State Department's Office of Fuels and Energy wrote in 1968, the companies were "disinvesting" rather than investing in Iraq: "They are taking as much oil out of Iraq as they can while it is still there to take, but there is no question of growth or new facilities".[2]

Another country that felt hard done by during the 1960s was Kuwait, which attributed the stagnation in its production in the mid-1960s to retaliation by the companies against the National Assembly's refusal to ratify the royalty expensing agreement. In 1966 Kuwait and Iraq jointly sponsored an OPEC Resolution (No. XI. 73) which, after noting that the unsatisfactory rate of production growth in some Member Countries could not be ascribed to lack of international outlets and deploring the "manipulation" of production by the oil companies concerned, declared that "should these rates of growth not be improved to satisfactory levels during the year 1966, full support of all OPEC Members shall be given to efforts made by the countries concerned to safeguard their legitimate national interests." After the issue of the Resolution, production rates in the two countries did show a marginal improvement in the second half of 1966.

As regards the three big-volume achievers during the 1960s — Iran, Saudi Arabia and Libya — the spectacular growth in Libya from zero in 1960 to 3.3 million b/d in 1970 was a natural result of the bonanza-type situation in that country, being a newly discovered oil province where a wide diversity of companies, including quite a few US independents striking it rich with foreign oil for the first time, were eager to recover their investment and start the profits rolling in the shortest possible time. In the Middle East, on the other hand, the centre of gravity of the oil industry, the two contenders for the lion's share of the growth were Iran and Saudi Arabia. The former (having itself been penalized by the companies with zero exports during the 1951-53 nationalization crisis) was anxious to regain its position as the leading producer in the Middle East — a position to which, in the Shah's eyes, Iran had a "right" by virtue of its having the largest population among the Middle East countries and therefore the greatest needs and potential for development. For its part Saudi Arabia, though in a more comfortable financial situation than Iran, was anxious not to fall behind in the production growth stakes.

At the time of the 1954 agreement the Consortium members had given Iran a commitment that its production increases would keep pace with Middle East growth as a whole, and in particular with the growth in liftings by Consortium members from other Middle East countries. But this was not sufficient for the Shah. In 1960, he had maintained that at least half of Middle Eastern oil production growth should accrue to Iran; and when Iran's expenditure requirements began to outpace oil revenues, the Shah's demands grew more insistent as the decade progressed. From 1966 to 1971, an annual row took place between the government and the Consortium on production levels. In 1966, the Iranians initially demanded a 17% annual output growth in order to meet the needs of Iran's budget and development plan, not to mention the burgeoning expenditure on armaments necessitated by the Shah's ambition to transform Iran into a major conventional military power with dominant regional responsibility for the security of the Gulf. In December 1966, agreement was reached on the basis that the Consortium would ensure Iran an 11% annual increment in its programmed production for 1967 and 1968, plus relinquishment of 25% of its concession area, and delivery to the National Iranian Oil Company of 20 million tons of royalty oil over the five-year period 1967-71 on preferential terms (a price half-way between tax-paid cost and the posted price, rather than the full posted price) with its use by NIOC specifically restricted to barter deals with certain East European countries. In fact, owing to the disruptions of the 1967 Arab-Israeli war, Iran's production increased by 22% in 1967, followed by 9% in 1968.

Early in 1968, the Shah changed the focus of his demands from oil production to meeting Iran's financial needs. Henceforth, the Consortium would be required either to raise production to satisfy the budget or, failing that, provide the equivalent in cash revenue by one means or another. To this end, the Consortium was presented with a formal notification specifying the annual revenue requirements of the 1968-72 five-year plan which it would be expected to meet.

From then on, various expedients were employed to bridge the gap between projected Consortium production and Iran's revenue needs, among them: changeover from the Gregorian to the Persian calendar which allowed for a one-shot boost of an extra three months revenue for the 1968-69 financial year; various payment advances on future revenues; increase of the Consortium's throughput and liftings of refined products; and a liberalization of the financial rules for "overlifting" as between the member companies of the Consortium (the crude-short members of the group had long been pressing for a reduction in the extra cost of oil lifted in excess of their equity entitlements). Finally, the annual confrontation between Iran and the oil companies on production and revenues was defused by the price increases of the early 1970s.

The Saudis, although at times patently irked by the Shah's successful campaign to boost Iran's share of oil output growth, did not make too much fuss about it. They could rest secure in the knowledge that, whereas Iran's production was fast nearing its physical peak, their own future oil primacy was assured by virtue of Saudi Arabia's enormous reserves.

Although the oil companies evidently had trouble in allocating the shares of individual producing countries in the overall demand growth of the 1960s, they were to be criticized later on for not having expanded capacity sufficiently during this period, thereby opening the way for the supply crunch of 1972-73.[3] It is true that, despite their pleas about unanticipated production constraints beyond their control in various countries, the companies did badly understimate the strength of oil demand in their forecasts for the late Sixties and early Seventies. On the other hand, it is also true to observe that the crunch was bound to come sooner or later, because supply could never have kept up with that unrestrained pace of demand for very long, even under the most favourable circumstances.

OPEC Production Programming 1965-66

From the producers' point of view, the major companies failed rather dismally in one aspect of their balancing act with regard to oil supplies in the 1960s. They were not able, as they had been at times in the past, to regulate supplies in such a way as to keep the downward pressure off prices. So, in 1965, OPEC made a rather half-hearted effort at doing the job itself by means of production programming.

It will be recalled (Chapter III) that, by a gentlemen's agreement between Venezuela and the Middle East Members of OPEC, the subject of the production programming (or prorationing as it was then generally called) had been left aside pending the settlement of the royalty expensing problem, on the understanding that it should be taken up again afterwards. So, in the mid-1960s with realized prices for crude oil still weak and subject to heavy discounts off postings, pressure from Venezuela finally succeeded in persuading the still reluctant Middle Eastern and African producers to give the idea a try.

As well as helping to firm up prices, another aim of the programme was to wrest the controlling power over offtake decisions out of the hands of the major companies, and thereby provide individual Member Countries with a greater degree of predictability in forecasting their oil production and revenues and consequently in planning their budget and development expenditure. Although, the overall rate of growth for Middle East crude as a whole did not vary very greatly from year to year during the Sixties, output figures of individual producers fluctuated widely — often for reasons other than commercial, as we have seen. "Is it reasonable," declared a 1965 OPEC explanatory memorandum in defence of the production programme, "to ask the producing countries, whose future must depend on the planned and orderly use of revenues from one source, to sit by and watch their revenues fluctuate unpredictably from year to year, simply because the power to shift around offtake programmes is solely in the hands of the major international companies?"[4]

Thus it was at its IX Conference in Tripoli, Libya, in July 1965, that OPEC formally adopted — as a "transitory measure" with a view to counteracting the continuing erosion of crude and product prices — what it described as a "production plan calling for rational increases in production from the OPEC area to meet estimated increases in world demand."

The price problem in the 1960s was not, of course, a question of surplus production as such (in the oil business it never is — unsold oil simply remains in the ground), but rather of surplus producing capacity which the companies concerned (both independent newcomers and the established majors), themselves often under pressure from individual governments to step up production, were prepared to put on offer competitively in the hope of enlarging their market shares and turning a profit on the incremental barrel. In short, for every five barrels needed to supply the market, there were six on offer. And it was to endeavour to remove this overhang of surplus capacity from the market that OPEC tried its hand at production programming.

The object of the exercise, as OPEC went to great pains to point out at the time, was not to peg the level of supply below anticipated demand or in any way to curtail overall supplies to the consumers, but to allocate the share-out of the demand growth among individual producing countries on a more equitable basis.

However praiseworthy in theory, an exercise of this kind faced severe practical difficulties — far more so when attempted on a global basis than in the widely differing circumstances of the State of Texas where a successful prorationing scheme, based on simple and well-defined technical criteria enforceable by the state authorities, had been in operation since the 1930s.

First of all, it was essential that the forecast of overall demand for the plan period as a whole should be almost uncannily accurate, and that the programme itself should be subject to fine tuning to cope with changing circumstances with the passage of time.

Secondly, there was the problem as to what criteria should be used for the allocation of increment quotas. To devise a formula for the equitable share-out of production growth between governments is a thankless task in any case since, among other things, the technical criteria (existing and historical production levels, size of reserves, future production potential, quality and locational advantages, etc.) tend to conflict with the socio-economic factors (population, financial and development needs, the importance of oil in the overall economy of the country, etc.) that are also required to be taken into consideration.

Finally, in the absence of any strict enforceability, it was indispensable that both the governments concerned and their concessionaire oil companies should have been convinced of the benefits and feasability of the programme and committed to its strict application.

None of these prerequisites were present in OPEC's trial production programme covering the 12-month period July 1, 1965, to June 30, 1966. Demand for the plan period was overestimated by a significant margin. The increment allocations seem to have been drawn up as an uneasy compromise between oil company projections (though the oil companies were not actually consulted in advance) and government aspirations. And finally the plan suffered fatally from lack of support from some of the high-growth producing countries and downright hostility from the concessionaire companies.

Although still sceptical about the usefulness of international prorationing as a means of price stabilization,[5] the Iranians were delighted with the increment quota of 304,000 b/d, or 17.5% (24% of the estimated total OPEC increase), allocated to Iran under the OPEC 1965-66 programme. This was not only the highest single-country allocation in OPEC, both in volume and percentage terms, but it also represented a substantial advance on what the oil companies planned to produce. The Iranians were thus able to use the OPEC-sanctioned 17.5% increase as a lever to induce the Consortium to boost output by this percentage on an annual basis, not just for 1965-66 but for the next five years as well, so that Iranian production would reach the Shah's target of 4 million b/d in 1970 (as against 1.8 million b/d in 1965). In an official letter to the Consortium in November 1965, NIOC Chairman Manuchehr Eghbal drew attention to the OPEC programme and called upon the companies to increase oil exports so as to meet the 4 million b/d target in 1970. Regarding the OPEC allocation Eghbal had the following to say:

"The Consortium member companies have at times intimated that the fact that they have somewhat similar commitments in other major oil producing countries would make them reluctant to take action which would increase Iran's oil production at a rate out of keeping with the rest of the Middle Eastern oil producing countries and expose them to criticism. Fortunately in this respect the OPEC Member Countries themselves have come to recognize Iran's special circumstances, and her rightful need for a higher oil income required for the execution of projects planned to develop the vast area and provide her large population with better living conditions, in that they have agreed to allocate some 24% of the estimated increment of oil production over the previous year of the total OPEC area to this country. Such recognition by countries that are in fact vying with Iran for the sale of their oil in world markets is evidence of the firm basis upon which Iran's long-standing claims are founded, namely, that her special circumstances demand that the production of oil from the Agreement Area should be rapidly increased."[6]

It was only after the OPEC production programme collapsed that Iran began its annual bilateral battles with the Consortium. However, it is worth noting that both the 1965-66 and 1970 Iranian production targets came very close to fulfillment.

Like Iran, Venezuela also found that its oil companies did not plan to produce as much as the increase allocated by OPEC (115,000 b/d or 3.3% above the previous 12 months). By contrast, the reaction of Venezuela — for some time back more conservation-oriented than its Middle Eastern OPEC partners — was simply to accept the lower figure as its new quota.

On the other side of the fence, Saudi Arabia and Libya, both of whom had been troubled by serious reservations about the programme all along, were faced with the opposite problem. Both found that the output projections of their operating oil companies for the plan period were substantially in excess of their OPEC quotas, and both effectively backed out of the programme.

Saudi Arabia had in the first place only agreed to abide by the OPEC programme for the first six months, its commitment for the second six months being dependent upon receiving an increase in its quota allocation. Since this was not forthcoming, Saudi Arabia let it be known in February 1966 that it was no longer bound by the programme. Announcing this, Sheikh Yamani criticized the production plan on two counts. Firstly, Saudi Arabia's quota was too low (an increase of 254,000 b/d or 12% for the year), being less than Aramco's production forecast, whereas Iran was using its OPEC quota figure to pressure the companies into producing more than their original forecast. Secondly, the OPEC programme would not be very effective as a price stabilization measure so long as it was restricted to OPEC Members, leaving other oil exporters outside, such as Nigeria, Algeria and Abu Dhabi (these countries not yet having joined the Organization).

It also became clear before the programme period was far advanced that Libya's production − then in the throes of headlong growth with the encouragement of the monarchical regime − could not be contained within the 20% increase allocated by OPEC. However, the then Libyan Oil Minister, Fuad Kabazi, declared that his government did not accept any limit on its production as a result of the OPEC programme.[8]

Meanwhile, in April 1966, those Member Countries whose production growth had fallen far behind the OPEC allocations − notably Iraq and Kuwait − sponsored an OPEC Resolution calling for the improvement of these rates of growth to satisfactory levels during 1966.

As for the oil companies, they were not surprisingly up in arms against the OPEC production programme, which they held to be a violation of the terms of the concession agreements. These, it was claimed, gave the companies the legal right to produce and export whatever quantities of oil they deemed fit without government intervention. In a number of producing countries − Saudi Arabia, Iran, Libya and Qatar − the companies made strong representations to the governments concerned on the subject accompanied, in the case of Saudi Arabia at least, by a formal request for arbitration, though no follow-up ensued.

With so many disparate views and interests involved in the affair, it is small wonder that such a yawning gap should have developed between the projections of the programme and the reality of the actual production performances over the 12-month period, as shown in the following table:

OPEC's Transitory Production Programme 1965-66
Plan vs. Performance
(Thousand b/d)

	Actual Production		Actual Incr.		Quota Incr. in OPEC Programme	
	July — 1965-66	June 1964-65	Volume	%	Volume	%
S. Arabia	2,406	2,091	315	15.1	254	12.0
Kuwait	2,351	2,355	(4)	(0.2)	157	6.5
Iran	2,044	1,754	290	16.5	304	17.5
Iraq	1,350	1,294	56	4.3	125	10.0
Qatar	261	221	40	18.1	67	32.0
Libya	1,344	1,062	282	26.6	210	20.0
Indonesia	496	474	22	4.6	48	10.0
Venezuela	3,453	3,445	8	0.2	115	3.3
TOTAL	**13,705**	**12,696**	**1,009**	**7.9**	**1,270**	**10.0**

As can be seen, overall demand was overestimated by two full percentage points or 260,000 b/d. Nevertheless, two countries — Saudi Arabia and Libya — substantially exceeded their quotas, while Iran came close to achieving its allocated increment. Three others — Kuwait, Iraq and Venezuela — fell a long way short of the quota level, and it is probably no coincidence that these were the countries where government relations with the oil companies were under the greatest strain at the time.*

Although some effort was made to prolong the programme for another year, it was to all intents and purposes abandoned in the summer of 1966. Thus came to an end OPEC's first and only tentative attempt at a formal production programme.

* By mid-1965 a draft agreement had been reached between an Iraqi negotiating team headed by the then Iraqi Oil Minister, Mr. Abdul Aziz Al-Wattari (now, in 1980, Assistant Secretary General of OAPEC), settling all outstanding issues between them. Had it been implemented, a sizeable increase in Iraqi production would have ensued. But the deal ran into a political blockage and was never ratified. Kuwait at the time was engaged in a tussle with the companies arising from the National Assembly's refusal to ratify the royalty expensing agreement.

Of course, the issue was to be raised again on numerous occasions down the years. In 1970, again under Venezuelan instigation, the OPEC Conference agreed in principle to a renewed effort at production programming, this time for five years, but there was no concrete follow-up and the idea melted away in the excitement of the 1971 price increases. Since then attempts to discuss regulations of production at OPEC Conferences — by Iraq and Libya, among others — have generally fallen foul of a veto by Saudi Arabia, which holds that decisions on production levels are matters involving national sovereignty, not to be discussed at OPEC.

Probably the root cause of the failure of the 1965-66 production plan was simply that it was premature. The OPEC Countries did not yet have the necessary sophistication, experience and self-confidence to carry through such a delicate enterprise. They were still not able or willing to challenge the companies' supremacy in decision making on offtake levels. Nor had the essential conviction of the desirability of production restraint taken hold anywhere outside Venezuela.

Ten years later things were very different. The OPEC producers had won the battle with the companies as regards the determination of production and export volumes, and through direct experience had themselves gained a better idea of the complexities of the supply process. At the same time, finances were more secure and the general OPEC outlook on production was permeated by a more conservationist ethos.

It was no doubt this enhanced expertise and feel for market conditions which permitted the OPEC Members to arrive at a reasonably equitable distribution of the output cutbacks necessitated by the big dips in oil demand in 1975 and the first half of 1978, even though there was no attempt at production programming, formal or informal.

The Conservationist 1970s

Venezuela's comparatively modest oil reserves position had led that South American producer to adopt a conservationist line in the late 1950s, well in advance of the rest of OPEC. By contrast Middle East reserves seemed almost limitless and, as we have seen, all the producers there were anxious to enlarge their share of the booming oil demand growth of the 1960s.

But even the Middle East producers were obliged to think again as increasing production, annual and cumulative, combined with shrinking discovery rates for new reserves, made sharp inroads into their reserves to production ratios. From a high of 135:1 (i.e. reserves sufficient to sustain 135 years of production at the then current rate) in 1957, the average reserves to production ratio for OPEC's six Middle Eastern members had slipped to 42:1 by 1979, with Kuwait at 76:1, Iran at 51:1, Saudi Arabia at 48:1, the UAE at 44:1, Iraq at 24:1 and Qatar at 20:1. Moreover, the contraction in the lifespan of the Middle East's oil reserves could be exacerbated in the future unless production rates are regulated in the light of additions to reserves. In the 1950s additions to Middle East reserves totalled 100 billion barrels, as against cumulative production of 12 billion barrels. In the 1960s, a total of 180 billion barrels was added to OPEC Middle East reserves as against cumulative production of 33 billion barrels during the decade. But in the 1970s the trend of additions to reserves substantially exceeding production was completely reversed. From 1971 to 1979 additions to Middle East reserves amounted to around 50 billion barrels, whereas cumulative production during the period reached 65 billion barrels.

For the rest of OPEC, the oil reserves position is far less comfortable than in the Middle East. For example, Algeria, Venezuela and Nigeria are all currently operating on an R/P ratio of only 20 years, while in Indonesia it is as low as 16.5 years.

For OPEC as a whole the average lifespan of Member Countries' oil reserves at current production rates has fallen from nearly 70 years in 1960 to under 40 years in 1979. Depletion has reached the point where more than a quarter of OPEC's total accumulated oil reserves has already been exhausted and in some countries, like Venezuela, this figure has passed the half-way mark. (For details of reserves, production and R/P ratios, see Statistical Appendix.)

It is true that depletion of oil reserves in non-OPEC producing countries — mainly industrialized nations of the West and East — is proceeding at a faster pace. The average R/P ratio of the non-OPEC producers is around 17 years, with the US registering as low as 9 years, and depletion spans of 10 to 15 years are regarded as quite acceptable even for major oilfields.

But there is a big difference between the relative positions of the industrialized world and the developing countries in this regard. In the case of the former, domestic energy production is used to serve an already going concern; a dynamic process of growth is already in train and the conversion of depleting oil reserves into new sources of income generation is rapid (or perhaps one should say ought to be rapid, in view of the fact that Britain, for example, seems to be developing many of the rentier attitudes usually associated with the traditional underdeveloped oil producers). In the developing oil producing countries, on the other hand, no such alchemical transformation of the extracted oil into diversified economic growth can take place overnight. At worst, the oil money may be frittered away on current expenditure and ill-conceived schemes. At best it can serve as the basis for a longer term process of structural change which is itself a prerequisite for the desired objective of diversified economic growth.[9] But this is a long job which cannot be properly started, let alone completed, unless the essential injection of capital from the exported oil wealth is spun out over a sufficiently extended period of time. If the rate of injection is too fast for productive absorption, much is wasted on inessential extravagance; if it is too slow, the development process never gains the necessary momentum for takeoff. Moreover, even when and if the desired developmental momentum is achieved, there arises the further problem of ensuring that the country concerned retains sufficient oil and energy resources to provide fuel and raw material for the new-style economy on a long-term basis.

Another related factor militating in favour of output restraint by revenue-surplus oil producers stems, of course, from the lack of investment instruments capable of maintaining the purchasing power of the petrodollar surpluses.

Such problems provided ample food for thought for the OPEC producers as the 1970s progressed, and horizons broadened with the easing of immediate financial constraints. After the initial conservationist steps taken by Libya and Kuwait in 1970-72, other governments too began to find that conservation made good sense not only for the economic reasons already indicated but from the domestic political standpoints as well. Any policy designed to lengthen the lifespan of a producing country's oil resources to the benefit of future generations is likely to strike a popular chord with public opinion, traumatized as it is by the nightmare prospect of "the day the oil runs out". A lower production profile would also help to apply a touch of the brake to the explosively hectic pace of change which always carries seeds of danger for traditional societies.

This emerging climate of opinion represents a very significant change from the "macho" attitude towards oil output volume which was prevalent until recently and has by no means entirely disappeared even now, when each producer was wont to measure his power and prestige in terms of barrels exported. Many a lesson is implicit in the career of the Shah of Iran, whose downfall so eloquently emphasized the dangers of grandiose conceptions.

Such a sea-change in basic outlook, gaining ground steadily through the 1970s, was bound to have profound global repercussions. The sparks which ignited the oil supply/price crises of 1973-74 and 1979-80 came from political tinderboxes, but the underlying economic verity in both cases was the growing reluctance of the oil producers to continue expanding supply at anything like the historic or consumer-projected rates of demand growth. It is the recognition of this fact, together with its price implications, that is at long last beginning to convince the consumers that it really is essential to curb excessive oil consumption through conservation and the development of alternative energy.

Some idea of the extent of the conservation trend on the producers' side may be gained from the table on page 214, which shows estimated preferred levels of crude production by OPEC and its individual Members, as compared with actual current output, full capacity and annual historical peaks. It can be seen that, at 27.8 million b/d, the estimated preferred level for all OPEC in mid-1980 is 3.5 million b/d below the peak annual output in 1977 and 6.1 million b/d below rated physical capacity. These figures alone do not give an adequate idea of the extent to which earlier production levels and projections have been scaled down. If, for example, we add up the annual production peaks attained by each country during the 1970s, regardless of the actual years in which they were attained, the total comes to 37.5 million b/d – nearly 10 million b/d above the mid-1980 preferred level. And if we go further and compare the mid-1980 preferred level with the capacity and output figures that were being projected by the oil companies in the early 1970s – which were envisaging a total OPEC production of something like 50 million b/d for the early 1980s (including 20 million from Saudi Arabia) – the contrast is truly staggering. And here it should be noted that it was consumer demand that perforce scaled itself down in response to the supply/price effects of the OPEC phenomenon, rather than the other way round.

Obviously, at some point there has to be a limit to the contraction of OPEC supply, but where? Kuwait, which is in the vanguard of the conservation drive, advocates the gearing of long-term production to an R/P ratio of 100:1, and has itself comfortably achieved that target with the reduction in April 1980 of its long-range output ceiling from 2 million b/d to 1.5 million b/d (excluding the Neutral Zone). But, if extended to the whole of OPEC or major producers like Saudi Arabia, this R/P ratio objective would entail halving production – which, for the time being at any rate, is unthinkable. (Yet who would have regarded the more than halving of Iranian production as thinkable a couple of years ago?)

True, every major oil price rise is likely to bring in its train a temporary drop in demand and the reappearance of an equally temporary semblance of surplus supply. But this yields no real comfort to the consumers in the longer term, since there is the danger that, with the producer governments fortified by higher prices, the interim lower production levels will solidify into new ceilings which may prove difficult to adjust when demand picks up again.

Theoretically, the limits of producer conservancy are dictated by the current financial needs of the governments concerned, though there is obviously room for debate about the proper determination of what those needs ought to be. For example, according to the Head of OPEC's Economics and Finance Department, Mr. Adnan Al-Janabi, the amount of OPEC production needed to cover domestic consumption and development expenditure in Member Countries would be only about half the 1979 output level.[10] In practice, there are overriding politico-economic imperatives of a global character which are likely to ensure that these limits are not reached so long as the satisfaction of bed-rock world demand requires that some producers be prepared to keep on supplying more oil than is essential for their own needs. Such imperatives are more keenly felt by key producers like Saudi Arabia; whereas smaller OPEC exporters, not so much in the world spotlight, have rather more latitude to pursue oil production policies based on strict national interest considerations.

OPEC's record in the matter of supply has been characterized by a sense of international responsibility and accommodation to the needs of the industrialized world. During the 1978-79 Iran supply crisis major producers, like Saudi Arabia and Iraq, showed themselves willing to boost production in order to fill the supply gap; in 1979 in fact, despite the Iranian shortfall, OPEC as a whole raised production by 1 million b/d, or 3.5%, to 30.8 million b/d from the 1978 level of 29.8 million b/d. As we have noted in Chapter VIII, the crisis was the product of fear and uncertainty over supplies rather than a genuine supply problem.

In the longer term, however, the production policies of OPEC Countries must be based on national interest considerations — public opinion in these countries will insist on that. This means that production levels will tend to be related to genuine development needs and the oil reserves balance. Exactly where the levels will be pitched will depend on a whole gamut of political and economic factors, including whatever incentives may be forthcoming to OPEC Countries to produce in excess of their needs,[11] and the rate of discovery of new reserves to offset the depletion of existing reservoirs.

The standard methodology for forecasting oil supplies has been first to estimate total demand for energy, then to add up the estimated contributions of all non-OPEC sources of energy, including non-OPEC oil, and finally the residual gap is labelled as OPEC production. This designation of OPEC as the world's residual supplier of energy is clearly unsatisfactory since, among other things, it takes no account of likely constraints on the level of OPEC supplies.

The table on page 215 lists some of the forecasts of "required" residual oil supply from OPEC made by various bodies over the past few years. Here the absurdity of the "OPEC as residual supplier" approach to forecasting becomes apparent. Most of the forecasts made in 1977-78, before the Iranian crisis, put required production from OPEC by 1985-90 in the 40 to 50 million b/d bracket. These figures were clearly a very long way above what OPEC would be willing, or indeed physically able, to produce. In mid-1980 OPEC physical capacity was estimated at around 34 million b/d (see table), and the report of the OPEC Long-Term Strategy Committee reckoned that 1985 capacity would be in the neighbourhood of 35 million b/d "and any significant increase in this figure is difficult to envisage in the absence of a substantial change in the fundamental circumstances which determine capacity at present. There are few signs that such changes will occur."

Forecasts made after the 1979-80 price surge represent a scaling down of the estimated requirement from OPEC to more realistic levels. In Exxon's 1980 forecast the requirement from OPEC is estimated at 33 million b/d by 1990, staying constant at that level until the end of the century. This would at least be within the limits of OPEC's physical capacity to supply. Shell, in its 1980 forecast, also predicts a no-growth future for OPEC, with an estimated output requirement of 29.5 million b/d in 1984.

However, there is more than a whiff of wishful thinking about these forecasts, which abolish the energy crisis with the stroke of a pen. Exxon now sees low growth in world energy demand (2.5% annually from 1978 to 2000 on world GNP growth of 3.5%), and even less growth in oil demand, with coal and nuclear energy taking up the bulk of the increase. Overall energy demand is estimated at 130 million b/d of oil equivalent in 1990 — an astounding 18 million b/d below the Exxon forecast two years previously in April 1978.

Other forecasts are more pessimistic. In 1980, the International Energy Agency (IEA) put out a forecast with the figure for OPEC supply based on what the Organization's Members might be prepared to produce, rather than the residual supplier approach. It estimated OPEC willingness to supply at 30.8 million b/d in 1985 and 31.6 million b/d in 1990, and on that basis postulates a supply shortfall in meeting OECD demand of between 2.1 and 3.8 million b/d in 1985 and between 3.6 and 5.7 million b/d in 1990. The implication is that without some incremental OPEC supply, the world is in for a crunch.

Obviously, one way or another and at some as yet uncertain price level, there will have to be some accommodation between world demand and what OPEC is prepared to supply. What is perhaps not yet sufficiently realized is the extent to which the industrialized countries grouped within the OECD are the residual recipients of OPEC oil, since it is OPEC policy to give priority in allocating supplies first (naturally enough) to the domestic needs of the OPEC Members themselves, and second to the other developing countries of the Third World. This means that, in addition to the supply constraints on the OPEC Countries already described, availability of oil for export to the OECD bloc will be further diminished by increases in oil demand in the Third World and the OPEC area itself.

According to OPEC estimates,[12] demand for petroleum products in the OPEC Countries, which is running at about 2.5 million b/d in 1980, may well exceed 6 million b/d by 1990. Assuming an OPEC production level of 30 million b/d, this would mean that only 24 million b/d would be available for export. On top of this, the oil requirements of the non-oil producing developing countries (which were consuming about 8 million b/d of oil in 1980 and importing 4 to 5 million b/d) may increase by over 4 million b/d by 1990. If a significant volume of the increment were to be supplied by OPEC, the impact on the availability of supplies to the OECD countries could be dramatic.

In the short term, as a result of the recessionary current and higher oil price levels of 1980, there could be a dip in demand, perhaps to 26 to 27 million b/d in the second half of 1980, which could possibly put some strain on prices and OPEC's production management. But, in the longer term, OPEC's propensity to reduce output will always be greater than any conceivable reduction in demand.

OPEC Crude Oil Production
Peak, Actual, Preferred and Capacity Levels
(Thousand b/d)

	Peak Production Year	Peak Production Volume	Actual 1979	Actual 1st Half 1980	Preferred Mid-1980(1)	Capacity Mid-1980(2)
S. Arabia(3)	1979	9,532	9,532	9,775	8,750	10,800
Iran	1974	6,022	3,121	1,850	3,000	3,000
Iraq	1979	3,477	3,477	3,500	3,000	4,000
Kuwait(3)	1972	3,283	2,457	1,855	1,750	2,800
UAE	1977	1,999	1,831	1,730	1,640	2,485
Qatar	1973	570	508	480	500	650
Venezuela	1970	3,708	2,367	2,120	2,200	2,400
Nigeria	1979	2,305	2,305	2,150	2,150	2,400
Libya	1970	3,318	2,090	1,900	1,750	2,100
Indonesia	1977	1,686	1,591	1,565	1,600	1,600
Algeria	1978	1,161	1,584	985	1,000	1,200
Gabon	1975	223	203	200	200	250
Ecuador	1979	214	214	230	250	250
All OPEC	1977	31,278	30,840	28,340	27,790	33,935

(1) Denotes either government allowablle ceiling or indicated preferred level of production.
(2) Source: Petroleum Intelligence Weekly. Defined as PIW's assessment of maximum production sustainable for several months without regard to government ceilings. This is less than installed capacity and does not necessarily reflect maximum production sustainable for long periods without damage to fields.
(3) Includes share of Neutral Zone output.

Some Forecasts of Required OPEC Production

Forecast By	Year Made	Required OPEC Production Volume (Mil. b/d)	Year
CIA	1977	47 - 51	1988
WAES	1977	40 - 45	1985
US Congressional Research Service	1977	42.8	1985
PIRINC	1978	36.6	1985
		39.8 - 51.7	1990
IEA	1978	42.9	1985
Exxon	1978	40	1985
EEC	1979	38	1985
US Energy Dept.	1979	28 - 36	1985
Exxon	1980	33	1990
		33	2000
Shell	1980	29.5	1984
CIA*	1979	30.2	1982
IEA*	1980	30.8	1985
		31.6	1990

*   Both these forecasts are based on estimates of what the OPEC Countries are likely to be willing to produce, rather than the residual requirement from OPEC. Both postulate a supply shortfall in meeting OECD demand with OPEC production at the indicated level. The CIA estimates a shortfall at an OECD GNP growth rate of anything over 2% — with 3 to 5 million b/d shortfall by 1982 at a growth rate of 3%. The IEA forecasts a shortfall of 2.1 to 3.8 million b/d in 1985 and 3.6 to 5.7 million b/d by 1990.

CHAPTER X

CONTROL OF MANAGEMENT AND OPERATIONS

The desire of host governments for equity participation with the concessionaire companies in the oil producing ventures goes back a long way before the foundation of OPEC. But this was a demand that the major oil companies always resisted with all the power and guile at their command, sensing no doubt that such a development would strike at the very roots of their control over the supply arteries of the world oil industry. In the end, it required a collective impetus on the part of OPEC to unblock the path towards participation and the takeover by the host governments of control over crude oil production operations.

Some of the early concession agreements — those in Iraq and Iran, for example — did contain clauses envisaging the possibility of national shareholdings in the producing ventures; but these were phrased in such a way as to make them incapable of fulfillment in practice. For example, Article 34 of the 1925 agreement between Iraq and the Iraq Petroleum Company (IPC) stipulates: "Whenever an issue of shares is offered by the company to the general public, subscription lists shall be opened in Iraq simultaneously with lists opened elsewhere, and Iraqis in Iraq shall be given a preference to the extent of at least 20% of such an issue."[1] Catch-22 in this Machiavellian formulation was that IPC was a closed private company whose shares were tightly held by a group of international majors (British Petroleum, Shell, CFP of France, Exxon, Mobil and the Gulbenkian interests), and therefore did not, and indeed under its constitutional set-up could not, issue shares to the public.

In the late 1950s and early 1960s, various Middle East producing countries concluded agreements for the exploration and development of new oil acreage, which included provisions for government equity participation in the ventures in the event of the discovery of oil in commercial quantities. The companies involved were mainly independent newcomers — the 1957 entrants being ENI of Italy and Amoco of the US in offshore Iran (with the government participation set at 50%) and the Japanese-owned Arabian Oil Company in the Saudi Arabia-Kuwait Neutral Zone (20% government participation) — but in 1961 one of the majors, namely Shell, accepted the principle of participation when it agreed to a 20% government shareholding option in the terms of its new concession covering offshore Kuwait. Shell, of course, was motivated by its comparative penury of access to owned sources of crude oil supply relative to its strong downstream position on the refining and product marketing side. But, notwithstanding Shell's willingness to break fresh ground in a new exploration venture, the majors as a whole still preserved a solid front against allowing such innovations to percolate to the established producing concessions where all the most prolific oilfields were located. Against mounting pressure from their host governments on this score, the companies maintained that the terms of the new joint ventures could not create a precedent under the most-favoured-nation clauses contained in some Middle East agreements unless and until it could be shown that their yield in revenue per barrel to the governments exceeded that of the traditional concessions; and this was an unlikely eventuality because, even when production was developed, the new ventures were low-volume, high-cost operations when compared to the major oilfields.

Nevertheless, as the years rolled by, the participation aspiration broke surface again and again with ever-increasing intensity. In 1961, participation was one of the Iraqi Government's demands which figured in the breakdown of General Qasim's negotiations with IPC, culminating in the promulgation of the celebrated Law No. 80 of 1961. And in 1965, when government and IPC negotiators succeeded in drafting a compre-hensive settlement, one of its main features was to be the setting up of a new company to explore and develop good-potential acreage (outside IPC's exclusive oilfield areas) in which the Iraq National Oil Company (INOC) would have one-third and the IPC owners two-thirds participation. Significantly, Exxon − at one and the same time the world's largest oil company, a major (30%) shareholder in Aramco, and a determined opponent, in deepest principle, of any governmental participation in the management of its affairs − opted out of the joint venture part of the Iraqi deal, evidently to a large extent out of trepidation about the effect that such a precedent might have in Saudi Arabia. However, the other US member of the IPC group − Mobil Oil (a 10% shareholder in Aramco) − retained its interest in the projected joint venture in Iraq.

In the event, the 1965 Iraqi-IPC draft settlement − involving as it did the return of the proven but as yet unexploited North Rumaila oilfield to the exclusive control of the IPC group (this being an issue of political and economic dynamite in Iraq at the time) − failed to gain the necessary governmental ratification and subsided into a historical limbo. But it was true that the Saudis were watching the Iraqi scene very carefully; if the joint venture in Iraq had gone through, Saudi Arabia would have insisted on some similar exploration deal with Aramco.

For Saudi Arabia, too, participation was a long-standing aspiration. It assumed even greater importance after the 1967 Arab-Israeli war, with the intensification of popular agitation in the Arab world for nationalization of western oil interests, of which one of the leading advocates was the former Saudi Oil Minister, Abdullah Al-Tariki.

However, in practical terms, outright nationalization was not a feasible option for Saudi Arabia. For one thing, it went totally against the grain of the Kingdom's pro-western political orientation and private-enterprise economic philosophy. For another, Saudi Arabia was still very dependent on the technical expertise of the Aramco companies for the operation and expansion of its mammoth oil industry. And finally, the weak market conditions of the 1960s, plagued by surplus producing capacity and falling crude prices, did not provide an ideal timing for a confrontation with the oil companies, as the experience of Iraq had shown.

As far as the Saudis were concerned, therefore, participation — progressive nationalization by agreement with the companies, one might almost call it — was the only viable path towards the fulfillment of the vital national aspiration of the oil producing countries for control over their natural resources and an expanding government role in the running of the oil industry, while retaining the essential expertise, services and markets that only the major oil companies could provide. Sheikh Yamani was to speak of participation as "a catholic marriage between the producers on the one hand and the consumers and the majors or independent oil companies on the other hand by linking both of them to an extent where it is almost impossible for any of them to divorce."[2]

In the summer of 1968, at a seminar at the American University of Beirut, Yamani launched a determined Saudi campaign for government participation in Aramco. But on this particular matter Aramco proved a tough nut to crack, and it became necessary to reinforce Saudi Arabia's individual effort with the collective force of OPEC.

In the 1960s and early 1970s, participation and nationalization were usually presented as rival alternatives — the moderate versus the radical solution to the problem of national sovereignty and control over oil resources. So, at the time, they certainly were. But, viewed in a historical perspective, they look more like just different paths leading to the same end.

OPEC and the Participation Negotiations

OPEC's first formal involvement with the participation issue came in the June 1968 Declaratory Statement of Petroleum Policy in Member

Countries, which stipulated that "where provision for governmental participation in the ownership of the concession-holding company under any of the present petroleum contracts has not be made, the Government may acquire a reasonable participation on the grounds of the principle of changing circumstances." The legal principle of changing circumstances *(rebus sic stantibus)* was frequently cited by the producer governments in those days as grounds for the revision of concession terms, while the companies were wont to make appeal to the opposing principle of the sancity of contracts *(pacta sunt servanda)*.

However, the participation drive did not really develop momentum until 1971 when, after the conclusion of the Tehran/Tripoli five-year price agreements, it reached the top of OPEC's priority list for action. In July 1971, the Organization's Twenty-Fourth Conference in Vienna resolved that Member Countries should take immediate steps towards the implementation of participation, and in September an extraordinary Conference was convened in Beirut to decide on a strategy for negotiations with the oil companies to this end.

As was only to be expected, there were differing ideas as to what the participation target should be: the Gulf producers (Saudi Arabia, Iran, Iraq, Kuwait, the UAE and Qatar) were inclined to think in terms of an initial 20% which, after some period of stability, would be subject to progression towards ultimate 51% majority control; for its part, Libya insisted that nothing less than immediate 51% majority control would be acceptable (thereby following the pattern set by Algeria which had nationalized 51% of the French-owned concessions in February 1971); while Nigeria favoured an initial target of around 35%. The other three Members were not directly involved in the participation drive: Venezuela was looking towards the expiry of its existing concessions by 1983; Algeria had already nationalized 51%; and Indonesia was operating under its own production-sharing arrangements.

Two other important points were agreed upon at the Beirut Meeting as bases for the OPEC negotiating position: firstly that the cost of acquisition of the governments' equity holding should be assessed on the basis of the book value of net fixed assets; and secondly that, to avoid disruption of markets and prices in the initial stages of the participation process while the OPEC National Oil Companies were establishing markets of their own, there should be guaranteed "buy-back" arrangements with the concessionaires under which the latter would purchase a substantial portion of the governments' share of production at a price half-way between tax-paid cost and the posted price, possibly less some discount or sales commission. The "half-way price", which was used as the price yardstick for overlifters as between the members of some of the operating groups in the Middle East, was at that time slightly above the realized market price.

The Beirut Meeting decided that OPEC Members should negotiate with the oil companies "either individually or in groups", and that the results should be submitted to the Conference for co-ordination. This meant in practice that, as in the price talks earlier in 1971, the Gulf producers would negotiate as a group, while Libya would go it alone with a more ambitious target.

Meanwhile, after initial manifestations of outrage at this new demand so soon after the Tehran five-year price deal, the oil companies set about organizing themselves for the fray. In October 1971, the same group of 23 international oil companies as had combined together for the Tehran and Tripoli price talks once again grouped in London, complete with another anti-trust waiver from the US Department of Justice, to prepare for the new negotiations with OPEC on participation (as well as on compensation for the depreciation of the US dollar, which was settled by the Geneva I currency agreement in January 1972).

The companies' initial reaction was to try to resist any kind of government participation as far as the presently producing oilfields were concerned. However, in the event they had to concede some percentage participation to the OPEC Governments, they wanted to keep the deal as far as possible within the following parameters:

(a) To resist at all costs the principle of compensation on the basis of net book value — which some company officials described as tantamount to virtual confiscation — and to insist that the cost of acquisition should be fixed at a "fair market price" reflecting the companies' anticipated loss of profit as a result of the sale. (This would have been tantamount, in effect, to the government paying compensation for the repossession and use of the nation's own oil reserves — a suggestion which naturally found no echo whatever on the OPEC side.) The gap between net book value and a loss of profit formula in any of the major producing countries of the Middle East would, of course, have been enormous. The net book value of Aramco's fixed assets at that time was probably in the region of $500 million, whereas the present value of Armaco's potential future profit from Saudi Arabia's 1971 proved reserves could have been reckoned at 10 times that figure.

(b) To keep the percentage participation as low as possible and stop short of any progression to majority control.

(c) To retain access to as much as possible of the government's participation entitlements of crude via buy-back arrangements, and to pay the minimum price uplift above tax-paid cost for such crude.

Not surprisingly, in view of the chasm between the conceptions of two sides, the negotiations were long and arduous as compared with the Tehran price talks, and from time to time required deblocking by means of interventions by King Faisal of Saudi Arabia individually or OPEC collectively.

The government-company negotiations got underway early in 1972, and the Saudi Oil Minister, Sheikh Ahmed Zaki Yamani, was delegated by the Gulf producers to pursue the talks on their behalf, as a result of which various meetings were held with company representatives in Saudi Arabia in February. Here, Aramco tried to sidestep the OPEC participation demand altogether; instead, on February 15, it offered Saudi Arabia 50% government participation with the Aramco shareholders in developing and operating certain proved but as yet undeveloped oilfields in Saudi Arabia.[3] In other circumstances, particularly if it had been put forward a few years earlier, such a proposal might have held some attraction for Saudi Arabia. But since it had little to do with the immediate matter in hand, namely the participation of all the Gulf OPEC Governments in the producing oilfields, as well as undeveloped acreage, the Saudis rejected the offer categorically without further ado.

The very next day, February 16, King Faisal made his first intervention by instructing Oil Minister Yamani to deliver the following stern royal warning to the assembled company negotiators: "The implementation of effective participation is imperative, and we expect the companies to co-operate with us with a view to reaching a satisfactory agreement. They should not oblige us to take measures in order to put into effect the implementation of participation". Coming direct from the King, the clearly implied threat of unilateral legislative measures to achieve participation, so uncharacteristic of the usual Saudi approach in its terse bluntness, gave the companies a severe jolt.

The next step for OPEC was to schedule an extraordinary Conference for March 11 in Beirut, in line with the Resolution of the previous Beirut Meeting in September 1971 (XXV. 139) which stipulated that, in case of failure of the negotiations, the Conference should "determine a procedure with a view to enforcing and achieving the objectives of effective participation through concerted action".

The evening before the Conference was due to begin, however, Yamani received a letter from the four parent companies of Aramco accepting the principle of a 20% participation by the Saudi Arabian Government in the company's concession. This declaration of acceptance

221

of the principle of 20% participation was also communicated by to the Governments of Kuwait, Abu Dhabi, Iraq and Qatar by the concessionaire oil companies operating in those countries.

This last-minute initiative by the companies — reminiscent of other occasions in the past — averted the activation of a pre-arranged OPEC plan for implementing participation by means of legislated partial nationalization. Under this plan, some of the more militant OPEC Countries — Libya and perhaps Iraq — would have started by nationalizing 51% of one or more of their concessionaires with the full backing of the OPEC Conference and a pledge of practical support, including sanctions, from the other Member States in case the company or companies in question resorted to retaliatory measures, either individually or in concert with the London group of 23 companies. In the ensuing climate of ferment, the more moderate Gulf producers would also have found themselves obliged to follow suit by legislating for 51% participation. OPEC sources emphasized at the time that, as a consequence of the companies' acceptance of 20% participation, the plan was being held in abeyance but had by no means been abandoned.[4] In fact, an essential element of the plan — the automatic provision of mutual support, including sanctions, in cases where the companies resist measures taken by a Member State in application of a Conference decision — was adopted in the form of a Resolution by the March 1972 Beirut Conference.

In terms of history, the acceptance by the companies — particularly Aramco — of the principle 20% government participation was a big breakthrough. This seemingly impregnable fortress of company inviolability had at last been breached. But, as is often the case with breakthroughs of this sort, it came at a time when the whole established system was about to be overwhelmed by the forces of change. So an enforced concession by the companies, however great a departure from the past, could do nothing to stem the tide; it was, in fact, the old story of too little, too late.

Meanwhile, however, the mere acceptance by the companies of 20% government participation in principle did not mean that the negotiations were now plain sailing. As already indicated, the two sides were still far apart as regards the terms of the deal — compensation, buy-back, timing of progression to majority control, etc. Talks between Yamani and the companies from April to the end of June in various parts of the globe — San Francisco, Riyadh, Geneva and London — made little progress; and further warnings of impending unilateral action were forthcoming from the OPEC Conference at its regular mid-year session in

Vienna in June and the Saudi Arabian Royal Cabinet in July.

About this time a number of significant events took place which rather altered the complexion of the participation talks, one of them being Iraq's nationalization of IPC on June 1, 1972.

The Iraqi nationalization followed yet one more abortive attempt at a comprehensive settlement of the formidable backlog of disputed issues between Iraq and the IPC group which had piled up over the years since Law No. 80 of 1961 and even before.[5] Most of these issues were peculiar to Iraq with no direct bearing on the OPEC scene; but there was one crucial element which was both a major factor in the collapse of the final Iraqi-IPC negotiations and at the same time directly related to the OPEC participation question. This was IPC's insistence on compensation for its loss of the oil reserves contained in the proved but undeveloped North Rumaila oilfield which was taken over by the government under Law No. 80. As part of its final offer for a package settlement of all disputes, the company was demanding compensation for its "loss of rights" in respect of oil discoveries made before 1961 in the form of 7% (down from 12.5% in an earlier offer) of all the oil produced by the Iraq National Oil Company, excluding certain guaranteed sales to the IPC parent companies themselves. Iraq, on the other hand, was prepared to offer nothing more than net book value for the exploration work done by the IPC group on North Rumaila prior to 1961.

That the compensation issue was the principal cause of Iraq's rejection of the IPC package was confirmed by Iraqi sources at the time, as well as by IPC Managing Director Geoffrey Stockwell. According to Stockwell, the compensation issue "was, without the slightest shadow of a doubt, the most crucial element. They were offering compensation on a net book value basis. It would have amounted to an insignificant figure. We proposed a figure based on the oil produced. We felt 7% would take care of it ...... We could have done a deal, but only by complete capitulation. We would have sold the pass in the current industry talks on participation. Equally, if the Iraqis had met our terms they would have sold the pass on the OPEC side. The question of participation and compensation in Law 80 were obviously intermingled. Both sides had their hands tied by the attitudes of OPEC and the oil industry."[6]

In retrospect, the IPC stand has a somewhat Quixotic air about it considering that all the companies eventually obtained as compensation for government participation was net book value anyway.

Although Iraq did not immediately drop out of the OPEC Gulf

participation group after its nationalization of IPC's northern oilfields, it declined to apply the Gulf participation formula to the southern Iraqi oilfields which remained, for the time being, in the hands of the companies.

A few months earlier Libya, too, had made its mark by nationalizing British Petroleum's producing interests. Although the motivation for this nationalization was not directly related to the participation issue — the reason given was that the British Government, as the departing protecting power in the lower Gulf, had allowed Iran to occupy three Arab islands — it nevertheless served as a reminder that Libya was always a force to be reckoned with.

Another defector from the Gulf participation front at mid-year was Iran, which decided to go it alone with a new deal with the Consortium, though the finalization of this would await the outcome of the Gulf participation talks. Although the Iranian move caused a certain amount of initial dismay in OPEC circles, the Iranians were at pains to reassure their OPEC colleagues that its purpose was in no way directed against the participation scheme, but should rather be regarded as a parallel alternative more suited to the particular circumstances of Iran which, among other things, had already nationalized its oil industry in 1951 and paid due compensation.

The nationalization of IPC, along with the renewed warnings from OPEC and King Faisal, seemed to have convinced the companies that a negotiated deal with the Gulf producers was the least of the possible evils facing them. From then on they stopped dragging their feet and started actively working towards a settlement.

By early October 1972, a draft agreement had been reached between Sheikh Yamani and the companies which provided for government participation in the existing concessions on the following terms:

- 25% initial government participation with effect from January 1, 1973, with stability for five years, then rising to 30% on January 1, 1978, 35% on January 1, 1979, 40% on January 1, 1980, 45% on January 1, 1981 and 51% on January 1, 1982.
- On compensation, a compromise was reached providing for payment for acquisition of the government shareholdings on the basis of "updated book value", which essentially meant written down book value adjusted for inflation to bring it more in line with present-day replacement cost (this apparently was a familiar feature in French accounting practice). Although a long way below the companies' original "loss of future profits" contention, the updated book value formula nevertheless gave the companies two or three times more than they would have obtained under strict net book

value. The amounts payable by the governments concerned for their initial 25% shareholdings were calculated under the updated book value formula as follows: $500 million for Saudi Arabia (Aramco); $150 million for Kuwait (KOC); $68 million for Iraq (southern BPC fields); $71 million for Qatar (QPC and Shell); and $162 million for Abu Dhabi (ADPC and ADMA).* (Iraq and Kuwait, of course, did not sign the agreement.)

— It was agreed that the companies would buy back the bulk of the governments' entitlements of crude for the first four years, partly at the market price (so-called bridging crude) and partly at a small discount off the market price (so-called phase-in crude). The share of total production to be marketed directly by the governments would rise from 2.5% in 1973 to 7.5% in 1976.

All that now remained was to gain the blessing of OPEC for the Gulf deal, which came to be known as the General Agreement on Participation. This was done at an extraordinary session of the OPEC Conference in Riyadh, Saudi Arabia, on October 26-27, 1972, which issued a communique congratulating the four Gulf states which intended to become parties to the General Agreement — i.e. Saudi Arabia, Kuwait, Abu Dhabi and Qatar — on their attainment of the participation objective.

As expected, Libya made it clear that, while it wished the Gulf countries luck, it was, for its own part far from satisfied with the Gulf participation terms, particularly as regards the percentage government interest and the formula for compensation. Libya, said Oil Minister Ezzedin Mabruk, would insist on participation with its concessionaires on terms similar to those of the deal it had recently concluded with the Italian state firm ENI, namely, a minimum of 50% participation with cost of acquisition assessed on a strict net book value basis.[7]

Owing mainly to domestic political opposition from the National Assembly (Parliament) which found the Gulf deal altogether too tame for its liking, Kuwait too began to have second thoughts and the prospect of it ever signing the General Agreement gradually receded.

Finally, after some delay for the completion of buy-back price talks (see Chapter V), three countries — Saudi Arabia, Abu Dhabi and Qatar — signed the General Agreement. Supposedly it was to be followed up by

* *It should be noted, however, that when in 1974 government participation was raised to 60%, the acquisition cost basis was switched to strict net book value, and payments for the first 25% by Saudi Arabia, Abu Dhabi and Qatar were readjusted accordingly.*

detailed implementing agreements in each country, but events were to move too fast for this ever to be accomplished.

Landslide Towards Majority Control

With the endorsement of the General Agreement by the Gulf states concerned, OPEC's direct involvement in the participation issue came to an end. But, as it turned out, that agreement was to mark only the beginning of a general landslide towards majority control and in many cases 100% ownership of the producing ventures by the OPEC Governments.

Ultimately, each OPEC Member chose the kind of arrangement best suited to its own particular circumstances. Basically, the shape of the arrangement arrived at would usually depend on the extent to which the producing country in question was in need of the technical and managerial services of the oil companies for the efficient functioning of its day-to-day production and export operations. Iraq, for example, found nationalization a relatively painless transition on the operational side, simply because it had no further need for the companies' expertise. Well before nationalization, apart from a handful of foreigners, the operating companies were staffed completely by Iraqis from top to bottom; so nationalization was a matter of business as usual at the oilfields and terminals. Some of the other OPEC Countries are, on the other hand, highly dependent on the services provided by the multinational companies.

Events in 1973 moved thick and fast. In March, Iraq and the IPC group agreed on a wide-ranging settlement covering compensation for the nationalized northern fields and expansion of production and export capacity for the Basrah fields in the south. Compensation for the IPC nationalization was to be effected in the form of crude oil deliveries (some 15 million tons over 15 months). This turned out to be a better-than-expected deal from the companies' point of view since the price of the crude happened to quadruple during the period of the deliveries. However, by and large, one could not help but observe that the major companies, which had strained at the gnat of 20% participation early in 1972, were being obliged to swallow the camel of total nationalization one year later. Among other factors, much of the rationale behind this *volte face* could be traced to the dramatic tightening of the crude oil supply situation in 1972-73.

Back on the participation front, the next round began in Libya in

January 1973, when some of the concessionaire companies, under the overall direction of the supposedly united front formed by the group of 23 international oil companies, formally presented the Libyan Government with an offer of participation on the Gulf model. As can be imagined, this charade went down with the Libyan leadership like a lead balloon.

The Libyan Government then focused its attention on the most vulnerable of the operating companies — Bunker Hunt which, originally in partnership with the new nationalized BP, held a 50% interest in the prolific Sarir oilfields — with a demand for immediate 50% participation on Libyan terms. (The Bunker Hunt oil company was essentially a family affair owned by the Texas tycoon Nelson Bunker Hunt, which owed its oil bonanza in Libya more to historical good fortune than to any weighty position in the international oil industry.) In solidarity with the collective stand of the group of 23, Hunt resisted the Libyan demand for immediate 50% participation; but all he got for his pains was nationalization by the Libyan Government on the one hand, and on the other scant satisfaction from the rest of the oil companies as regards oil supply support from the much-vaunted inter-company "safety net" agreement.

When, shortly afterwards, Libya zeroed in on the larger, but still highly vulnerable, independents like Occidental and the participants in the Oasis group (Continental, Marathon and Amerada-Hess) with the threat of a production cut, the latter — wisely judging discretion to be the better part of valour, whatever the by now disintegrating group of 23 might have to say — came to a deal on the basis of voluntary acquiescence to a government law nationalizing 51% of their assets. After an initial period of resistance, some of the majors, notably Exxon and Mobil, followed the same path around nine months later, by which time the Gulf states had gone even further ahead than Libya in terms of majority control.

In July 1973, meanwhile, Iran had finalized its new deal with the Consortium which, in addition to providing for increased production capacity, assured Iran of an income per barrel no less favourable than than of the other Gulf producers.

Thus by the late summer of 1973 the Gulf participation deal was being outflanked on all fronts: the Libyans had induced some companies (albeit not the majors) to accept 51% government control at net book value; the Kuwaitis, biding their time, were preparing to outdistance Libya's 51%; Iraq's full nationalization of IPC had been accepted by the majors; in June Nigeria had obtained an initial 35% interest in its major concessions; and the Shah was presenting his deal to the public as an assumption of 100% control by Iran.

It was small wonder then that, even before the October 1973 war and the quantum leap in oil prices further changed the picture, Saudi Arabia and the other signatories of the General Agreement had become aware that the deal was doomed. In Saudi Arabia, the idea was beginning to take root that the only way to put an end to the constant leapfrogging as regards participation terms was for the Kingdom to move towards a 100% takeover, while retaining full access to the essential expertise and technology that only the Aramco parents could provide.

In the changed situation of 1974, the takeover momentum intensified, and the companies had little alternative but to acquiesce. First Kuwait, then Saudi Arabia, Qatar and Abu Dhabi raised their participation level to 60%. Subsequently, Kuwait reached agreement with BP and Gulf for a 100% takeover of KOC in December 1975, and Qatar followed suit with QPC and Shell in 1976-77. Saudi Arabia completed negotiations for 100% ownership of the Aramco venture in 1977 and, though the documents have not yet been finalized, the financial provisions of the new deal have been in effect since January 1, 1976.

Meanwhile, Iraq completed its nationalization of the Basrah oilfields by 1975; and Venezuela formally nationalized its oil industry on January 1, 1976, after concluding marketing and technical service agreements with the former concessionaires.

As for those OPEC Countries which opted to retain their concessionaires as equity holders, the standard patterns has remained 60-40 in Abu Dhabi, 51-49 in Libya and 55-45 in Nigeria. Indonesia, meanwhile, has retained its complex production-sharing system.

In some OPEC Countries, concessionaires or ex-concessionaires still receive either profit margins on their equity crude or fees for services. In others, such payments either never existed or have been phased out in the course of time. As of mid-1980, the positions in the leading OPEC producers in this regard were as follows:

Saudi Arabia:
Under the 1976 takeover arrangement, the Aramco parents — Exxon, Socal, Texaco and Mobil — receive service fees initially totalling between 18 and 19 cents per barrel of production. By 1980 this had escalated to around 27 cents/barrel.

Iraq:
No margins or discounts for ex-concessionaires.

228

Iran:
From 1975 up to 1978 Consortium members were entitled to a margin/
discount of 22 cents per barrel of liftings for export (minus interest
payments on investment obligations fulfilled on their behalf by NIOC).
Such discounts were discontinued after the revolution.

Kuwait:
For their first five-year crude oil purchase contract (1975-80) after the
government takeover, the ex-concessionaires, BP and Gulf Oil, were
allowed a discount of 15 cents on each barrel lifted. This has been
discontinued in the new crude contracts as of April 1, 1980.

Qatar:
Under the 1976-77 takeover deals, ex-concessionaires — QPC and Shell —
get a service fee per barrel of production, starting at 15 cents and
escalating with the price of crude oil. By mid-1980 the fee had
presumably escalated to around 42 cents/barrel.

Abu Dhabi:
Equity holding companies get a margin (between tax-paid cost and the
government sale price) on their 40% equity crude entitlement. With the
1979-80 increases in the crude price, this has escalated from about 65
cents/barrel in 1978 to around $1.60/barrel in July 1980.

Libya:
Equity holders get a margin (between TPC and GSP) on their 49%
equity crude entitlement, estimated at around 60 cents/barrel in mid-
1980.

Nigeria:
Equity holders get a margin (between TPC and GSP) on their 45% equity
crude entitlement, estimated at around 80 cents/barrel in mid-1980.

Algeria:
No equity margins or service fees, except for France's CFP which retains
a 49% equity stake in some oilfields.

Venezuela:
After nationalization in 1976, ex-concessionaires were paid service fees
of up to 15 cents per barrel of crude produced plus a similar amount per
barrel refined. Such across-the-board payments were discontinued at the

end of 1979, and services provided by the oil companies are now paid for on a job to job basis.

The Changing Structure of the Oil Market

The widespread assumption of operational control by the producer governments over the upstream (i.e. crude producing) segment of the oil industry from 1974 onwards naturally gave rise to expectations of an upheaval in the structure of the oil market, with the OPEC National Oil Companies (NOCs) taking over from the international companies as purveyors of crude oil to the world.

However, the change was slow in coming about. The takeovers coincided with a period of surplus in the market and, with so much else on their minds at the time, the OPEC Governments were in no mood for too much experimentation with regard to their crude oil marketing patterns. The international majors represented safe, secure outlets for large volumes of crude through well-established channels to their own downstream affiliates and to third parties. So, with their relative lack of experience at the time, it was hardly surprisingly that most of the governments and their NOCs should have opted for security, preferring the devils they knew to the perils of the unknown. The result was that in 1974-75 the international oil companies made a relatively painless transition from being big offtakers of owned crude within the concession system to becoming bulk purchasers of large volumes from the producer governments. Formally speaking, their position had changed from owners to buyers, but the volumes of crude oil that ran through their channels to the ultimate customers had not greatly diminished.

Nevertheless, eventually the expected structural change in the oil market did materialize, slowly at first, then rising to a crescendo in 1979-80 when the tight supply situation gave the OPEC Governments and NOCs — by now much more sophisticated in the mechanics of the oil business — the opportunity to reorganize their marketing patterns in line with their own long-range economic and political objectives.

Traditionally, of the total crude supply at the disposal of the international companies, about 70 to 75% was channeled to their own affiliates and the remaining 25 to 30% sold to third parties. This third-party market, consisting basically of refiner/marketers, both private and state-owned, without adequate access to crude oil supplies of their own, was something that was inevitably likely to gravitate into the orbit of the new OPEC Government sellers of the first resort.

230

This was a two-way process ending up with the elimination of the middleman. Taking stock of the changed status of the major companies and the essential weakness of their position under the new set-up, crude-short refiners — particularly national companies in the consuming countries with the backing of their governments — began making direct approaches to the producer governments with a view to cementing long-term supply relationships.

On the other side, the producer governments, or some of them at least, were interested in taking over the third-party market for a variety of economic and political motives. For one thing there was a desire to cut the majors down to size, since the continued preponderance of their crude offtake in the governments' marketing patterns left the companies with a not inconsiderable leverage over the governments, particularly in times of surplus. Secondly, the producers were aware that there were political and economic benefits to be gained from being a direct supplier of oil to a consuming country, either on a government to government or a national company to national company basis.

Some erosion in the majors' position was already evident during the 1976-78 period. But in 1979-80 came the deluge. Firstly, there was the loss to the Consortium members of automatic preferred access to over 4 million b/d of Iranian oil. Then in late 1979 and early 1980, the majors found their contract volumes being slashed all over the place. In Kuwait, in the new contracts starting in the second quarter of 1980, total deliveries to Kuwait's three major customers — BP, Shell and Gulf Oil — were cut by more than two-thirds, to only 400,000 b/d from the previous level of over 1.3 million b/d. In other countries too — Venezuela, Iraq and Abu Dhabi, among others — the contract volumes of the majors were substantially reduced, though not as dramatically as in Iran or Kuwait.

As a result, the majors have had to carry out a drastic pruning of their third-party sales, while their former customers have, as it were, been recycled to the OPEC NOCs. Some of the majors — those like Shell, BP and Gulf Oil which are outside the charmed circle of Aramco — probably no longer have enough preferred-access and secure contract crude to meet their own integrated needs.

In fact — apart from the pockets of equity and semi-equity crude still available to the international companies in places like Abu Dhabi, Qatar, Nigeria, Indonesia and Libya — Saudi Arabia remains the last really large pool of oil availability to which the majors (that is the lucky four) have automatic preferential access. And even this is being pared down. Direct crude sales by the Saudi national company Petromin, mainly on a government-to-government or government-sponsored basis, have risen from around 500,000 b/d in 1978 to getting on for 2 million b/d in mid-1980; and this, with the increasing quantities lifted by Petromin for local refining and processing deals, has entailed a reduction in the residual Aramco entitlement. In mid-1980, with Saudi production at the 9.5 million b/d level, the Aramco companies are able to lift about 6.8 million b/d. But if output is cut back to 8.5 million b/d (as seems likely) and Petromin's sales increase as scheduled, with deliveries of "incentive" crude to companies investing in refining and petrochemical projects in the Kingdom, the amount remaining for Aramco could fall to less than 5 million b/d, subject to even further erosion with the passage of time.

As well as restructuring their sales patterns, the OPEC NOCs have tightened up the terms of sales contracts to a considerable degree. Volumes are often subject to change at the sellers' option; the traditional margins of tolerance for liftings — usually 10% above or below the contract volume, thus catering for seasonal and other potential fluctuations in demand — have been abolished and customers are required to lift evenly throughout the year. Also, strict destination controls and restrictions on resale or exchange of crude have been introduced in many cases, along with preferential employment for tankers owned by OPEC Countries.

The figures in the table on page 235 give some idea of the trend away from the international oil companies (majors and big independents) and in favour of the OPEC NOCs with regard to supplies of oil moving in the world export trade during the years 1973-79. According to this analysis, made by Petroleum Intelligence Weekly on the basis of one major company's data, the international companies' access to crude oil on a preferential basis (i.e. equity or guaranteed buy-back) has shrunk from 92% of total supply in 1973 to less than 58% in 1979, while the share of producing countries' NOCs has risen from 8% to over 42% during the same period.[8]

Nor do these figures reflect the full extent of the change which has been further accelerating in 1980. According to one well-known petroleum consultant, the majors' share, under secure contracts, of non-Communist crude exports has fallen to as low as 35%, only about two-thirds of their downstream requirements.[9]

It would be difficult to exaggerate the importance of the structural change in the world oil industry signified by these trends. For the consuming countries and their governments the main change, apart from some loss of flexibility in the actual mechanism of the supply system, will be strategic and qualitative rather than quantitative, in that effective control of their oil supplies has passed from western-based, western-oriented oil companies into the hands of a group of Third World governments with a totally different set of priorities and preoccupations. For the majors themselves, it will entail a more or less severe disturbance of equilibrium and orientation, from which recovery will not be easy. For OPEC and its national companies, on the other hand, it should signal a general takeoff into new realms of international power and influence.

The loss of flexibility comes as an inevitable consequence of the break-up of the majors' system. For example, as wholesaling middlemen par excellence, each of the big companies could offer its customers the choice of a whole range of different quality crudes, and tailor qualities and volumes to the needs of individual refiners. This is more difficult for the OPEC NOC suppliers because, unless and until they can work out some kind of exchange or entrepot system between them, the range of crude qualities available in each individual producing country is limited. Other characteristics of the emerging system, inevitably involving a degree of higher costs, include some loss of economy of scale in tanker transportation and a higher level of stocks (one major company has estimated this requirement at an extra 10 days worldwide) to cater for the consequences of fragmentation and upstream uncertainties and rigidity of lifting schedules.

Basically, these are all signs that an industry which has hitherto been characterized by an abnormally high degree of integration right from the production of the raw material to the sale of the final processed product, is now in the process of dis-integration — not in the sense of collapsing or falling apart, but simply that the various segments, upstream and downstream, are drawing away from one another under their now separate centres of control. This could mean that oil will in time begin to exhibit more of the features of other raw material industries (even with futures markets and things like that). On the other hand, one should not underestimate the centripetal drive towards integration in an industry as closely-knit and strategic as oil. The OPEC producers are themselves engaging in a certain degree of downstream integration, by means of expanding refining and petrochemical export capacity in their own countries and entering into crude processing deals with refineries in the consuming areas.

For the majors themselves, as functioning organizations, the change will be hard to digest. Their structures were designed to take advantage of the benefits accruing from the integrated management, handling and processing of oil from the wellhead to the consumer. But the whole edifice was based on ownership and control of the sources of crude oil, and now that base has largely been eroded. They will have to — indeed are having to — scrabble in the market like everyone else, even to meet the needs of their own refineries. Their impressive logistical systems — ultra-large tankers, trans-shipment depots, etc. — were designed to handle bulk volumes which are no longer available to them. So, to the extent that they are unable to replace their lost availability of OPEC oil with owned crude supplies from elsewhere, they will have to restructure themselves to adapt to the new realities. Given their technical expertise, flexibility and financial resources, this task should not be beyond them.

At the same time, there are a number of ways in which the big oil companies can make use of the technological, managerial and financial trump cards at their disposal to improve their prospects in the OPEC Countries or at least ensure that their positions are not undermined any further. One way is for the companies to involve themselves in high-technology oil or gas-based projects for which their expertise is really needed — i.e. in areas such as exploitation, enhanced recover, advanced refining, petrochemicals, etc. To a certain extent this is already happening. For example, companies are investing in exploration in Algeria and Libya as a condition for maintaining their crude oil supply contracts. In Abu Dhabi, France's CFP is the contractor for a huge project to produce oil from an offshore low-energy reservoir (Upper Zakum). And Saudi Arabia is offering extra incentive crude supplies to companies like Shell, Mobil, Exxon and Caltex, which are investing in refining and petro-chemical ventures in the Kingdom.

For OPEC and its national companies, this is a time of unparalleled opportunity. Although domestically in their own countries many of the NOCs are huge concerns in their own right, until recently their impact on the international scene has been limited owing to the continued dominance of the majors in the world oil trade. Now that they have taken charge of the mechanics of the world's crude oil supply and are energetically diversifying into refined product sales as well, there is really nothing that can stop them becoming a force to be reckoned with on the international oil scene.

Changes in the Pattern of World Oil Supplies 1973-79

	% Supply Mix		Volumes in Million Barrels Daily							Chg. 1979/73
	1973	1979	1973	1974	1975	1976	1977	1978	1979	
Producer Nations										
State-to-State	5.0	16.5	1.5	2.0	2.3	3.8	3.7	4.6	5.0	+3.5
Commercial	2.9	25.7	0.9	1.7	2.2	3.3	5.9	5.1	7.8	+6.9
Total	**7.9**	**42.2**	**2.4**	**3.7**	**4.5**	**7.1**	**9.6**	**9.7**	**12.8**	**+10.4**
Oil Companies										
Affiliates	69.6	46.6	21.1	20.0	18.1	17.1	14.2	14.5	14.1	-7.0
Third-Party	22.5	11.2	6.8	6.3	3.9	4.7	5.9	4.8	3.4	-3.4
Total	**92.1**	**57.8**	**27.9**	**26.3**	**22.0**	**21.8**	**20.1**	**19.3**	**17.5**	**-10.4**
Grand Total	**100.0**	**100.0**	**30.3**	**30.0**	**26.5**	**28.9**	**29.7**	**29.0**	**30.3**	

Source: Petroleum Intelligence Weekly, February 25, 1980.

CHAPTER XI

OPEC AID PROGRAMMES

The developing world's principal sources of concessionary finance are the Western industrialized states grouped together in the OECD's Development Assistance Committee (DAC); countries with centrally planned economies (CPEs); and members of OPEC, unique among the major foreign aid donors in themselves being developing countries. OPEC aid programmes, which are not new, have since 1973 undergone dramatic expansion, not only in terms of volume, but also as regards the number of recipients and forms of channels of aid. The story of that growth is outlined in this chapter.

OPEC Aid before 1973

The creation of the Kuwait Fund for Arab Economic Development (KFAED) in 1961, shortly after Kuwait gained full independence and just one year after the foundation of OPEC itself, is generally taken to mark the beginning of the history of OPEC Member State aid programmes. But even before that date, Kuwait had for a number of years been assisting other developing countries in the fields of health and education through its smaller and less well-known aid agency, the General Authority for the Gulf and Southern Arabia (GAGSA). Libya and Saudi Arabia joined Kuwait as substantial OPEC aid donors in 1967, followed by Abu Dhabi in 1971. Algeria, Iran, Iraq and Venezuela were in addition small-scale providers of financial assistance to other less developed countries (LDCs) already before 1973.

Annual aid disbursements by OPEC Members in the period 1967-1972 fluctuated between about $400 million and $700 million. For the principal OPEC donors even then this represented a high share of their GNP, though of course by comparison to present levels volume was small and OPEC Members remained on the periphery of world concessional finance.

Expansion: 1973 To Date

The upward revision of oil prices in 1973, however, enabled OPEC[1] to emerge as a major source of aid to the Third World. Total official flows (concessional and non-concessional) from OPEC Members to other LDCs and multilateral organizations amounted in 1973 to $1.7 billion, three times the level achieved in 1970. A further more than threefold increase in 1974 brought the figure to $5.9 billion, followed in 1975 by peak disbursements of $8.2 billion, or over 4% of the collective OPEC GNP. Cumulative concessional and non-concessional flows from OPEC for 1973-1978 came to some $37 billion, or $43 billion if lending to the IMF Oil Facility is included.[2] About 70% of the former figure, or over $26 billion during 1973-1978, was made available by OPEC Members on concessional terms, that is in the form of official development assistance (ODA), or "aid".[3]

On a disbursement basis, concessional assistance from OPEC Members passed the $1 billion mark in 1973, increasing almost threefold the following year to $3.4 billion. Between 1975 and 1977, annual disbursements ranged between $5.5 billion and $5.9 billion. But (according to provisional OECD data) in 1978, after a period of continually rising volume, OPEC ODA disbursements fell 26% (or $1.5 billion) below their 1977 peak. The fall in disbursements, coinciding with an ebb in OPEC financial surpluses, was in fact largely confined to flows from Kuwait, Saudi Arabia and UAE, which together provide almost 80% of total OPEC aid. Several other smaller OPEC donors (Iraq, Libya and Venezuela) by contrast significantly stepped up disbursements.

The year 1979 saw a further dramatic increase in disbursements by Iraq, a partial recovery in the level of concessional flows from Saudi Arabia, and redoubled aid efforts by Qatar. These developments more than offset a decline in disbursements by other OPEC donors and total OPEC aid disbursements for the year amounted to some $4.7 billion. The table below summarizes the volume of OPEC aid in the 1970s.

Concessional Assistance* by OPEC Members
1970, 1973-1979
(Billion US$)

1970	1973	1974	1975	1976	1977	1978[p]	1979[p]
0.4	1.3	3.4	5.5	5.6	5.9	4.3	4.7

*   net disbursements
p   provisional
Source: OECD

237

OPEC as a result of this expansion is now the world's second largest donor group, a position it has held since 1974, when it provided more than one-fifth of developing countries' net receipts of ODA from all sources. During 1975-1977 OPEC flows accounted for well over one-quarter of net receipts, though in 1978 and 1979 the proportion fell back to about 20% of net receipts. In every year since 1974, two OPEC Members (Kuwait and Saudi Arabia) have ranked among the world's top seven aid-givers in absolute terms, as until 1979 did the UAE; and in both 1976 and 1977 Saudi Arabia was the world's second largest aid donor.

OPEC Aid in Context

There are several possible ways in which the aid efforts of OPEC Member States can be evaluated. The annual volume of OPEC assistance is for example often unfavourably compared to the level of oil importing developing countries' (OIDCs') aggregated net oil import bill, which in 1978 stood at about $20 billion and perhaps reached $35 billion in 1979. However, the aid programmes of OPEC Member States were not conceived solely as vehicles for compensating other LDCs for higher oil prices. If that had been their purpose, the handful of the richest, semi-industrialized LDCs[4] (which together account for over 55% of Third World net oil imports) would have received the bulk of OPEC financial assistance, to the detriment of those LDCs most in need of aid, the 50 "least developed" and "most seriously affected" countries (which take one-fifth of OIDCs' net oil imports), upon which OPEC ODA has in fact been concentrated. Substantial volumes of OPEC aid (perhaps as much as one-half of total flows since 1973) have moreoever been made available to LDCs which are either net exporters of oil or largely self-sufficient in that commodity, but which nevertheless continue to require financial support. Several OPEC Members, it should also be repeated, were well-established aid donors already before the 1973-74 oil price adjustments.

Two more familiar measures of aid-giving performance are the proportion of donor GNP taken up by net aid disbursements (ODA/GNP ratio) and the grant element of aid commitments. The first is primarily an indicator of the donor's effort, while the second focuses on the value of the assistance to the recipient.

As part of a strategy for the Second Development Decade, industrialized countries were called upon by the UN General Assembly at the end of 1970 to increase their official development assistance to a minimum net amount of 0.7% of GNP by the mid-1970s. Most DAC members have endorsed the 0.7% of GNP target; yet since 1970 as a group they have failed to provide more than one-half this amount (see table below). The performance of CPEs makes even this disappointing record seem generous by contrast: aid disbursements by CPEs, accounting for less than 0.1% of their GNP in the early 1970s have slipped to 0.04% of their collective GNP, roughly one-ninth the DAC average.

OPEC donors on the other hand have, as is well-known, sustained uniquely high levels of aid in relation to national income throughout the decade. Already in 1970, the OPEC ODA/GNP ratio was unmatched by the other aid-giving groups. Net ODA disbursements by OPEC Members, 1.24% of their GNP in 1973, equalled roughly 2% of GNP or more during 1974-1977, peaking in 1975 at over 2.7% of GNP. In every year since 1973, the world's four most important aid donors relative to GNP have all been Members of OPEC. In 1977, the combined ODA/GNP ratio of these four countries (Kuwait 10.6%, Qatar 7.93%, Saudi Arabia 4.3% and UAE 10.2%) exceeded 6%; in 1978 it stood at 4% and in 1979 amounted to 3.5% or ten times the corresponding average for DAC countries. Another OPEC Member (Libya) also ranks among the world's top ten donors relative to GNP.

As shown in the table below, the OPEC ODA/GNP ratio steadily declined after its 1975 peak of 2.71%, reflecting the fall in real terms of the value of oil revenues and the growing absorptive capacity of OPEC Members during this period (1975-1978). From provisional OECD data it appears that in 1978 OPEC's ODA/GNP ratio fell below its 1973 level, and showed a further decline in 1979. However, OPEC donors both in 1978 and 1979 were still reserving well over 1% of their collective GNP for their aid programmes and giving more than three times as much aid as DAC countries in relation to GNP.

Net ODA Disbursements of Major Donor Groups, 1970, 1973-1979 (As % of Donor GNP)

	1970	1973	1974	1975	1976	1977	1978	1979
OPEC	0.43	1.24	1.96	2.71	2.27	1.96	1.35[p]	1.28[p]
DAC	0.34	0.30	0.33	0.35	0.33	0.31	0.35	0.34
CPE[e]	0.09	0.09	0.07	0.05	0.03	0.04	0.04	na

e *estimated*
p *provisional*
Source: OECD

The so-called grant element, calculated on the basis of the financial terms of a transaction at the commitment stage and expressed as a percentage, is employed by the OECD to measure the concessionality of aid flows when compared to alternate commercial financing. A grant is said to have a 100% grant element, and according to OECD criteria a loan conveying a grant element of 25% or below fails to qualify as concessional.

In 1973 and before, the overall grant element of OPEC concessional assistance was very high (about 95%) due to the large share of grants in total commitments. The financial terms of OPEC aid hardened considerably in 1974 and 1975, but improved thereafter. With an 88% overall grant element they nevertheless remain marginally less favourable than the terms of DAC assistance.

Such indicators as the ratio of aid to GNP and the grant element, evolved by the OECD to measure the aid-giving performance of DAC countries, are however inadquate to evaluate fairly the OPEC record owing to fundamental differences between OPEC and other donor groups. For example, the OPEC ODA/GNP ratio, impressive though it is, tends to understate the extent of the sacrifice made by OPEC Members through their aid programmes, because these are made possible by the depletion of a finite natural resource that is more in the nature of a capital endowment than the source of indefinitely recurring income. DAC and CPE aid programmes are by contrast overwhelming derived from renewable sources of wealth. The grant element, reflecting interest, grace period and maturity, is furthermore arrived at without reference to the tying status of aid flows. Almost one-half of DAC gross ODA disbursements is tied or partially tied to procurement in the donor country, and its value to the recipient or true grant element is correspondingly reduced. The concessionality of OPEC aid is on the other hand enhanced by the fact that it is essentially untied to source. This may be making a virtue of necessity, though pressures have not been unknown in OPEC Member States to make aid available only for the purchase of goods produced locally.[5] A uniquely high proportion of OPEC aid is moreover untied to use, i.e. made available in the form of quick-disbursing general support assistance which, it has been suggested[6], may be of more real value to the recipient than project aid disbursed over a period of years. If, in short, allowance were made for tying status, the terms of OPEC aid would be seen to be at least as soft as DAC terms.

By boosting demand among Third World countries for the donors' goods and services, DAC states themselves derive economic benefits from their aid programmes. As the DAC area is the major source of procurement for LDCs, this is in a large part true even for untied assistance. OPEC aid flows also indirectly benefit western industrialized countries by creating markets for their exports; but OPEC assistance brings its donors no such material returns. This raises the question of the motivations of OPEC Members to provide foreign aid. Lacking global commercial or strategic interests to promote through their economic assistance programmes, OPEC Countries instead appear to be motivated largely by moral and religious considerations and by their political interest in Third World international solidarity.

Geographic Distribution

Inter-regional solidarity has been of particular importance to individual OPEC Members, and this has shown itself in the geographic distribution of OPEC aid flows. Thus, for example, the Venezuelan aid programme has revealed a preference for other Latin American countries while Nigeria's has concentrated on other sub-Saharan African nations. Since, however, OPEC aid is overwhelmingly provided by Arab Members of the Organization, it is essentially their geographic preferences (as well as other aspects of their aid policies) which the overall picture of OPEC flows portrays; and for these donors, as for others both in and outside of OPEC, charity naturally began "at home": but it by no means ended there.

Of bilateral ODA from OPEC Members as a whole, only 3% went to non-Arab countries in 1973. Increasing diversification of bilateral flows up to 1976, however, raised the share of non-Arab recipients to well over 35% of the total. One sign of this new orientation towards non-Arab nations occurred in 1974. In that year, the statutes of both the Kuwait and Abu Dhabi Funds (previously limited in their operations to Arab countries) were amended to permit the former to lend to all developing countries and the latter to extend assistance to countries throughout Africa and Asia.[7] The more recently established external development funds of OPEC Members, the Iraq and Saudi Funds, have from the beginning had no geographic limitation on their lending operations. Since 1976, the share of Arab countries in bilaterial OPEC aid flows has again increased to about 70% of the total, but this has been paralleled by the growth of aid channelled through the major OPEC-financed multilateral institutions, only two of which lend exclusively to Arab countries.

OPEC bilateral and multilateral flows have now reached at least 76 developing countries since 1973, when only about 20 benefited from

241

OPEC assistance. It is true that certain less developed regions have as yet received comparatively little in the way of assistance from OPEC: the share of Latin American countries for example in OPEC aid comes to little more than 2%. But the African and Asian countries upon which OPEC aid is concentrated are among the world's poorest. Indeed, the distribution of OPEC aid flows appears to be more sensitive to recipients' income levels (i.e. their relative poverty) — and thus more equitable — than the distribution of DAC flows. Only about 12% of OPEC bilateral ODA goes to the higher income LDCs;[8] and over 55% is channelled to the poorest developing countries.[9] By contrast, over one-quarter of DAC bilateral ODA resources is earmarked for higher income LDCs, with little more than one-half going to the poorest.

The Forms of OPEC Aid

OPEC aid to other Third World countries takes a variety of forms, including disaster relief, technical assistance (which for obvious reasons is small), contributions to multilateral organizations, and project assistance. OPEC aid has additionally been made available in the form of concessional credits for the sale of oil, though not to date on a large scale. It may also be recalled in this connection that at a time when there were supply shortfalls and a widening discrepancy between Members' official oil prices and spot market prices, OPEC decided in March 1979 to take action to guarantee lower-income LDCs adequate oil supplies at prices consistent with official postings.

But the distinguishing feature of OPEC aid programmes as regards allocation by purpose is the large share of general budget or balance of payments support assistance.[10] Its relative importance has, however, been declining. In the early years, OPEC aid was composed largely of general support assistance, with well over four-fifths of commitments allocated for this purpose in 1973. Since then, there has been a steady decline in the share of budget or balance of payments support, though it still accounts for a high proportion of the overall total.

This decline is the consequence of the increasing importance of project lending. The shift away from quick-disbursing general support assistance towards project lending has had two immediate effects. First, it has reduced the rate of OPEC aid disbursements and led to the building up of a "pipeline" of undisbursed commitments. This is a common problem for new aid donors; but in view of the fact that most OPEC institutions for the programming of aid are as yet in their infancy, project aid has been disbursed with remarkable speed. Second, it brought about the overall hardening of financial conditions observed earlier, as much of general support assistance (but not project aid) is made available in grant form or on very soft terms.

OPEC project assistance as a whole has emphasized physical and social infrastructure[11] over the industrial and agricultural sectors, though agriculture is gaining favour. Infrastructure has to date received about 60% of the project assistance of the principal OPEC-sponsored aid agencies.[12] The philosophy lying behind this sectoral distribution seems to have been that industry and even agro-business can more readily attract commercial financing, while infrastructural improvements, which cannot, are the most urgent need of the recipients of OPEC project aid. Within infrastructure, energy and transport and roads are the top priorities, accounting for almost one-half of total cumulative project lending to the end of 1977. The energy projects have mainly been power projects, with only a handful of loans provided for the development of hydrocarbons or other fuel mineral resources.

The trend towards increased programming of aid flows since 1973 has been associated with a steady growth in the importance of the multilateral component of OPEC aid programmes. In 1973, most aid was distributed on a bilateral basis, with contributions to multilateral development agencies accounting for less than 8% of total ODA disbursements. The share of multilateral organizations in concessional assistance from OPEC Members had more than doubled by 1976, and now represents about one-third of total ODA disbursements. This is approximately the same position occupied by multilateral disbursements in DAC programmes.

The shift towards project lending and the increased multilateralisation of aid flows are largely explained by the growth of the institutions of OPEC aid. On the bilateral level, more aid is channelled through strengthened or newly-created national agencies whose principal concern is project assistance. Similarly, the creation after 1973 of most of OPEC's multilateral aid agencies (also project orientated) has enhanced the role of project lending and at the same time made it possible for the multilateral component of OPEC aid programmes to assume greater importance. Together these bilateral and multilateral OPEC institutions now command resources exceeding $17 billion.

But before examining these institutions in greater detail, it is important to remember that only approximately one-third of OPEC aid is committed through these channels: most OPEC donors have decided against establishing their own specialized national aid agencies; and the bulk of the bilateral flows of even those OPEC States that have such institutions continues to be distributed on a direct government-to-government basis. The very substantial volumes of OPEC general support assistance in particular are by and large not handled by the organizations described below. The OPEC Fund apart, several OPEC Members furthermore have no or only slight participation in the new multilateral agencies; and a significant (30%) proportion of OPEC multilateral disbursements goes to the traditional, non-OPEC international aid institutions.

The Institutions of OPEC Aid

Prior to 1973, only two OPEC Members, Abu Dhabi and Kuwait, possessed specialized national aid agencies. Kuwait's principal fund, the Kuwait Fund for Arab Economic Development (KFAED) is not only the oldest major OPEC aid agency, but also until recently the largest (bilateral or multilateral), with an authorized capital of $3.6 billion. In its flexibility, aid-giving philosophy, and the autonomy it enjoys from its sponsoring government, KFAED has served as a model for other OPEC institutions, which also actively draw on its experience. In 1971, a decade after KFAED was founded, Abu Dhabi established its Fund for Arab Economic Development (ADFAED) which has an authorized capital of $516 million. The names of these two institutions are of course anachronistic since, as mentioned earlier, they can now lend to non-Arab countries.

Two further external development funds were created by OPEC Members in 1974: the Iraqi Fund for External Development (IFED) and the Saudi Fund for Development (SFD). SFD, with resources of $2.9 billion, is the third largest (bilateral or multilateral) OPEC aid agency. The average grant element of assistance extended by the Abu Dhabi, Kuwait, Iraq and Saudi Funds (mostly for infrastructural projects) ranges from 36% to 49%. Their combined cumulative aid commitments for the period 1973-1978 amounted to almost $5 billion. Other OPEC Countries lack specialized national aid agencies, though some have institutions which combine external assistance with domestic investment such as the Iran Organization for Investment and Economic and Technical Assistance and the Venezuelan Investment Fund, both set up in 1974.

The comparatively limited aid-giving capacity of several of OPEC's "higher absorbers", namely Algeria, Nigeria and Venezuela, has resulted in their pursuing external assistance policies which differ in structure from the overall pattern of OPEC aid flows. Not having the machinery to administer large-scale lending abroad, they have channelled virtually all of their aid through multilateral institutions such as the OPEC Fund, agencies belonging to the UN system, and regional development banks. A noteworthy form of the aid programmes of Algeria, Nigeria and Venezuela has been the establishment of trust funds with non-OPEC regional development banks – assistance from the funds then being given by the banks (the trustees) to their developing country members in accordance with the terms of the trust agreements. The first such fund was Algeria's $14 million Arab Oil Trust Fund, created in 1974 to provide balance of payments support for non-Arab African countries and administered by the African Development Bank (ADB). ADB also administers the Nigeria Trust Fund, set up in 1976 with a capital of approximately $90 million. Its resources are earmarked primarily for the long-term financing of agricultural development and infrastructural projects. The largest of the trust funds is Venezuela's $500 million facility established in 1975 with the Inter-American Development Bank (IDB). Venezuela in the same year also set up a smaller ($25 million) fund with the Caribbean Development Bank (CDB). The resources of the Venezuelan funds are *inter alia* allocated for the financing of projects furthering the exploitation of natural resources, especially non-renewable ones. In order to maximize the coverage of assistance from the funds, the trust instruments of the Nigerian and Venezuelan facilities require the trustees to give priority to projects benefiting several countries simultaneously, projects which promote inter-regional economic co-operation and integration. The combined resources of these regional trust funds (including that of Algeria, now fully drawn down by disbursements) amounts to some $630 million, $370 million of which had been committed by the end of 1978..

In addition to such arrangements, OPEC support for the traditional, non-OPEC multilateral aid agencies has been substantial in recent years. In 1978, disbursements of concessional assistance by OPEC Members to UN agencies and the World Bank exceeded $270 million. But most (about 70% – and over $810 million in 1978) of OPEC's growing assistance to multilateral organizations since 1973 has gone to institutions wholly or largely financed by OPEC Members.

There was only one such institution in existence in 1973. This was the Arab Fund for Economic and Social Development (AFESD), founded in 1971. Based in Kuwait, AFESD has an authorized capital of $1.4 billion, almost 80% of which was pledged by Arab OPEC Members.

Its operations are confined to Arab countries, and its priority object is the financing of inter-Arab infrastructural projects.

Since 1973, a further nine OPEC-financed multilateral aid institutions or special accounts have been created, though three of these are now terminated or merged with other organizations. In addition, there is an array of recently-established OPEC multilateral institutions whose principal task is not concessional finance, but from which non-OPEC LDCs obtain capital that might otherwise not be forthcoming at any price (e.g., Arab Monetary Fund).

Of the newer multilateral aid agencies, the Islamic Development Bank (IsDB), set up in 1974, is second in size only to the OPEC Fund: capitalized at $2.6 billion, it is 80% financed by OPEC Members. IsDB seeks to conduct its operations in accordance with the principles of the Shari'a and undertakes equity investment and interest free lending for industry and infrastructure in Islamic countries. The Arab Bank for Economic Development in Africa (generally known as BADEA, the acronym formed from the French version of its title) was founded in 1975 to strengthen economic, financial and technical co-operation between Arab and African countries. Its capital (some $740 million) is entirely subscribed by members of the League of Arab States (of which over three-quarters by OPEC Countries). Eligible recipients of BADEA assistance on the other hand are African countries not belonging to the Arab League. Of BADEA aid commitments cumulative to the end of 1978, 60% had been allocated for infrastructural and agricultural projects. Now in terms of resources the biggest OPEC-financed aid agency, the $4 billion OPEC Fund (OF) was created in 1976, and is 100% financed by OPEC Members. Its organization and activities are examined in some detail below.

Cumulative concessional disbursements by OPEC's multilateral development agencies exceeded $3 billion by the end of 1978. But in addition to being aid givers in their own right, several have also served as fora for the co-ordination of OPEC Members' aid flows and policies. Periodic meetings of the external development funds of OPEC's Arab Members help them to co-ordinate their operations; BADEA acts as the co-ordinating body for the flow of Arab resources to non-Arab Africa; and one of OF's principal functions is the concertation of Member States' aid programmes.

One sign of this co-operation, and a distinguished feature of OPEC bilateral and multilateral project assistance, has been the prevalence of co-financing arrangements, both among OPEC agencies and between them and traditional sources of concessionary finance such as the World

Bank. Through cofinancing, OPEC donors have played a catalytic role in attracting additional non-OPEC finance to large-scale projects. They have as a result also been able to influence the sectoral composition of non-OPEC aid flows. Moreoever, cofinancing has enabled OPEC aid agencies to overcome their relative lack of experience and qualified staff by taking advantage of project evaluation and supervision undertaken by established development agencies, as well as by avoiding a duplication of preparatory and follow-up work among OPEC-sponsored institutions. This extensive co-operation largely accounts for the swiftness with which OPEC's newly-created aid agencies have been able to disburse project assistance. Several OPEC aid-giving institutions expect eventually to acquire the administrative machinery necessary for independent project appraisal and loan administration. But a reliance on project appraisal and loan administration undertaken by other agencies has thus far been an integral part of the structure of OPEC's collective aid facility, the OPEC Fund, as one of the principal concerns of its founders was to avoid the creation of a full-blown bureaucracy which would constitute a drain on manpower resources and slow down the aid-giving process.

The OPEC Fund

Following proposals by Algeria, Iran and Venezuela, the OPEC Fund (OF) was founded in early 1976 as an international special account collectively owned by the contributing parties, i.e. all 13 OPEC Members. Uncertainty within OPEC at the time as to whether the OF should become a permanent feature on the international aid scene is reflected by the fact that it lacked its own juridical personality, as well as by its initial title ("The OPEC Special Fund"). However in September 1979, the OF's constinent Agreement was amended in order to permit the Fund to use loan repayments to finance future operations, thus providing for the agency's indefinite continuity. More symbolically perhaps, OF's permanence was ensured in January 1980 when OPEC Finance Ministers decided to convert the Fund into "an international agency for financial assistance to other developing countries" and to endow it with legal personality.

Now known formally as "The OPEC Fund for International Development", OF is administered by a Ministerial Council and a Governing Board, on which all Member States of OPEC are represented. Its activities are managed by a Director-General assisted by a small staff. Contributions to OF have been channelled through accounts held in the name of the Fund by Members' Executing National Agencies" (ENAs), several of which are also Members' external development funds. For the appraisal of OF-supported projects and the implementation of OF project lending programmes, the Fund relies heavily on ENAs and on other OPEC and non-OPEC national and international agencies. OF was initially endowed with contributions totalling some $800 million, the bulk of which was provided by Iran, Saudi Arabia and Venezuela. Three further general contributions since 1976, with contributions channelled through OF to other multilateral agencies, have boosted the resources committed to the Fund to approximately $4 billion, making it the largest bilateral or multilateral OPEC aid agency. At the end of August 1980, cumulative OF commitments of concessional assistance to LDCs and multilateral institutions amounted to some $1.4 billion, $745 million of which had been disbursed. Aid channelled through OF has been fairly evenly divided between contributions to other multilateral organizations and, through OF's lending programmes, direct financial assistance to non-OPEC LDCs.

Four lending programmes were launched by OF during 1976-80. These, in contrast to the usual practice of other aid agencies, were pre-designed, both as regards eligible beneficiaries and allocation by purpose. Although all non-OPEC LDCs are in principle eligible to benefit from OF assistance, the Fund drew up priority lists of beneficiaries and allocated to each a pre-determined maximum proportion of the total set aside for the programmes. Economic critera with a regard for broad geographical coverage determined the country limits set by OF, which then invited eligible countries to participate in its programmes. Most of the other funds by contrast consider applications on an ad hoc basis as they are received, limiting the amount that may be loaned for a single project to a proportion of the Fund's capital (usually about 10%) or a proportion of the project's overall cost (usually 50%).

Primarily addressed to those developing countries most in need, the "least developed", "most seriously affected", and other low-income countries, OF lending programmes have consisted of both project assistance and balance of payments support for the importation of essential capital and consumer goods. With an overall average grant element in the 60 to 70% range, the terms of OF lending have been highly concessional. Loans have borne long-term maturities and most have been interest-free, though a small (0.5 to 0.75%) service charge has been made. Almost $200 million was allocated for OF's first lending programme, initiated at the end of 1976 and designed to provide balance of payments support for the 49 most seriously affected countries. A very rapid rate of disbursement led to the virtual completion of the programme within one year of its implementation. The second ($142 million) lending programme, started up in early 1977, was for project assistance to a priority list of 38 lower income LDCs. With the shift to project lending, the rate of disbursements slowed significantly and, by the end of 1978, less than one-half of the total committed had been disbursed. Sixty-two developing countries have benefited from OF's Third Lending Programme,. Started up in mid-1978, it has consisted of both balance of payments loans and project aid. Including an uncommitted portion of the sum allocated for the Second Programme, over $430 million was earmarked for the Third Lending Programme, making it the largest undertaken by OF to date. A Fourth Lending Programme, for which $345 million has been set aside, was approved for implementation starting January 1, 1980. By September 1980, the Fund had committed $807 million through its lending programmes since their inception at the end of 1976, $425 million of which had been disbursed.

Additional resources are mobilized for development under OF balance of payments loans. Under the terms of these loans, borrowers are required to deposit an amount equivalent in their own currencies to the value of the OF foreign exchange loan for the purpose of financing local costs of development projects of programmes and projects mutually agreed upon by them and the OF management. The borrower may opt against this course if he accepts a five-year reduction of the maturity of the loan, but few have done so: OF balance of payments loans amounting to some $400 million have so far generated local counterpart funds equivalent of which $250 million have so far been committed to specific development projects.

The impact of OF direct lending has also been magnified through its cofinancing of development projects already appraised and approved by other development agencies. OF has entered into cofinancing arrangements in support of about $8 billion — worth of projects with a wide variety of institutions — cofinanciers have included national aid agencies of OECD states, the traditional mulilateral development organizations, as well as other OPEC institutions.

Agriculture and energy have together been a main focus of OF project assistance, receiving almost 60% of total commitments. This sectoral preference for "basic needs" has also made itself apparent in the allocation by purpose of the local counterpart funds generated by OF balance of payments support. As of mid-June 1980 over 50% of these funds were destined for agricultural or energy projects chosen by borrowers in co-operation with the Fund's management.

Considerable grant aid moreover has been channelled by OPEC Members, through OF to other multilateral institutions, in particular the IMF

Trust Fund, the United Nations Development Programme (UNDP), and the International Fund for Agricultural Development (IFAD).

The IMF Trust Fund was established in May 1976 to provide additional balance of payments support on concessionary terms to eligible developing IMF member countries. The Trust Fund's resources comprise profits realized from the sale of IMF gold for the benefit of LDCs. As LDCs themselves, OPEC Members were entitled to retain their share of these profits, but seven instead arranged to donate their shares (totalling $108 million at mid-1980) to the Trust Fund through OF.

OF has furthermore to date allocated $40 million on a grant basis to finance regional and inter-regional technical assistance projects. Technical assistance provided through the Fund is mostly conducted in collaboration with UNDP, and 17 such projects have been approved since the autumn of 1977. The accent in these OF programmes for technical assistance has been on regional ventures aimed at increasing food and energy production, again reflecting OF's interest in these sectors.

Out of OF resources, OPEC Members have also committed some $436 million to IFAD, which promotes agricultural progress and increased food production in the Third World. The OPEC contribution (representing over 40% of IFAD resources) was initially made conditional on donations of $600 million from industrialized countries, and was instrumental in making the establishment of IFAD possible.

OF has also been active in institution-building for the new international economic order through its support for the UNCTAD-sponsored Integrated Programme for Commodities and its main component, the proposed Common Fund for the Stabilization of Prices of Primary Commodities. OF has recently expressed its willingness to assist the least developed countries in meeting their contributions to the Common Fund and to make a sizeable voluntary contribution to that Fund. OF's support for the reform of international economic relations is also evident in the research activities its funds, such as those undertaken by the Centre for Research on the New International Economic Order.

OF, finally, plays an important role in co-ordinating the policies and programmes of national aid agencies of OPEC Members, a task entrusted to it by the OPEC Ministerial Committee on Financial and Monetary Matters in August 1977. In order to avoid duplication in carrying out this duty, OF has established links with existing co-ordination mechanisms of OPEC donors. OF management additionally helps to co-ordinate the policies of OPEC Members' representatives on IFAD's governing boards, with the OF Director-General as OPEC's spokesman within IFAD on issues where a common stance has been adopted.

250

Concessional Assistance by OPEC Members 1973-79
Net Disbursements
(In US$ million)

Donor Country	1973	1974	1975	1976	1977	1978[p]	1979[p]
Algeria	25.4	46.9	40.7	53.6	47.2	44.1	45.1
Iran	1.9	408.3	593.1	752.5	221.2	277.6	20.7
Iraq	11.1	422.9	218.4	231.7	61.1	172.0	860.5
Kuwait	345.2	622.5	976.3	615.3	1,517.4	1,268.3	1,098.6
Libyan Jamahiriya	214.6	147.0	261.1	93.6	114.8	169.3	145.6
Nigeria	4.7	15.3	13.9	82.9	64.4	38.0	27.5
Qatar	93.7	185.2	338.9	195.0	196.9	105.7	251.1
Saudi Arabia	304.9	1,029.1	1,997.4	2,407.1	2,408.7	1,470.0	1,969.9
United Arab Emirates	288.6	510.6	1,046.1	1,060.2	1,177.1	690.1	206.6
Venezuela	17.7	58.8	31.0	102.8	51.5	108.9	82.6
TOTAL	**1,307.8**	**3,446.6**	**5,516.9**	**5,594.7**	**5,860.3**	**4,344.0**	**4,708.2**

p = provisional
Source: Flows of Resources from OPEC Members to Developing Countries, Statistical Tables, OECD, Paris, June 1980.

Concessional Assistance by OPEC Members 1973-79

Net Disbursements
(As percent of GNP)

Donor Country	1973	1974	1975	1976	1977	1978[p]	1979[p]
Algeria	0.29	0.37	0.28	0.33	0.25	0.18	0.14
Iran	0.01	0.88	1.13	1.13	0.27	(0.33)	(0.03)
Iraq	0.21	3.98	1.65	1.44	0.32	0.76	2.94
Kuwait	5.72	5.72	8.12	4.36	10.61	6.35	5.14
Libyan Jamahiriya	3.32	1.23	2.31	0.63	0.65	0.93	0.58
Nigeria	0.04	0.07	0.05	0.25	0.16	0.08	0.05
Qatar	15.62	9.26	15.62	7.95	7.93	3.65	5.60
Saudi Arabia	4.04	4.46	5.40	5.73	4.32	2.76	3.15
United Arab Emirates	15.96	7.57	14.12	11.02	10.22	5.60	1.58
Venezuela	0.11	0.20	0.11	0.33	0.14	0.28	0.18
TOTAL	**1.42**	**1.96**	**2.71**	**2.27**	**1.96**	**1.35**	**1.28**

p = provisional

Source: *Flows of Resources from OPEC Members to Developing Countries, Statistical Tables, OECD, Paris, June 1980*

Concessional Assistance by Ten Major Donors* to Developing Countries and Multilateral Agencies 1974-79 (Net Disbursements as percent of GNP)

Country	1974	1975	1976	1977	1978^p	1979^p
UAE	7.57	14.12	11.02	10.22	5.60	1.58
Kuwait	5.72	8.12	4.36	10.61	6.35	5.14
Qatar	9.26	15.62	7.95	7.93	3.65	5.60
Saudi Arabia	4.46	5.40	5.73	4.32	2.76	3.15
Sweden	0.72	0.82	0.82	0.99	0.90	0.94
Netherlands	0.63	0.75	0.82	0.85	0.82	0.93
Norway	0.57	0.66	0.70	0.83	0.90	0.93
Libya	1.23	2.31	0.63	0.65	0.93	0.58
Denmark	0.55	0.58	0.56	0.60	0.75	0.75
France	0.59	0.62	0.62	0.60	0.57	0.59

* *In terms of the proportion of their GNP represented by their aid.*
p = provisional and incomplete data
Sources: Development Co-operation, 1979 Review, Organization for Economic Co-operation and Development (OECD), Paris, and OECD Press Release A(80) 39, June 19, 1980.

Concessional Assistance by Ten Major Donors* to Developing Countries and Multilateral Agencies 1974-79 (Net Disbursements in US$ million)

Country	1974	1975	1976	1977	1978p	1979p
United States	3,437	4,007	4,334	4,159	5,664	4,567
France	1,616	2,093	2,145	2,267	2,705	3,358
Saudi Arabia	1,029	1,997	2,407	2,401	1,470	1,970
Kuwait	622	976	615	1,443	1,268	1,099
Japan	1,126	1,148	1,105	1,424	2,215	2,368
Germany	1,433	1,689	1,384	1,386	2,347	3,350
UAE	511	1,046	1,060	1,229	690	207
Canada	713	880	886	991	1,060	1,042
United Kingdom	717	863	835	914	1,456	2,067
Netherlands	436	604	720	900	1,074	1,404

* In terms of the absolute amounts of aid provided.

p = provisional

Sources: Development Co-operation, 1979 Review, Organization for Economic Co-operation and Development (OECD), Paris, and OECD Press Release A(80)39, June 19, 1980.

Institutions of OPEC Aid
(By Size of Authorized/Subscribed Capital)

Institution	Year Established	Authorized/Subscribed Capital — Amount as of May 79 (bn. $)	Proportion provided by OPEC Members (%)	Geographical Mandate	Sectoral Priorities	Cumulative Aid Commitments, 1973-78 (bn. $)	Estimated Average Grant Element of Assistance (%)
OF	1976	4.0 (a)	100	all non-OPEC LDCs	infrastructure/agriculture	1.2 (b)	61
KFAED	1961	3.6	100	all LDCs	infrastructure	1.7	47
SFD	1974	2.9	100	all LDCs	infrastructure	2.3	49
IsDB	1975	2.6	82	Islamic countries	infrastructure/industry	0.1	50
AFESD	1972	1.4	77	Arab countries	infrastructure	1.0	32
BADEA	1974	0.7	76	non-Arab Africa	agriculture	0.2	42
AAAID	1977	0.5	87	Arab countries	agriculture	n/a	n/a
ADFAED	1971	0.5	100	all LDCs except Latin America	industry	0.6	36
IFED	1974	0.3	100	all LDCs	n/a	0.7 (c)	45
ISF	1974	0.3	93	Islamic countries	education/relief aid	n/a	n/a
AFTAAC	1975	0.3	96	Arab and African countries	education/technical assistance	n/a	n/a
GAGSA	1953	n/a	100	Arab countries	education/health	0.9 (d)	100
Note: IFAD	1976	1.0	43	member LDCs	agriculture	0.1	n/a

(a) As of May 80
(b) Cumulative to December 79
(c) Cumulative to July 79
(d) Cumulative to December 76 (partly estimated).

255

Abbreviations:

KFAED:	Kuwait Fund for Arab Economic Development
SFD:	Saudi Fund for Development
IsDB:	Islamic Development Bank
OF:	The OPEC Fund for International Development
AFESD:	Arab Fund for Economic and Social Development
BADEA:	Arab Bank for Economic Development in Africa
AAAID:	Arab Authority for Agricultural Investment and Development
ADFAED:	Abu Dhabi Fund for Arab Economic Development
IFED:	Iraqi Fund for External Development
ISF:	Islamic Solidarity Fund
AFTAAC:	Arab Fund for Technical Assistance to Arab and African Countries
GAGSA:	General Authority for the Gulf and Southern Arabia
IFAD:	International Fund for Agricultural Development

Operations terminated/merged with other institutions:
Gulf Organization for the Development of Egypt (GODE)
Special Arab Aid Fund for Africa (SAAFA)
OAPEC Special Account (OAPEC Sp. Acc.)

Sources: *KFAED, Chase World Information Corpn., MEES, OECD*

CHAPTER XII

OPEC AND THE NORTH–SOUTH DIALOGUE

In the early days, OPEC's horizons did not extend much beyond the oil companies which were the focus of their initial struggles. But the great transformation of 1973-74 obliged the Member States to take heed of a much wider spectrum of international realities, problems and pressures.

Moves towards some sort of international economic dialogue in the wake of the oil price increase got underway early in 1974, with active encouragement from Iran and Saudi Arabia on the one side and France on the other. The need for some such dialogue became more and more evident as the anti-OPEC campaign in the western oil consuming nations — orchestrated by US Secretary of State Henry Kissinger and culminating in the formation of the International Energy Agency (IEA) in November 1974 — gathered in intensity.

The initial approaches on the possibility of a dialogue centered on an exchange limited to oil producers and western industrialized consumers. This was the way the industrial powers wanted it and continued to want it. But it soon became clear to the OPEC Countries that no such dialogue would be feasible without the participation of the rest of the Third World.

The OPEC Members had always been highly conscious of themselves as an integral part of the Third World. Moreover, as the recent victors in the oil price battle, which marked the first time that a group of Third World raw material producers had, through collective action, scored a resounding economic success against the West, the oil exporters saw themselves as the vanguard which alone had the necessary global weight to lead their fellow developing countries towards the attainment of a better economic deal vis-à-vis the industrialized world.

The ensuing alliance between the oil exporting developing countries (OPEC) and the oil importing developing countries (OIDCs) was not something based on sentiment and fellow-feeling alone. There was a solid backing of practical good sense to it. The OIDCs needed the bargaining strength that only oil could provide in order to have any chance at all of making any impression on the industrial powers. On the other hand, OPEC was in need of political backing from the Third World as a whole in order to counterbalance the pressures and threats to which they were being subjected by the West.

The first step towards cementing this alliance and paving the way towards an international economic dialogue, in which a unified Third World front would face the industrialized nations, was taken in April-May 1974 at the Sixth Special Session of the UN General Assembly devoted to the problems of raw materials and development, which called for the establishment of a "new international economic order". Further progress in this direction was registered at the First Summit Conference of Sovereigns and Heads of State of OPEC Member Countries in Algiers in March 1975, which agreed in principle to holding an "international conference bringing together the developed and developing countries."

The Algiers Summit

In agreeing in principle to the holding of an international conference between the developed and the developing worlds, the Algiers Summit in its concluding Solemn Declaration made it clear that "the objective of such a conference should be to make a significant advance in action designed to alleviate the major difficulties existing in the world economy, and that consequently the conference should pay equal attention to the problems facing both the developed and developing countries."

"Therefore," the Declaration went on, "the agenda of the aforementioned conference can in no case be confined to an examination of the question of energy; it evidently includes the questions of raw materials of the developing countries, the reform of the international monetary system and international co-operation in favour of development in order to achieve world stability."

As regards oil prices, the Declaration stated that these should be determined taking into account the following factors: "the imperatives of conservation of petroleum, including its depletion and increasing scarcity in the future; the value of oil in terms of its non-energy uses; and the conditions of availability, utilization and cost of alternative sources of energy. Moreover, the price of petroleum must be maintained by linking it to certain objective criteria, including the prices of manufactured goods, the rate of inflation, the terms of transfer of goods and technology for the development of OPEC Member Countries."

As regards the supply of oil, the Summit Declaration reaffirmed the readiness of the OPEC Countries "to ensure supplies that will meet the essential requirements of the economies of the developed countries, provided that the consuming countries do not use artificial barriers to distort the normal operation of the laws of supply and demand," while also noting in this context with regard to prices that the OPEC Countries "are prepared to negotiate the conditions for the stabilization of oil prices which will enable the consuming countries to make necessary adjustments to their economies."

The Declaration also listed a number of Third World demands on the developed countries, many of them deriving from the Programme of Action adopted by the UN Sixth Special Session. These included:

— Support by developed countries for measures taken by developing countries to stabilize the prices of their exports of raw materials and other basic commodities at equitable and remunerative levels.
— Fulfillment by the developed countries of the international aid commitments for the Second UN Development Decade.
— Implementation of an effective food programme under which the developed countries should extend grants and assistance to the most seriously affected developing countries with respect to their food and agricultural requirements.
— Acceleration of the development processes of the developing countries, particularly through the adequate and timely transfer of modern technology.
— Co-operation of the industrialized nations in building a major portion of the planned new petrochemical complexes, oil refineries and fertilizer plants in the territories of OPEC Members, with guaranteed access for the products of such plants to the markets of the developed countries.
— Adequate protection against depreciation of the value of the external reserves of OPEC Members, as well as assurance of the security of their investments in the developed countries.
— Opening of the markets of developed countries to primary commodities and manufactured goods produced by the developing countries.
— Reform of the world monetary system to allow for participation in decision-making by the developing countries on a basis of equality.

These requirements constituted the foundation upon which the OPEC Members and other developing countries built their case in the North-South Dialogue which was to come.

In a nutshell, what was being proposed by the OPEC Summit was a blueprint for a new relationship between the Third World (including OPEC) and the industrialized nations, involving guarantees on the part of OPEC regarding (a) the stabilization of oil prices (for the proposed Algerian formula in this regard, see Chapter VII), (b) adequate supplies of oil, and (c) recycling of petrodollars, in return for certain engagements on the part of the industrialized world in favour of the developing countries. At the same time it was made very clear that what was being proposed was a package deal to help to solve the economic problems of both the West and the Third World, and that failure by the West to implement its side of the deal would undermine the whole proposal.

The North-South Dialogue

Hard on the heels of the Algiers Summit, a preparatory meeting for what was later to be known as the Conference on International Economic Co-operation (CIEC) or North-South Dialogue convened in Paris early in April 1975, with a view to preparing the ground for the conference envisaged in the Summit Declaration. Represented at the Paris meeting were seven developing countries – four from OPEC (Algeria, Saudi Arabia, Iran and Venezuela) and three OIDCs (Zaire, India and Brazil) – and the industrialized bloc composed of the nine-nation European Economic Community (EEC), the USA and Japan.

The meetings got off to a bad start with an acrimonious hassle over what it was to be called. Originally billed as "Preparatory Meeting for the International Conference on Energy and Related Economic Problems", the title was changed, after the seven had objected to the focus on energy, to the anodyne but meaningless formulation "Preparatory Meeting for the International Conference Proposed by the President of the French Republic". Trivial though it was, the dispute over the title of the meeting encapsulated a basic difference in orientation between the West and the Third World which persisted all the way through the two long years of the Paris North-South Dialogue: the Third World wanted a broad discussion of all relevant economic issues leading to positive action towards the new international economic order, whereas the West was really only interested in talking about energy. In the circumstances it was not surprising that the meeting broke up without being able to agree on either a format or an agenda for the proposed conference.

Agreement on procedure was finally arrived at in October 1975. Representation at CIEC was to number 27 (counting the nine-nation EEC as one bloc), among which were 19 developing countries – 7 oil exporters (Saudi Arabia, Iran, Venezuela, Nigeria, Iraq, Algeria and Indonesia) and 12 OIDCs (India, Pakistan, Yugoslavia, Egypt, Zambia, Zaire, Cameroon, Brazil, Argentina, Mexico, Peru and Jamaica) – and

8 industrialized participants (the USA, Japan, the EEC, Canada, Australia, Sweden, Spain, and Switzerland). Four commissions were set up on energy, raw materials, development, and financial affairs, each with 15 members (10 from the Third World and 5 from the industrial bloc).

In order to make sure that the group of 8 (G8) did not focus all their efforts on the Energy Commission to the detriment of the other issues, the group of 19 (G19) insisted on the concept of "linkage" between the work of the four commissions. This meant that the commissions would function in parallel, and that progress in any one of the commissions would have to be matched by similar progress in the others. In this manner the OPEC Countries were seeking to use their oil leverage in the Energy Commission to obtain parallel concessions and benefits for the other developing countries.

Disagreements between the two groups over agendas for the commissions were resolved by simply merging the respective agendas proposed by the two sides and permitting any delegation to "raise any subject relevant to the themes of the Dialogue for discussion in the commissions".

For their part, the OPEC participants categorically vetoed any discussion or negotiation about oil price levels as such in the Energy Commission. The setting of oil prices, they pointed out, was the prerogative of OPEC and could not in any way be usurped by CIEC or any other body. However, it was permissible for the question of oil prices to be touched upon indirectly as one of the factors influencing supply and in the context of consideration of the competitive costs of alternative sources of energy, or protection of the purchasing power of energy export earnings (i.e. via indexation to maintain value in real terms).

On their side, the G8 participants were equally adamant in their refusal to consider indexation as a means of protecting the purchasing power of Third World export earnings, either from oil or from any other raw material or commodity.

Despite all the procedural wrangles, CIEC was launched in Paris with a ministerial meeting of the participating nations in mid-December 1975.

Even at this early stage, there were disturbing indications that the much-vaunted North-South Dialogue would not amount to anything more than a talking shop. Heartened by the reappearance of surplus conditions in the oil market, with real prices on the decline, the hardliners among the G8 — the US in particular — were pushing the view that there was no need to concede anything at all to OPEC or the rest of the Third World.

Between December 1975 and July 1976 the four commissions convened five times, with each session lasting about 10 days. During this period — later to be known as the "analytical phase" — the commission participants submitted and discussed position papers on various agenda items. The meagre progress in this phase, which coincided with the inconclusive UNCTAD IV Conference in Nairobi, prompted the G19 to issue statements deploring both the slow pace of CIEC and the disappointing results of UNCTAD IV.

In order to review progress to date and set guidelines for future work, a meeting of senior officials of the 27 CIEC participating entities was held early in July 1976. This meeting directed that the second phase of CIEC must be "action oriented", and that the commissions should formulate "concrete proposals for action" for submission to the final ministerial meeting. However, the senior officials failed to agree on specific areas of co-operation in any of the commissions, and the commission members were in turn unable to draw up their own timetables and priorities.

In September 1976, after extensive consultations by the CIEC co-presidents, the commissions finally adopted a "programme of work." G19 presented detailed papers on all major items of the work programme, and left the choice of negotiations on any or all of them up to the G8 to decide. The latter, however, were unable to agree among themselves on a suitable package. As a result, the final ministerial meeting, which had been scheduled for December 1976, had to be postponed and the commissions adjourned for three months.

In April 1977, negotiations were resumed at the level of contact groups assigned to draft the final areas of agreement in each of the four commissions. But, here again, very little was agreed upon. The senior officials met once more at the end of May, with the object of improving upon the work of the contact groups and drafting common texts on agreed proposals, as well as indentifying areas of disagreement. A report of limited scope was prepared on non-controversial issues; but almost all questions of substance were referred to the Ministers for action. At their concluding meeting (May 31 to June 2, 1977), the Ministers did an enormous amount of hard bargaining, but these last-minute efforts did not have the necessary force to overcome the combination of rigid positions and sheer inertia which had built up over the many months of sterile debate.

The Demise of the Dialogue

With disagreement having been registered on virtually all of the major issues that the North-South Dialogue was set up to tackle, only three tiny crumbs of tangible accord could be salvaged from the debris:

- G8 undertook to contribute, subject to the necessary legislative approval, $1 billion for a special action programme to help to meet the urgent needs of individual low-income countries "facing general problems of transfer of resources."
- G8 agreed in principle to underwrite a common fund for the purpose of financing buffer stock for certain raw materials exported by LDCs, with the details left for further negotiation in UNCTAD.
- Industrial donor countries pledged to increase their flow of official development assistance (ODA) "effectively and substantially" in real terms. The governments that had not yet accepted the UN target of 0.7% of GNP as their annual aid objective, committed themselves to work towards that goal.

By any standards this was a dismal result to show for two years' work. Even those commitments that were made by the G8 were not binding and were never in fact carried out in practice. As can be seen from the table on page 239, the industrialized countries have never reached anywhere near the aid target figure of 0.7% of GNP.

The question then arose as to whether, and in what form, there should be any continuation or follow-up of the CIEC Dialogue. G8 specifically hoped to persuade G19 to agree to the setting up of a new consultative forum for energy. Ostensibly, the idea was to "establish a framework of co-operation aimed at developing under optimal conditions the world's energy resources." This was to be achieved through continued regular discussion between the oil producers and the oil consumers. But the intention of making use of the proposed forum as a counterweight to OPEC was only too transparent, and the idea was turned down by G19.

A compromise put forward by Saudi Arabia proposed that an institution should be set up under the aegis of the UN to deal with questions of transfer of technology in general, in which energy matters could also be discussed, including long-term forecasting of supply and demand, but definitely not matters concerning oil prices or oil production decisions in the near to medium term. This compromise proposal was reportedly well viewed by G19, but was rejected by G8.[1]

Meanwhile, among themselves G19 had been debating whether there should be any effort at continuation of the Dialogue within the CIEC framework or something like it. Some, like Saudi Arabia, were in favour because they felt that meagre though the results had been, some movement had nevertheless been achieved, and that, owing to the presence of the oil leverage, CIEC provided a better framework for negotiating economic issues to the advantage of the Third World than any existing UN forum. However, the G19 majority felt that CIEC had served its term and opted for a return of the campaign for a new international economic order to the Group of 77 and the appropriate UN bodies.

Since then the UN Committee of the Whole has been following up the issues which were raised inconclusively in CIEC, but progress has been minimal and prospects for a breakthrough are practically non-existent.

As for the admirable report of the Brandt Commission with its clear-sighted warnings of impending disaster if nothing is done quickly to alleviate the plight of the Third World, and its clarion call for an immediate emergency action programme for 1980-85, this has been publicly reviled and rejected in a number of western capitals.[2]

All in all things have rarely looked bleaker on the North-South Dialogue front.

Prospects for the Baghdad Summit

With the renewed surge in oil prices in 1979-80, and a fresh set of politico-economic problems in its train, the time is certainly ripe for the holding of a Second Summit Conference of OPEC Heads of State.

Of all the problems facing the OPEC leaders, none is more serious and urgent than the economic plight of the Third World — in particular, of course, the oil importing developing countries. After the first oil price rise, the OPEC Countries embarked upon the most generous aid-giving programme in history. This, together with recycling of petro-dollars via western banks, enabled the OIDCs to weather the storm during 1974-78. Now, as a result of the new oil price increase, the oil import bill of the OIDCs has risen by some $25 billion (or 2.5% of GNP — roughly the same impact in GNP terms as with the 1973-74 crisis) from $26 billion in 1978 to $51 billion in 1980, with oil imports accounting for 25% of total export earnings as against 19% in 1978.[3] And this time, though it is too early to judge properly, recycling may prove to be more problematical.

So, undoubtedly, something more in the way of help is required for the affected Third World countries. The OPEC Members are well aware of this, and it is certain that they will not lag behind in fulfilling their responsibility in this regard. But OPEC by itself cannot fill the whole gap; unless and until the industrialized countries also do their fair share, there can be no satisfactory solution.

Where the question of aid to developing countries is concerned, OPEC is not the problem. The problem lies in the industrialized world whose miserable aid-giving performance – scarcely reaching even half the often proclaimed and acknowledged target of 0.7% of GNP – has been little short of shameful.

One thing that can be done for the OIDCs, and done without delay because for once everyone – OPEC, the industrialized countries, the World Bank and the OIDCs themselves – agrees that it is a good idea, is a massive aid programme to promote exploration for and development of indigenous energy resources in the energy-deficient developing countries.

Everybody has something to gain from boosting the energy resources of the OIDCs. Apart from the obvious benefits to the OIDCs themselves, it is in OPEC's interest because otherwise the rapidly increasing energy consumption of these countries will be an extra drain (and a subsidised drain at that) on OPEC oil revenues. The industrialized countries also benefit because every priority barrel of OPEC oil imported by an OIDC means that much less OPEC oil availability for the western consumers.

Meanwhile, some OPEC (notably Iraq and Venezuela), and non-OPEC (Mexico) producers have been refunding to developing country customers part of the full cost of their oil imports in the form of soft loans.

On an altogether broader scale, two imaginative and comprehensive proposals for large-scale OPEC aid to the Third World are to be put before the Baghdad Summit via the report of the Long-Term Strategy Committee.

Algeria and Venezuela have proposed the creation of an international development agency with an initial authorized capital of $20 billion which would assist developing countries in the following fields:
- Loans and grants to assist OIDCs in covering the cost of their oil imports.
- Financing of projects on favourable terms, particularly those relating to the development of indigenous energy resources in OIDCs.
- Underwriting of loans and credits for developing countries on financial markets.

A second proposal tabled by Iraq would fairly and squarely divide the burden of aid to the OIDCs between the industrialized countries and OPEC according to the direct responsibility of each. The contribution of the industrialized countries would be based on the rate of inflation of the prices of their exports to developing countries, while that of OPEC would be based on any new price increases calculated on the quantities of oil exported to developing countries. The proceeds of these contributions would be paid into a "joint fund for energy and development" which would: provide grants and soft loans for the least developed countries; finance exploration for and development of energy resources in developing countries endowed with some energy potential; and extend commercial and semi-commercial loans to relatively well-off developing countries which might face problems in finding short-term finance for oil imports and other deficits.

The Iraqi proposal certainly has the smack of equity and justice about it (provided of course that the industrialized countries can be persuaded to do their bit) and has been well received in preliminary soundings with Third World leaders.

The Long-Term Strategy Committee's Report does not rule out the possibility of some direct dialogue between OPEC and the industrialized world on problems of bilateral concern — in fact, it feels that some such development is probably inevitable. It is, however, recognized that the satisfaction of the pressing needs of the developing countries should be given priority.

According to the Report, OPEC should participate as a bloc in any such dialogue with the industrialized countries with a view to obtaining the following: access to western markets for OPEC refined products and petrochemicals; access to existing and advanced technology for OPEC industries; increased involvement of industrialized countries in oil and gas exploration operations in the OPEC area; OPEC participation in joint research and development activities; the location of energy intensive industries in areas of natural gas production in OPEC Countries; and the lifting of trade barriers against non-oil exports from oil producing countries.

In addition to these questions of North-South Dialogue, however, the OPEC Summit will also be pondering the weighty problem of a long-term pricing policy along the lines of the formula described in Chapter VIII.

Finally, whatever blueprint for the future is unveiled by the OPEC leaders at their November 1980 Summit, it is fitting that they should proclaim it in Baghdad — the city that witnessed the birth of the oil exporters' Organization 20 years previously. In 1980, however, it is not just the fate of their own countries that they decide upon, but the fate of the world as well.

STATISTICAL APPENDIX

ALGERIA

Year	Cumulative discoveries (million bbl)	Remaining proven reserves (million bbl)	Production Daily average (1,000 b/d)	Production Annual (million bbl)	Cumulative (million bbl)	Percentage produced from cumulative reserves (%)	Reserve/production ratio (years)
1960	5,266.3	5,200.0	181.1	66.3	66.3	1.3	78.4
1961	5,687.1	5,500.0	330.9	120.8	187.1	3.3	45.5
1962	6,846.6	6,500.0	436.9	159.5	346.6	5.1	40.8
1963	7,530.6	7,000.0	504.3	184.1	530.6	7.0	38.0
1964	8,234.8	7,500.0	557.8	204.1	734.8	8.9	36.7
1965	8,338.7	7,400.0	558.7	203.9	938.7	11.3	36.3
1966	8,451.0	7,250.0	718.7	262.3	1,201.0	14.2	27.6
1967	8,402.4	6,900.0	825.7	301.4	1,502.4	17.9	22.9
1968	8,833.4	7,000.0	904.2	331.0	1,833.4	20.8	21.1
1969	10,178.8	8,000.0	946.4	345.4	2,178.8	21.4	23.2
1970	10,652.4	8,098.0	1,029.1	375.6	2,554.4	24.0	21.6
1971	12,681.1	9,840.0	785.4	286.7	2,841.1	22.4	34.3
1972	12,979.9	9,750.0	1,062.3	388.8	3,229.9	24.9	25.1
1973	11,270.4	7,640.0	1,097.3	400.5	3,630.4	32.2	19.1
1974	11,698.5	7,700.0	1,008.6	368.1	3,998.5	34.2	20.9
1975	11,727.2	7,370.0	982.6	358.6	4,357.2	37.2	20.5
1976	11,550.7	6,800.0	1,075.1	393.5	4,750.7	41.1	17.3
1977	11,771.2	6,600.0	1,152.3	420.6	5,171.2	43.9	15.7
1978	11,895.1	6,300.0	1,161.2	423.8	5,595.1	47.0	14.9
1979	14,456.2	8,440.0	1,153.8	421.1	6,016.2	41.6	20.0

ECUADOR

Year	Cumulative discoveries (million bbl)	Remaining proven reserves (million bbl)	Production Daily average (1,000 b/d)	Production Annual (million bbl)	Cumulative (million bbl)	Percentage produced from cumulative reserves (%)	Reserve/production ratio (years)
1960	32.7	30.0	7.5	2.7	2.7	8.3	11.0
1961	35.7	30.0	8.0	2.9	5.7	15.9	10.3
1962	33.2	25.0	7.0	2.6	8.2	24.8	9.7
1963	35.7	25.0	6.8	2.5	10.7	30.0	10.1
1964	38.5	25.0	7.6	2.8	13.5	35.0	8.9
1965	36.3	20.0	7.8	2.8	16.3	45.0	7.0
1966	37.0	18.0	7.3	2.7	19.0	51.4	6.8
1967	46.3	25.0	6.2	2.3	21.3	46.0	11.0
1968	348.1	325.0	5.0	1.8	23.1	6.6	179.1
1969	524.7	500.0	4.4	1.6	24.7	4.7	310.9
1970	776.2	750.0	4.1	1.5	26.2	3.4	506.8
1971	5,775.5	5,748.0	3.7	1.4	27.5	0.5	4,245.2
1972	5,806.1	5,750.0	78.1	28.6	56.1	1.0	201.2
1973	5,807.3	5,675.0	208.8	76.2	132.3	2.3	74.5
1974	2,696.9	2,500.0	177.0	64.7	196.9	7.3	38.7
1975	2,705.7	2,450.0	160.9	58.7	255.7	9.4	41.7
1976	2,024.4	1,700.0	187.8	68.8	324.4	16.0	24.7
1977	2,031.3	1,640.0	183.4	66.9	391.3	19.3	24.5
1978	1,635.0	1,170.0	201.8	73.7	465.0	28.4	15.9
1979	1,643.2	1,100.0	214.2	78.1	543.2	33.1	14.1

GABON

Year	Cumulative discoveries (million bbl)	Remaining proven reserves (million bbl)	Production Daily average (1,000 b/d)	Production Annual (million bbl)	Cumulative (million bbl)	Percentage produced from cumulative reserves (%)	Reserve/production ratio (years)
1960	155.6	150.0	15.4	5.6	5.6	3.6	26.7
1961	161.1	150.0	14.9	5.4	11.1	6.9	27.5
1962	167.1	150.0	16.4	6.0	17.1	10.2	25.0
1963	173.5	150.0	17.7	6.4	23.5	13.5	23.3
1964	201.2	170.0	21.0	7.7	31.2	15.5	22.2
1965	215.3	175.0	24.9	9.1	40.3	18.7	19.2
1966	250.7	200.0	28.6	10.4	50.7	20.2	19.2
1967	425.9	350.0	69.0	25.2	75.9	17.8	13.9
1968	574.6	465.0	91.9	33.6	109.6	19.1	13.8
1969	646.0	500.0	99.8	36.4	146.0	22.6	13.7
1970	882.7	700.0	108.8	36.7	182.7	20.7	19.1
1971	974.5	750.0	114.6	41.8	224.5	23.0	17.9
1972	1,370.4	1,100.0	125.2	45.8	270.4	19.7	24.0
1973	1,825.2	1,500.0	150.2	54.8	325.2	17.8	27.4
1974	2,148.7	1,750.0	201.5	73.5	398.7	18.6	23.8
1975	2,680.1	2,200.0	223.0	81.4	480.1	17.9	27.0
1976	2,686.7	2,125.0	222.8	81.5	561.7	20.9	26.1
1977	2,692.7	2,050.0	222.0	81.0	642.7	23.9	25.3
1978	2,688.9	1,970.0	208.7	76.2	718.9	26.7	25.9
1979	1,293.1	500.0	203.4	74.2	793.1	61.3	6.7

INDONESIA

Year	Cumulative discoveries (million bbl)	Remaining proven reserves (million bbl)	Production Daily average (1,000 b/d)	Production Annual (million bbl)	Cumulative (million bbl)	Percentage produced from cumulative reserves (%)	Reserve/production ratio (years)
1960	9,649.9	9,500.0	409.6	149.9	149.9	1.6	63.4
1961	9,804.8	9,500.0	424.3	154.9	304.8	3.1	61.3
1962	10,470.3	10,000.0	453.4	165.5	470.3	4.5	60.4
1963	10,632.3	10,000.0	444.0	162.1	632.3	5.9	61.7
1964	10,799.4	10,000.0	456.6	167.1	799.4	7.4	59.8
1965	10,474.9	9,500.0	480.6	175.4	974.9	9.3	54.2
1966	10,244.4	9,100.0	464.6	169.6	1,144.4	11.2	53.7
1967	10,328.9	9,000.0	505.4	184.5	1,328.9	12.9	48.8
1968	10,398.8	8,850.0	600.7	219.9	1,548.8	14.9	40.3
1969	10,819.7	9,000.0	742.3	270.9	1,819.7	16.8	33.2
1970	12,131.3	10,000.0	853.6	311.5	2,131.3	17.6	32.1
1971	12,856.9	10,400.0	892.1	325.6	2,456.9	19.1	31.9
1972	12,857.5	10,005.0	1,080.8	395.6	2,852.5	22.2	25.3
1973	13,841.0	10,500.0	1,338.5	488.6	3,341.0	24.1	21.5
1974	18,842.7	15,000.0	1,374.5	501.7	3,842.7	20.4	29.9
1975	18,319.6	14,000.0	1,306.5	476.9	4,319.6	23.6	29.4
1976	15,369.9	10,500.0	1,503.6	550.3	4,869.9	31.7	19.1
1977	15,485.3	10,000.0	1,686.1	615.4	5,485.3	35.4	16.2
1978	16,282.2	10,200.0	1,635.2	596.8	6,082.2	37.4	17.1
1979	16,262.8	9,600.0	1,590.8	580.6	6,662.8	41.0	16.5

IRAN

Year	Cumulative discoveries (million bbl)	Remaining proven reserves (million bbl)	Production Daily average (1,000 b/d)	Production Annual (million bbl)	Cumulative (million bbl)	Percentage produced from cumulative reserves (%)	Reserve/production ratio (years)
1960	35,390.8	35,000.0	1,067.7	390.8	390.8	1.1	89.6
1961	35,829.6	35,000.0	1,202.2	438.8	829.6	2.3	79.8
1962	38,316.7	37,000.0	1,334.5	487.1	1,316.7	3.4	76.0
1963	38,861.0	37,000.0	1,491.3	544.3	1,861.0	4.8	68.0
1964	40,487.1	38,000.0	1,710.7	626.1	2,487.1	6.1	60.7
1965	43,183.6	40,000.0	1,908.3	696.5	3,183.6	7.4	57.4
1966	48,161.7	44,200.0	2,131.8	778.1	3,961.7	8.2	56.8
1967	48,711.9	43,800.0	2,603.2	950.2	4,911.9	10.1	46.1
1968	59,951.3	54,000.0	2,839.8	1,039.4	5,951.3	9.9	52.0
1969	62,183.4	55,000.0	3,375.8	1,232.2	7,183.4	11.6	44.6
1970	78,581.0	70,000.0	3,829.0	1,397.6	8,581.0	10.9	50.1
1971	65,737.9	55,500.0	4,539.5	1,656.9	10,237.9	15.6	33.5
1972	77,076.4	65,000.0	5,023.1	1,838.5	12,076.4	15.7	35.4
1973	74,215.6	60,000.0	5,860.9	2,139.2	14,215.6	19.2	28.0
1974	82,413.5	66,000.0	6,021.6	2,197.9	16,413.5	19.9	30.0
1975	82,866.3	64,500.0	5,350.1	1,952.8	18,366.3	22.2	33.0
1976	83,519.4	63,000.0	5,882.9	2,153.1	20,519.4	24.6	29.3
1977	84,586.4	62,000.0	5,662.8	2,066.9	22,586.4	26.7	30.0
1978	83,499.6	59,000.0	5,241.7	1,913.2	24,499.6	29.3	30.8
1979	83,638.8	58,000.0	3,121.2	1,139.2	25,638.8	30.7	50.9

IRAQ

Year	Cumulative discoveries (million bbl)	Remaining proven reserves (million bbl)	Production		Cumulative (million bbl)	Percentage produced from cumulative reserves (%)	Reserve/production ratio (years)
			Daily average (1,000 b/d)	Annual (million bbl)			
1960	27,355.8	27,000.0	972.2	355.8	355.8	1.3	75.9
1961	27,223.7	26,500.0	1,007.1	367.9	723.7	2.7	72.0
1962	27,092.0	26,000.0	1,009.2	368.4	1,092.0	4.0	70.6
1963	27,016.1	25,500.0	1,161.9	424.1	1,516.1	5.6	60.1
1964	26,975.5	25,000.0	1,255.2	459.4	1,975.5	7.3	54.4
1965	27,454.6	25,000.0	1,312.6	479.1	2,454.6	8.9	52.2
1966	26,962.8	24,000.0	1,392.2	508.1	2,962.8	11.0	47.2
1967	26,911.0	23,500.0	1,228.1	448.2	3,411.0	12.7	52.4
1968	31,961.2	28,000.0	1,503.3	550.2	3,961.2	12.4	50.9
1969	32,016.5	27,500.0	1,521.2	555.2	4,516.5	14.1	49.5
1970	37,081.7	32,000.0	1,548.6	565.2	5,081.7	13.7	56.6
1971	41,690.0	35,990.0	1,694.1	618.3	5,700.0	13.7	58.2
1972	35,236.4	29,000.0	1,465.5	536.4	6,236.4	17.7	54.1
1973	38,473.0	31,500.0	2,018.1	736.6	6,973.0	18.1	42.8
1974	42,692.3	35,000.0	1,970.6	719.3	7,692.3	18.0	48.7
1975	42,817.8	34,300.0	2,261.7	825.5	8,517.8	19.9	41.5
1976	43,401.8	34,000.0	2,415.4	884.0	9,401.8	21.7	38.5
1977	44,758.9	34,500.0	2,348.2	857.1	10,258.9	22.9	40.3
1978	43,294.1	32,100.0	2,562.0	935.1	11,194.1	25.9	34.3
1979	43,463.1	31,000.0	3,476.9	1,269.1	12,463.1	28.7	24.4

KUWAIT

Year	Cumulative discoveries (million bbl)	Remaining proven reserves (million bbl)	Production Daily average (1,000 b/d)	Production Annual (million bbl)	Cumulative (million bbl)	Percentage produced from cumulative reserves (%)	Reserve/production ratio (years)
1960	65,619.2	65,000.0	1,691.8	619.2	619.2	0.9	105.0
1961	66,252.5	65,000.0	1,735.0	633.3	1,252.5	1.9	102.6
1962	68,717.1	66,750.0	1,957.8	714.6	1,967.1	2.9	93.4
1963	71,232.2	68,500.0	2,096.3	765.2	2,732.2	3.8	89.5
1964	72,824.4	69,250.0	2,301.0	842.2	3,574.4	4.9	82.2
1965	73,135.9	68,700.0	2,360.3	861.5	4,435.9	6.1	79.7
1966	80,542.6	75,200.0	2,484.1	906.7	5,342.6	6.6	82.9
1967	83,005.0	76,750.0	2,499.8	912.4	6,255.0	7.5	84.1
1968	83,711.6	76,500.0	2,613.5	956.5	7,211.6	8.6	80.0
1969	82,723.9	74,500.0	2,773.4	1,012.3	8,223.9	9.9	73.6
1970	89,265.1	79,950.0	2,989.6	1,091.2	9,315.1	10.4	73.3
1971	88,679.9	78,198.0	3,196.7	1,166.8	10,481.9	11.8	67.0
1972	84,583.5	72,900.0	3,283.0	1,201.6	11,683.5	13.8	60.7
1973	85,535.9	72,750.0	3,020.4	1,102.4	12,785.9	14.9	66.0
1974	95,165.2	81,450.0	2,546.1	929.3	13,715.2	14.4	87.6
1975	85,676.0	71,200.0	2,084.2	760.7	14,476.0	16.9	93.6
1976	85,811.2	70,550.0	2,145.4	785.2	15,261.2	17.8	89.8
1977	86,079.9	70,100.0	1,969.0	718.7	15,979.9	18.6	97.5
1978	86,197.8	69,440.0	2,131.4	778.0	16,757.8	19.4	89.3
1979	86,184.5	68,530.0	2,456.6	896.7	17,654.5	20.5	76.4

SOCIALIST PEOPLES LIBYAN ARAB JAMAHIRIYA

Year	Cumulative discoveries (million bbl)	Remaining proven reserves (million bbl)	Production Daily average (1,000 b/d)	Production Annual (million bbl)	Cumulative (million bbl)	Percentage produced from cumulative reserves (%)	Reserve/production ratio (years)
1960	2,000.0	2,000.0	0.0	0.0	0.0	0.0	0.0
1961	3,006.6	3,000.0	18.2	6.6	6.6	0.2	451.7
1962	4,573.2	4,500.0	182.3	66.5	73.2	1.6	67.6
1963	7,234.5	7,000.0	441.8	161.3	234.5	3.2	43.4
1964	9,550.1	9,000.0	862.4	315.6	550.1	5.8	28.5
1965	10,994.9	10,000.0	1,218.8	444.9	994.9	9.0	22.5
1966	21,542.8	20,000.0	1,501.1	547.9	1,542.8	7.2	36.5
1967	31,378.1	29,200.0	1,740.5	635.3	2,178.1	6.9	46.0
1968	33,130.5	30,000.0	2,602.1	952.4	3,130.5	9.4	31.5
1969	39,265.3	35,000.0	3,109.1	1,134.8	4,265.3	10.9	30.8
1970	34,676.4	29,200.0	3,318.0	1,211.1	5,476.4	15.8	24.1
1971	31,484.1	25,000.0	2,760.8	1,007.7	6,484.1	20.6	24.8
1972	37,703.7	30,400.0	2,239.4	819.6	7,303.7	19.4	37.1
1973	33,597.6	25,500.0	2,174.9	793.9	8,097.6	24.1	32.1
1974	35,252.9	26,600.0	1,521.3	555.3	8,652.9	24.5	47.9
1975	35,293.0	26,100.0	1,479.8	540.1	9,193.0	26.0	48.3
1976	35,400.3	25,500.0	1,932.6	707.3	9,900.3	28.0	36.1
1977	35,653.5	25,000.0	2,063.4	753.1	10,653.5	29.9	33.2
1978	35,677.1	24,300.0	1,982.5	723.6	11,377.1	31.9	33.6
1979	35,640.0	23,500.0	2,090.1	762.9	12,140.0	34.1	30.8

NIGERIA

Year	Cumulative discoveries (million bbl)	Remaining proven reserves (million bbl)	Daily average (1,000 b/d)	Production Annual (million bbl)	Cumulative (million bbl)	Percentage produced from cumulative reserves (%)	Reserve/production ratio (years)
1960	156.4	150.0	17.4	6.4	6.4	4.1	23.6
1961	323.2	300.0	46.0	16.8	23.2	7.2	17.9
1962	447.8	400.0	67.5	24.6	47.8	10.7	16.2
1963	575.7	500.0	76.5	27.9	75.7	13.2	17.9
1964	1,119.7	1,000.0	120.2	44.0	119.7	10.7	22.7
1965	3,219.8	3,000.0	274.2	100.1	219.8	6.8	30.0
1966	3,872.2	3,500.0	417.6	152.4	372.2	9.6	23.0
1967	4,038.7	3,550.0	319.1	116.5	488.7	12.1	30.5
1968	4,540.4	4,000.0	141.3	51.7	540.4	11.9	77.3
1969	5,737.6	5,000.0	540.3	197.2	737.6	12.9	25.4
1970	10,432.9	9,300.0	1,083.1	395.3	1,132.9	10.9	23.5
1971	13,371.8	11,680.0	1,531.2	558.9	1,691.8	12.7	20.9
1972	17,356.4	15,000.0	1,815.7	664.5	2,356.4	13.6	22.6
1973	23,106.2	20,000.0	2,054.3	749.8	3,106.2	13.4	26.7
1974	24,829.2	20,900.0	2,255.0	823.1	3,929.2	15.8	25.4
1975	24,780.1	20,200.0	1,783.2	650.9	4,580.1	18.5	31.0
1976	24,836.6	19,500.0	2,066.8	756.4	5,336.6	21.5	25.8
1977	24,797.6	18,700.0	2,085.1	761.1	6,097.6	24.6	24.6
1978	24,990.0	18,200.0	1,897.0	692.4	6,790.0	27.2	26.3
1979	25,031.3	17,400.0	2,304.9	841.3	7,631.3	30.5	20.7

QATAR

Year	Cumulative discoveries (million bbl)	Remaining proven reserves (million bbl)	Production Daily average (1,000 b/d)	Production Annual (million bbl)	Cumulative (million bbl)	Percentage produced from cumulative reserves (%)	Reserve/production ratio (years)
1960	2,563.9	2,500.0	174.6	63.9	63.9	2.5	39.1
1961	2,878.6	2,750.0	177.2	64.7	128.6	4.5	42.5
1962	3,196.6	3,000.0	186.2	68.0	196.6	6.1	44.1
1963	3,216.4	2,950.0	191.5	69.9	266.4	8.3	42.2
1964	3,845.3	3,500.0	215.3	78.8	345.3	9.0	44.4
1965	3,430.2	3,000.0	232.6	84.9	430.2	12.5	35.3
1966	4,536.5	4,000.0	291.3	106.3	536.5	11.8	37.6
1967	4,404.6	3,750.0	323.6	118.1	654.6	14.9	31.8
1968	4,653.8	3,875.0	339.5	124.3	778.8	16.7	31.2
1969	6,408.6	5,500.0	355.5	129.7	908.6	14.2	42.4
1970	5,340.8	4,300.0	362.4	132.3	1,040.8	19.5	32.5
1971	7,198.0	6,000.0	430.7	157.2	1,198.0	16.6	38.2
1972	8,374.6	7,000.0	482.4	176.5	1,374.6	16.4	39.7
1973	8,082.8	6,500.0	570.3	208.2	1,582.8	19.6	31.2
1974	7,772.0	6,000.0	518.4	189.2	1,772.0	22.8	31.7
1975	7,781.7	5,850.0	437.6	159.7	1,931.7	24.8	36.6
1976	7,813.7	5,700.0	497.3	182.0	2,113.7	27.1	31.3
1977	7,876.0	5,600.0	444.6	162.3	2,276.0	28.9	34.5
1978	6,453.6	4,000.0	486.7	177.6	2,453.6	38.0	22.5
1979	6,399.1	3,760.0	508.1	185.5	2,639.1	41.2	20.3

SAUDI ARABIA

Year	Cumulative discoveries (million bbl)	Remaining proven reserves (million bbl)	Production Daily average (1,000 b/d)	Production Annual (million bbl)	Cumulative (million bbl)	Percentage produced from cumulative reserves (%)	Reserve/pro-duction ratio (years)
1960	53,480.7	53,000.0	1,313.5	480.7	480.7	0.9	110.2
1961	56,021.0	55,000.0	1,480.1	540.2	1,021.0	1.8	101.8
1962	57,370.6	55,750.0	1,642.9	599.7	1,620.6	2.8	93.0
1963	67,272.5	65,000.0	1,786.0	651.9	2,272.5	3.4	99.7
1964	69,716.7	66,750.0	1,896.5	694.1	2,966.7	4.3	96.2
1965	69,971.6	66,200.0	2,205.3	804.9	3,771.6	5.4	82.2
1966	77,221.3	72,500.0	2,601.8	949.7	4,721.3	6.1	76.3
1967	87,195.1	81,450.0	2,805.0	1,023.8	5,745.1	6.6	79.6
1968	91,358.8	84,500.0	3,042.9	1,113.7	6,858.8	7.5	75.9
1969	154,532.7	146,500.0	3,216.2	1,173.9	8,032.7	5.2	124.8
1970	150,769.4	141,350.0	3,799.1	1,386.7	9,419.4	6.2	101.9
1971	168,635.0	157,475.0	4,768.9	1,740.6	11,160.0	6.6	90.5
1972	159,362.0	146,000.0	6,016.3	2,202.0	13,362.0	8.4	66.3
1973	156,884.6	140,750.0	7,596.2	2,772.6	16,134.6	10.3	50.8
1974	192,379.7	173,150.0	8,479.7	3,095.1	19,229.7	10.0	55.9
1975	173,612.2	151,800.0	7,075.4	2,582.5	21,812.2	12.6	58.8
1976	138,101.5	113,150.0	8,577.2	3,139.3	24,951.5	18.1	36.0
1977	181,418.4	153,100.0	9,224.5	3,367.0	28,318.4	15.6	45.5
1978	200,288.3	168,940.0	8,301.0	3,029.9	31,348.3	15.7	55.8
1979	201,307.5	166,480.0	9,532.0	3,479.2	34,827.5	17.3	47.9

UNITED ARAB EMIRATES

Year	Cumulative discoveries (million bbl)	Remaining proven reserves (million bbl)	Production		Cumulative (million bbl)	Percentage produced from cumulative reserves (%)	Reserve/production ratio (years)
			Daily average (1,000 b/d)	Annual (million bbl)			
1960	0.0	0.0	0.0	0.0	0.0	0.0	0.0
1961	0.0	0.0	0.0	0.0	0.0	0.0	0.0
1962	5,005.2	5,000.0	14.2	5.2	5.2	0.1	964.7
1963	7,522.8	7,500.0	48.2	17.6	22.8	0.3	426.3
1964	7,791.1	7,700.0	186.8	68.4	91.1	1.2	112.6
1965	10,194.1	10,000.0	282.2	103.0	194.1	1.9	97.1
1966	12,825.5	12,500.0	360.0	131.4	325.5	2.5	95.1
1967	15,465.0	15,000.0	382.1	139.5	465.0	3.0	107.6
1968	19,646.8	19,000.0	496.6	181.8	646.8	3.3	104.5
1969	17,875.9	17,000.0	627.8	229.1	875.9	4.9	74.2
1970	13,943.5	12,783.0	779.6	284.6	1,160.5	8.3	44.9
1971	22,049.2	20,502.0	1,059.5	386.7	1,547.2	7.0	53.0
1972	24,755.4	22,768.0	1,202.7	440.2	1,987.4	8.0	51.7
1973	28,046.8	25,500.0	1,532.6	559.4	2546.8	9.1	45.6
1974	37,079.5	33,920.0	1,678.6	612.7	3,159.5	8.5	55.4
1975	35,966.8	32,200.0	1,663.8	607.3	3,766.8	10.5	53.0
1976	35,675.5	31,200.0	1,936.4	708.7	4,475.5	12.5	44.0
1977	37,630.0	32,425.0	1,998.7	729.5	5,205.0	13.8	44.4
1978	37,209.1	31,316.0	1,830.5	688.1	5,893.1	15.8	45.5
1979	35,972.6	29,411.3	1,830.7	668.2	6,561.3	18.2	44.0

VENEZUELA

Year	Cumulative discoveries (million bbl)	Remaining proven reserves (million bbl)	Production Daily average (1,000 b/d)	Production Annual (million bbl)	Cumulative (million bbl)	Percentage produced from cumulative reserves (%)	Reserve/production ratio (years)
1960	19,451.7	18,500.0	2,846.1	1,041.7	1,041.7	5.3	17.8
1961	19,657.4	17,550.0	2,919.9	1,065.8	2,107.4	10.7	16.5
1962	20,275.3	17,000.0	3,199.8	1,167.9	3,275.3	16.2	14.6
1963	21,460.9	17,000.0	3,247.9	1,185.5	4,460.9	20.8	14.3
1964	22,702.6	17,000.0	3,392.8	1,241.8	5,702.6	25.1	13.7
1965	24,220.2	17,250.0	3,472.9	1,267.6	6,970.2	28.8	13.6
1966	25,600.7	17,400.0	3,371.1	1,230.5	8,200.7	32.0	14.1
1967	26,493.6	17,000.0	3,542.1	1,292.9	9,493.6	35.8	13.1
1968	26,312.9	15,500.0	3,604.8	1,319.4	10,812.9	41.1	11.7
1969	26,874.8	14,750.0	3,594.1	1,311.8	12,124.8	45.1	11.2
1970	27,478.2	14,000.0	3,708.0	1,353.4	13,478.2	49.1	10.3
1971	28,673.6	13,900.0	3,549.1	1,295.4	14,773.6	51.5	10.7
1972	29,652.1	13,700.0	3,219.9	1,178.5	15,952.1	53.8	11.6
1973	31,180.7	14,000.0	3,366.0	1,228.6	17,180.7	55.1	11.4
1974	33,267.0	15,000.0	2,976.3	1,086.4	18,267.0	54.9	13.8
1975	36,823.4	17,700.0	2,346.2	856.4	19,123.4	51.9	20.7
1976	35,233.1	15,270.0	2,294.4	839.7	19,963.1	56.7	18.2
1977	38,979.9	18,200.0	2,237.9	816.8	20,779.9	53.3	22.3
1978	39,570.3	18,000.0	2,165.5	790.4	21,570.3	54.5	22.8
1979	40,300.8	17,870.0	2,367.4	860.5	22,430.8	55.7	20.8

TOTAL OPEC

Year	Cumulative discoveries (million bbl)	Remaining proven reserves (million bbl)	Production			Percentage produced from cumulative reserves (%)	Reserve/production ratio (years)
			Daily average (1,000 b/d)	Annual (million bbl)	Cumulative (million bbl)		
1960	221,213.0	218,030.0	8,696.9	3,183.0	3,183.0	1.4	68.5
1961	226,881.1	220,280.0	9,363.8	3,418.0	6,601.1	2.9	64.4
1962	242,511.6	232,075.0	10,508.1	3,835.5	10,436.6	4.3	60.5
1963	262,764.2	248,125.0	11,514.2	4,202.7	14,639.2	5.6	59.0
1964	274,286.3	254,895.0	12,983.9	4,752.1	19,391.3	7.1	53.6
1965	284,870.2	260,245.0	14,339.2	5,233.8	24,625.2	8.6	49.7
1966	320,249.2	289,868.0	15,770.2	5,756.1	30,381.2	9.5	50.4
1967	346,806.5	310,275.0	16,849.8	6,150.2	36,531.5	10.5	50.4
1968	375,422.1	332,015.0	18,785.6	6,875.6	43,407.1	11.6	48.3
1969	449,787.8	398,750.0	20,906.3	7,630.8	51,037.8	11.3	52.3
1970	472,011.5	412,431.0	23,413.0	8,542.7	59,580.5	12.6	48.3
1971	499,807.6	430,983.0	25,326.3	9,244.1	68,824.6	13.8	46.6
1972	507,114.1	428,373.0	27,094.4	9,916.5	78,741.1	15.5	43.2
1973	511,866.9	421,815.0	30,988.5	11,310.8	90,051.9	17.6	37.3
1974	586,238.1	484,970.0	30,729.2	11,216.2	101,268.1	17.3	43.2
1975	561,049.7	449,870.0	27,155.0	9,911.6	111,179.7	19.8	45.4
1976	521,424.7	398,995.0	30,737.7	11,250.0	122,429.7	23.5	35.5
1977	573,761.2	439,915.0	31,278.0	11,416.5	133,846.2	23.3	38.5
1978	589,681.1	444,936.0	29,805.2	10,898.9	144,745.1	24.5	40.8
1979	591,593.0	435,591.3	30,840.1	11,256.6	156,001.7	26.4	38.7

NON-OPEC COUNTRIES

Year	Cumulative discoveries (million bbl)	Remaining proven reserves (million bbl)	Production Daily average (1,000 b/d)	Production Annual (million bbl)	Cumulative (million bbl)	Percentage produced from cumulative reserves (%)	Reserve/production ratio (years)
1960	87,405.0	82,956.8	12,186.8	4,448.2	4,448.2	5.1	18.6
1961	99,621.3	89,695.1	15,008.2	5,478.0	9,926.2	10.0	16.4
1962	96,375.2	81,469.1	13,643.6	4,979.9	14,906.1	15.5	16.4
1963	103,121.1	82,917.3	14,514.2	5,297.7	20,203.8	19.6	15.7
1964	112,022.0	86,377.9	14,904.9	5,440.3	25,644.1	22.9	15.9
1965	124,208.6	92,813.3	15,756.9	5,751.3	31,395.3	25.3	16.1
1966	136,837.6	99,182.4	17,150.3	6,259.9	37,655.2	27.5	15.8
1967	148,415.0	104,065.2	18,341.3	6,694.6	44,349.8	29.9	15.5
1968	177,577.8	126,030.8	19,718.6	7,197.3	51,547.0	29.0	17.5
1969	184,109.4	125,030.4	20,635.6	7,532.0	59,079.0	32.1	16.6
1970	266,027.8	198,966.5	21,869.2	7,982.3	67,061.3	25.2	24.9
1971	276,264.2	200,873.2	22,821.0	8,329.7	75,391.0	27.3	24.1
1972	322,539.4	238,510.3	23,666.2	8,638.2	84,029.1	26.1	27.6
1973	298,933.1	206,041.5	24,280.9	8,862.5	92,891.6	31.1	23.2
1974	332,713.4	230,727.2	24,916.5	9,094.5	101,986.2	30.7	25.4
1975	320,288.4	208,815.7	25,990.6	9,486.6	111,472.7	34.8	22.0
1976	319,297.7	197,995.3	26,930.5	9,829.6	121,302.4	38.0	20.1
1977	337,739.2	205,932.9	28,777.8	10,503.9	131,806.3	39.0	19.6
1978	339,621.3	196,671.8	30,529.3	11,143.2	142,949.5	42.1	17.6
1979	360,658.5	206,032.2	31,991.4	11,676.9	154,626.3	42.9	17.6

TOTAL WORLD

Year	Cumulative discoveries (million bbl)	Remaining proven reserves (million bbl)	Production			Percentage produced from cumulative reserves (%)	Reserve/production ratio (years)
			Daily average (1,000 b/d)	Annual (million bbl)	Cumulative (million bbl)		
1960	308,618.0	300,986.8	20,883.7	7,631.2	7,631.2	2.5	39.4
1961	326,502.4	309,975.1	24,372.0	8,896.1	16,527.3	5.1	34.8
1962	338,866.8	313,544.1	24,151.7	8,815.4	25,342.7	7.5	35.6
1963	365,885.3	331,042.3	26,028.4	9,500.3	34,843.0	9.5	34.8
1964	386,308.3	341,272.9	27,888.8	10,192.4	45,035.4	11.7	33.5
1965	409,078.8	353,058.3	30,096.1	10,985.1	56,020.5	13.7	32.1
1966	457,086.8	389,050.4	32,920.5	12,016.0	68,036.4	14.9	32.4
1967	495,221.4	414,340.2	35,191.1	12,844.8	80,881.2	16.3	32.3
1968	552,999.9	458,045.8	38,504.1	14,072.9	94,954.1	17.2	32.5
1969	633,897.3	523,780.4	41,541.9	15,162.8	110,116.9	17.4	34.5
1970	738,039.3	611,397.5	45,282.2	16,525.0	126,641.8	17.2	37.0
1971	776,071.8	631,856.2	48,147.3	17,573.7	144,215.6	18.6	36.0
1972	829,653.6	666,883.3	50,760.6	18,554.7	162,770.3	19.6	35.9
1973	810,800.1	627,856.5	55,269.4	20,173.3	182,943.6	22.6	31.1
1974	918,951.5	715,697.2	55,645.7	20,310.7	203,254.3	22.1	35.2
1975	881,338.1	658,685.7	53,145.6	19,398.2	222,652.4	25.3	34.0
1976	840,722.4	596,990.3	57,668.2	21,079.7	243,732.1	29.0	28.3
1977	911,500.3	645,847.9	60,055.8	21,920.3	265,652.4	29.1	29.5
1978	929,302.3	641,607.8	60,334.5	22,042.1	287,694.5	31.0	29.1
1979	952,251.5	641,623.5	62,831.5	22,933.5	310,628.0	32.6	28.0

OPEC: Selected Posted Crude Oil Prices
(Dollars/Barrel FOB Port of Export)

Effective Date		Kuwait 31°	Saudi Arabian Light 34°	Abu Dhabi Murban 39°	Libyan 40°
1950	Oct. 2	—	—	—	—
	Nov. 1	—	1.75	—	—
1951	Year	—	"	—	—
1952	July 24	—	"	—	—
1953	Feb. 5	—	1.93	—	—
	April 1	1.50	"	—	—
	June 23	"	"	—	—
	July 16	1.72	"	—	—
1954	Year	"	"	—	—
1955	Feb. 18	"	"	—	—
1956	Feb. 9	"	"	—	—
1957	Jan. 15	"	"	—	—
	May 28	1.85	"	—	—
	June 7	"	2.08	—	—
	Sept. 10	"	"	—	—
1958	Jan. 31	"	"	—	—
1959	Feb. 6	"	"	—	—
	Feb. 13	1.67	1.90	—	—
	April 4	"	"	—	—
1960	Aug. 9	1.59	1.80	—	—
	Aug. 16	"	"	—	—
1961	Aug. 12	"	"	—	2.23
1963	Year	"	"	—	"
1964	Jan. 1	"	"	1.88	"
1965	Year	"	"	—	"
1966	Year	"	"	—	"
1967	Year	"	"	—	"
1968	Year	"	"	—	"
1969	Year	"	"	—	"
1970	Jan. 1	"	"	—	2.53
	Sept. 1	"	"	—	"
	Nov. 14	1.68	"	—	"
1971	Jan. 1	"	"	—	"

Effective Date		Kuwait 31°	Saudi Arabian Light 34°	Abu Dhabi Murban 39°	Libyan 40°
1971	Feb. 15	2.085	2.18	2.235	"
	March 18	"	"	"	"
	March 20	"	"	"	3.447
	June 1	2.187	2.285	2.341	"
	July 1	"	"	"	3.423
	Oct. 1	"	"	"	3.399
1972	Jan. 1	"	"	"	3.386
	Jan. 2	2.373	"	"	"
	Jan. 20	"	2.479	2.54	3.673
	April 1	"	"	"	3.642
	July 1	"	"	"	3.620
1973	Jan. 1	2.482	2.591	2.654	3.777
	March 13	"	"	"	"
	April 1	2.626	2.742	2.808	4.024
	June 1	2.776	2.898	2.968	4.252
	July 1	2.830	2.955	3.026	4.416
	Aug. 1	2.936	3.066	3.140	4.582
	Oct. 1	2.884	3.011	3.144	4.604
	Oct. 16	4.903	5.119	6.045	"
	Oct. 19	"	"	"	8.925
	Nov. 1	4.957	5.176	6.113	9.061
	Dec. 1	4.822	5.036	5.944	"
1974	Jan. 1	11.545	11.651	12.636	15.768
	July 1	"	"	"	"
	Nov. 1	11.145	11.251	12.236	14.60

OPEC: Selected Official Government Sale Prices for Crude
(Dollars/Barrel FOB Port of Export)

Effective Date		Kuwait 31°	Saudi Arabian Light 34°	Abu Dhabi Murban 39°	Libyan Brega 40°
1975	Jan. 1	10.36	10.46	10.87	11.86
	April 1	"	"	"	11.56
	June 1	"	"	"	11.20
	Oct. 1	11.30	11.51	11.92	12.32
1976	June 1	11.23	"	"	"
	July 1	"	"	"	12.62
1977	Jan. 1	12.37	12.09	12.50	14.00
	July 1	"	12.70	13.26	14.25
1978	Jan. 1	12.27	"	"	14.05
	April 1	12.22	"	"	13.90
1979	Jan. 1	12.83	13.34	14.10	14.69
	Feb. 15	"	"	15.12	"
	Feb. 20	14.03	"	"	"
	Feb. 21	"	"	"	15.37
	March 3	"	"	"	16.07
	April 1	15.80	14.55	17.10	18.25
	May 15	16.40	"	"	"
	May 16	"	"	"	18.95
	May 17	"	"	17.90	"
	May 27	"	"	"	21.26
	June 1	"	18.00	"	"
	July 1	19.49	"	21.56	23.45
	Oct. 1	21.43	"	"	"
	Oct. 15	"	"	"	26.27
	Nov. 1	25.50	24.00	27.56	"
	Dec. 13	"	"	"	30.00
1980	Jan. 1	27.50	26.00	29.56	34.72
	April 1	"	28.00	"	"
	May 1	29.50	"	31.56	"
	May 15	"	"	"	36.72
	July 1	31.50	"	"	37.00

Government Selling Prices and Differentials
(Dollars/Barrel)

	Govt. Selling Prices		Diff. vs. Arabian Light		Increase	
	July '80	Dec. '78	July '80	Dec. '78	$/B	%
GULF						
Saudi Arabia						
Arabian Berri (39°)	29.52	13.22	+1.52	+0.52	16.30	123.3
Arabian Light (34°)	28.00	12.70	—	—	15.30	120.5
Arabian Medium (31°)	27.45	12.32	-0.55	-0.38	15.13	122.8
Arabian Heavy (27°)	27.00	12.02	-1.00	-0.68	14.98	124.6
Iran						
Iranian Light (34°)	35.00	12.81	+7.00	+0.11	22.19	173.2
Iranian Heavy (31°)	34.00	12.49	+6.00	-0.21	21.15	172.2
Iraq						
Kirkuk (36°)	32.18	12.88	+4.18	+0.18	19.30	149.8
Basrah Light (35°)	31.96	12.66	+3.96	-0.04	19.30	152.4
Basrah Medium (30°)	31.30	12.00	+3.30	-0.70	19.30	160.8
Basrah Heavy (24°)	30.65	11.35	+2.65	-1.35	19.30	170.0
Kuwait						
Kuwait (31°)	31.50	12.22	+3.50	-0.48	19.28	157.8
Neutral Zone						
Khafji (28°)	31.20	12.03	+3.20	-0.67	19.17	159.4
Hout (35°)	32.00	12.69	+4.00	-0.01	19.31	152.2
UAE						
Murban (39°)	31.56	13.26	+3.56	+0.56	18.30	138.0
Zakum (40°)	31.46	13.17	+3.46	+0.47	18.29	138.9
Umm Shaif (37°)	31.36	13.04	+3.36	+0.34	18.32	140.5
Dubai Fateh (32°)	31.93	12.64	+3.93	-0.06	19.29	152.6
Qatar						
Dukhan (40°)	33.42	13.19	+5.42	+0.49	20.23	153.4
Marine (36°)	33.23	13.00	+5.23	+0.30	20.23	155.6

| | Govt. Selling Prices | | Diff. vs. Arabian Light | | Increase | |
	July '80	Dec. '78	July '80	Dec. '78	$/B	%
Oman						
Oman (34°)	32.20	13.00	+4.20	+0.30	19.20	147.7
MED. AND AFRICA						
Libya						
Zuetina (40.5^O)	37.00	13.90	+9.00	+1.20	23.10	166.2
Brega (40°)	37.00	13.85	+9.00	+1.15	23.15	167.1
Es Sider (37°)	36.78	13.68	+8.78	+0.98	23.10	168.9
Sarir (38.5^O)	36.40	13.29	+8.40	+0.59	23.11	173.9
Bu Attifel (40°)	36.32	13.21	+8.32	+0.51	23.11	174.9
Amna (36°)	36.30	13.19	+8.30	+0.49	23.11	175.2
Algeria						
Saharan Blend (44°)	37.00	14.10	+9.00	+1.40	22.90	+162.4
Zarzaitine (42°)	37.00	14.05	+9.00	+1.35	22.95	+163.3
Nigeria						
Brass River (41.5^O)	37.00	14.13	+9.00	+1.43	22.87	+161.8
Bonny Light (37°)	37.00	14.10	+9.00	+1.40	22.90	162.4
Forcados (31°)	36.83	13.70	+8.83	+1.00	23.13	168.8
Medium (26°)	35.73	13.55	+7.73	+0.85	22.18	163.7
SOUTH AMERICA						
Venezuela						
Lago Light (41°)	36.10	14.35	+8.10	+1.65	21.75	151.6
Oficina (34°)	34.85	13.99	+6.85	+1.29	20.86	149.1
Lago Medio (32°)	33.32	13.64	+5.32	+0.94	19.68	144.3
Tia Juana (31°)	33.00	13.54	+5.00	+0.84	19.46	143.7
Ceuta (30°)	32.58	13.39	+4.58	+0.69	19.19	143.3
Tia Juana (26°)	29.88	12.72	+1.88	+0.02	17.16	134.9
Tia Juana (24°)	29.03	12.39	+1.03	-0.31	16.64	134.3
Bachaquero (17°)	24.95	11.38	-3.05	-1.32	13.57	119.2
Bachaquero (13°)	21.80	10.96	-6.20	-1.74	10.84	98.9
Boscan (10°)	17.90	9.75	-10.10	-2.95	8.15	83.6
Ecuador						
Oriente (30°)	na	12.35	—	-0.35	—	—

	Govt. Selling Prices		Diff. vs. Arabian Light		Increase	
	July '80	Dec. '78	July '80	Dec. '78	$/B	%

FAR EAST

Indonesia

	July '80	Dec. '78	July '80	Dec. '78	$/B	%
Attaka (44°)	34.25	14.10	+6.25	+1.40	20.15	142.9
Ardjuna (37°)	32.95	13.70	+4.95	+1.00	19.25	140.5
Sumatra Light (34°)	31.50	13.55	+3.50	+0.85	17.95	132.5
Handil (37°)	31.55	13.30	+3.55	+0.60	18.25	137.2
Cinta (34°)	31.50	13.15	+3.50	+0.45	18.35	139.5

Distribution of Main Cost Elements of Final Price of
Refined Products to European Consumers

Year	Final Price ($/B)*	Oil FOB	Freight	Refining	Distrib.	Dealer	Tax**
				% Distribution of Main Cost Elements			
1962	12.90	7.61	7.11	5.59	22.70	4.54	52.45
1963	12.07	8.21	7.60	5.86	21.43	6.90	50.00
1964	11.90	8.69	7.70	5.90	19.64	7.38	50.69
1965	12.00	8.65	7.64	6.11	16.09	7.36	54.14
1966	12.18	8.55	7.53	5.92	14.76	7.48	55.76
1967	12.66	8.23	7.25	5.77	16.16	7.52	55.08
1968	12.64	8.32	7.25	5.74	15.48	7.87	55.34
1969	13.06	8.11	7.02	5.60	12.78	8.57	57.91
1970	12.73	8.02	7.21	6.28	16.66	7.89	53.95
1971	14.55	8.93	7.15	5.66	20.24	7.56	50.46
1972	15.73	9.85	5.83	5.28	19.13	8.21	51.70
1973	19.05	11.28	6.80	4.63	20.86	7.47	48.96
1974	26.62	36.68	3.87	4.21	8.71	5.00	41.52
1975	30.97	34.73	3.54	4.29	8.83	5.67	42.94
1976	32.26	34.94	3.33	4.55	8.43	6.35	42.41
1977	36.63	33.52	2.93	4.37	10.88	6.81	41.49
1978	41.47	30.50	2.56	4.04	13.71	6.10	43.09
1979	54.09	31.94	2.14	3.24	18.82	3.54	40.32

* i.e. the final price to consumers of an average barrel of refined petroleum products in Western European markets.
** i.e. excise and other government-levied taxes in the Western European countries concerned.

Source: Petroleum Product Prices and their Components in Europe 1962-79, published by OPEC.

OPEC: Area, Population, GNP and Crude Production

Country	Area '000 Sq. Kms.	Population '000 Mid-1979	Inhabitants per Sq. Km.	GNP at Mkt. Prices 1979, $ Mil.	GNP per Capita 1978, $	Crude Prod., 1979 '000 b/d
Algeria	2,382	19,130	8	22,290	1,260	1,154
Ecuador	281	8,080	29	6,890	880	214
Gabon	268	540	2	1,930	3,580	203
Indonesia	1,904	139,376	73	48,820	360	1,591
Iran	1,648	37,140	23	80,000*	1,648	3,168
Iraq	438	12,770	29	22,720	1,860	3,477
Kuwait	18	1,272	71	18,040	14,890	2,500
S.P.L.A.J.	1,760	2,860	2	18,960	6,910	2,092
Nigeria	924	82,700	90	45,720	560	2,302
Qatar	11	210	19	2,840	12,740	508
Saudi Arabia	2,150	8,110	4	63,310	7,690	9,532
UAE	84	885	11	11,440	14,230	1,831
Venezuela	916	13,520	15	40,710	2,910	2,356
Total OPEC	**12,784**	**326,593**	**26**	**383,670**	**1,208 (Average)**	**30,928**

* *Estimated*

NOTES

CHAPTER I

1 Helmut J. Frank: *Crude Oil Prices in the Middle East*, New York, Praeger, 1966, p. 129.

2 In particular US Senate, Select Committee on Small Business: *The International Petroleum Cartel*, Staff Report to the Federal Trade Commission, 82nd Congress, 2nd Session, Committee Print No. 6, August 22, 1952 (hereafter referred to as FTC Staff Report), p. 199 et seq.

3 Frank, op. cit., p. 32. FTC Staff Report, pp. 362-3. Also see M.A. Adelman: *The World Petroleum Market*, Baltimore, Johns Hopkins University Press, 1972, p. 134 et seq.

4 Frank, op. cit., p. 35. FTC Staff Report, p. 363. Also Adelman, op. cit. p. 134 et seq.

5 Frank, op. cit., pp. 54 and 55-60. FTC Staff Report, pp. 364-368. For discussion of the rationale for the 1948-49 reductions in Middle East crude prices, see also Adelman, op. cit., pp. 138-39; and Edith T. Penrose: *The Large International Firm in Developing Countries – The International Petroleum Industry*, London, George Allen and Unwin, 1968, pp. 183-188.

6 FTC Staff Report, p. 368.

7 See also Taki Rifai: *The Pricing of Crude Oil*, New York, Praeger, 1974, p. 51-52.

8 *Radical Changes in the International Oil Industry During the Past Decade* (hereafter referred to as Radical Changes), paper presented by OPEC at the Fourth Arab Petroleum Congress, Beirut, November 5-12, 1963.

CHAPTER II

1 Adelman, op. cit., p. 385 et seq.

2 *New York Times*, April 7 and 10, 1959.

3 Frank, op. cit, pp. 106-107.

4 *Financial Times*, London, February 14, 1959.

5 *Venezuela and OPEC*, collection of documents published by the Venezuelan Government, Caracas, 1961, pp. 99-101.

6 Ibid, pp. 97-98.

7 *Petroleum Week*, October 16 and 23, 1959, interview by Wanda Jablonski.

8 *Petroleum Week*, July 22, 1960.

9 Ibid

10 *Venezuela and OPEC*, op. cit., pp. 99-101.

11 *Radical Changes*, OPEC, op. cit., p. 16.

12 *Radical Changes*, p. 10; November 1962 Aramco Memorandum; Saudi Arabian Monetary Agency (SAMA) Bulletins.

13 *Petroleum Week*, October 16, 1959.

14 Interview in *Petroleum Week*, May 6, 1960.

15 Supplement to *Middle East Economic Survey* (MEES), November 4, 1960.

16 MEES Supplement, January 8, 1960.

17 *Petroleum Week*, May 6, 1960.

18 The text of the document was published in *Venezuela and OPEC*, op. cit. pp. 103-104.

19 *Petroleum Week*, May 6, 1960.

20 *Petroleum Week*, December 2, 1960.

21 A lively account of the goings-on in the Exxon boardroom is given in Anthony Sampson's *The Seven Sisters* (London, Hodder and Stoughton, 1975), pp.156-158.

22 *Petroleum Week*, December 9, 1960.

23 MEES, September 16, 1960.

24 MEES, November 4, 1960.

CHAPTER III

1 For documentation on these ideas, see interviews with Perez Alfonzo in the London *Times* and *Financial Times*, September 27, 1960, and MEES, October 28, 1960. Also the paper delivered by Tariki at the Second Arab Petroleum Congress, Beirut, October 1960, entitled: *The Pricing of Crude Oil and Refined Products*.

2 Interview with Wanda Jablonski in *Petroleum Week*, December 9, 1960.

3 *Petroleum Week*, December 30, 1960.

4 Not surprisingly in view of the enormity of the task, the search for a rational price structure has so far been unavailing. But for the record, it is instructive to recall the views of the OPEC Secretariat in 1963. An OPEC paper (appropriately entitled: *The Price of Crude Oil: A Rational Approach*) presented to the Fourth Arab Petroleum Congress in Cairo in November of that year said that any such rational price structure must take into account the following considerations:

   "The demand for crude oil at the source is virtually insensitive to price changes and the price of crude oil should therefore be free from severe fluctuations. Such fluctuations would entail serious consequences in the long run for both producing and consuming nations.

   "Prices should bear a reasonably close relationship to prices existing today, because any violent change over a short period of time would precipitate either too great a drop in the revenue of producing countries or too sharp an increase in the energy costs of the consuming nations.

"Prices should, within reasonable limits, be predictable, because predictability within these limits and over a period of a few years would confer on the producing nations the benefit of being able to plan their economic development with a greater measure of certainty and would confer on the consuming nations the benefit of the additional security to be derived from the knowledge that prices would not fluctuate erratically.

"Prices should take into account, and in some manner compensate for, the continually increasing prices of manufactured goods, because it is only in this way that the petroleum exporting nations, which share in common with other exporters of primary commodities the problem of a trend towards deteriorating prices, can achieve the long-term stability required for their economic development."

5   A frank account of these negotiations from an OPEC point of view can be found in an OPEC paper entitled: *OPEC and the Principle of Negotiation*, presented at the Fifth Arab Petroleum Congress in Cairo, March 1965.

6   See *Petroleum Intelligence Weekly* (PIW), September 2, 1963, and MEES, September 6, 1963.

7   Supplement to MEES, August 28, 1964.

8   MEES, January 8, 1964.

9   *OPEC and the Principle of Negotiation*, op. cit.

10   MEES, January 12, 1968.

11   MEES, December 3, 1965.

CHAPTER IV

1   Hearings (1973-74) Before the Sub-committee on Multinational Corporations of the Committee on Foreign Relations, United States Senate, 93rd Congress, First and Second Sessions, on Multinational Petroleum Companies and Foreign Policy (hereafter referred to as MNC Hearings), Part 6, p. 70.

2   MEES, May 29, 1970.

3   MEES, June 6, 1970; PIW, June 8, 1970.

4   The whole controversy is expertly explained and analysed by Dr. Taki Rifai in his book *The Pricing of Crude Oil* (published by Praeger, New York, 1974) pages 89-99. Dr. Rifai, who acted as economic adviser to the Libyan Ministry of Petroleum from 1969 to 1971, assesses the arguments put forward by Esso in a 1962 memorandum justifying its Brega posting. He finds the Esso arguments confusing and at times self-contradictory, and concludes that the $2.21/barrel posting could only be justified if one were to accept Intascale minus 55% as a representative average freight rate in 1960-61, which was not in order since this

rate applied only to spot charters at the time (not term charters as claimed by Esso). If other more appropriate freight rates were to be used, the Libyan posting would be undervalued by between 9 cents (at Intascale minus 33% based on the historical predecent for East Mediterranean postings) and 20 cents (using Intascale minus 7.6% as the average AFRA rate for the period 1960-61).

5 Rifai, op. cit., p. 95.

6 MEES, August 15, 1969.

7 MNC Hearings, Part 5, pp. 2-4.

8 MNC Hearings (Testimony of Exxon Senior Vice President George Piercy), Part 5, pp. 196-198 and 214. Also Report (January 1975) on Multinational Oil Corporations and US Foreign Policy to the Committee on Foreign Relations, United States Senate, 92nd Congress, Second Session, by the Sub-committee on Multinational Oil Corporations (hereafter referred to as MNC Report), p. 123.

9 MNC Report, p. 123. Also Sampson, op. cit., p. 212.

10 Letter from Sir David Barran of Shell to Senator Frank Church, MNC Hearings, Part 8, pp. 771-773.

11 Sampson, op. cit., p. 214.

12 Barran Letter to Church, op. cit. Sampson, op. cit., p 214.

13 Testimony by James Akins, MNC Hearings, Part 5, pp. 6 and 12-13.

14 Letter from the Companies' attorney, John J. McCloy, to the Church Committee, MNC Hearings, Part 8, pp. 777-779.

15 *Platt's Oilgram*, October 7, 1970.

16 MNC Hearings, Part 6, pp. 63-65.

17 Barran Letter to Church, op. cit.

18 MNC Hearings, Part 5, p. 263.

19 MNC Hearings, Part 5, p. 169.

20 Irwin Testimony, MNC Hearings, Part 5, p. 149.

21 MNC Hearings, Part 6, p. 79.

22 Statement to MEES, February 12, 1971.

23 The minutes of this particular meeting were published in MNC Hearings, Part 6, pp. 215-222. They make riveting reading — in Anthony Sampson's words a "classic dialogue" of government-company oil negotiations.

CHAPTER V

1 For the restrospective analysis of one major company — Standard Oil of California — see MNC Hearings Part 7, pp. 370-373. The company's 1968 forecast underestimated 1973 non-Communist world demand by 10.5% or 4.7 million b/d.

2 Statement by George Piercy of Exxon, MNC Hearings, Part 7, p. 337.

3 The 1973 Aramco programme for expansion of producing capacity envisaged the

attainment of 10.5 million b/d by year-end 1974, 11.6 million b/d by year-end 1975 and 13.5 million b/d by year-end 1977; and there was even talk at the time of expanding to 20 million b/d by the early 1980s. Such numbers turned out to be fanciful, and Aramco's more ambitious expansion proposals were turned down by the government in the interests of a more extended production profile for the oilfields. In early 1980 Aramco's maximum sustainable capacity was estimated at around 10.5 million b/d, scheduled to reach around 12 million b/d (with a facility capacity of some 14 million b/d) by the mid-1980s. This is the maximum that is planned for the presently producing oilfields.

4   Supplement to MEES, September 7, 1973.

5   Anwar el-Sadat: *In Search of Identity*, London, Collins, 1978, p. 238.

6   Mohamed Heikal: *The Road to Ramadan*, London, Collins, 1975, p. 266.

7   The Cairo weekly *al-Musawwar*, August 4, 1972; MEES, August 4, 1972.

8   MEES, October 6, 1972.

9   *The Washington Post*, April 19, 1973.

10 MNC Hearings, Part 7, pp. 504-509.

11 See *The Washington Post* and *Christian Science Monitor*, July 6, 1973, and *Newsweek*, September 10, 1973.

12 MNC Hearings, Part 7, p. 509.

13 See in particular Akin's celebrated article *The Oil Crisis: This Time The Wolf Is Here*, published in *Foreign Affairs* magazine, April 1973.

14 Nixon at White House News Conference, September 5, 1973. See MEES, September 7, 1973 and PIW, September 10, 1973.

15 Ian Seymour in *The New York Times*, October 7, 1973.

16 PIW, October 22, 1973.

17 MNC Report, p. 149.

18 For full documentation on the Arab oil measures see MEES, October 1973 to March 1974.

19 For official statements on Iraqi policy in this regard, see MEES October 26 and November 9, 1973.

20 PIW, December 3, 1973.

21 MEES, December 21, 1973.

22 Sampson, op. cit., p. 258.

23 MEES, December 28, 1973.

CHAPTER VI

1   Expressing this Saudi scepticism with regard to US intentions on prices, Sheikh Yamani remarked in an interview with *Events* magazine, January 14, 1977: "The real interest for the US is in higher oil prices. I do not recall that Dr. Henry

Kissinger ever raised the subject of oil prices with us although he talks to us frequently. These are well-known facts. Their whole interest is in raising the price of oil. This is a political decision in the first instance, then an economic one."

2   The then US Assistant Secretary of State for Economic Affairs, Thomas Enders, publicly acknowledged, in April 1975, that the aim of the US administration was to "break the OPEC cartel".

3   See *The Kissinger Proposals: Squaring the Crude?* in MEES, February 7, 1975.

4   For detailed account of the Quito Conference, see MEES, June 21, 1974.

5   MEES, July 26, 1974.

6   MEES, August 2, 1974.

7   MEES, September 6, 1974.

8   For a report on the London Meeting of OPEC NOCs, see MEES, August 23, 1974.

9   Supplement to MEES, September 13, 1974.

10 For a report on the Abu Dhabi Meeting, see supplement to MEES, November 15, 1974.

11 Supplement to MEES, February 11, 1980.

CHAPTER VII

1   Interview with *Events* magazine, January 14, 1977.

2   For a detailed report on Algeria's "Overall Proposal for Measures in Favour of Development and International Co-operation", see Supplement to MEES, January 31, 1975.

3   OECD Economic Outlook, No. 27, July 1980.

4   Ibid, p. 119.

5   Ibid, p. 120.

6   For analyses of domestic markets in the UK, West Germany and Italy during this period, see PIW, June 2 and December 22, 1975, and July 12, 1976.

7   *International Crude Oil and Product Prices*, (ICOPP), April 15, 1975, p. iii. ICOPP is a biannual review of oil price trends published in Beirut up to 1976 and since then in Cyprus.

8   MEES, June 13, 1975.

9   For an account of the September 1975 Conference, see MEES September 19/ 26, 1975.

10 MEES, June 7, 1976.

11 For a detailed report on the Doha Conference, see supplement to MEES, December 20, 1976.

12 Supplement to MEES, January 10, 1977, p. 22

13 Supplement to MEES, December 20, 1976, p. 7.

14 MEES, January 24, 1977.

15 Interview with the Arabic-language Beirut daily *al-Anwar*, December 22, 1976; translation in MEES, January 3, 1977.

16 At a press conference just after the Doha Conference — see Supplement to MEES, January 10, 1977 — Sheikh Yamani had the following question and answer exchange:

Q: Can you describe the substance of any meetings you had, or representatives of your Government had, with officials from the US Government, including persons from the Administration of President-elect Carter; and say if the price decision was made on any arrangements or commitments on promises from these people?

A: We don't have any arrangements, but I want you to know that we expect the West to appreciate what we did, and especially the United States, and that appreciation has to be shown on two different fronts: (1) the North-South Dialogue in Paris; and (2) the Arab-Israeli conflict; and there must be peace in the area as a sign of appreciation.

17 A detailed 1979 US Senate Staff Report claims that Aramco's actual sustainable capacity was only 9.3 million b/d in January 1977, rising to 9.8 million in April when actual production reached 10 million b/d. As production increased to this level, according to the Report, the surface facilities experienced breakdowns.

After the first-half 1977 production experience, the Saudi Government re-evaluated its capacity ratings, particularly in the light of pressure problems encountered in some of the major oilfields producing Arabian Light; and this led to the decision in February 1978 to restrict production of Arabian Light to 65% of total output, as well as the imposition of strict allowable production and pressure maintenance rules for the oilfields. The full background may be found in the Report referred to above, published in PIW, April 23, 1979, under the title: *The Future of Saudi Arabian Oil Production* (A Staff Report to the Sub-committee on International Economic Policy Committee on Foreign Relations, United States Senate).

In 1980, Aramco's maximum sustainable capacity is probably in the region of 10 to 10.5 million b/d. Basically, the planned expansion to reach 12 million b/d of sustainable capacity, with a facility capacity of 14 million b/d, remains in effect.

18 MEES, May 16, 1977.

19 MEES, June 6, 1977.

20 MEES, November 21, 1977; PIW November 21, 1977.

21 MEES, May 15, 1978.

22 Fadhil J. Al-Chalabi: *OPEC and the International Oil Industry: A Changing Structure*, Oxford, Oxford University Press, 1980, p. 95.

23 Adnan A. Al-Janabi: *Equilibrium of External Balances Between Oil Producing Countries and Industrialized Countries*, paper published in MEES, November 19, 1979, and *OPEC Review*, Winter 1979/ Spring 1980.

24 *The Economist*, January 5, 1974. The article in question (a leader no less), entitled "The Coming Glut of Energy", makes bizarre reading, particularly the concluding paragraph which makes the following curious prophesies: "Most of this article should not be regarded as good news for Britain. A main implication is that Britain's North Sea oil 'bonanza' may very well come on full flow just when oil is coming towards glut. Another is that the £1 billion being spent on Britain's coal mines will be wasted, because it will be surprising if by the mid-1980s any man-operated coal mines should remain open at all. A more tragic implication is that the most deserving charity of Christmas, 1980, will probably be to relieve Arab states ruined by the monoculture of unwanted oil – a charity which is likely to be mainly subscribed by rich Jews. Not enough tears seem to be raised by that."

25 Sheikh Ali Khalifa Al-Sabah: *Conceptual Perspective for a Long-Range Oil Policy*, published in MEES, September 17, 1979.

CHAPTER VIII

1   PIW, August 18, 1980.
2   MEES, May 12, 1980.

CHAPTER IX

1   MNC Hearings, Part 7, pp. 308-309; MNC Report, p. 101.
2   MNC Report, p. 100.
3   See in particular the exchange between Senator Muskie and George Piercy of Exxon in MNC Hearings, Part 5, p. 178.
4   *Note on Resolution IX. 61*, OPEC, 1965.
5   Interview with NIOC Director Reza Fallah in PIW, May 17, 1965.
6   PIW, November 29, 1965.
7   MEES, February 11, 1966.
8   PIW, August 30, 1965.
9   For a penetrating analysis of these problems, see paper by OPEC's Deputy Secretary General, Dr. Fadhil Al-Chalabi, entitled *The Concept of Conservation in OPEC Member Countries*, published in *OPEC Review*, Autumn 1979.
10 See paper by Adnan Al-Janabi, Head of OPEC's Economics and Finance Department, entitled *The Supply of OPEC Oil in the 1980s*, published in *OPEC Review*,

Summer 1980.

11 For example, the internationally issued indexed energy bonds for surplus funds of oil producing countries, as proposed by petroleum consultant Walter J. Levy — see Supplement to MEES, April 7, 1980.

12 Janabi, op. cit.

CHAPTER X

1 In theory, this provision in the 1925 Iraqi-IPC Agreement was supposed to give expression to the clause in the 1920 San Remo Oil Agreement between the Governments of Britain and France which envisaged national participation in any oil development company in Iraq. But whereas the San Remo Agreement (Article 8) speaks unconditionally of a 20% participation for the Iraqi Government in any private petroleum company set up to develop Mesopotamian oil, the Iraqi-IPC Agreement simply evades the issue entirely.

2 Address to North Sea Conference in London, September 1972 — published in MEES, September 22, 1972.

3 Supplement to MEES, March 10, 1972.

4 MEES, March 17, 1972.

5 For detailed background, see MEES, June 16, 1972.

6 *Platt's Oilgram*, June 6, 1972.

7 Supplement to MEES, November 3, 1972.

8 PIW, February 25, 1980.

9 J.E. Hartshorn: *From Multinational to National Oil — The Structural Change*, paper published in MEES, April 28, 1980.

CHAPTER XI

1 Unless indicated otherwise, the term "OPEC" in this Chapter means OPEC's 10 major aid donors, i.e. all Members except Ecuador, Gabon and Indonesia, although those three countries have all contributed to the resources of the OPEC Fund.

2 OECD, the principal compilers of data on financial flows from OPEC Members, argue that disbursements by OPEC Members to the IMF Oil Facility are not to be regarded as resource flows "partly because they benefit developed as well as developing countries." For a contrary view, see R. Mabro and I.F.I. Shihata: "The OPEC Aid Record" in M. Abdel-Fadil, (ed), *Papers on the Economics of Oil: A Producer's View* (Oxford: 1979).

3 "Aid", "assistance" or ODA (according to OECD criteria) refer to grants or

loans on concessional terms, undertaken by the official sector for the promotion of economic development in developing countries. Excluded are private voluntary contributions, military assistance and loans conveying a grant element below 25%.

4 Brazil, South Korea, Singapore, Taiwan and Turkey.

5 See A.Y. Al-Hamad: *Some Aspects of the Kuwait Fund's Approach to International Development Finance* (KFAED: 1977), p. 6.

6 R. Mabro and I.F.I. Shihata, op. cit., p. 96.

7 Law No. 25 1974 (Kuwait); Law No. 7 1974 (Abu Dhabi).

8 1976 per capita income above US$1,000.

9 1976 per capita income below US$400.

10 R. Mabro and I.F.I. Shihata, op. cit. p. 99.

11 Includes energy, transport and roads, water and sewage, telecommunications, schools and hospitals.

12 Source: Chase World Information Corporation.

CHAPTER XII

1 MEES, June 6, 1977.

2 *North-South: A Programme for Survival*, Report of the Independent Commission on International Development Issues under the chairmanship of Willy Brandt, published by Pan Books, London, 1980.

3 OECD Economic Outlook, July 1980.

INDEX

301